Seeds
of Change

Edited by PRISCILLA LEDER

CRITICAL ESSAYS ON
Barbara Kingsolver

Seeds
of Change

The University of Tennessee Press
Knoxville

"Contingency, Cultivation, and Choice: The Garden Ethic in Barbara Kingsolver's *Prodigal Summer*" was published, in different form, in *ISLE: Interdisciplinary Studies in Literature and Environment* 16.2 (Spring 2009): 227–43, and is reprinted by permission of the editors.

"Gardens of Auto Parts: Kingsolver's Merger of American Western Myth and Native American Myth in *The Bean Trees*" was published, in different form, in the *Southern Literary Journal* 39.2 (2007): 119–39, and is reprinted by permission of the editors.

"Trauma and Memory in Kingsolver's *Animal Dreams*" was first published in *LIT (Literature, Interpretation, Theory)* 11.4 (2001): 327–50, and is reprinted here by permission of Taylor & Francis.

The paper in this book meets the requirements of American National Standards Institute / National Information Standards Organization specification Z39.48-1992 (Permanence of Paper). It contains 30 percent post-consumer waste and is certified by the Forest Stewardship Council.

Library of Congress Cataloging-in-Publication Data

Seeds of change: critical essays on Barbara Kingsolver / edited by Priscilla Leder. — 1st ed.
    p. cm.
Includes bibliographical references and index.
ISBN-13: 978-1-57233-719-0 (alk. paper)
ISBN-10: 1-57233-719-2 (alk. paper)
    1. Kingsolver, Barbara—Criticism and interpretation.
    2. Identity (Psychology) in literature.
    3. Social justice in literature.
    4. Ecology in literature.
    I. Leder, Priscilla Gay.

PS3561.I496Z87 2010
813'.54—dc22   2010015358

CONTENTS

Preface   vii
Introduction   1
Priscilla Leder

PART 1 IDENTITY

Gardens of Auto Parts: American Western Myth
and Native American Myth in *The Bean Trees*   27
Catherine Himmelwright

To Live Deliberately: Feminist Theory in Action in
High Tide in Tucson   47
Maureen Meharg Kentoff

Women, a Dark Continent? *The Poisonwood Bible*
as a Feminist Response to Conrad's *Heart
of Darkness*   71
Héloïse Meire

Trauma and Memory in *Animal Dreams*   87
Sheryl Stevenson

"Hemmed In": Place, Disability, and Maternity in
Animal Dreams and *The Poisonwood Bible*   109
Breyan Strickler

PART 2 SOCIAL JUSTICE

"Give Me Your Hand": Accessibility, Commitment,
and the Challenge of Cliché in Kingsolver's
Poetry   129
Meagan Evans

Wild Indians: Kingsolver's Representation of Native
    America   145
    Robin Cohen

The White Imagination at Work in *Pigs in Heaven*   157
    Jeanne Sokolowski

Imagined Geographies   175
    Kristin J. Jacobson

Earthbound Rhetoric and Praxis: Authentic
    Patriotism in a Time of Abstractions   199
    Wes Berry

PART 3 ECOLOGY

Remembering Our Ecological Place: Environmental
    Engagement in Kingsolver's Nonfiction   213
    Christine Cusick

Contingency, Cultivation, and Choice: The Garden
    Ethic in *Prodigal Summer*   233
    Priscilla Leder

Celebrating a Lively Earth: Children, Nature, and the
    Role of Mentors in *Prodigal Summer*   251
    Susan Hanson

Together at the Table: *Animal, Vegetable, Miracle*
    and Thoreau's *Wild Fruits*   263
    Gioia Woods

Works Cited   277
Contributors   293
Index   297

PREFACE

I n a sense, this book began in my mother's kitchen, where I experienced two different courses of instruction. In the present, spiced with the smell of chopped celery or the taste of beaten egg whites, I learned to cook. My mother's other lesson—get all the education you possibly can—addressed a future that she could only imagine, having left school at sixteen to marry my father. I absorbed both lessons, only to have them diverge. Like other women of my generation, I found that pursuing that higher education took me into a world where only intellectual nourishment mattered and kitchens seemed beneath notice. Beginning graduate school in the seventies, I became part of the effort to bring women, women writers, and women's experience into the academy. The women writers closest to my heart—Harriet Beecher Stowe, Sarah Orne Jewett, Toni Morrison, and others—not only depicted the kitchen but also found there recipes for feeding the hungry and healing a wounded world. Studying them, for me, reconnected divergent paths and reintegrated life and work.

Of all the writers who recognized and explored the connections between personal and political, Barbara Kingsolver engaged me most, with the immediacy of her language and her conviction, always present but never belabored, that human beings bear some responsibility for the world we have inherited. Some of her descriptions also engage my earliest memories: I grew up in Tucson, formed by the landscape, the city, and the people who shaped her as a writer. I believe I once lived for a time in one of the "falling-down stone houses" in the "little colony" "in the desert at the edge of town" where Taylor lives at the beginning of *Pigs in Heaven*. Of course, the little colony may be imaginary, but I lived there just the same. So, I'm deeply gratified to have been able to assemble and offer this guidebook to all of Kingsolver's landscapes, real and imaginary.

Throughout the process, I've received invaluable help and support. In the early stages, Allan Chavkin and Huey Guagliardo initiated me into the mysteries of creating an essay collection and seeking a publisher. Texas State University–San Marcos awarded me developmental leave for the spring semester of 2008, without which I could not have completed the project. Michael Hennessy, my chair, has been consistently encouraging and genuinely interested. Ricardo Bach shared his own experiences as editor of two collections. Teya Rosenberg read a draft of the introduction and offered characteristically astute editorial suggestions; Nevin Leder read and commented wisely on an early version of my essay. To a person, the contributors brought not only their insightful essays but also patience, good humor, and a generous spirit. Though absent from the table of contents, Isabel Fernandes Alves and C. Lynne Fulmer gave much of themselves. Susan Hanson, the lady on the other side of the woods, contributed not only her lyrical essay but also her extraordinary gift for listening and her knowledge of publishing. Memories of Deborah Guagliardo and Hans Leder also shaped this book, though neither will see it. Finally, I'm grateful to José Alfredo Bach, who presides over our kitchen with love and garlic, sustaining me body and soul.

INTRODUCTION

Priscilla Leder

Though best known for her novels, Barbara Kingsolver
has also penned a popular food memoir and even that
publishing rarity, a best-selling essay collection, as well
as a book of poems, a short story collection, and a nonfiction account of a labor action. Amid this impressive variety, two basic themes emerge: an appreciation of the natural world that not only celebrates its nurturing beauty but
also explores it as a biological system, and an appreciation
of human diversity that considers how people of different
backgrounds and perspectives can learn from each other.
Increased understanding, Kingsolver believes, can create a
better world. To foster that understanding, she addresses
her readers through their own experience to reveal the possibilities for that better world as well as the imperfections of
this one.

Her beliefs and concerns have emerged from her life and
through her work. She was born Barbara Ellen Kingsolver,
April 8, 1955, in Annapolis, Maryland, the second of three
children of Dr. Wendell and Virginia Lee Henry Kingsolver.[1]
After Dr. Kingsolver completed the military service that had
taken him to Annapolis, the family returned to Kentucky,
their original home, taking a farm just outside of Carlisle,
in Nicholas County. Kingsolver grew up exploring the surrounding woods with her older brother, Rob, and, later, her
younger sister, Ann—collecting leaves, watching birds, eating crawfish and wild onions. In her essay "The Memory
Place," she affirms the formative power of "the experience
of nature, with its powerful lessons in static change and predictable surprise" (171). Those paradoxes express her deeply

felt fascination with the natural world—wonder at its apparently inexhaustible variety and respect for the life cycle that drives and unifies it.

When Kingsolver was seven, her father undertook a medical exchange to the Congo, "a place that was even more desperately in need of medical care than Nicholas County" (Mendes 309). What the parents presented to their children as a family adventure turned out to be more arduous than they had anticipated: there was no running water; supplies were dropped from a small plane once a month; "[n]othing was clean, and nothing was safe" (Wagner-Martin 18). Though the village children found the young Americans exotic, pulling at Kingsolver's long hair because it didn't look real to them, they accepted and played with their visitors (Wagner-Martin 18). Her experience in Africa permanently widened her sense of what was "normal," in physical appearance or in material culture. "For the first time I faced the possibility that everything I had assumed to be true . . . could be absolutely false, in another place" (Rehm interview quoted in Wagner-Martin 19). After the Congo, human variety, like the variety of the natural world, became lived experience, something to be explored and celebrated rather than observed at a distance.

Later on, when Kingsolver was in the seventh grade, her family undertook another medical mission, shorter and relatively more comfortable, to the island of St. Lucia in the Caribbean, among the Windward Islands. Both missions grew out of Dr. Kingsolver's "magnificent compunction to be useful in the world," as his daughter describes it (Mendes 309). Kingsolver assimilated that compunction along with her appreciation of the natural world and of human variety: "My parents always gave me to know I could make a difference—and I'd better make one" (Kerr 54).

Kingsolver's upbringing expanded her horizons through reading as well as through adventures abroad and in the nearby woods: "When I was growing up our TV broke, and it took twelve years to get it fixed because my dad just hated TV and really didn't want one in the house" (Perry 149). Instead, the whole family read books, including the *Encyclopedia Britannica*; "[m]y parents read aloud to us for years, I mean, even into adolescence" (Mendes 308). Home entertainment included music: her parents and siblings played a variety of instruments; Kingsolver studied piano assiduously and played clarinet in the school band. Like many avid readers, she began to write as a child, in "little diaries and spiral-bound notebooks" (Mendes 307). Later, she entered and won essay contests, waxing so enthusiastic about topics like soil conservation that she imagined that "the judges got together and said,

'This child is histrionic about soil conservation—we better give her the prize again'" (Mendes 310).

Though her modest, rural, intellectual home brought Kingsolver lasting gifts, it did not prepare her especially well for the experience of adolescence in the 1960s South. Her frugal, practical parents dressed her in a cousin's hand-me-downs and "black lace-up oxfords," which they "perceived to have orthopedic value" but which made her "the Bride of Frankenstein" to her classmates ("Life without Go-Go Boots" 54–55). Her appearance, five foot nine by sixth grade, and very thin, exacerbated her image of herself as "a collection of all the wrong things: too tall and shy to be interesting to boys. Too bookish" ("Letter to a Daughter" 145). Attention from boys was dangerous as well as desirable: "The story I got from the world around me on how to behave with boys . . . boiled down to this: Boys want only one thing, which is to have sex with you, which is too nasty even to talk about, and it's your job to prevent it" ("Letter to a Daughter" 151). The painful self-doubt and confusion of this period, like her more positive early experiences, expanded the range of her vision—this time, to encompass the wounded and the outcast. "From the vantage point of invisibility I explored the psychology of the underdog, the one who can't be what others desire but who might still learn to chart her own hopes" ("In Case" 42).

In "How Mr. Dewey Decimal Saved My Life," Kingsolver explains how an expanded range of reading assuaged much of her adolescent isolation. Set to the task of cataloging the books in the Nicholas County High School library, she discovered first *Gone with the Wind,* then Poe, then William Saroyan's *The Human Comedy,* mis-shelved between "Human Anatomy" and "Human Physiology." Reading Doris Lessing's *Martha Quest* showed her that literature could not only open alternate worlds but also provide perspectives on her own experience. Puzzling over the unfamiliar words "colour bar," she "eventually figured out it meant . . . the thing that had forced some of the kids in my county to go to a separate school . . . and grow up without plumbing or the hope of owning a farm" (51). She also admired, and continues to admire, writers closer to home—Eudora Welty, Carson McCullers, and Flannery O'Connor, but cites Lessing most often, for her insights into the position of women as well as for waking her from her "placid color-blind coma" (53) by focusing her attention on the everyday injustices of her segregated world (Perry 150).

Like other introspective, intellectually inclined young people, Kingsolver became less isolated when she went to college and found others

4

with similar interests and attitudes. In 1973, she entered DePauw University in Greencastle, Indiana, on a music scholarship, meeting and befriending music majors and other readers who introduced her to new books (Wagner-Martin 32–33). "Finally, I [had] a genuine social life" ("Letter to My Mother" 167). Typically concerned with injustice, she joined the movement to end the war in Vietnam. As the movement grew and Nixon left office, she recalls, "I felt that I had helped that happen. To this day, when I see something that makes me angry or makes me sad, my impulse is to act, to change it" (Mendes 311). That impulse—the need to make a difference—pervades both her life and her writing.

In her sophomore year, Kingsolver endured an experience that remains all too common for college women: a man she had met in a bar came to her apartment two nights later, where he raped her. "In 1974," Linda Wagner-Martin points out, "there was no such term as 'acquaintance rape . . . no way the college woman could have reported her attacker" (37). Kingsolver revealed her ordeal publicly only much later, first in poems in 1992, and then in "Letter to my Mother," part of the 2002 essay collection *Small Wonder.* As she describes it in that essay, her reaction reveals an attitude that pervades her writing, as well as her life. Initially, she lies curled on her bed, annihilated, "a dot of nothingness." "My bones are weak. I am trapped in a room with no flowers, no light, and a ceiling of lead so low I can never again straighten up" ("Letter to My Mother" 168). She escapes this unbearable state only by consciously, deliberately, taking a position of strength: "I will be able to get up from this bed only if I can get up angry. . . . I have to be someone else. Not you [my mother] and not even me" (168). Though she retains compassion for the figure on the bed, as for all the wounded and outcast, she must refuse to identify with that defeated figure by taking the position of power and acting.

She began to dress as a powerful "someone else," cutting off the long hair that had attracted the man's notice and walking around campus in an army surplus overcoat and a green pith helmet she found in her parents' attic. Also during her sophomore year, she changed her major from music to biology, taking required science classes by examination to avoid falling behind schedule and losing her scholarship. "[I]t occurred to me that all the classical pianists in the U.S. were going to have a shot at, maybe, eleven good jobs, and the rest of us would wind up tinkling through 'The Shadow of Your Smile' in a hotel lobby" ("Confessions" 130). The practical choice of biology would lead to economic power; in addition, the biologist possesses the power of knowledge of life itself. "I think biology is my religion. Understanding the processes of the natural world and how all living things are related is the way that I answer those questions that are the basis of religion" (Perry 147).

Kingsolver's early experiences had taught her the horizon-expanding possibilities of immersion in another culture, and she looked forward to participating in DePauw's exchange program in her junior year. Once in Europe, she did not want to leave, prolonging her stay by working as an archeological assistant in France and England, returning to DePauw in 1977 to complete her requirements and graduate, and immediately turning back to France, where she worked at a variety of jobs, including translator, housecleaner, and artist's model, until her work visa could no longer be renewed.

Back in the United States in 1978, she once again sought out new territory, this time within the country but nevertheless vastly distant geographically and culturally from Kentucky. "I moved to Tucson [Arizona]," she recalls, "for no good reason. I knew someone in Tucson, and I kind of had a theoretical interest in the Southwest" (Beattie 157). That interest may well have been biological; for the landscape she found expanded her sense of ecological diversity. "I was driving and driving and driving, and I didn't see any desert because I thought desert looked like the funny papers. I thought it would be rolling sandy hills with one cactus sticking up here and another one there, and I didn't see anything like that. And I got to Tucson and said 'Where is the desert?'" (Mendes 312). As she came to know the desert and to love its biological variety, she also discovered the city's "cultural heterogeneity . . . like this big rowdy unweeded flower garden" with a university in the middle. It was in Tucson that Kingsolver developed into a professional writer.

Her first job, as a medical technician for the University of Arizona, gave her a good income and left her time to write. Drawing on her one creative writing class at DePauw, she wrote poetry and short stories and even began a novel. Typically politically active, she joined the Sanctuary movement, which advocated for political refugees from Latin America, many of whom had fled dictatorships supported by the United States. Action took written form: she "wrote broadsides. I cranked out broadsides on a mimeograph machine . . . and I wrote poems" (Mendes 312). She also retained her interest in biology and ecology; encouraged by Joseph Hoffmann, the chemistry professor whom she would later marry, she applied and was accepted to the university's doctoral program in ecology and evolutionary biology in 1979. Supported by a teaching assistantship, she completed her coursework, passed her exams, and began exploring her dissertation topic, which involved research on termites.

Though she was well on her way to a career as a biologist, her path took an abrupt turn. First, life as an academic scientist came to seem too constricting: "I didn't want that kind of ultracompetitive kind of very, very narrow focus, devoting myself to writing this dissertation that possibly eleven people in the universe are going to read" (Beattie 159). Fortuitously, she discovered a job opening as a scientific writer for the university, took a terminal master's degree, and went to work translating the research reports of scientists into English, as she described it (Beattie 159). Though she experienced some "boring days" as a science writer, her Friday paychecks validated her efforts. Still pursuing other types of writing, she audited a fiction-writing workshop with the novelist Francine Prose. Eventually, success with a range of audiences showed her that writing could satisfy both her need for action and her fascination with biological and human diversity: she published scientific articles (Wagner-Martin 47), read her poetry in coffeehouses and won a poetry prize in 1981 (Beattie 158), published political writing in the national alternative press, and sent the short story "Rose-Johnny" to the *Virginia Quarterly Review*, where it was accepted without revision (Wagner-Martin 48).[2] At that point, she turned over a new page of her journal and in the middle wrote "I am a writer" (Beattie 158).

Writing for the *Progressive* and other journals, Kingsolver began covering a bitter strike against the Phelps-Dodge copper company, beginning in 1983. As she spent time in the mining towns of Clifton and Morenci, the assignment became more than just an ideal story for an activist journalist. It revealed the unfolding narrative of a sea change in the lives of the women, traditional Mexican American wives and mothers who left their kitchens to stand on the picket line when their striking husbands were forbidden to do so by injunction. Subjects as well as subject matter suggested a full-length book: As she drove around Clifton, "[t]hey'd all say, 'Oh, it's that girl that's writing the book.' So I had to at least pretend I was writing a book, and it occurred to me that I would like to . . ." (Beattie 161). Knowing nothing about marketing a book, she consulted a listing of literary agents and was caught by one that began, "I do not represent any material that is sexist, racist, ageist, homophobic, or gratuitously violent." Thus began Kingsolver's long and fruitful association with independent agent Francis Goldin, which continues to the present (Beattie 161).

Busy with her freelance work, Kingsolver couldn't find the uninterrupted time she needed to complete the proposed book on the mine strike. Other distractions arose: she married Joe Hoffmann in 1985 and became pregnant with her first child in 1986. From the beginning of her pregnancy, she suffered acute insomnia. Her doctor suggested that she spend her wakeful hours on some distasteful task such as scrubbing the grout in the bathroom tile so as not to reward herself for wakefulness. "So I did that one night, and then I said, 'Screw this; I'm writing a novel'" (Perry 151). Shutting herself in the closet because the sound of her typewriter keys kept her husband awake, she reached the end of the novel before the end of her protracted pregnancy, and, "in a mad fit of housekeeping, to be done with it," sent it off to Goldin ("In Case" 37). Entranced, Goldin called Kingsolver at 6 A.M., promising to auction the work for what seemed an astonishing amount of money. On the day she returned from the hospital with her daughter, Camille, Kingsolver accepted a lucrative offer from HarperCollins [then Harper and Row] for *The Bean Trees*. The writer was now an author.

The novel features Taylor Greer, younger and much less educated than her creator, but no less curious and resourceful. Taylor narrates the story of her journey from Kentucky to Tucson, her establishment there, and her adoption of the three-year-old Cherokee girl she calls Turtle. Expressing Taylor's penetrating intelligence through her limited vocabulary proved difficult, but Kingsolver "wanted to write a book that my family or my neighbors or the guy that runs [the] . . . Service Station in Carlisle . . . could read" (Perry 153). Like her creator, Taylor discovers and celebrates the diverse ecology of the desert, describing the long-awaited coming of the summer rains with a typically homely metaphor: "[The storm] looked something like a huge blue-gray shower being drawn along by the hand of God" (161). Also like her creator, Taylor is drawn into the Sanctuary movement, and her friendship with the Guatemalan refugees Estevan and Esperanza broadens her sense of human diversity. In addition, Taylor manifests Kingsolver's own penchant for creating and asserting herself through action—she travels into the unknown, takes in Turtle, and later risks arrest by driving Estevan and Esperanza to a safe house in Oklahoma.

To express "the vantage point of the underdog" that she learned to assume in high school, Kingsolver created Lou Ann Ruiz, also a Kentuckian

8

and a single parent, whose "dreadful insecurities" contrast with Taylor's habitual confidence ("In Case" 42). Kingsolver cherishes Lou Ann ("I liked her") but, employing her typical strategy for dealing with wounded and damaged characters, limits and contains her point of view in two third-person chapters. As *The Bean Trees* unfolds, Taylor herself displays a vulnerability that, according to Kingsolver, made the book "more humane and probably more interesting for most people. . . . [A]s I got farther and farther from my keyboard throughout this pregnancy, . . . the terror of becoming a parent, the emotional inadequacy we feel facing the possibility of raising a child, . . . became a bigger and bigger part of the book" (Beattie 160). The theme becomes explicit late in the novel, when Taylor, temporarily depressed and discouraged, feels that she has "no business just assuming I could take the responsibility for a child's life," but it develops implicitly from the moment a complete stranger puts Turtle on the seat of Taylor's Volkswagen (177). However anticipated and prepared for, parenthood must seem at times like a trip with a mysterious, unknown, vulnerable passenger. Typically for a Kingsolver protagonist, Taylor copes with her doubts by taking action, seeking Turtle's family in Oklahoma and then devising a solution that allows her to adopt Turtle.

After signing with Harper for *The Bean Trees*, Kingsolver recalls, "I realized about a month later that I didn't have to go back to work as a journalist because I was getting this nice fat check . . . and I could write another book (Perry 151). Sharing child care duties with Joe and hiring part-time help, she actually wrote two books, both of which incorporated previous writing. First was the account of the mine strike, developed into a chronological narrative that focused on the experiences of the women. In keeping with its sociological, participant observer perspective, the nonfiction *Holding the Line: Women in the Great Arizona Mine Strike of 1983*, which appeared in 1989, went to an academic press—ILR Press, sponsored by the New York State School of Industrial and Labor Relations and by Cornell University.

Along with *Holding the Line*, Kingsolver developed a collection of short stories, also published in 1989, which again drew on some of her previous work. "I got to pull these scenes out of a drawer and say, 'now, who could say this?'" (Perry 156). She had begun the title story of *Homeland*, an imaginary re-creation of her Cherokee great-grandmother, fifteen years before in her one creative writing class at DePauw and had rewritten that story "every single year" until she finally found "a rhythm and a tone of voice" by im-

1

mersing herself in the tribe's legends (Perry 158). The other stories offer a variety of voices and perspectives, from a male, middle-class biology teacher to a striking woman miner, and draw on a range of Kingsolver's experiences, past, present, and even future—she must have imagined the infant Camille growing up into the adult daughter who complains about her activist mother: "'It's morbid. All those war marches she goes on. How can you think all the time about nuclear winter wiping out life as we know it, and still go on making your car payments?'" ("Islands" 124). The stories of *Homeland* also reflect literary influences: "I depend really heavily on other writers," Kingsolver told Donna Perry, citing Flannery O'Connor, Virginia Woolf, Bobbie Ann Mason, and Ethan Canin, and explaining that she turned to them for solutions to "tricky writing situation[s]" that arose "because I was doing things I had never done before" in the collection (157–58).

Kingsolver remarked that she turned to other writers "[p]ossibly because I didn't study writing in school," and the collection resembles the work of a promising writing workshop student experimenting with forms and voices (Perry 157). To create it, Kingsolver purposely stifled the distinct voice she had already developed: "Taylor wanted to tell every story I wrote, so I quite deliberately put her in the closet, and I moved out" (156). Why abandon a successful strategy in favor of experimentation? "I was scared to death . . ." (155). Apparently, she feared exposure, as well as confinement in the closet of a single literary point of view. In creating Taylor, she was "unself-conscious," revealing much of herself. When the novel became successful, she faced writing her next book "with the awareness that my mother and my neighbors and other people were going to read it" (155). Feeling exposed, she experimented with a concealing wardrobe of narrative strategies before returning to the novel form.

She also feared failing to meet the high expectations generated by a promising first novel. After completing *Holding the Line* and *Homeland,* she thought, "Well, maybe by now they've forgotten that I wrote a novel, so maybe I can hazard another one" (Beattie 163). In that novel, *Animal Dreams,* she reimagined the mining towns of *Holding the Line* as Grace, Arizona, paid tribute to the tenacious women of the strike with the fictitious Stitch and Bitch club, and incorporated her ecological perspective by reinventing the strike as a dispute with a mining company that had been polluting the river, threatening the fruit trees that helped sustain the town. Kingsolver gives the women the victory that was denied their real-life counterparts with the unfavorable resolution of the Phelps-Dodge strike: their energetic fund-raising and the resulting publicity pressure the company into ceasing operations.

Though it ends with a resolution, *Animal Dreams* explores pain, loss, isolation, and injustice through its three main characters—Dr. Homer Noline and his daughters, Hallie and Codi. The brief third-person chapters that develop Doc Homer's point of view reveal both the increasing confusion between past and present that results from Alzheimer's and the painful isolation of his stubborn self-reliance. The activist Hallie appears only in memory and speaks only through letters; she has departed for Nicaragua to serve as an agricultural consultant to the struggling Sandinista government and is first kidnapped, then killed, by the Contras. Kingsolver identified Hallie, who expresses herself through action, as the "most like me" of "all the characters I've written [up to 1996]" (Beattie 164). Yet Kingsolver's own action in writing the book to expose the abuses of the Contras meant that Hallie could not tell the story because she "had to die because that's part of what the book is about" (Perry 161). In allowing Codi, the "walking wounded," alienated sister, to tell most of the story in the first person, Kingsolver struggled with her own reluctance to identify with the wounded and damaged. "Codi's . . . personality scared me because she so detached, she's so wounded, and she's so cynical. . . . I feel [her cynicism] always walking along beside me; and if I ever once turned and embraced it, I couldn't let go" (Perry 160). Through Codi, she acknowledges annihilation as a possibility—"You could be nowhere at all"—but never embraces it (*Animal Dreams* 204). Gradually, Codi begins to heal, helped by taking part in the effort to save the river and by discovering the Native American sense of connection with the natural world through her Pueblo/Apache boyfriend, Loyd Peregrina. By the end of the novel Codi, like the river, loses her corrosive acid and becomes part of the life of Grace.

Animal Dreams appeared in 1990. As she had done after *The Bean Trees*, Kingsolver turned to another form, developing a collection of poetry—*Another America/Otra America*, which appeared in 1992. Like the stories of *Homeland*, most of the poems were new, but some had been written years before. In contrast to "big, complicated ideas that lend themselves to novels," poems for Kingsolver express "deeply felt moments that don't necessarily have a beginning or an end" (Perry 161). Those might be moments of rage or anguish she considers too intense for a novel or short story—"little steam

Priscilla Leder

vents on the pressure cooker" in which the prose work simmers gently (162).
Within the limited scope of a poem, she can speak freely as the wounded,
outcast, or outraged.

Intended to reveal the "other" America of poverty and exploitation hidden from non-Americans by cultural exports such as *Dallas,* the poems also
present a linguistic "other" in the form of facing-page Spanish translations
by Rebeca Cartes, a Chilean poet then living in Tucson. For Kingsolver, the
Spanish versions celebrate the rich possibilities that result from knowledge
of another culture and the language that expresses it. "My poems always
sound better to me in Spanish" (Perry 162). In addition, the visual presence of Spanish embodies the cultural presence so inextricably a part of
Kingsolver's adopted Southwest and testifies to its importance. In *The Bean
Trees,* Lou Ann Ruiz thinks of sending the bilingual pamphlet on prenatal
care that she receives from her doctor to her mother in Kentucky, to prove to
her that "[in] Tucson, there were so many Mexicans that people didn't think
of them as a foreign race" (*Bean Trees* 27). *Another America/Otra America*
offers a literary version of that "proof."

Among the gifts of other cultures are alternative ways of looking at
families and child rearing. For instance, Kingsolver pointed out to an interviewer, the "terrible twos" don't exist in the Spanish language or culture, perhaps, she speculated, because Hispanic children are not so rigidly
scheduled as Anglo children (R. Epstein 34). Reading local headlines about
a Yaqui child who was taken from her Hispanic adoptive parents to be returned to the tribe, she noted that the media focused only on the individual
child, while the tribe considered the child as part of a community and wondered, "In this dialogue, is there any point of intersection?" (Beattie 170). For
her, novels grow out of questions like this one, and she "completely formed
[her] idea . . . for this novel," before, she insists, "I realized that I'd already
set up the situation perfectly with *The Bean Trees*" (Beattie 170). She could
satisfy readers who clamored for a sequel and, more important, address the
moral dilemma she had set up earlier, "without paying any attention," with
Taylor Greer's illegal adoption of Turtle (Beattie 170).

Pigs in Heaven confronts Taylor with the Cherokee attorney Annawake
Fourkiller, who wants to return Turtle to the tribe. Because she believed
"that these antagonists are both right," Kingsolver felt she had to create an
omniscient narrator, "[s]omeone looking down on all these characters, loving them equally" (Mendes 319). In doing so, she employs the third-person

perspectives of Turtle's grandfather Cash Stillwater, Taylor's mother Alice, and Taylor's boyfriend, Jax, as well as those of Annawake and Taylor herself. Besides the unfamiliar omniscient point of view, *Pigs in Heaven* required Kingsolver to deal with direct conflict between people, something difficult for her. "[I]t seemed to me that I might mature as a writer if I forced myself to write about two people who have a conflict of interest who have to work it out . . . [o]n the page, not off" (Beattie 170). The working out takes place through a series of confrontations, a hearing, and finally a compromise in which Taylor and Cash share custody of Turtle, who becomes part of the tribe without losing Taylor, the only mother she knows.

After *Pigs in Heaven*, which appeared in 1993, Kingsolver again took a break from fiction with the essay collection *High Tide in Tucson: Essays From Now or Never*. Some of the essays were expanded versions of previously published magazine features or speeches, but all were recent. Many reflect her experiences as a successful writer—a book tour, a stint as keyboardist for the all-writers' band the Rock Bottom Remainders, correspondence with readers—as well as documenting life in Tucson and her relationship with Camille. Whatever the subject, the essays draw a larger meaning: in "Stone Soup," for instance, her own divorce becomes not only a painful personal ordeal ("as much *fun* as amputating your own gangrenous leg") but also part of a defense of nontraditional families of all sorts (138). This blend of personal and political, everyday and theoretical, gives the essays their power. What begins as detailed personal observation, sometimes lighthearted and funny, moves imperceptibly into something larger: after a pleasant cruise through familiar territory, readers find themselves at a higher vantage point, the cultural and political landscape spread out before them, without perceptible braking, shifting, or grinding of gears.

Through the essays in *High Tide in Tucson*, Kingsolver also returns to her Kentucky origins. A triumphant homecoming celebration in Carlisle, where "boys" who once alternately teased and ignored her lined up for her autograph, left her feeling "so cherished, so aware of old anguish, and so ready to let go of the past" ("In Case" 43). Other essays recall her adolescence with humor, and in "The Memory Place" she affirms her spiritual connection to the woods she explored as a child, revisiting them with Camille. Given an opportunity serve as visiting writer, she chose Emory and Henry College in Virginia, near her parents and her former home. There she met Steven Hopp, the ornithology professor who became her second husband.

Coming to know him and his southwestern Virginia farm was at once a homecoming and a new birth, celebrated in the final essay of *High Tide in Tucson*.

Established as a writer, settled into a life spent alternating between Tucson and Virginia with her newly blended family, Kingsolver at last confronted a subject she had thought of for years. "For about half my life," she told Elisabeth Beattie in 1993, "I have wanted to write a novel about and set in Africa, owing to the piece of my childhood that I spent there" (171). Political conviction, as well as childhood memories, shaped *The Poisonwood Bible*. The story of the arrogant preacher Nathan Price, who undertakes a mission to the Congo in the 1950s with his wife and four daughters, functions as "a political allegory, in which the small incidents of characters' lives shed light on larger events in our world. The Prices carry into Africa a whole collection of beliefs about religion, technology, health, politics, and agriculture, just as industrialized nations have often carried these beliefs into the developing world in an extremely arrogant way . . . even when . . . those attitudes are useless, offensive or inapplicable" ("FAQ"). Once again, personal and political blend, as coercion and exploitation within the family plays out in the context of coercion and exploitation within and between nations.

To bring story to life, Kingsolver undertook extensive research, immersing herself in historical and fictional accounts of the Congo and drawing upon "two remarkable sources of literary inspiration, approximately equal in size"—the King James Bible and a Kikongo-French dictionary ("Author's Note," *Poisonwood* ix). Though she could not visit the Congo (then called Zaire), she took two research trips to Africa, staying with local residents whenever she could, volunteering to cook dinner so she could experience the sights, smells, and rituals of the markets firsthand ("FAQ"). The resulting imagery lends the novel immediacy, but it is Kingsolver's narration, in which Nathan Price's wife and four daughters tell their individual stories, that gives it power. With the spontaneity of childhood, some of those voices play with language: the self-absorbed malaprop Rachel descends into "the sloop of despond," missing "simple things in [American] life that I have took for granite"; the hemiplegic Adah reverses words and sentences, deconstructing the W/word by imagining her father's weekly spiritual purgation as the "Amen enema." (*Poisonwood* 23, 69). Rachel and Adah's language distances readers from these flawed characters; in contrast, the activist Leah speaks clearly and straightforwardly. At the end of the novel, a mysterious, unidentified narrator, possibly the spirit of the dead sister Ruth May, speaks from the trees, drawing readers into a magical realm. *The Poisonwood Bible,* which appeared in 1998, remains Kingsolver's most acclaimed, most discussed novel, continually compelling because the luminous wonder of childhood illuminates the astute historical vision of the concerned, informed adult.

Her next novel represents a return to familiar geography and a shift in emphasis in which ecology, always an essential element in her work, becomes its central focus. "After the enormous effort of researching that very exotic book [*The Poisonwood Bible*]," Kingsolver wrote on her Web site, "I think I needed the comfort of looking homeward"("FAQ"). She looked to landscape of her childhood and the farm she shared with Stephen and Camille and her second daughter Lily, born in 1996. *Prodigal Summer,* which appeared in 2000, celebrates one fecund summer in a fictionalized bit of Appalachia. Its three parallel plots function like the interrelated lives of species in the same ecosystem, and Kingsolver's third-person limited narration reveals how biological exigencies—sex for Deanna Woolf, aging for Garnett Walker, adaptation for Lusa Landowska—drive its main characters.

In *Prodigal Summer,* all of Kingsolver's recurring themes take on an ecological perspective. For instance, human diversity expresses itself through food preferences and rituals: Lusa's vegetable garden looks *"pretty"* to her sister-in-law Jewel because the fava beans and eggplant varieties she grows for her mother's Middle Eastern delicacies harmonize visually with the carrots and corn. When Lusa offers to adopt the dying Jewel's two children, she creates the kind of blended family that Kingsolver often advocates. By settling the farm on the children and thus keeping it in the family, Lusa literally grounds that family in the relationship to the land that her husband's family has cultivated through generations. Love, care, and mindfulness forge fruitful relationships among all creatures, human and otherwise.

After *Prodigal Summer,* Kingsolver returned to the essay form, and the collection *Small Wonder* appeared in 2002. Like *High Tide in Tucson,* the work included recent pieces, some previously published in different versions. As with the earlier work, some essays explore her experiences as a writer—traveling to Japan, judging the Best American Short Stories contest, and writing explicitly about sex for the first time in *Prodigal Summer.* Many others, the largest group in fact, continue her focus on ecology, celebrating the wonders of the natural world and considering how humans might relate more responsibly to it. Still other essays, those that drew the most attention, express grief at the attacks of September 11, 2001, and frustration at the Bush administration's violent response to them.

That grief and frustration shadows much of *Small Wonder,* which seems haunted by an implicit question: Why does our culture so often seem to lack respect for life—to view it as a commodity or to see violence as a solution? The struggle to confront this difficult question shapes form as well as content: the essays of *Small Wonder* are darker, longer, less often playful, and more stringently analytical than those of the earlier collection. Characteristically, though, Kingsolver seeks out and calls for solutions, documenting efforts to preserve the San Pedro River in Arizona and a program that encourages people to grow native crops in an endangered forest in Yucatán, and advocating less violence on television, responsible eating, and communal actions of all kinds. The human drive for self-preservation can overcome our destructive tendencies. "We got here," she reminds us, "by being social animals, bipedal animals, tool users, seed savers, cagey mate choosers, bearers of live, big-brained young. . . . We are much too clever an animal, it seems to me, to kill ourselves now" ("God's Wife's" 263).

Ecological interests drove the other work Kingsolver completed in 2002—the text accompanying Annie Griffiths Belt's photographs in the large-format book *Last Stand: America's Virgin Lands.* Her introduction to the book first evokes her own childhood in the woods, then pays tribute to "a few Americans who could see far beyond their time on the matter of wilderness conservation" (16). She draws on five of these visionaries, William Bartram, Henry David Thoreau, John Muir, Aldo Leopold, and Edward Abbey, in introducing the five sections of *Last Stand,* each of which covers a different ecosystem—wetlands, woodlands, coasts, grasslands, and drylands (deserts). Introductions to the individual sections describe each ecosystem and our effects on it, touch on the work and thought of one of the visionaries, and call for the preservation of the system. That bald summary does little justice to the text, which is as infused with Kingsolver's lyricism as Belt's photographs are infused with light, and which manifests her gift for uniting concrete and abstract. For instance, the form of a tree recalls its chemistry. "A tree stands as a lung in reverse. Its uplifted trunk, branches, and leaves form an architectural opposite to the downward reaching trachea and alveoli rooted in our own chests" (62).

Kingsolver's next work, *Animal, Vegetable, Miracle,* which appeared in 2007, employed a new form to develop her ecological concerns. Subtitled *A Year of Food Life,* this full-length nonfiction memoir documents her family's permanent move to their Virginia farm and their effort to eat only food produced locally, by themselves or by nearby farms. Its subject perfectly exemplifies the connection between political and personal, large and small that characterizes Kingsolver's perspective; for instance, reliance on industrial farming subjects the whole society to pollution and waste at the same time as it insults the individual's taste buds with bland, mushy tomatoes. Similarly, the book juxtaposes intimate details of the farm family's life—coaxing turkeys to breed, weeding, or sneaking zucchini into the cookies, with informative discussions by Kingsolver's husband, Stephen Hopp, that deal with more technical subjects such as mad cow disease and farm subsidies.

Like Thoreau's *Walden,* the book moves through the year from spring to spring, and the ongoing chronicle of emerging and ripening plants, like the emphasis on family, grounds the narrative in the life cycle that encompasses plants and animals, writer(s) and readers. Lily and her chickens grow and mature, making her presence in the narrative inescapable. Camille's recipes round out the family circle with her input and draw readers into it by inviting them to prepare and enjoy the same foods. The writing of *Animal, Vegetable, Miracle,* typically for Kingsolver, constitutes an action that in this case grows out of her own life and encourages readers to undertake actions of their own—"searching out redemption where we can find it: recycling or carpooling or growing a garden or saving a species or *something.* Small, stepwise changes in personal habits aren't trivial. Ultimately they will, or won't, add up to having been the thing that mattered" (346).

Kingsolver's works encompass an impressive range of genres and settings, but, as we have seen, a network of interrelated themes, concerns, and strategies connects them all. She celebrates the captivating diversity of the natural world and reminds us that the life cycle unites that diversity and binds us to it. She finds human diversity similarly compelling and often embodies her belief in its possibilities as a blended family. Her imagination also embraces the wounded and the outcast but stops short of full immersion in moments of paralyzing despair because hopelessness is inimical to the sense of purpose that drives her work. Writing is action, undertaken to make a difference in the real world and to demonstrate that making a difference is possible for the reader. Action, "searching for redemption where we can find it," can take place at any level, because large political, social, and cultural issues manifest themselves in the everyday. Kingsolver's writing, both fiction and nonfiction, consistently addresses larger issues through immediate human experience, encompassing a range of readers, from a hypothetical English professor to "one of [her] relatives—who's never read anything but the Sears catalogue" (See 46).

Such accessibility, achieved through the fusion of artistry with purpose, poses a challenge to literary scholars, whose enterprise traditionally involves interpretation, articulating "hidden" meanings—showing, for example, how the alienated characters and inconclusive plots so common in contemporary writing symbolize the emptiness of our consumer society. Confronted with Kingsolver's texts, whose meanings manifest themselves clearly (though never simplistically), many scholars have focused instead on locating her work in contexts such as gender, region, culture, ecology, and disability.

Beginning with Donna Perry, who included her in *Backtalk: Women Writers Speak Out,* her 1993 collection of lively, in-depth interviews with women writers, scholars have often studied Kingsolver as a woman writer, noting her choice of women protagonists, emphasis on family, and depiction of everyday life.[3] Some writers, such as Loretta Martin Murrey and Roberta Rubenstein, have argued that she reimagines traditionally male myths from a woman's point of view.[4] Kingsolver herself readily embraces her gender identity, explaining that "our first responsibility, and also our first treasure, as writers, is to represent ourselves. So women are always dead center in my novels" (R. Epstein 34). Women's experiences—cooking, gardening, caring for children—serve to anchor her web of interrelated concerns. The potential for pregnancy and birth binds women to the biological life cycle, and the activities traditionally assigned to them give them responsibility for the family and, by extension, for survival itself. In "God's Wife's Measuring Spoons," she remarks wryly that "'when the going gets tough, seems like men reach for a weapon and women look in the pantry'" (263). It is the pantry, she implies, that holds the potential for sustaining continued existence.

Kingsolver's vivid evocations of place also encourage critics to study her as a regional writer, conferring upon her multiple regional identities. She has been classified as both a Southwestern and a Western writer and associated with Appalachia and Kentucky (Beattie).[5] Writing in the *Appalachian Journal,* Meredith Sue Willis attempts to resolve Kingsolver's geographic variety into a single, fundamental regional identity by pointing out an "Appalachian tradition [that] shapes much of her fiction, the fine old propensity for *moving on*" (80). Willis's hypothesis allows her to explain even the mobility of many of the characters in Kingsolver's early fiction in regional terms.

Scholars who consider Kingsolver as a regional writer have also noted her depictions of Native American and Mexican American cultures, but *The Poisonwood Bible* prompted the most extensive discussion of her treatment of cultures other than her own. Diane Kunz considers the novel in terms of the history of the Congo, while Kimberly Koza and Elaine Ognibene focus on Kingsolver's exploration of imperialist politics through relations within the family. After analyzing the language of the African novel, J. U. Jacobs concludes that it addresses the responsibility of the colonizers more than it reveals the reality of life in Africa.

In Kingsolver's fiction, meticulous attention to natural processes developed into open environmental advocacy, growing alongside and in concert with ecocriticism, a new interdisciplinary movement. The first issue of *ISLE (Interdisciplinary Studies in Literature and the Environment)*, the premier ecocritical journal, carried Patti Capel Swartz's essay "Saving Grace: Political and Environmental Issues and the Role of Connections in Barbara Kingsolver's *Animal Dreams*." Swartz praises Kingsolver's skillful interweaving of political, spiritual, and environmental themes and finally locates her in a women's tradition of environmental and political advocacy. Kingsolver's increasing focus on ecology, especially in *Prodigal Summer,* has inspired discussions of characters' mutual environmental education, comparisons with ecological writers, and an analysis of that novel as a model for saving the family farm (Murphy, Wenz, Jones).

After the publication of *The Poisonwood Bible,* Kingsolver's fiction drew the attention of another new interdisciplinary movement, disability studies. From that perspective, Stephen D. Fox lauded Kingsolver for giving the hemiplegic Adah her own voice, making her a full, complex human being, and even depicting the negative aspects of her eventual recovery. Earlier studies of *Animal Dreams* such as Lee Ann De Reus's "Exploring the Matrix of Identity" had prefigured the disability studies approach by focusing on the mental trauma of the troubled Codi Noline.

While Kingsolver can readily be considered in terms of gender, region, culture, ecocriticism, and disability studies, she herself identifies most strongly with an overarching category that can encompasses all the others—the political. She believes that this makes her an exception among writers in the United States, where, as she puts it, "art and politics got this divorce in the fifties, and there's never been a reconciliation" (Perry 155). Her atypical political commitment draws attention from interviewers: "When I'm inter-viewed about writing, I spend a good deal of time defending the possibility that such things as environmental ruin, child abuse, or the hypocrisy of U.S. immigration policy are appropriate subjects for a novel" ("Jabberwocky" 229). In essays such as "Jabberwocky" and "God's Wife's Measuring Spoons," she explains and defends her political commitment. She has also acted to support that commitment in others by founding the Bellwether Prize for socially responsible fiction.

Unlike the interviewers, who have apparently taken the "divorce" seri-ously, academics who study Kingsolver tend to accept her political commit-ment, perhaps because it often coincides with their own. Many scholars, like some of those cited above, compliment her skill in using literature to advo-cate responsible change. However, a few apparently believe that a political writer, because of her commitment to such change, must be judged by rigor-ous standards; they fault Kingsolver for offering hopeful visions along with bitter realities. Maureen Ryan, for example, complains that Kingsolver's books "leave all of us feeling just a bit too fine" (78). In other words, though they depict social and environmental problems, Kingsolver's works finally reassure readers instead of inciting them to action. According to Ryan, the books' endings invite complacency because "[o]ver and over, . . . her char-acters grapple with, and finally overcome hazards large and small" (79). Though characters often do overcome hazards, Kingsolver's endings never promise the easy "happy ever after" that Ryan implies. Rather, the endings are provisional compromises which open new possibilities that can be cel-ebrated in the moment, though they may fail. The resolution of *The Bean Trees* does fail, and others are incomplete or tenuous: Turtle may be unhappy with the shared custody arrangement of *Pigs in Heaven;* Anatole and Leah in *The Poisonwood Bible* may never be able to return to the Congo; the elderly Garnett Walker of *Prodigal Summer* may die before he can enjoy his grand-children or his budding friendship with his neighbor Nannie Rawley.

Though she focuses more specifically on the environment, Krista Comer makes some of the same criticisms that Ryan does. Both writers mistrust Kingsolver's depiction of family as a locus of mutual caring that potentially extends into the larger world in the form of equity and justice. Comer com-plains that the "female-gendered values" upheld in *Animal Dreams* "over-lap" in "obvious" ways with "traditional female gender roles" (231); Ryan feels that Kingsolver's "privileging of family values works to compromise her message about the injustices of our society" (81). Both writers apparently assume that readers, especially women readers, will experience Kingsolver's texts as a simple affirmation of their own experiences as women and thus remain complacent about larger social problems. However, in the absence of definitive psychological experiments on readers, assumptions about them always remain no more than that. In this case, for instance, one might just as plausibly assume that readers will never be moved to action by a text that does not in some way affirm their own experience.

These writers ultimately indict Kingsolver for idealism, arguing that she offers readers escape rather than the motivation to action that her political concerns demand. Carried to their logical extension, their standards for political writers would dismiss all imagined solutions as suspect, requiring that such writers depict only problems—painful realities such as exploitation, pollution, corruption, torture, and war. As we have seen, such a descent into despair is anathema to Kingsolver, for whom writing is an action, a movement toward some sort of resolution. "Move on," she writes at the end of *The Poisonwood Bible*. "Walk forward into the light" (543). Without the light of possibility, we remain without direction, in the dark.

Those who fault Kingsolver for idealism complain that she creates idyllic geographical and cultural spaces into which readers can escape. Comer, for instance, considers the fictionalized Grace, Arizona, to be unrealistically bucolic and free of racism. In "Barbara Kingsolver's Cherokee Nation: Problems of Representation in *Pigs in Heaven*," Kathleen Godfrey complains that the novelist "idealize[s]" and "ritualize[s]" the Cherokee (259). However, other scholars see Kingsolver's fictionalized locations and depictions of non-Western cultures not as escapist fantasies, but rather as narratives of possibility which create alternate worlds in order to reenvision this one. For instance, Naomi Jacobs demonstrates how *Animal Dreams* "unravels the Western's conventional approach to heroism, to violence and death, and to community." Deborah Clarke sees *The Bean Trees* as an example of "women's road novels" which both challenge the traditionally masculine form of the road novel and "unsettle" received notions of gender and domesticity (102).

The essays in this volume both extend already established lines of inquiry into Kingsolver's work and take them in new directions. Though her interwoven web of themes and concerns makes classification of her work necessarily arbitrary, the three sections that follow represent a movement outward from individual, to society, to the biosphere. Because ecology has become ever more central to her work, this organization also broadly reflects the chronology of her work, beginning with *The Bean Trees* and ending with *Animal, Vegetable, Miracle.*

In different ways, the essays in section one all consider how individuals define themselves and come to terms with their experiences within and against socially constructed norms. The first three approach Kingsolver as a woman writer. Catherine Himmelwright develops and extends the argument that Kingsolver reimagines patriarchal myths: she shows how *The Bean Trees* draws on Native American mythology to undo the traditional binary between the free, adventurous Western man and the static, domestic woman. Maureen Kentoff argues that the essays of *High Tide in Tucson* articulate and make concrete the complex, abstract concepts of identity, perspective, and agency postulated by contemporary feminist theory. Like Himmelwright, Héloïse Meire explores Kingsolver's revision of an arguably patriarchal narrative; like Kentoff, she aligns Kingsolver with feminist theory: her essay analyzes *The Poisonwood Bible* as a feminist response to Joseph Conrad's *Heart of Darkness.*

The other two essays in part 1 examine Kingsolver's depictions of damaged or disabled characters. Sheryl Stevenson considers *Animal Dreams* in light of trauma theory, showing that Codi's discourse, memory, and relationships depict the experience of trauma survivors and reveal the relevance of trauma theory for the larger society. In comparing Codi to the disabled character Adah from *The Poisonwood Bible,* Breyan Strickler draws on both feminism and disability studies to show how Kingsolver calls into question distinctions between "normal" and disabled, "healthy" nature and "toxic" city.

The essays in part 2 focus on Kingsolver's political commitment, exploring her calls for change and visions for a better world and analyzing her methods for engaging her readers. In the first extensive treatment of her poetry collection, *Another America/Otra America,* Meagan Evans shows how Kingsolver reconciles the activist's need to convey a clear message with the expectation that poetry must require readers to construct meaning for themselves. Evans demonstrates how Kingsolver reimagines familiar clichés; similarly, Robin Cohen reveals how Kingsolver's depiction of Native America calls stereotypes into question. In considering the interactions between Anglo and Native Americans in *Pigs in Heaven,* Jeanne Sokolowski reveals the subtlety of Kingsolver's political rhetoric, which reminds Anglo readers of the history of exploitation of Native Americans without holding them responsible for it. Kristen Jacobson uses cultural geography to analyze Kingsolver's fictional spaces, showing that, rather than offering easy escapes, they "challenge the reader to envision alternative realities." In the final essay, Wes Berry responds to critics who accuse Kingsolver of disrespect for American institutions by showing how, in her nonfiction, she reimagines loyalty to "God, family, and country" as her own version of patriotism.

The essays in the final section consider the various ways in which Kingsolver explores the operation of natural systems and demonstrates how humans might best participate in those systems. My essay argues that *Prodigal Summer* presents a version of Michael Pollan's garden ethic, which advocates responsible interaction with the natural world rather than the isolation of some areas as inviolable "wilderness," leaving the rest vulnerable to exploitation. As Christine Cusick explains, Kingsolver's nonfiction illustrates how we might draw upon the personal memories and stories of specific places that form the basis of our attachment to the land to address the current environmental crisis. Attachment to the land grows out of a sense of wonder that must be discovered and fostered in childhood: Susan Hanson reveals how Kingsolver models that process in *Prodigal Summer* and in her essays. Finally, Gioia Woods envisions that attitude as an "environmental aesthetic" and shows how, in *Animal, Vegetable, Miracle,* Kingsolver and her coauthors blend the discourses of science, economics, politics, and art to create that aesthetic.

Taken together, these essays demonstrate how Kingsolver's work reconsiders and reimagines the discourses of our culture to reveal possibilities for a better world. In doing so, they also offer new perspectives on Kingsolver to her readers.

Notes

1. Unless otherwise indicated, biographical information in the introduction is taken from Linda Wagner-Martin's thoughtful and informative work *Barbara Kingsolver.*
2. A search of the Alternative Press Index turns up articles by Kingsolver in the national socialist newsweekly *The Militant* as early as 1979 and 1980.
3. Ruth Smith explores the multiple possibilities of home in several of Kingsolver's works; Patricia Goldblatt compares the marriages of Nathan and Orleanna and Leah and Anatole in *The Poisonwood Bible;* Mary Jean DeMarr discusses the gender roles of mothers and children in *The Bean Trees.*

Priscilla Leder

4. Murrey argues that Kingsolver reimagines the familiar American theme of the wandering loner by relating it to the matriarchal community in *The Bean Trees* and *Pigs in Heaven;* Rubenstein analyzes *Animal Dreams* as a reenvisioning of the Homeric quest.

5. David Dunaway and Susan Quick both identify Kingsolver as a Southwestern writer; Charlotte Wright and Gioia Woods have each contributed essays on Kingsolver to collections on contemporary Western writers.

Part 1
Identity

Gardens of Auto Parts: American Western Myth and Native American Myth in *The Bean Trees*

Catherine Himmelwright

> *Outside was a bright, wild wonderland of flowers and vegetables and auto parts. Heads of cabbage and lettuce sprouted out of old tires. An entire rusted out Thunderbird, minus the wheels, had nasturtiums blooming out the windows like Mama's hen-and-chicks pot on the front porch at home. A kind of teepee frame made of CB antennas was all overgrown with cherry-tomato vines.*
>
> —The Bean Trees

Junkyards and gardens: How could two such diametrically opposed worlds flourish together? Seemingly, one would preclude the possibility of the other. Abandoned wrecks would jeopardize new tomatoes, while spilled oil would poison the fertile ground, debilitating the delicate burgeoning of a squash blossom. How can anyone tend a garden in the midst of rusted auto parts? How can growth occur in the midst of abandonment?

In the mythology that surrounds the American West, one of the primary expressions of the Western experience has been the male's desire to move. Whether by horse, pioneer wagon, raft, or even later by car, action typifies the male Western hero, who feels a powerful desire to hit the open road. Action and adventure are tied tightly to the need to be mobile. Adventures do not happen at home; you have to go find them. In contrast, women have been connected rather loosely to the male Western archetype despite their presence on the frontier. As opposed to symbols of movement, the female experience has been firmly rooted in the image of the garden. Annette Kolodny has perhaps furthered this construction the most by exploring women's idealization of the garden on the frontier. She states in *The Land Before Her* that women gained access to the West by connecting themselves both literarily and figuratively with the garden. Embodying both the characteristics of the natural and procreative, gardens evolved into symbols of the home. Cultivating a garden in the West provided women a claim or admittance into a masculine world, if only to a portion of the experience. As a garden must have constant attention, motion is difficult for those who garden. Women, therefore, gained access to the frontier yet were excluded from the adventure that men sought.

Despite the obvious oppositions, Barbara Kingsolver finds a way to bring them together in *The Bean Trees*. Merging these characteristics: the desire for movement and the desire to tend a home, Kingsolver is able to express a female voice that has heretofore been lost or subsumed by the white male experience. In many ways, Kingsolver creates a character who becomes that individual Kolodny speaks of at the end of *The Land Before Her,* for Kingsolver's main character becomes both "adventurer and domesticator" (Kolodny 240). By combining these two figures, Kingsolver fashions a new American mythology that unites both male and female imaginative constructs. The attempt is not an easy one, as access to the West has almost always been achieved, whether the individual is male or female, through white masculine constructs. In *West of Everything*, Jane Tompkins points out the difficulty women have had in gaining admittance to this masculine world, especially access to the role of the hero. Although Tompkins deals chiefly with the genre of the Western, she does question the type of connection women have to the genre as a whole. Her findings reveal the female desire for this access through their own attempts to "imagine" themselves within the Western. Tompkins found that some women found imagining inclusion impossible, but for those who could, awkward manipulations would take place in order to create a place for the female within this world:

> One friend said she loved "Bonanza" so much that she had to invent a female character so that she could participate as a woman. ... Another friend told me she could identify with male heroes but only the nonwhite, non-WASP ones, Tonto and Zorro. (16)

Clearly, the struggle to find inclusion in this myth of adventure is difficult; still the passage demonstrates women's desire to claim in some "real" sense the ideology represented in our imaginative construction of the American

West. Yet how does one write about a female's experience in the West? The West has become so "masculinized" in connotation that the very word evokes images of the male. Thus, finding negotiated space from which to express the female experience in the West is difficult. Although attempts have been made which include the female presence, traditionally these representations privilege a male voice.

Historically, a woman's presence in the "frontier experience" occurs *hysterically,* as she is seen bemoaning the fact that her recent husband or father has forced her to leave everyone and everything she loves to "go west." Rarely is she seen as a willing participant in her removal to the wide-open spaces. Lillian Schlissel states in *Women's Diaries of the Westward Journey* that "[t]he overland journey wrenched women from the domestic circle that had encased much of their lives in stable communities" (28). Schlissel provides many examples that emphasize this devastating separation. Often the separation from a domestic community proved to be one of the most difficult challenges. As Melody Graulich states, "Adventure, independence, and freedom belong to male characters, while women 'endure,' as does the long-suffering pioneer helpmate who tries to re-create 'home' in the West, memorialized as the Madonna of the plains" (187). Janis Stout in *Through the Window, Out the Door* states that "narrative conventions and assumptions (of journeys and departures) are so deeply rooted in masculine paradigms that reshaping them to serve a woman's own desire is an enormous challenge" (4). As for some of the women described by Tompkins, active participation seems difficult to imagine within the historical accounts of Western experience.[1]

Rejecting the limited representations of women on the frontier that are given by history and literature, many contemporary writers have tried their hand at the "anti-Western." Michael Johnson in *New Westers* defines the "anti-Western" as "going against the grain in pretty direct fashion." The anti-Western emerges as a vehicle to manipulate that literary construction or archetype that has been fashioned within the American imagination. Johnson states, "They portrayed the underside and . . . suggested that the idealist assumptions of the traditional Western formula were naïve and masked the racism, violence, and greed of the historical conquest of the West" (215). Most who have chosen to write the anti-Western have remained within the parameters of a masculine world. In writing about the female experience, they have simply written about a woman who, when faced with the challenges that normally face the male protagonist, reacts in a similar way.

30

Such narratives still privilege the masculine experience and undermine how the female experience might be separate from the archetype. In essence, the female figure simply becomes a man, or at least a more androgynous figure who can adopt masculine characteristics in order to experience the West.

Kingsolver does adopt the approach of the anti-Western; however, she brings a new twist to her approach. Envisioning a new Western archetype, she is able to leave behind the standard forms of male adventure by finding access to an alternate mythology. Like Tompkins's friends who find access through the alter-hero, "the nonwhite, non-WASP ones, Tonto and Zorro," Kingsolver uses a similarly alternative perspective by evoking a nonwhite mythology that will allow for the participation of the female. By choosing the "ultimate anti-Western," Kingsolver is able to explore a world that gives voice to the female through the Native American experience. Adapting Native American mythology to her novel provides Kingsolver access to a world prior to the development of a white masculine construction. Gaining access to a world and mythology that preexists the white male construction, she is able to navigate a space in which the female story has not yet been defined by the masculine voice.

Kingsolver begins her novel by following the male archetype of Western myth, the only initial difference being that her main character is female. Kingsolver creates a strong-minded independent woman in search of a better life. Turning away from Kentucky, Missy Greer, at twenty-three, heads West with the hope of finding a life that will provide new opportunities. Popular Western heroes such as Daniel Boone, Huck Finn, and Natty Bumppo are all brought to mind in Kingsolver's initial description of Missy. She is strong and independent and appears fully capable of clearing her path in order to achieve her own desires, but most important, she, like them, desires to leave civilization and "light out for the territory" (Twain 283). Similar to Leslie Fiedler's depictions of westering men in *The Return of the Vanishing American,* Kingsolver creates a protagonist who yearns for escape. Many male literary figures "together constitute the image of the runaway from home and civilization whom we long to be when we are our most authentic selves"; their female counterparts "add up to the image of his dearest enemy, spokesman for the culture and the European inheritance he flees" (118). Men leave their homes in order to flee women; women represent for them an opposition to the fulfillment of their identity. Building on this tradition, Kingsolver inverts the usual pattern in order to explore the female search for identity.

Catherine Himmelwright

Important to note, as well, is the fact that *The Bean Trees* is a Southern novel, or certainly a novel that begins in the South. Taking place initially in Kentucky, it is replete with rural images and the vivid dialogue of the South. However, Missy's southern origins take up very little of this novel. Giving the reader only a glimpse, Kingsolver shows us the impetus for Missy's search and an explanation for the Western novel that *The Bean Trees* becomes. The nasturtiums might bloom like "Mama's hen-and-chicks pot on the front porch at home," but by the end of the novel, Missy is not in Kentucky anymore. And in leaving Kentucky, Missy and *The Bean Trees* leave the South behind in an attempt to head West and craft a Western adventure. How can a southern novel be a Western novel? Robert Brinkmeyer explores this question in *Remapping Southern Literature*. He notes the proliferation of Western novels written by southerners and their interests in exploring notions of southern place and Western space. For the most part, he investigates this merging or blending of the two. In *The Bean Trees,* Brinkmeyer sees the main character as forming a place in the West, as finding some type of regeneration that comes through "reintegration–reintegration into family and community that closes . . . *The Bean Trees*" (101). While the novel might certainly be read in this way, it neglects to consider the true lack of place provided by the southern community described. Missy Greer may find something typically considered "southern" in Arizona, but the remarkable thing is she does not find this "typically southern" place in Kentucky. For this reason, a "reintegration" does not seem possible; instead she crafts a new place, her own place, out of the space she finds. Much of what sparks the events of *The Bean Trees* proves a dramatic reaction against the main character's southern upbringing.

Unlike the societal pressures depicted in traditional Western novels, *The Bean Trees* reveals how the demands of civilization or society are no longer represented by women. As men are often depicted as seeking freedom away from the demands of women, Kingsolver suggests a world in which women and children feel limited by the demands of the father. Although Kingsolver creates no father figure for Missy (her father leaves long before she is born), she does paint a vivid picture of another family in town, Newt Harbine's. Missy sees many likenesses between herself and Newt. "If you were to look at the two of us . . . you could have pegged us for brother and sister" (2). Due to these similarities, Kingsolver suggests that the events that occur in Newt's family are at least partially responsible for Missy's flight. Missy relates the story of watching Newt Harbine's father propelled "over the top

32

of the Standard Oil sign" due to his inability to fill a tire correctly. Despite the comedy provided for the reader, this experience leaves a lasting impression on Missy. "I had this feeling about what Newt's whole life was going to amount to, and I felt sorry for him. Before that exact moment I don't believe I had given much thought to the future" (1). And it is later, after Newt Harbine dies due to an altercation with his father that Missy saves her money in an attempt to leave Pittman County. Jolene, Newt's wife, tells Missy that Newt's father was responsible for everything. She claims that "he [Newt's father] beat him up, beat her up, and even . . . hit the baby with a coal scuttle" (9). As similarities have already been drawn between Newt and Missy, it is difficult not to see the feelings of being trapped and lost to all opportunity for Newt as well. Escaping "daddy" is seen as a difficult feat, as in Newt's eventual demise, as well as Jolene's challenges of escaping her own father's abuse. Learning Jolene's past, Missy feels she may have been lucky: "I told her I didn't know, because I didn't have a daddy. That I was lucky that way. She said yeah" (9).

In addition to this pressure, Missy is also desperate to escape the pressures to conform to the woman's role as seen in Pittman County, Kentucky. Most of the women at Missy's high school have become pregnant before their senior year: "Believe me in those days the girls were dropping by the wayside like seeds off a poppyseed bun and you learned to look at every day as a prize" (3). Graduating from high school, Missy describes herself as incredibly lucky to have been given a job at the local hospital. In fact, she says that her science teacher who helped her get the job, "changed my life, there is no doubt" (3). In an environment where most young girls marry and become pregnant, Missy describes a place where opportunities for a different kind of life are limiting or nonexistent. Her mother cleans homes for people in town, and before finding a job at the hospital, Missy's only options for gaining money are helping her mother with other people's laundry, babysitting, or picking bugs off farmers' beans. Missy prizes the job at the hospital, as it dramatically contrasts the dead end jobs she has had before. She states: "But this was a real job at the Pittman County Hospital, which was one of the most important and cleanest places for about a hundred miles" (4). Missy pursues a life that deviates from the ones around her: "Mama always said barefoot and pregnant was not my style. She knew" (3). Escaping pregnancy, Missy feels she has the opportunity to flee Pittman County and the dim future it represents for her.

Catherine Himmelwright

Perhaps more telling than the lack of opportunity is the lack of community found in this novel. Nowhere does Kingsolver describe this southern community in a positive way. Unlike other southern novels that seem rife with the close, although sometimes smothering bonds of family and community, Kingsolver describes no close friends or caring extended family in Missy's life. The only positive forces are her mother, who always acted as if her daughter "hung [the moon] up in the sky and plugged in all the stars," and her teacher, who is "from out of state, from some city college up north" (3). They are the only ones described who are able to envision a life larger than Pittman County, Kentucky. Telling, too, is the fact that Missy's teacher is not even from the South. He seems easily able to imagine a larger more expansive world due to his outsider's perspective. That a southern community might be found stifling is not necessarily surprising or strange; southern literature abounds with such descriptions. What is considerably more notable is that this small southern county is completely devoid of any representation of community. Perhaps Missy is denied admittance; yet she never mentions a positive view of community for anyone, including her mother or her school friends. Regardless of this larger absence found within Pittman County, the focus remains on Missy's lack of community. Take out Missy's mother and her northern teacher, and she has no one. Within this environment, Missy Greer is well fostered to become a self-sufficient and independent individual. She has no real choice. Missy's society prescribes a role that she does not desire and that denies her a sense of community. For these reasons, the dream of freedom that has always loomed large for the westering man is now sought by the woman in her equally powerful desire to escape. Southern society threatens her vision of personal identity. Flight is essential.

Missy will be like the fish she finds in the "old mud-bottomed ponds" of Kentucky—"The ones nobody was ever going to hook, slipping away under the water like dark-brown dreams" (3). She will not be the "hooked bass" that remains. After working at the hospital for over five years, she makes enough money to buy a modern-day horse, a "55 Volkswagen bug with no windows to speak of, and no back seat and no starter" (10). She leaves Kentucky unaided and relying on her own abilities: "I would drive west until my car stopped running, and there I would stay" (12).

Soon after she leaves, Missy decides she will change her name. "I wasn't crazy about anything I had been called up to this point in life, and this seemed like the time to make a clean break. I didn't have any special name in mind, but just wanted a change" (11). The name change certainly marks Missy's desire to "re-create" herself, or at least her attempts toward that recreation, but it also marks Missy's recognition of her own success at leaving Pittman County, and similar to other Western figures, her ability to claim her own autonomy due to her escape. R. W. B. Lewis notes in *The American Adam* this pivotal moment in Cooper's *Deerslayer*. Once "the trial is successfully passed—the trial of honor, courage and self-reliance—Deerslayer earns his symbolic reward of a new name" (104). Missy's name change is equally pivotal. She decides to name herself for the nearest town in which her car runs out of gas. Although she claims to desire leaving this decision to the fates, she proves she has control over what her destiny will be. "I came pretty close to being named after Homer, Illinois, but kept pushing it. I kept my fingers crossed through Sidney, Sadorus, Cerro Gordo, Decatur, and Blue Mound, and coasted into Taylorsville on the fumes" (12). She chooses the name, Taylor. She has fashioned her own name, which denotes not only Western movement but also someone empowered and able to adapt or create. This change further marks Taylor as a creative participant in her new identity.

Taylor's adventure west continues to follow this male pattern at the beginning of the novel. Just as she leaves society behind and begins to create her own identity, she crosses the path of the Native American. As Fiedler states: "The heart of the Western is not the confrontation with the alien landscape . . . but the encounter with the Indian" (21). Much has been written concerning the white male's relationship with the Indian. Smith states in *Virgin Land,* "As the literary Western hero moves beyond the Mississippi he is becoming more and more fully assimilated into the mores of the Indian. At the same time, he is conceived as more and more completely autonomous, isolated, and self-contained" (91). Regardless of the result, which has often been dramatic, the exchange between whites and Native Americans has taken place *only* between men.[2]

Kingsolver's *The Bean Trees* places equal importance on this confrontation, but its approach differs dramatically from earlier literary representations. Just as Taylor begins to feel she has left Pittman County behind, she is surprised by a Cherokee woman who emerges out of the night to leave a small child with her as she is leaving a diner. Taylor is confused and muddled about what she should do. A child is not part of her plan, and she quickly feels the promise of her new life threatened: "If I wanted a baby I would have stayed in Kentucky. . . . I could have had babies coming out of my ears by now" (18). Yet Taylor does not leave the child, and she continues on her journey with baby in tow. Once she realizes that the child has been abused, Taylor becomes more convinced that she really has no choice: "I thought I knew about every ugly thing that one person does to another, but I had never even thought about such things being done to a baby girl" (23). Finding "bruises and worse" on the child's body, Taylor confronts the dark shadows of abuse that have tormented the child's young life.

Important to note, as well, is the fact that Kingsolver has chosen that the Native American child should be Cherokee. Through this choice, Kingsolver evokes the forced removal of Native Americans, including Cherokee, along the Trail of Tears (1813–55). Allusions to this historical event intensify Kingsolver's questioning of an American mythology of conquest and control. Facing car trouble on Cherokee lands in Oklahoma, Taylor states, "It was not a place you'd ever go to live without some kind of lethal weapon aimed at your hind end. It was clear to me that the whole intention of bringing the Cherokees here was to get them to lie down and die without a fight" (13). Sympathizing with the Native American plight, Taylor is perhaps further moved due to her own belief that she is one-eighth Cherokee. Raised by her mother, Taylor has been brought up to believe that if times grew tough she could always claim her "head rights." On viewing the reservation, Taylor realizes that these "rights" promise very little. When she writes home she informs her mother: "No offense, but the Cherokee Nation is crap. Headed west" (15). Kingsolver emphasizes the despair Taylor finds at the Oklahoma reservation. "I sat in the parking lot looking out over that godless stretch of nothing and came the closest I have ever come to cashing in and plowing under" (13). What her mother has described as possible freedom, Taylor discovers to be a life of stagnation and ultimate despair. Claiming the child, however, ties Taylor to this heritage, regardless of her rejection of reservation life.

The acquisition of the child is pivotal in Kingsolver's novel, for at this point Kingsolver breaks from the male archetypal construction. Although the confrontation with the Native American is comparable in importance, Taylor's experience no longer mirrors that of the masculine. Choosing to adapt a Cherokee creation myth, Kingsolver severs her previous connection to a white masculine perspective and investigates the female experience through Cherokee mythology. Traditionally in American literature the male experience has been closely defined through his relation to the Native American. Much of the white male interaction has relied heavily on the physical component of that relationship. The white male gained from his experience with the Native American by modeling many of his physical abilities. Learning the ways of the woods, the white male would learn how to navigate the frontier landscape through the guidance and expertise of the Native American. Although these behaviors were often successfully modeled, males tended to stray from the spiritual nature of their "borrowed" behavior. The inner workings of the Native American mythology had no place in the white world and in many ways frightened white males in their search to gain access and control of a mysterious wilderness.

Fiedler comments on the threat of Indian mythology in *The Return of the Vanishing American:*

> The really disturbing threat of the Indian, technologically backward and eternally surprised at the white man's treachery, was never military—nor even, despite the unexpectedness of the pox, venereal—but mythological, which is to say, based not on what he did, only on what he was. (39)

Kingsolver explores levels of Native American mythology and Native American spirituality which have been traditionally avoided in literary representations. Even as her character follows the male pattern of confrontation with the Native American, the encounter and the ramifications of that encounter will differ vastly from the male approach. Rather than confronting and adopting the *physical* attributes of a Native American world, Kingsolver creates a character who explores the *spiritual* or mythological ways of Native Americans.[3] Despite the radical differences in the contact, a growing sense of identity still emerges from this experience.

Important to note, as well, is the fact that the specific myth that Kingsolver incorporates is based on female deities. By looking to the Cherokee world, Kingsolver's story further gains strength by employing a myth derived from a society in which women are empowered. Historically, Cherokee society was matrilineal. The influence of the woman in Cherokee culture is seen through the power demonstrated by females in the area of kinship. "The only permanent members of a household were women. Husbands were outsiders; that is they were not kinsmen. When a man married, he moved from the household of his mother to that of his wife" (Perdue 43). Empowerment of women in areas of kinship is equally represented in the mythology that surrounds Cherokee thought. Some critics state that "the existence of an important female deity indicates the acceptance of female rights, privileges, and even power" (Perdue 40). Many of the deities that exist in the Cherokee world reflect the essential role of the woman in Cherokee society. Two examples include the deity of corn and the deity of creation.[4] Commanding a role in the Native American's main source of food, as well as in the act of creation, exemplifies the unequivocal importance of the female within Cherokee society.

Kingsolver's choice of myth not only describes the female experience but also glorifies the power of the woman and her ability to create. The central figure of the Cherokee myth of creation is Star Woman; she creates not only gardens but also new worlds. In the ancient Cherokee myth, Star Woman is responsible for the creation of the natural world and for bringing consciousness to those around her:

> Many people say it was Star Woman who was the primal cause. One story says she was in her father's garden, that is in Galunlati, when she heard drumming under a tree and dug a hole to see what was going on. Star Woman fell through the hole and spun toward the earth. At that time the earth was under the primeval flood, and earth creatures lacked the spark of deep consciousness or understanding. They did have feelings, however.
>
> The father watched his daughter fall and called on the winds to get the earth creatures to help her. Turtle suggested that his back become a landing place for her, so the animals dove into the depths to find something soft to place on Turtle's back.
>
> Now the earth on Turtle's back grew. . . . All was ready for Star Woman, who landed on Turtle's back and immediately produced corn, beans, other plants, and rivers from her body. Most of all, she brought the spark of consciousness, symbolized by the Cherokee's sacred fire, which is always kept alive for the ceremonies. (Leeming 47)

Kingsolver's knowledge of this myth is revealed on a variety of levels due to the emphasis placed on certain themes. The myth details the empowerment of the female, which is central to the human connection to a natural world, as well as the importance of community. In choosing and adapting this myth to her novel, Kingsolver dramatically opposes the traditional themes of the Western archetypal tradition.

In both the myth and the novel, women leave the world they have previously known for another. Star Woman falls through a hole from her father's world, while Taylor also leaves a patriarchal southern world that restricts her. After their departure, their journeys are radically changed through their meeting with (the) Turtle. Star Woman is saved from the destructive "primeval flood," where no land mass exists, through the concerted efforts of the natural world to find a means for her survival. She enters a world in which the human and natural world come together in a communal effort.

In Kingsolver's novel, Taylor has a similar experience. Soon after receiving the Cherokee child, Taylor names her Turtle due to her powerful grip:

> The most amazing thing was the way that child held on. From the first moment I picked it up out of its nest of wet blanket, it attached itself to me by its little hands like roots sucking on dry dirt. I think it would have been easier to separate me from my hair. . . . You're like a mud turtle. If a mud turtle bites you, it won't let go till it thunders. (22)

Difficult to ignore is the similarity that emerges between the relationship between the two (Star Woman and the turtle, and Taylor and Turtle). Both lives are dramatically changed due to the productivity that arises through their meeting.

Although Kingsolver focuses on the relationships that occur in the human world, she describes these relationships in terms that reflect the natural world. By doing so, Kingsolver compares the connections between people with the relationships essential in the plant and animal world, as seen in Taylor's description of Turtle's holding on. Despite the fact that the dirt is "dry," there is still the powerfully natural connection between soil and plant and the creative act that occurs between the two. Whether between people and plants or between soil and animals, productivity only occurs through relationship. Unlike mythic adventures of the male, creation is the goal rather than acquisition or destruction.

In many ways Kingsolver enacts the Indian belief of the Sacred Hoop through her choice of creation myth. The myth, and thus the novel, function as reminders that the individual belongs to a larger body. As Paula Gunn Allen states in *The Sacred Hoop:*

> At base, every story, every song, every ceremony tells the Indian that each creature is part of a living whole and that all parts of that whole are related to one another by virtue of their participation in the whole of being. . . . Beauty is wholeness. . . . The circle of being is not physical, but it is dynamic and alive. It is what lives and moves and knows, and all the life forms we recognize— animals, plants, rocks, winds—partake of this greater life. (241)

Therefore the natural world and the human world often reflect and combine to emphasize the vital interconnectedness of a larger, spiritual world.

Kingsolver continually mixes and merges images of nature with people. Often the very act of nature described is the spark for bringing the characters together. One such powerful instance occurs when the drought in Tucson finally ends. "Around 4 o'clock we heard thunder. Mattie turned over the 'closed' sign in the window and said 'Come on. I want you to smell this'" (160). Hustling everyone to come along, Mattie brings Taylor, Lou Anne, Esperanza, and Estevan to witness the Indian New Year. Mattie explains to Taylor, "They celebrated it on whatever day the summer's first rain fell" (161). Taylor's small community is again drawn together by nature's instigation. Knocking on her door late at night, Virgie Mae, her older neighbor, comes to announce the appearance of her night-blooming cereus.[5] Gathering up the children, Taylor and Lou Ann walk over to Virgie Mae and Edna's to witness the amazingly rare natural occurrence. "The petals stood out in starry rays, and in the center of each flower there was a complicated construction of silvery threads shaped like a pair of cupped hands catching moonlight. A fairy boat, ready to be launched into the darkness" (186). Lou Ann states that "it's a sign . . . (of) something good" (186). Occurring in the midst of personal challenges, the cereus unites community and proves the existence of beauty, even in the darkness.

Taylor's relationships are strengthened due to their communal participation in nature, but it is also important to realize that the community that exists around her results through Taylor's own relationship with Turtle. Just as vegetative productivity is the result of the connection between Star Woman and Turtle, so is communal productivity the result of the connection between Taylor and Turtle. Kingsolver challenges Taylor by confronting her directly with the challenges of motherhood as well as her growing comprehension of the difficulties in the world around her. Although these difficulties surround Taylor, she is strengthened by the group that encompasses her due to Turtle's presence. When Taylor has questions about mothering or needs a babysitter, her community provides support.

On first meeting Mattie at Jesus Is Lord Used Tires, Taylor and Mattie bond over discussing Turtle. Mattie quickly informs Taylor, as she gives more juice to Turtle, that "[i]t's so dry out here kids will dehydrate real fast.... You have to watch out for that" (44). Taylor slowly begins to realize the enormous responsibility she has assumed: "I wondered how many other things were lurking around waiting to take a child's life when you weren't paying attention. I was useless" (45). Fortunately for Taylor, she is surrounded by a group of strong women. Although Taylor's mother is also depicted as a strong woman, community is not described as a source of support in Kentucky. In Tucson, Taylor finds a world where women aid those around them. Quickly meeting Lou Ann when she moves to Tucson, Taylor shares rent with her in order to afford raising two small children as single parents. Child care and meals are often shared and the burden seems lighter due to the bond that grows between these two initial strangers. Lou Ann and Taylor soon meet others who are invited to share meals and discuss their lives and personal struggles. Estevan tells a story one evening that epitomizes Kingsolver's growing point concerning the bonds and need of community.

> If you go to visit hell, you will see a room like this kitchen. There is a pot of delicious stew on the table, with the most delicate aroma you can imagine. All around, people sit, like us. Only they are dying of starvation.... They are starving because they only have spoons with very long handles.... With these ridiculous, terrible spoons, the people in hell can reach into the pot but they cannot put the food in their mouths. Oh, how hungry they are! ... you can visit heaven.... You see a room just like the first one, the same table, the same pot of stew, the same spoons as long as a sponge mop. But these people are all happy and fat.... Why do you think?
>
> He pinched up a chunk of pineapple in his chopsticks, neat as you please, and reached all the way across the table to offer it to Turtle. She took it like a newborn bird. (108)

Struggles still surround, yet they are able to make their way with each other's help. Amid these powerful women is Mattie, the matriarchal leader who runs a used tire shop. Although Mattie runs her own business, she also uses her store as a safe sanctuary for illegal aliens. Providing food and care for those who need it, Mattie's home and business thrive as a means of support for those who find themselves hiding from the law. Repairing and selling tires emerges as a fitting metaphor symbolizing the importance of action. This is seen most clearly through Mattie's ability to "control" tires. This power scares Taylor initially, as she is haunted by Newt Harbine's father's own inability to control them. However, Mattie is able to rid Taylor of her fears and ultimately teach her the importance and need for the power tires possess, if one only knows how to control them.

Much of the male Western myth has been founded on the desire to explore adventure on the edges of a shifting frontier. As men gain and cultivate, the frontier moves outward while civilization slowly follows. Male characters must travel farther and farther away from civilization in order to confront those explosive areas that exist on the ever-moving frontier. Kingsolver also explores this occurrence; however, she finds a movement that shifts inwardly as opposed to one that continues outwardly. The dangers come from within areas close to the home, those areas that have already been settled and defined as safe. For Taylor, adventures emerge in the challenge to survive within the domestic frontier. Although in Taylor's adventure the landscape no longer presents an overt threat, the landscape does hide would-be molesters who jeopardize the physical as well as the spiritual growth of children. Escaping one danger that occurs within her own biological family, Turtle is further threatened by an unknown assailant's attack. While Taylor is at work, Edna, an older blind neighbor, takes Turtle to the park. During their day there, Edna hears Turtle being attacked, yet even in her blindness she is able to strike the attacker with her cane and drive him away. Those places that appear to be the safest hide sinister elements of violence and destruction.

Taylor's adventures multiply as she gains a greater understanding of the challenges of those individuals who live around her. Her naiveté quickly explodes when she learns of the plight of illegal aliens like Estevan, who tells Taylor one evening what happened to him and his wife in Guatemala. After the police killed Estevan's brother and two of his friends, they looked to Esperanza and Estevan for the names of the remaining members of a teacher's union to which they belonged. When they refused to release the seventeen names, Estevan and Esperanza's child was taken from them as a leveraging tool. Without proof of the malevolent treatment that awaits their return to Central America, Estevan and Esperanza become fugitives who must hide from an American government that refuses them aid. Threatened with their removal and return, the illegal aliens depend upon Taylor's ability to guide them to a sanctuary hidden from the law. Opening her eyes to the world around her, Taylor vents her frustration with those who question the safety of such an expedition: "Just stop it okay? . . . I can't see why I shouldn't do this. If I saw somebody was going to get hit by a truck I'd push them out of the way. Wouldn't anybody? It's a sad day for us all if I'm being a hero here" (188). Taylor is confronted with the fact that she must finally grow up and face the real world, which is often dangerous and cruel. There seems no need to look very far for adventure. Dangers and threats circle and impinge on life for the individual and the community, even in the perceived safety of society.

Some critics believe that Kingsolver's story appears too politically correct in its approach.[6] Occasionally the tension or conflict created is rather too easily resolved, given that the real world is often more messy than neat. Some also argue that her easy incorporation of multicultural communities exists primarily to provide images rather than to attempt to confront realistic representations of these integrations. However, to be blinded by these shortcomings would certainly be a loss. For Kingsolver has found a way to give voice to that experience which has yet to be explored. By rewriting the Western experience through the female mythology of the Cherokee, Kingsolver has gained access to that part of our American experience that has been lamentably absent in our imaginative constructions of the American West.

Many critics have noted the importance of the Native American in the development of our American identity, yet few have fully explored that legacy. Through *The Bean Trees,* Kingsolver launches our pursuit of that complete voice by providing the voice of the female as well as the spiritual legacy of the Native American. Despite Taylor's re-creation of self, her metamorphosis is radically different from the creation of self found in stories of Western male adventure. Rather than relying on the power of the individual and the individual's ability to conquer challenges on his own, Kingsolver creates a female character who is empowered and able to transform herself and others through the act of creation through community. As Allen states in *The Sacred Hoop*, mothering brings that power:

> A strong attitude integrally connects the power of Original Thinking or Creation Thinking to the power of mothering. That power is not so much the power to give birth, as we have noted, but the power to make, to create, to transform. Ritual, as noted elsewhere, means transforming something from one state or condition to another, and that ability is inherent in the action of mothering. . . . And as the cultures that are woman-centered and Mother-ritual based are also cultures that value peacefulness, harmony, cooperation, health, and general prosperity, they are systems of thought and practice that would bear deeper study in our troubled, conflict-ridden time. (29)

And it is through this experience that Taylor is empowered. Facing a role she initially tried so doggedly to avoid, Taylor has been initiated in the role of mother. Through this acceptance of responsibility she has dramatically transformed a small, abused, silent little girl into a growing child who is able to play, sing, and dance. Yet Turtle's life is not the only life to be transformed; Taylor has also created a new identity for herself by becoming a mother. She has turned her back on an individual approach for one of nurturing help and assistance through community. As the traditional male approach depicts the need of males to explore their own individual desires and powers, it also depicts a turning away from social responsibility. Desiring freedom from the demands that such a responsibility entails, men have exemplified an individualistic search. Although Kingsolver describes a similar desire to explore individual pursuits, she does not depict a woman who is able to turn her back on responsibility. Through this acceptance, Taylor gains the powers of motherhood as well as the essential powers of community.

This delicate natural system is described by Taylor to Turtle when she attempts to define their family. As in the Cherokee creation myth, ideas of community and the natural world are combined:

> But this is the most interesting part: wisteria vines, like other legumes, often thrive in poor soil, the book said. Their secret is something called rhizobia. These are microscopic bugs that live

> underground in little knots on the roots. They suck nitrogen gas right out of the soil and turn it into fertilizer for the plant.
> . . ."It's like this. . . . There's a whole invisible system for helping out the plant that you'd never guess is there." I loved this idea. "It's just the same as with people. The way Edna has Virgie, and Virgie has Edna, and Sandi has Kid Central Station, and everybody has Mattie. And on and on." These wisteria vines on their own would just barely get by, is how I explained it to Turtle, but put them together with rhizobia and they make miracles. (227–28)

Kingsolver ends the novel in much the same way as the ending of the Cherokee myth. Both end with the production that arises through relationship. Star Woman is surrounded by the "corn, beans, other plants, and rivers from her body," while Taylor is amazed by the profusion of friends, family, and a larger body of community that surrounds her. Kingsolver formulates the idea of regeneration through communal productivity. As the organic relationship serves to symbolize the power of community in Taylor's life, it also seems to speak to the larger messages of a changing mythology that exists throughout.

The relation between the wisteria and rhizobia in many ways represents Mattie's garden as described at the beginning of the novel. Wisteria "thrives in poor soil" just as Mattie's vegetables grow within auto parts. Both plants are surrounded by elements that would seem to impede their growth. However, something invisible exists which nourishes and enables their productivity. In much the same way, Kingsolver addresses the American mythology of the West. By turning from the male archetype, Kingsolver claims a new mythology that proves in her novel to be a productive means of experience. On their own, the American myths of the West are weakened by their inability to produce a viable future, yet by adapting the Native American myth to the American experience, the rhizobia, balance is possible.

As Star Woman brings consciousness to the natural world, Kingsolver's archetype is created with the same hope. In this way, Taylor becomes like Star Woman bringing the world consciousness and, perhaps more important, balance. And by expressing that hope, Kingsolver has succeeded in creating an archetype that melds the two myths together. By attempting a "new" archetype, she has initiated the process of finding a new mythic model from which to view the American experience. Although Taylor's initial story seems to be her attempt to escape her southern past, her story grows into a much larger vision. Taylor's move enlarges her scope and understanding of herself in relation to the world as a whole. Her story is certainly an escape from the South, but Kingsolver uses this regional move to express the need to escape any type of limited vision. A vision of wholeness in relation to America and the world as a whole is needed in order to gain understanding. Through her creation of Taylor, she molds an individual who empowers the American experience by stitching together two mythologies, the male Western myth and the Native American one, in order to reveal the need for balance within our American mythology. By doing so, Kingsolver provides a vision of the feminine as well as the masculine. The hero is both adventurer and domesticator. The power of creation and motherhood, as well as the need for action and adventure, are essential for growth and productivity. The garden no longer symbolizes that space relegated as a safe portion outside the male experience, nor does it symbolize a limited place in which women are empowered to create. Adventures and dangers abound in the communal garden.

Rusted Thunderbirds and certainly CB antennae for tomato vines imply that the movement these auto parts once shared has been dismantled. Motion has subsided in order to provide support. Whether for nasturtiums, cabbage, or tomatoes, all come together to aid in the growth of the garden. This image certainly strengthens the image of the garden as a place of power and support, yet it is important to keep in mind that this garden exists directly outside of a car shop. There may be a lot of cars that have been dismantled into parts, yet these parts still provide the potential to go when needed. This garden is prepared for action when the need arises, which is exemplified with Taylor's departure to help Estevan and Esperanza. When those are in danger within the community, action must be taken. However, action takes place on behalf of the community, as opposed to an individual's departure in search of adventure. And with that hope, Kingsolver has developed a new Western archetype, a hero who is both a mother and an adventurer.

Notes

1. There are times when westering women found some liberation through their experience. Sandra Myers and to a lesser degree Schlissel reveal some examples of women "who greeted the adventure of the western frontier with zeal and independent spirit" (Schlissel 155). However, they are not the norm.

2. Women certainly experienced meetings with the Indian, yet this introduction rarely resulted in any dramatic change in female behavior. As men are described as becoming more assimilated to Indian behaviors, women's encounters more often reflect a reaction that reflects their own white femininity. Often they are shown as becoming frightened, or in contrast they become more sympathetic to the Indian. Rarely, however, do they become more like the Indian—unless of course they are captured and forced into assimilation. This lack of self-willed assimilation shows a marked difference in this encounter.

3. Richard Slotkin exemplifies the contrasting *physical* version. In learning the physical prowess of the Indian, the male also learns the ways of the wilderness. Learning the ways of the Indian, the male then turns his newfound knowledge against the Indian. He claims that this kinship is justified in that it makes the hunter more effective as the destroyer of the Indian, as the exorcist of the wilderness's darkness. "He comes to know the Indian only in the act of destroying him" (*Regeneration through Violence* 563).

4. In the Cherokee myth of Corn Mother, as told by Joseph Bruchac, he relates the story of a grandmother mysteriously able to provide corn for her family by rubbing her sides. Once her secret is found out, she must leave, but she makes her grandson promise to clear the land and bury her body in the cultivated field, "wherever a drop of blood fell, a small plant grew up" (97). In this act, she promised to always be with her people. This myth exemplifies the importance of the female in that a female deity provides for her community through her act of giving.

5. Cereus is also known as the "Queen of the Night." Kingsolver positions this natural occurrence happening the night before Taylor is to attempt to take Estevan and Esperanza to safer sanctuary, in the midst of their own personal and political turmoil. The natural image works well in showing light amid the darkness. The Latin root of *cereus* is candle. The common name also works well in this scene, evoking the power of women to handle and persevere in difficulties.

6. Maureen Ryan provides the best example of this attitude.

Catherine Himmelwright

To Live Deliberately: Feminist Theory in Action in *High Tide in Tucson*

Maureen Meharg Kentoff

The essays collected in *High Tide in Tucson* were written at the cusp of a new millennium—a time when those at the helm of American political and economic institutions were heralding an era of unprecedented wealth and power. Yet this swaggering fin de siècle exuberance belied an unstable national infrastructure and increasingly precarious relationships with other cultures around the globe. Despite clear signs of local and international unrest, many conservative ideologues were peddling the notion that "we"—the United States—had rightfully achieved our abiding place as uncontested "leader of the free world." Even some of our more dissident pundits were optimistic, capitulating with a presumably objective media that America's collective conscience had been raised sufficiently to justify whatever actions our nationalist ideals dictated.[1] But there remained a few social critics who never lost sight of the consequences of this sweeping sense of entitlement. Through art, poetry, and prose they revealed how often our ostensibly modern humanitarian ideologies reflected only a cursory nod toward "non-Western," immigrant, or indigenous cultures, and an often specious (when not self-serving) concern for the welfare of marginalized Others. With a keen eye trained on the zeitgeist, Barbara Kingsolver stands out as a popular author whose work has persistently questioned the paradigms of moral certitude, material meritocracy, and cultural dominance that constitute "the American way."

For readers more familiar with her novels, *High Tide in Tucson* serves as a classic example of how Kingsolver's nonfiction is as unconventional, thought provoking, and compellingly readable as her fiction. Through her depictions of living in what she describes as an incredibly wondrous and complicated world, Kingsolver's essays capture that wonder, in her own voice, as she illuminates the myriad challenges and possibilities of the human condition. In this (her first) collection of personal narratives, she deftly balances social criticism—one that refuses to settle for blind optimism or misdirected nostalgia—with the hopeful determination that social progress is, in fact, achievable. And if her efforts inspire just one reader to think anew or to take action, then the urgently subtitled "Essays from Now or Never" have succeeded in communicating her message and making a difference.

With both an artist's passion and a critic's vigilance, Kingsolver addresses the complexity of her project when she asks, "How does the animal mind construct a poetry for the modern artifice in which we now reside?" ("High Tide in Tucson" 13). In the hands of a less approachable author, this question might be glossed over as just another rhetorical device. But set in Kingsolver's personable and vivid prose, it is a sincere apostrophe—one that urges the most passive reader to stop for a moment and consider the rich tapestry of human memory, perspective, and imagination. Then, having grabbed our attention, Kingsolver's underlying message begins to take hold: Despite our climb to the top of the food chain and our "fundamental" (read: self-appointed) right to survive and conquer, humans still know very little about the world. As a result, *High Tide* succeeds in raising questions that both caution against and hope for what is possible in an infinitely interconnected, infinitely unknowable universe.

Of course any social critic worth her salt is bound to pose more questions than answers. But perhaps the most effective communicators are those whose queries are simultaneously subtle, as they suggest alternative viewpoints, and bold, as they compel us to act on our desire for social change. From an artfully expressive and intellectually incisive (yet never nihilistic) position, Kingsolver's narratives consistently strike a balance between thought and action, passion and reason, the personal and the political. As she strives "to construct a poetry for the modern human condition," She often finds inspiration in the works of early American naturalist thinkers who sought this same balance. For example, reflecting on Thoreau's musings in *Walden*, Kingsolver recognizes her own desires and experiences echoed in the Transcendentalist's quest "to live deliberately" ("Making Peace" 23). Yet given the degree to which authors must deliberate over their choice of words in order to convey a certain meaning, this term is something of a con-

Maureen Meharg Kentoff

tradiction within itself—especially as employed by Kingsolver. In common usage, to do something *deliberately* might suggest quick and decisive action. On the other hand, it can imply unhurried and careful consideration. With similar ambiguity, the verb *to deliberate* might mean to introspectively weigh a thing in mind, *or* to openly discuss, debate, or decide collectively. And more obsolete uses include to secure or set down a resolution, *or* to liberate or set free. As with much of Kingsolver's prose, her use of Thoreau's phrase may seem straightforward at first; but throughout the collection, her rich perspective complicates these ostensibly simple words, thereby engaging, to varying degrees, all of the aforesaid permutations. As Kingsolver's deliberate writing encourages her readers to deliberate meaning, she actively illustrates the reflexive relationships between writer and reader, text and context. The result is a collection of creative yet accessible personal narratives that reveal multidimensional, interrelational, and actionable interpretations of living and writing deliberately.

While Kingsolver's work celebrates Thoreau's message, her diverse manifestations of living deliberately are a radical departure from those that tend toward a "self-in-the-wilderness" individualist interpretation of Transcendentalism. For example, Kingsolver's naturalist essays may open with an idyllic paean to the surrounding landscape but then diverge from metaphysical reflection toward a practical call for the conservation of our devolving ecosystems via individual *and* institutional accountability. When addressing other social issues, she might begin with a captivating observation, moving personal encounter, or self-deprecating anecdote, any of which can then lead to a fervid discussion of identity-based discrimination and the psychological, cultural, or material consequences of sociopolitical oppression. As these essays assert an alternative vision of living deliberately—one that is collective, nondeterministic, and transformative—we have our first illustration of the author's ability to embrace the ambiguous multiple truths of human consciousness: a viewpoint shared among scholars of postmodernist thought, and postmodern feminists in particular. Throughout the collection, Kingsolver provides myriad examples of how human experience is inextricably bound to the ecological and social systems from which we construct our sense of reality. Thus, as her personal narratives convey the infinite dimensionality, reflexivity, and undecidability of human experience, we begin to see how *High Tide in Tucson* emerges as an archetype of postmodern feminist literature.

If we concede that any effective articulation of postmodern feminism must address diverse, often contradictory perspectives, then the following expanded version of bell hooks's definition is perhaps the most appropriate for the discussion at hand: Feminism is a movement dedicated to critiquing, countering, and ultimately ending all forms of sociopolitical oppression (see hooks viii). Furthermore, postmodern feminisms contend that "each of us, in our manifold positions in discursive fields, inhabits margins and centers simultaneously" (Smith 16). For an explication of these positions, we turn to the work of feminist philosopher Elizabeth Grosz, who critically assesses the deeply embedded cultural rules restricting who humans should be, how they should think, and what they should do.

In *Space, Time, and Perversion,* Grosz presents a cogent analysis of the effects of hegemonic social-identity norms on human experience.[2] In particular, she illuminates how identity-based oppression is defined and operationalized in society. First, she contends that social oppression is the production of systematically differentiated identities, positions, and hierarchies, which often confer privilege on groups deemed to be statistically or arbitrarily "normative." Next, these social systems perpetuate assumptions that group attributes are fixed, innate, and merited, and therefore linked to certain values. As a result, normative groups are empowered with the authority to produce and maintain paradigms of truth and representation for all groups. But Grosz also contends that our awareness of identity-based oppression is a potential site for social change: As marginalized groups recognize and reject systems of discrimination, they can more effectively influence power structures and act on opportunities for resistance and transformation. In sum, postmodern feminist theory directly relates social oppression, and its resistance, to society's interpretations of human exper-ience, identity, perspective, and agency. With these four themes serving as a framework, we continue our discussion of how Kingsolver (wittingly or not) engages with feminist scholarship as we return to her earlier query: *How does the animal mind construct a poetry for the modern artifice in which we now reside?*

Maureen Meharg Kentoff

TO BE HUMAN

Kingsolver's fiction is often celebrated for the emotional candor and perceptual clarity with which she relates a character's human experience. In her nonfiction, that experience is vividly captured and embraced as distinctively her own:

> I gained things from my rocky school years: A fierce wish to look inside of people. An aptitude for listening. The habit of my own company. The companionship of keeping a diary, in which I gossiped, fantasized, and invented myself. From the vantage point of invisibility I explored the psychology of the underdog, the one who can't be what others desire but who might still learn to chart her own hopes. ("In Case" 42)

Throughout *High Tide,* Kingsolver often describes experiences of feeling like an outcast. But, rather than merely ruminating, or seeking ways to numb the sting of oppression, she deliberately attends to the sharpness of its bite and to the adaptive awareness—at once self-protective, forgiving, and requiring—that these mysteries and revelations engender. Although "it's human, to want the world to see us as we think we ought to be seen," she asserts, "in the broad valley between real life and propriety, whole herds of important truths can steal away into the underbrush. I hold that valley to be my home territory as a writer" (36). Kingsolver suggests that to write deliberately, one must be able to negotiate the constantly shifting terrain of competing realities, beliefs, and values. Then, as the writer corrals these wide-ranging, amorphous herds of varying perspectives, she begins to expand her creative potential and its influence on others through the reflexive act of authorship. Kingsolver accomplishes this by writing multivalent social commentary, without apology, and with little encumbrance save the desire to tell a good story, and to tell it well.

When considering Kingsolver's aforementioned home territory of human aporia and liminality, it is useful to borrow from postmodern theory the seemingly redundant phrase "lived experience." Philosophical discussions of lived experience attend to the sociocognitive awareness of one's own existence—of how it feels, and what it means "to be" in a world teeming with other humans, species, systems, places, and things. More to the point, many feminist scholars suggest that lived experience is the confluence of one's various perceptions of self—which include our sense of identity, perspective, and agency. Given that theoretical abstractions, such as "lived experience," characterize a good deal of contemporary philosophy, Kingsolver's direct and uncomplicated prose may seem an unlikely candidate for a postmodern feminist analysis of the text. Yet, while *High Tide* may (deliberately) appeal to a diverse and widespread audience, the essays also (perhaps just as deliberately) stand up to critical literary scholarship as they balance deeply personal stories with trenchant political commentary.

For example, when Kingsolver suggests that humans possess an "animal mind," her language may seem common at first, almost quaint; but soon it becomes evident that the juxtaposition of these basic terms is loaded with both concrete and abstract meaning. Consider the book's cryptic title essay, "High Tide in Tucson." Here Kingsolver alludes to her unwitting displacement of a hermit crab from its home shores in the Bahamas to the *unheimlich* landscape of the American Southwest. Through careful observation, she ponders the crab's refugee status, empathizes with its situation, imagines its inner life, and marvels at its adaptability. As with all animal minds about which Kingsolver writes, the crab's point of view *matters* to this author. She not only welcomes "Buster" (a conventionally male name chosen to enhance gender diversity at home), she also hopes to learn a thing or two from the little guy.

In philosophical terms, Kingsolver's experience of closely identifying with animals, even quiet crustaceans, can be interpreted as one possible iteration of a feminist antihumanism. In contrast to the human-centricity of anthropomorphism, antihumanist theory maintains that human existence is no more or less important than that of any other species or ecosystem; that the sense of privilege and entitlement we grant humans as the more sentient or advanced species is erroneously hierarchical and deterministic. On the other hand, within the same essay, Kingsolver embraces the position that humans are accountable for having and using their conscious, multidimensional minds: "In the best of times, I hold in mind the need to care for things beyond the self: poetry, humanity, grace" (13). Here she adopts a feminist humanist stance, which contends that we do have some control of our existence and environment, and that we are pointedly aware of and responsible for that agency. So from the very first chapter, the simple phrase "animal mind" suggests a much broader paradox: Is the author's point of view humanist, antihumanist, both, neither?[3] As we shall see, the essays collected

Maureen Meharg Kentoff

in *High Tide* provide a constellation of perspectives from which to consider the inextricable, reflexive, and protean relationships between civilization and nature.

In "Creation Stories," Kingsolver marvels at human adaptation and the astounding variety of cultural myths we contrive to explain the unexplainable. With simultaneous expressions of respect, amusement, and empathy, she considers the countless palimpsests of human existence that leave indelible yet constantly rewritten traces of ourselves in the world. Upon returning home from a brief drive through the culturally diverse neighborhoods of Tucson, the author reflects on her rapid journey "through all these lands, all these creation stories." Never one to ignore life's existential contradictions, she concludes:

> [I] stare out my window at a landscape of wonders thrown to-
> gether with no more thought than a rainstorm or a volcano can
> invoke on its own behalf. It's exactly as John Muir said, as if
> "nature in wildest extravagance held her bravest structures as
> common as gravel-piles." (22)

Kingsolver asserts that, despite our daily agendas and power struggles, some natural event is bound to intercede. Yet nature is not entirely in control either. Rather, life's ironies are often just a matter of circumstance, be it happy coincidence or unfortunate accident. Hence, Kingsolver challenges proponents of metaphysical or symbolic dualities by eschewing the traditional notion of a romantic struggle between humanity and nature. In contrast to a linear or teleological dialectic, she posits a multivalent and anarchic interpretation of life in which human interventions and natural events coexist and commingle on a more or less even playing field, for better or worse.

Ultimately Kingsolver is most interested in what we learn from and how we respond to these chaotic circumstances—a concern shared by feminist philosopher Donna Haraway. In *Simians, Cyborgs, and Women,* Haraway contends:

> Actors come in many and wonderful forms. Accounts of a "real"
> world do not, then, depend on a logic of "discovery," but on a
> power-charged social relation of "conversation." . . . The codes of

the world are not still, waiting only to be read. The world is not
raw material for humanization. (198)

Both Haraway and Kingsolver suggest that our human "conversations"—
the richly told and, at times, hotly contested creation myths we employ to
make sense of the world—serve as the genealogical stepping stones that
perpetuate social constructions of what we deem to be scientific, religious,
or cultural truths. These tensions between society and nature, desire and
necessity, agency and survival, provide plenty of fodder for what Haraway
calls "the world's independent sense of humour." She elaborates with a folklore analogy: "The Coyote or Trickster, embodied in American Southwest
Indian accounts, suggests our situation when we give up mastery but keep
searching for fidelity, knowing all the while we will be hoodwinked" (199).
Like Kingsolver, Haraway contends that as humans vie with nature for this
"mastery," it is the random circumstance of our mutual existence that can
trip up even our most altruistic efforts. Moreover, the Trickster cautions, as
our adaptive success perpetuates a self-generated illusion of mastery over
nature, our fidelity often leads to the ultimate irony: in many cases, we are
the ones hoodwinking ourselves.

Kingsolver underscores this arbitrary balance between civilization and
nature in "Infernal Paradise" when she asserts that the human diaspora was
due to a combination of "stamina and spectacular accident" (197). She too
marvels at the sheer audacity of human fidelity and commends our determination to survive and progress, despite knowing there is no guarantee
that our efforts will pay off. Likewise, Haraway concludes, "the world's sense
of humor is not comfortable for humanists and others committed to the
world as a resource" (*SWC* 199); which returns us to the question of where
Kingsolver stands along the humanist-antihumanist continuum.

Kingsolver's ability to effectively embrace more than one position is exemplified in her assertion that *if* human consciousness has the potential
to impact the world, then it is what we intend to do with that consciousness that really matters. In search of practical answers, she muses, "when it
seems difficult merely to survive and be happy about it, the condition of my
thought tastes as simple as this: let me be a good animal today" ("Creation
Stories" 13). But, as usual, her thoughts are never quite that simple.

Here, and elsewhere, Kingsolver employs the compound subject *good-
animal-human* as a catachrestic trope—one that deliberately troubles a few
seemingly simple, commonplace words whose dominant meanings gener-

ally go uncontested. As her narratives creatively interweave traditionally opposed or unrelated ideas, she challenges conventional epistemologies, such as the biological determinism inscribed in binarial representations of animal *versus* human. In so doing, she effectively steers clear of the dualist "either/or" thinking found in Hegel's dialectic, as well as the indecisive "neither/nor" thinking repudiated by Roland Barthes. And yet, some feminist scholars might argue that, despite Kingsolver's multivalent usage, any assertion of a good-animal-human capitulates to an intolerant moral idealism or conveys subtle iterations of an essentialist ontological hierarchy. (For example, Grosz and others, such as Martha Saxton and Gayatri Spivak, would remind us that the privileged few maintain the power to impose standards of "goodness" or "humanness" against which subordinated populations are judged unfairly or inequitably.) But Kingsolver tacitly addresses these issues by employing the "both/and" thinking championed by Patricia Hill Collins and other postmodern feminists. Throughout *High Tide,* she asserts the admittedly contradictory claim that despite our subjectivity, humans are merely one of a countless number of species vying for space in the world, and despite our objectivity, we always have the potential to change our minds and act according to conscience. From this both/and position she suggests what we might call a kind of "co-humanism." The flexibility of a co-humanist stance allows Kingsolver to eschew the passivity of relativism and the dominance of idealism by engaging deeply with context, paradox, and ambiguity in order to expand our perspective and generate equitable, co-rational solutions.

In *Literature after Feminism,* Rita Felski extols this multidimensional way of observing and writing about lived experience, asserting that "literature is one of the cultural languages through which we make sense of the world; it helps to create our sense of reality rather than simply reflecting it. At the same time, it also draws on, echoes, modifies, and bounces off our other frameworks of sense-making. No text is an island" (13). In this same spirit, Kingsolver's style of personal narrative moves the author and reader beyond isolated introspection toward a more reflexive engagement with the world—one that emphasizes the reciprocal, precarious, and fluid relationships between all species, systems, places, and things. With this co-humanist, multivalent perspective in mind, we next address Kingsolver's commentary on the similarities and differences within and across human populations; that is, our *social identities.*

IDENTITY

When exploring the impact of social identity and its norms on lived experience, postmodern theorists constantly wrestle with the issue of whether to
see or not to see those qualities through which we connect with or distinguish ourselves from others. Kingsolver repeatedly addresses this question
as she reflects on her life as an outsider and considers the lived experience
of those who are marginalized for being nonnormative, or just different.
Returning to the title essay, we find more evidence of co-humanist/feminist
thinking as Kingsolver observes her crustacean housemate and marvels at
what we can learn when we stop for a moment to consider the wonders of
physical and behavioral adaptation found in nature.

As Buster's biorhythms slowly adjust to what he senses is high tide in
Tucson (despite its dearth of beachfront), the displaced crab's experience
is an apt analogy for the author's own search for identity and belonging.
Growing up among the verdant hills of Kentucky, Kingsolver relocated as
an adult to the vast desert spaces of Arizona—wholly unfamiliar places she
has since come to love. She often feels disembodied in this new setting: "No
one here remembers how I was before I grew to my present height. I'm called
upon to reinvent my own childhood time and again; in the process, I wonder
how I can ever know the truth about who I am" ("High Tide in Tucson" 14).
But, like Buster's impulse to shed outgrown shells and inhabit new ones—be
they custom-fit carapaces or scrappy old shoeboxes—for Kingsolver there is
no one-size-fits-all answer to the human identity question, *who am I?* And
that's just fine with her.

In the amusing but cautionary tale "In Case You Ever Want to Go Home
Again," the author shares vivid examples of her early struggles with social
identity and adaptation:

> . . . I was not a hit in school, socially speaking. I was a bookworm
> who never quite fit her clothes. . . . Popularity remained a frus-
> trating mystery to me. . . . I've never gotten over high school, to
> the extent that I'm still a little surprised that my friends want to
> hang out with me. But it made me what I am, for better or worse.
> (40–42)

Despite some painful memories, Kingsolver's narratives go on to describe
how she has learned to make the most of her marginalized position. Rem-

iniscent of Grosz's theories of oppression, the future author resists hegemonic social identity norms by taking advantage of her invisible status. As
she observes, listens, reads, and writes, she begins to discover *multiple truths*
that can expand perspective and raise awareness of our myriad possible
selves. Thus we can read her remarks within a Foucauldian feminist framework which asserts that discrete and prescribed social identities are rarely,
if ever, representative of individual lived experience.

As Kingsolver recalls experiences of inventing herself and charting her
own hopes, despite what others expect or dictate, she contends that individuals are not composed of a single set of identity traits, with stable attributes
and limited possibilities. Kimberlé Crenshaw and other feminist scholars
refer to the constant negotiation of our inextricably linked multiple identities as our *intersectionality*. For, depending on the situation, human characteristics are constantly shifting in value: they may be more or less salient,
or celebrated, or ignored; deemed more or less propitious, or dysfunctional,
or even dangerous. As social institutions preserve myopic, one-dimensional
interpretations of identity, we are often required to conceal, suppress, assert, or promote the myriad parts of ourselves deemed nonnormative. This
theory highlights the ways in which multiply marginalized individuals suf-
fer compound oppressions, particularly in cultural settings that neither embrace nor allow for contradiction and ambiguity.

Throughout *High Tide,* Kingsolver illustrates the impact of conventional social mores that do not accommodate our experiences of intersectionality, such as those reflected in the ongoing debate over what constitutes
a family. In "Stone Soup," she debunks the myth of a nuclear family majority
and posits a more accurate account of contemporary family life. With characteristic intellectual empathy, she celebrates the nonnuclear, fragmented,
socially unacceptable, or illegal relationships that converge, necessarily or
by choice, to raise healthy, adaptive humans. Reflecting on her own patch-
work family, she concludes: "If there is a *normal* for humans, at all . . ." it is
that "we're social animals, deeply fond of companionship, and children love
best to run in packs. . . . The sooner we can let go the fairy tale of families
functioning perfectly in isolation, the better we might embrace the relief
of community" (144). Thus, with greater awareness and acceptance of our
intersectionality and multiple possible selves, we can do more to debunk
stereotypical thinking, center the margins, and reap the benefits of the complex diversities within and across individuals and groups.

In another essay, aptly titled "The Spaces Between," Kingsolver digs deeper into these issues as she addresses our perceptual and social habits of racial discrimination. En route to a Native American cultural center with her young daughter, Camille, she takes the opportunity to discuss the infinite manifestations of ethnic identity and cultural imagination. In the course of conversation, Kingsolver realizes that, despite her own Cherokee lineage and manifold Native American friends and neighbors, Camille has been exposed to too many storybooks and media images that contradict her actual lived experience with the message "Indians lived long ago, period" (147). Seeking early inoculation against overt prejudice and tacit discrimination, Kingsolver asserts, "I want my child to be so completely familiar with differences that she'll ignore *difference* per se and really see what she's looking at" (148). Yet the transition from acknowledging difference to perceptually ignoring it is an admittedly idealistic and precarious, but perhaps not impossible step.

Kingsolver insists that we must try to overcome the limitations of our neuro-cognitive habits of perception and find ways to more effectively interpret our world: "We humans have to grant the presence of some past adaptations, even in their unforgivable extremes, if only to admit they are permanent rocks in the stream we're obliged to navigate" ("High Tide in Tucson" 8). Here Kingsolver's language is simultaneously direct, subtle, and artful, as, in merely one sentence, she generates an apposite confluence of scientific detachment, human sensitivity, political passion, and ecological metaphor. As a result, her deliberately approachable text effectively echoes a complex philosophical abstraction—in this case, one asserted by Teresa de Lauretis, who asserts that our sense of self "is one constructed across a multiplicity of discourses, positions, and meanings, which are often in conflict with one another and inherently (historically) contradictory" (de Lauretis ix–x). Kingsolver continues:

> [We recognize] insider/outsider status, for example, starting with white vs. black and grading straight into distinctions so fine as to baffle the bystander—Serb and Bosnian, Hutu and Tutsi, Crip and Blood. . . . Deference to the physical superlative, a preference for the scent of our own clan: a thousand anachronisms dance down the strands of our DNA from a hidebound tribal past, guiding us toward the glories of survival, and some vainglories as well. ("High Tide in Tucson" 9)

Maureen Meharg Kentoff

Once again, Kingsolver employs both/and thinking to acknowledge the ways biological factors and social constructions intersect to constitute, complicate, and even contradict lived experience. She recognizes that we are embodied, that our bodies differ from each other, and that these differences are more adaptive in some ways, less so in others. But humans have developed an acuity for noticing and arbitrarily assigning value to these differences, "recognizing insider/outsider status, for example." This position recalls Grosz's claim that social constructions of normativity give dominant groups the authority and means to determine which differences are inferior, unhealthy, or threatening, and to enforce and perpetuate those judgments. Consequently, as nonnormative, subaltern groups strive for acceptance and enfranchisement, they are often faced with a double bind: either assimilate or fend for yourselves. Thus the actions desired or required for both self-expression and sociopolitical agency are significantly limited by the constraints that accompany traditional, one-dimensional identity constructions.

Effectively summarizing this conundrum, feminist philosopher Linda Martín Alcoff posits the question: *Are social identities necessary, or necessarily problematic?* In *Visible Identities,* Alcoff asserts that, while much of our sense of self is socially constructed, the facts of corporeal experience and biological difference present us with "embodied horizons from which we each must confront and negotiate our shared world and specific life condition. They are largely unchosen (just as our bodies are unchosen), but just as in the case of bodies, our identities can be reshaped, and they absolutely require interpretation" (*VI* 288). Expanding on this idea, Judith Butler suggests concrete strategies for resistance; namely, that we can wrest the power of language and meaning from dominant groups by actively *resignifying* social norms. In *Gender Trouble,* she asserts that our ability to "perform" multiple, ambiguous identities allows us to expand and even break out of prescribed social roles. So it is not a question of whether one *does* gender, or race, or any other social-identity performance, but what *shape* that performance will take along an infinite spectrum of possibilities.

Like Alcoff and Butler, Kingsolver recognizes the myriad socio-cognitive-biological tensions that complicate our understanding of the human condition. With distinctive humor, empathy, and enthusiasm, she acknowledges both the "glories" and " vainglories" of human adaptation as we habitually differentiate and evaluate our social identities. She concludes, "If we resent being bound by these ropes, the best hope is to seize them out like snakes, by the throat, look them in the eye and own up to their venom"

("High Tide in Tucson" 9). Never forcing a choice between society or nature, individualism or collectivism, our "hidebound tribal past" or multicultural present, Kingsolver's attentiveness to both the consequences and the possibilities of social identity exemplifies her facility in accepting the messiness of aporia and hybridity. Accordingly, with a heightened awareness of our all-too-human habits, perhaps the reader can begin to more effectively navigate and ultimately resignify the long and winding ropes of social oppression.

PERSPECTIVE

As feminist scholars reflect on the multiple dimensions and implications of social identity, they assert that dominant systems and paradigms often dictate not only *who* we should be, but what we should *believe* as we go about trying to make sense of the world. They contend that since the dawn of scientific methodology, the search for and alleged discovery of objective universal truths has given credence to social norms that impose these truths as the standard against which all thought and behavior should be judged. Donna Haraway and others theorize that, as each of us is situated in our own particular material conditions, our lived experience is significantly influenced by our position in relation to normative standards. In order to challenge these constraining norms, feminists insist that we look to the margins of society for more diverse perspectives and learn from the *multiple partial truths* that they can engender. Hence, as a writer attempts to construct a poetry for the modern artifice, one way of recognizing and resisting dominant systems of oppression is to raise awareness of what Haraway calls our *positionality*.

Throughout *High Tide,* Kingsolver depicts our modern artifice as something of a Potemkin Village: a cultural facade constructed by privileged groups who impose particular ideologies that mask uncomfortable realities and maintain systems of hierarchy. In her efforts to strip away the layers of these arbitrary, artificial standards, Kingsolver is quite candid about the limitations of her own positionality; but—determined to expand her perspective—she is driven by the desire to fathom how we know what we know (or think we know), and how much we really *don't* know about the world.

In "Semper Fi," Kingsolver pursues this quest with a trenchant analysis of Edward O. Wilson's *On Human Nature.* She debates Wilson's assertion that, "as science-based ethics replace those of religion, our unconscious motives will drop out, we'll know what we're really capable of, and the truth will set us free" (73). For Kingsolver, this begs so many questions: Which science? Whose ethics? Which truth? Whose truth? She concludes:

> Never in the deep blue sea will we ever be that conscious of
> our motives. The problem with identifying the biological roots
> of such things as sexism, aggression, and racism is that we're
> looking at our past through spectacles tinted with sexism,
> aggression, and racism. (73)

She goes on to cite numerous examples of the folly of traditional research methods and the consequences of unchecked personal bias. In response, she advocates theories and practices that counteract "science's deep roots in creative interpretation and selective oversight [such that] the expected winners *always* came out on top" (75).

Kingsolver's commentary reflects the call for a "strong objectivity" set forth by Haraway and fellow feminist scholars Sandra Harding, Nancy Harstock, and Patricia Hill Collins. Haraway argues:

> There is no single feminist standpoint because our maps require
> *too many dimensions* for that metaphor to ground our visions.
> But the feminist standpoint theorists' goal of an epistemology
> and politics of engaged, accountable positioning remains emi-
> nently potent. The goal is better accounts of the world, that is,
> "science." (Haraway 196; emphasis mine)

Hence feminist practitioners strive for an impartiality that (paradoxically) acknowledges multiple partial truths. While remaining constantly aware of the practitioner's own positionality, strong objectivity seeks a range of contextual scientific standards that are flexible and attentive to statistical majorities *and* minorities, as well as individual and collective needs. Similarly, as Kingsolver concedes that our unconscious motives and anachronistic adaptations sustain the modern artifice of socionormativity, she urges us to pursue—not Wilson's brand of absolute truth—but an awareness of and respect for the infinite manifestations of lived experience that constitute our world.

Of course this vision of strong objectivity gets somewhat blurry when applied to various forms of cultural representation, such as literature. In

"The Spaces Between," Kingsolver recognizes the irony of debating issues of scientific objectivity while grounded in a creative writer's subjective standpoint. She asserts:

> To write novels, to design a museum, to teach fourth-graders
> about history—all these enterprises require the interpretation of
> other lives. And all of them, historically, have been corrupted by
> privileges of race, class, and gender. (153)

So how does an author accomplish both an objective awareness of social construction and a subjective respect for individual difference? Kingsolver avers, "This is the dilemma upon whose horns I've built my house: I want to know, and to write, about the places where disparate points of view rub together—the spaces between" (154). Here, the possibility of strong objectivity within nonscientific domains is suggested via another both/and paradox of lived experience: While Kingsolver asserts that our subjective perspectives are socially constructed, and these constructions are usually influenced by those in power, she also insists that we must find ways to objectively interpret these perspectives without sacrificing a respect for differentiated cultures, beliefs, and values. Within these "spaces between," a writer can explore the murky, porous, and elastic boundaries of lived experience—she can acknowledge the gray areas of society and celebrate the ambiguous truths that constitute our multivalent existence. Evocative of Gloria Anzaldua's poignant metaphor of the "borderlands," Kingsolver's depiction of those who live in forgotten, ignored, or unimaginable places encourages us to embrace the infinite and undecidable manifestations of lived experience. Hence, from within these spaces between, the author can acknowledge her own biases and strive to overcome them with "a keen ear, empathy, caution, willingness to be criticized, and a passionate attraction to the subject" (154).

In her efforts to write novels that depict myriad cultures and life circumstances, Kingsolver has been both lauded and criticized for inventing and speaking for characters with whom she may have little in common. Willing to open the Pandora's box of who gets to write about whom, she contends:

> I can't speak in tongues I don't understand, and so there are a
> thousand tales I'll never tell: the waging of war; coming of age
> as a man; childhood on an Indian reservation. But when the

wounded veteran, the masculine disposition, and the reservation
child come into the place where I live, they enter my story. ("The
Spaces Between" 154–55)

As passionate as she is about the writer's accountability for what she calls
"bearing witness" to the people and places that enter her story, she is equally
adamant that authors should not presume to "take possession" of others'
lives. Instead, she is determined to write stories that try to make sense of
the world: "How wondrous, it seems to me, that someone else can live on
the same round egg of a world that I do but explain it differently—how it got
here, and what's to be done with it" (154).

In "How Mr. Dewey Decimal Saved My Life," Kingsolver describes feeling that same wonder since childhood. She reveled in books not considered
canonical at the time, but which offered a larger world perspective—those
written by authors such as Doris Lessing, who challenged social norms
and celebrated cultural difference. She muses, "What snapped me out of
my surly adolescence and moved me on were books that let me live other
people's lives" (51). Once again, the author's personal experience becomes
political commentary as she illustrates her own burgeoning awareness of
our multiple identities, limited perspectives, and infinite interconnections
within and across species, systems, places, and things. In sum, we might call
this complex sociocognitive awareness of lived experience our "interdimensionality."[4] As a result, Kingsolver's work encourages readers to push beyond
their own positionality and to embrace the interdimensionality within and
between us all.

AGENCY

Feminist theorists assert that, in addition to our multiple identities and perspectives, a third variable that significantly impacts our lived experience
is our sense of agency—that is, the freedom and ability to act (either individually or collectively) according to one's own volition. Hence, another way
systems of social oppression operate is by restricting individual or group
agency through overt and tacit processes of discrimination, exploitation,
and subordination. Complicating this notion of agency, however, is the
postmodernist Foucauldian principle that "freedom" itself is an existential impossibility—that social constructions of human corporeality, material circumstances, aptitude levels, and institutional standards will forever

constrain any absolute expression of fully capable or unfettered agency. Yet Grosz and other feminist scholars argue that opportunities for resistance can surface as we become more aware of the underlying processes that constrain our individual and collective agency. For Kingsolver, resistance is accomplished through her own act of writing political commentary via accessible and compelling personal narratives:

> I don't consider a novel to be a purely recreational vehicle. I think
> of it as an outlet for my despair, my delight, my considered opin-
> ions, and all the things that strike me as absolute and essential,
> worked out in words. ("Careful" 252)

Although some of Kingsolver's work has been dismissed at times as "popular women's fiction," its ubiquity has provided a sizable platform from which she can express her opinions and expand her reputation as a writer who does not shy away from contentious social debates. In "Jabberwocky," she insists that her responsibility as a writer of popular works is to raise social awareness and make a difference. She contends that "most of the rest of the world considers social criticism to be, absolutely, the most legitimate domain of art" (229). In contrast, when interviewed stateside about her own work, she laments spending "a good deal of time defending the possibility that such things as environmental ruin, child abuse, or the hypocrisy of U.S. immigration policy are appropriate subjects for a novel." Kingsolver responds by affirming the scope of an author's opportunities for resistance and agency: "Art is the antidote that can call us back from the edge of numbness, restoring the ability to feel for another. By virtue of that power, it is political, regardless of content" (232).

In "Careful What You Let in the Door," Kingsolver argues that the power of fiction provides a vital opportunity for authors to connect events with their consequences. She is concerned that all too often contemporary writers do not take this responsibility for their agency seriously:

> [Characters] fall off of things or they get shot and they are gone.
> ... We never knew the guy so we don't feel a thing, and we don't
> have to sit through the funeral. If you had to sit through all the
> funerals, most TV shows would be seven hours long. But you
> don't. (253)

Maureen Meharg Kentoff

On the other hand, she is also sensitive to the slippery slope of imposing her own (or anyone's) "absolute and essential" standards of good taste:

> I will not argue for censorship, except from the grassroots up:
> my argument is for making choices about what we consume.
> The artist is blessed and cursed with a kind of power, but so are
> the reader and viewer. The story no longer belongs to the author
> once it's come to live in your head. By then, it's a part of your life.
> So be careful what you let in the door, is my advice. (256)

Hence, the reader's perspective is just as critical as the writer's, and Kingsolver is adamant that the responsibility of literary agency flows both ways. "The artistic consummation of a novel is created by the author and reader together, in an act of joint imagination, and that's not to be taken lightly" (253). Here, in her deliberate choice and juxtaposition of words, we find another illustration of the reflexive relationship between reader and writer, text and context. For example, the phrase "artistic consummation" invokes the liminal spaces between two different yet inextricable actions—both the consumption and the production of art. Likewise, the "act of joint imagination" is one that is concurrently individual *and* collective, produced *and* consumed, contemplative *and* performative.

In "Jabberwocky," Kingsolver exemplifies this interdimensionality of the artist-consumer-institution-citizen connection as she excoriates the ways in which our government and the media wrest agency from the public by propagating adulterated "facts" via sanitized news. She is particularly troubled by the degree to which information is disseminated based on its universal palatability and shares her grassroots opinion passionately and directly.

> As a member of that all-important public, I'd like to state for the
> record that I'm offended. . . . I'm offended by the presumption
> that my honor as a citizen will crumple unless I'm protected from
> knowledge of my country's mistakes. . . . What kind of love is patri-
> otism, if it evaporates in the face of uncomfortable truths? (227)

Willing to risk the apostasy of confronting reactionary national ideologies, Kingsolver is determined, as an artist and a citizen, to address uncomfortable truths through her work. But not one merely to point fingers, she consistently holds up a mirror to her own potential culpability as an author: "Artists are as guilty as anyone in the conspiracy of self-censorship, if they succumb to the lure of producing only what's sure to sell" (227). She contends,

> The artist's maverick responsibility is sometimes to sugarcoat
> the bitter pill and slip it down our gullet, telling us what we
> didn't think we wanted to know. But in the U.S. we're establish-
> ing a modern tradition of tarpapering our messengers. (228)

As writer cum apostate, Kingsolver has had, and continues to have, her share of moments peeling off that tarpaper. In *The Terror Dream*, feminist cultural critic Susan Faludi dedicates three pages to the "fierce response" Kingsolver received for two op-ed pieces she wrote after 9/11. In these articles, Kingsolver "appealed to 'our capacity of mercy' and proposed that one of 'a hundred ways to be a good citizen' was to learn 'honest truths from wrongful deaths'" (Faludi 30). Faludi reports that letters were sent to the editors charging Kingsolver with "nothing less than another act of terror" and "pure sedition," and that "this little horror of a human being" needed to be "surveilled." No less threatening has been the frequent dismissal of Kingsolver's works as reactionary ecofeminist literature—a genre on which we dare not waste our time when, as Faludi sarcastically notes, "We're at war, sweetheart." Never one to back down, Kingsolver recognized the opportunity for resistance by responding quickly to all of these allegations with a second collection of incisive personal and political essays, entitled *Small Wonder.*

When addressing less overt forms of censorship, Kingsolver voices her concern over institutional standards that dictate which literary texts are worthy of canonical consideration in the United States: "Real art, the story goes, does not endorse a point of view" ("Jabberwocky" 229). Hence, works deemed to be excessively radical (or popular) by the experts are often boxed into (or completely excluded from) narrow, discrete, and inflexible categories of aesthetic or historic value. Over the years, as Kingsolver's books achieved best-seller status, it was almost a foregone conclusion that academia would ignore her fiction for its accessible narrative style, or its quotidian particularity, or grassroots radicalism. And here we have another double bind, in this case, of literary agency: It seems that if an author hopes to be considered canon-worthy, she must sacrifice works that are potentially *too* original, controversial, comprehensible, or popular (notably with women). But there may be hope yet.

Rita Felski recounts the impact that recent changes in social values have had on previously ignored texts. She contends that if our libraries and curricula are finally dedicating space to "critical volumes on [Virginia] Woolf and Edith Wharton and Toni Morrison, it is because feminist scholars have made a painstaking case for the importance of such writers *as writers*" (Felski 148–49). As Kingsolver is now gaining recognition for her artistic and substantive merit, we may be witnessing a sea change toward a literary canon willing to embrace her imaginative narrative style and the sociopolitical issues about which she writes so passionately. Thus, through her quest to construct a poetry for the modern artifice, Kingsolver's prose offers the artistic creativity, critical scrutiny, and interdimensional awareness required of any author who hopes to maintain her literary agency and have a lasting impact on society.

In the penultimate essay, "The Forest in the Seeds," Kingsolver returns to the works of Thoreau and his peers and commends them for eschewing "the notion that poetry and science are incompatible" (238). Given her desire to maintain this same balance, Kingsolver laments that present-day authors lack the nineteenth-century naturalist's "luxury of writing for an audience with an attention span" (237). With characteristic wit and sagacity, Kingsolver gives us pause to deeply consider our place in this world. She concludes: "Nature does not move in mysterious ways, really. She just moves so slowly we're inclined to lose patience and stop watching before she gets around to the revelations." Thus, through the act of living and writing deliberately, Kingsolver hopes to recapture for herself and modern readers "the simple wonder we hastily leave behind in the age of reason" (238).

In "Reprise," we are left with a final, intimate glimpse into Kingsolver's own sense of wonder in action:

> What to believe in, exactly, may never turn out to be half as important as the daring act of belief. A willingness to participate in sunlight, and the color red. An agreement to enter into a

> conspiracy with life, on behalf of both frog and snake, the
> predator and the prey, in order to come away changed. (268)

Kingsolver's narratives suggest that she has learned to push the limits of her own hermeneutic horizons in order to come away changed—for the metamorphosis endured by all creatures is even more required of the "good animal human." Through the act of exploring our chaotic, undecidable, and wondrous experiences in person and in writing, she reflexively conspires with her readers to challenge social conventions and envision the possibilities of our existence. Thus *High Tide* epitomizes the spirit of postmodern feminism as the author's expanding interdimensional awareness is effectively translated into individual and collective action. And although some may find these entreaties to be at times quixotic, sentimental, or strident, Kingsolver candidly admits that she is often visited by doubt, disappointment, and the specter of all she could lose. As an antidote, she has come to learn that "everywhere you look, joyful noise is clanging to drown out quiet desperation. The choice is draw the blinds and shut it all out, or believe" (267). It is in these moments that, with both a critical eye and a deliberate leap of faith, the writer can imagine life's limitless interdimensionality and craft stories that inspire the reader to question, to believe, and to change.[5]

Notes

1. For examples of liberal writers and pundits who softened (if not reversed) their critiques of social issues, government activity, and national policy, see Eric Alterman, *What Liberal Media? The Truth about Bias and the News.*
2. This paragraph summarizes Grosz's detailed discussion of sociopolitical oppression in *Space, Time, and Perversion* (208–10).
3. For feminist discussions of humanism and antihumanism, see Linda Martín Alcoff, *Visible Identities;* Judith Butler, *Undoing Gender;* Elizabeth Grosz, *Volatile Bodies;* and Donna Haraway, *Simians, Cyborgs, and Women.*
4. See Maureen Meharg Kentoff, "An Interdimensional Model for Coping with Identity-Based Oppression: Conversations with U.S. Feminist Activists." As theorized here, interdimensionality describes the ways in which our awareness of self is informed by three interconnected sociocognitive processes: (1) intersectionality—multiple identities, or who we are; (2) positionality—situated perspectives, or what we know; and (3) reciprocal agency—our reflexive actions, or what we do. From a qualitative study of feminist activists, it was found that an awareness and assertion of one's interdimensionality served as a coping mechanism for those facing and seeking to counter identity-based oppression.

Maureen Meharg Kentoff

This method of coping was a creative and effective alternative to the gender-normative coping styles touted in traditional psychology texts.

5. The author would like to thank Alyssa Zucker for encouraging nonconformity, James A. Miller for paving and re-paving the way, Phyllis Palmer and Teresa Murphy for illuminating the possibilities, Gayle Wald for reading between the lines, Priscilla Leder for suffering the infinite details, Sharon Lemke for rehabilitating the crumbling fort, and Michael Kentoff for creating the imaginative melodies that soothe and inspire the echoes of my mind.

Women, a Dark Continent? *The Poisonwood Bible* as a Feminist Response to Conrad's *Heart of Darkness*

Héloïse Meire

I n the past few years, the history of the Congo has caught many people's attention all over the world. One century ago, Belgium annexed the Congo as its colony, which lasted from 1908 until the Congo's independence in 1960. Since then, Western views on the colonial past have changed dramatically. In Belgium, recent exhibitions, plays, historical publications, and broadcasts demonstrate the difference between the modern debates on Africa and colonization and those witnessed by older generations fifty years ago.

Discussions of *Heart of Darkness,* arguably the most famous novel traditionally associated with the Congo, exemplify this ideological gap. Completed in 1899, this highly canonical novel has long been acclaimed, notably for its "visionary" indictment of imperialism. However, since the 1970s, the book's reputation has undergone two major critical assaults. The first came from postcolonial writers who claimed that *Heart of Darkness* presents a racist image of Africa and its people. In 1977, Nigerian novelist and scholar Chinua Achebe published "An Image of Africa," one of the most influential and controversial criticisms of *Heart of Darkness*. In this essay, Achebe labeled Conrad a "bloody racist" who contributed to the "Eurocentric" view that confirmed Africa as the negative antithesis of the West (787). A few years later, some feminist critics argued that the novel also presents a sexist image of women.

Since the beginning of the twentieth century, authors have also reassessed Conrad's novel by implicitly rewriting it. Writers from the colonial or the postcolonial period have taken this emblematic story of the encounter with alterity as a source of inspiration, as a basis for riposte, or both. In her master thesis *Colonial and Postcolonial Rewritings of Heart*

of Darkness: A Century of Dialogue with Joseph Conrad, Regelind Farn studies thirty rewritings of *Heart of Darkness,* from 1901 to 2000 and spanning
five continents.

The Poisonwood Bible, by Barbara Kingsolver, particularly crystallizes
the principal themes that have raised debate on Conrad's novel—race and
gender. Published in 1998, the novel soon became a critical success and a best
seller. *Heart of Darkness* appears explicitly in Kingsolver's bibliography at
the end of her novel, and both novels denounce the vices of Western imperialism through the adventures of white people in the Congo. Both novels pre-
saged public protests against abuses in the Congo, specifically the excesses of
the Leopoldian regime in the Congo and the involvement of Western powers
in the murder of Patrice Lumumba. Interestingly, *The Poisonwood Bible* was
published exactly a century after Conrad started to write *Heart of Darkness.*
Whereas *Heart of Darkness* tells the first chapter of the colonization in the
Congo, since the novel is set a few years after the creation of the Congo Free
State, ruled by King Leopold II, *The Poisonwood Bible* writes the last chapter
of colonization as the novel deals with the Congolese independence.

Despite their similarities, the two works differ in many ways, featur-
ing different protagonists and addressing different issues. Most important,
The Poisonwood Bible was written by a woman and is narrated by female
protagonists. In her article "Into the Heart of Light," Pamela Demory analyzes Kingsolver's novel as "an homage to Conrad" (181) but suggests also
that *The Poisonwood Bible*'s narrative perspective offers "the most intriguing commentary on *Heart of Darkness*" (183) as the first rewriting of *Heart
of Darkness* from a woman's point of view.[1] I maintain that *The Poisonwood
Bible* is not only an homage to Conrad's novel but also to the literary debate
surrounding *Heart of Darkness.* Kingsolver addresses themes that generated much discussion around the older novel; specifically, feminist debate
on *Heart of Darkness* is reflected in *The Poisonwood Bible.*

According to feminist critics such as Johanna Smith and Nina Pelikan
Straus, *Heart of Darkness* sustains patriarchal dominance on two different
levels: in Marlow's derogatory representation of female characters and in the
narrative perspectives and artistic conventions used by the author, which
impose male conventions on women readers. In *The Poisonwood Bible,*
Kingsolver seems to revise *Heart of Darkness* both through the novel's the-
matic approach to gender and through its narrative perspective.

Heart of Darkness tells the story of a sailor, Charlie Marlow, who describes his journey as a riverboat captain for a trading company on what

readers may assume is the Congo River. Marlow is sent there to bring back Kurtz, a company employee who, during his time looking for ivory in the jungle, has become a disturbing megalomaniac. Marlow describes his past experiences to a group of men aboard a ship on the Thames. One of these male listeners narrates this story that, as Susan Jones explains, predominantly targeted a male readership (171).

Like many of Conrad's other tales of the sea and economic conquests, which are often accepted as his major works, *Heart of Darkness* presents a world in which women are practically absent. Indeed, all the characters of the frame narrative, namely Marlow and the hearers on board the *Nellie,* are men. The embedded narrative, a story of exploration, power, and violence in Africa's ivory trade, leaves little room for female characters to be developed. The few scenes that involve women are narrated by Marlow, who seems to hold contradictory views of the other sex. Whereas the women in the domestic sphere (Marlow's aunt and Kurtz's intended) are described by Marlow as naive and idealistic, the women outside the home (the two women at the company's office, the native laundress, and the "savage" woman) reflect his underlying fear of and fascination with them. In true Victorian tradition, Marlow believes that the role of women should be confined to the domestic sphere and that they should not interfere in affairs outside of it. He says, for example, that "They—the women I mean—are out of it—should be out of it. We must help them to stay in that beautiful world of their own, lest ours gets worse" (76).

Whereas Western women were practically nonexistent in the Congo Conrad describes, *The Poisonwood Bible* deals with a period where many Western families, thus many Western women, lived in the Congo.[2] Unlike the Western women of *Heart of Darkness,* who stay at home admiring the men who have gone to the heart of Africa, the women of the Price family in *The Poisonwood Bible* follow the father, Nathan, to experience the reality of the Congo. However, as Demory points out, *The Poisonwood Bible,* like *Heart of Darkness,* presents a world where men and women are relegated to separate spheres (184). Orleanna, who represents the 1950s American housewife, is the counterpart of the two Western women living in the closed world of the domestic sphere in *Heart of Darkness.* But *The Poisonwood Bible* criticizes this gender division. While Orleanna's husband spends his time preaching his sermons unsuccessfully to the villagers, she has to work unremittingly to provide for the family's needs, not unlike African women, since Leah explains: "I'd noticed the Congolese men didn't treat even their own wives and daughters as if they were very sensible or important. Though as far as I could see the wives and daughters did just about all the work" (258).[3]

The novel takes thus the same stance as *Heart of Darkness*, that men are writing history while women remain hidden in the domestic sphere. However, this division between gender spheres in *The Poisonwood Bible* does not imply that women do not take action. They do, but on a different and, as it is suggested in the novel, more essential level. This is exemplified in Orleanna's speech:

> For women like me, it seems, it's not ours to take charge of beginnings and endings. Not the marriage proposal, the summit conquered, the first shot fired, nor the last one either—the treaty at Appomattox, the knife in the heart. Let men write those stories. I can't. I only know the middle ground where we live our lives. We whistle while Rome burns, or we scrub the floor, depending. Don't dare presume there's a shame in the lot of a woman who carries on. (435)

Moreover, the female protagonists of *The Poisonwood Bible* do not remain ignorant as those of *Heart of Darkness*. According to Straus, gender realms in *Heart of Darkness* create a world in which women are "dedicated to the maintenance of delusion" (199). Marlow seems to relegate all women to an imaginary world when he states, "It's queer how out of touch with truth women are. They live in a world of their own, and there had never been anything like it, and never can be" (40). He even participates in this "maintenance of delusion," since he lies to the Intended, substituting "your name" for Kurtz's actual last words "the horror, the horror," leaving her deluded while he knows the truth. Kingsolver rebuts Marlow's belief that the truth of the "horror" is inaccessible to women. Originally, the girls and the mother are as blind to the colonialist enterprise as the European women in *Heart of Darkness*. However, by caring for the household, Orleanna and her daughters mingle with the natives and begin to understand the truth— namely, the horror that is really going on in the foreign exploitation of the Congo—whereas Nathan rhapsodizes like Marlow's aunt about the Western civilizing mission.

According to Johanna Smith, Marlow regards the female characters who transgress the domestic sphere as a symbolic threat to men. In order to preserve his dominance, Marlow silences these women and shrouds them in mystery (172–75). In *Heart of Darkness,* the African woman, who is sometimes referred to as Kurtz's mistress, is said to be "like the wilderness itself" (89). Smith argues that the native woman, being associated with nature, represents a "menacing jungle sexuality" for Marlow (174). For Smith, this image serves both Marlow's masculinist and imperialist ends because it aims to "distance and conquer" the "savage woman's body" as well as the "mysterious life of the jungle" (174).[4] This comparison between the conquered land and the conquered body of the woman has appeared in feminist debates of the past three decades and is a leitmotif in *The Poisonwood Bible.* Like Marlow, the characters of *The Poisonwood Bible* often draw a parallel between the woman and the African land, rejecting the idea of threat, but keeping the idea of conquest.

The slogan "the personal is the political" from the feminist movement of the 1970s clearly echoes in *The Poisonwood Bible.* Throughout the novel, Kingsolver insists on drawing a parallel between the power relationships within the Price family and the power relationships of the colonial and neocolonial powers in the Congo. Orleanna's comment that she has been "swallowed by Nathan's mission, body and soul. Occupied as if by a foreign power" (226), that Nathan "was in full possession of the country once known as Orleanna Wharton" (228), or that Nathan could see "no way to have a daughter but to own her like a plot of land" (217), are just a few examples of this pervasive metaphor.[5]

The evocation of "mother Africa" has become a common feature in contemporary imagery, but in *The Poisonwood Bible* the feminine aspect of the Congo is specifically used to reinforce its victimization. For example, Orleanna says that "in the end, [her] lot was cast with the Congo. Poor Congo, barefoot bride of men who took her jewels and promised the Kingdom" (229). Later in the novel, Adah claims that "*Congo* was a woman in shadows, dark-hearted, moving to a drumbeat" and that its inhabitants cannot forget its colonial past because "if chained is where you have been, your arms will always bear marks of the shackles" (562).

These comparisons might give way to critical reactions. Indeed, Kingsolver's constant parallel between the Price women and the Congo could be seen as tactless, coming from a Western writer. In her book *Re-Orienting Western Feminisms,* Chilla Bulbeck warns against "radical feminism"—according to her, particularly based in the United States—which would see "women treated as much the same everywhere" (7). When Orleanna says that "we're all women, made of the same scarred earth" (101–2) or that "to resist occupation, whether you're a nation or merely a woman, you must understand the language of your enemy" (434), one might think that Kingsolver has fallen into the trap of romanticizing women into a broad sisterhood struggling together with the same issues.

Moreover, the image of a feminized and victimized Congo tends to give a romanticized vision of Africa and its inhabitants. Kingsolver seems to use the image of idealized African people to emphasize the evil of the West's imperial maneuvers. In her analysis of dualisms between First and Third Worlds, Bulbeck warns about writers who "have merely reversed the evaluative connotations of the former dualisms, so that west=bad and east=good" (18). Kingsolver seems to fall into the trap of reversing former dualisms, at least to a certain extent. While Belgium and the United States represent the rapacious exploiters of the Congo, none of the African characters possesses a single flaw. Of course, there is the evil figure of Mobutu, but he is not considered in the same light as the other African people; he is malevolent merely because he is under the yoke of Western imperialism. Indeed, Anatole's remark that Mobutu is "not even African now" because "he is the one wife belonging to many white men" makes him appear as a mere puppet at the service of the West and not as a dictator responsible for his acts (515). Kingsolver's tendency to idealize the African people and culture is evident in her treatment of the issue of physical impairment. In his article entitled "Disability, Family and Culture," Stephen Fox argues that the approval that disabled characters receive from other villagers would be highly unlikely in the Congo of the 1950 and concludes that Kingsolver's idealization of the Congolese unwittingly denies the people's "true natures and actual needs" (412).

But Kingsolver is careful enough to center most of her issues on her female Western characters, a representation she can depict with more assurance than the issues concerning her African characters. Though sisters, the Prices are clearly not "a broad sisterhood of women struggling with the same issues." All are victims of Nathan, but after their departure each one follows a different path and will have very different problems to deal with, from Rachel's concerns about her luxury hotel bathroom to Leah trying to survive with her family, so Kingsolver is able to paint a mixed image of (Western) womanhood.

By contrast, her description of the most important male character, Nathan Price, works as a caricature of patriarchal dominance, since he is not only the abusive father of the Price family, but also a fundamentalist representative for the Christian religion as a Baptist missionary (Adah calls him sarcastically "Our Father") and a jingoist American citizen (whose "fatherland" is governed by a "grandfather," as Adah calls Eisenhower) (338).

In some ways, Nathan's extremist character resembles that of Kurtz. First of all, both characters use violence to enforce their authority. Moreover, both tend to use rhetoric to justify their superiority over the natives. Nathan's report to the Baptist scholars in which he explains how "Congolese do not become attached to their children as we Americans do" (337) is somewhat reminiscent of Kurtz's report to the "International Society for the Suppression of Savage Customs" (77). But their descent into madness, caused by their megalomania, makes the most explicit parallel. At one point in the novel, Kingsolver hints at this similarity between Nathan and Kurtz when Rachel describes her father giving his sermon like "one of those gods they had in Roman times, fixing to send down the thunderbolts and the lightning" (31). This sentence recalls the description of Kurtz's weapons as "the thunderbolts of that pitiful Jupiter" (88). The metaphor represents in both cases the image of the extremist who is convinced of being entrusted by a superior power to carry out his mission.

However, Nathan's will to indoctrinate his family and the Congolese villagers does not succeed, since his evangelization mission is a failure: the villagers vote "against Jesus" in a general election and the Price girls, first blinded by their father, progressively distance themselves from him. Even Nathan's favorite daughter, Leah, says at the end of the novel, "that exacting, tyrannical God of his has left me for good" (594). Thus Nathan differs from Kurtz, who was considered as a "remarkable man" by the Europeans and as a divinity by the natives. Though evil, Kurtz evokes the image of a genius, whereas The Poisonwood Bible depicts Nathan as utterly ineffectual.

In her reader-response analysis of Heart of Darkness, Straus argues that the contrast between the African woman as flesh and the Intended as soul strikes a "jarring note of psychologically reductive simplicity in a text which, when referring to male characters, is psychologically dense" (203). In The Poisonwood Bible, Nathan's one-dimensionality may appear as reductive in contrast with the psychological development of each female Price character. Like the two Western women of Heart of Darkness, Nathan is remote in a world of his own, symbolizing imperialism and ignorance. Whereas most of the Price girls detach themselves from their Western-centrism, Nathan never learns the villagers' language, nor does he try to understand their culture.

Because he does not want to acknowledge the subtlety of Kikongo, the villagers' language, Nathan constantly mispronounces words. This brings us to the metaphor of the title, *The Poisonwood Bible:* in Kikongo, the word "bangala" signifies something dear, or with Nathan's pronunciation, a poisonwood tree. The fact that Nathan mispronounces *"Tata Jesus is bangala!"*— preaching that Jesus is a poisonwood tree and therefore to be feared—reveals Nathan's will to evangelize the Africans forcibly (81).

After the terrible event of Ruth May's death, the mother Orleanna recounts that "it happened finally by the grace of hell and brimstone that I had to keep moving. I moved, and he [Nathan] stood still" (436). In fact, Nathan is the only character that does not evolve from the beginning to the very end of the novel. As Brad Born notes, Nathan's inability to change is illustrated by the words of Adah, whose poetic but cynical mind, reinforced by her love for the poet Emily Dickinson, encourages her to read words backward to discover hidden meanings in them (par. 6). While reading the names of her peers backward, she realizes that only her father's name can be read almost identically in both ways: "Ruth May is not the same Ruth May she was. Yam Htur. None of us is the same: Lehcar, Hael, Hada. Annaelro. Only Nathan remains essentially himself, the same man however you look at him. The others of us have two sides" (312).

By designating Nathan as the only one of the Price members who does not get to narrate his version of the events, Kingsolver offers us one of her most important revisions of Conrad's novel. In *Heart of Darkness,* the relationship between speakers and hearers is exemplified through the transmission of knowledge by different "voices." The motif of the voice comes back many times in the novel, and Marlow's remark that Kurtz was "very little more than a voice" echoes the words of the narrator, who says, "for a long time already he [Marlow], sitting apart, had been no more to us than a voice" (76). Kurtz's voice transmits his revelation of the horror to Marlow. The latter transmits it to the hearers onboard the *Nellie,* one of whom transmits it to the readers. No link in the chain between speakers and hearers includes women, so that, in Straus's words, the "horror" becomes "the secret password in the brotherhood of men who know" (213).

Straus denounces the "peculiar density and inaccessibility" of *Heart of Darkness,* which is, according to her, due to "its extremely masculine historical referentiality, its insistence on a male circle of readers" (199). She argues that even though the horror is revealed to both male and female readers, the scene between Marlow and the Intended suggests that this truth should be hidden from women (199). Moreover, if the frame tale invites the reader to identify with the (male) hearers onboard the *Nellie,* women can only have an ambivalent attitude to the novel. Straus suggests three options for the woman reader of *Heart of Darkness.* One is to identify with the Intended as a symbol of purity and fidelity (but also, we might add, of ignorance). Another possibility is to identify with the native woman, which is highly unlikely because of her abstract character. Lastly, and most likely, the female reader can attempt what Karen Horney calls a "flight from womanhood" and try to identify with Marlow or Kurtz (qtd. in Straus 208). For Straus, all possibilities imply a self-degradation of the female reader, which contrasts with the "psychotherapeutic plenitude" a male reader experiences through his identification with the male characters of the novel (201). Though Straus acknowledges *Heart of Darkness* to be "High Art," she explains how such art requires the female reader "to abandon her own concerns" and impose on them its male conventions (208). She wonders whether *Heart of Darkness* is not primarily about "a certain kind of male self-mystification whose time is passing if not past" and hopes that new conventions for what constitutes "Art" will be created (215).

Kingsolver seems to answer Straus's call. As Linda Wagner-Martin notes, Kingsolver uses "the striking convention of choosing as narrators of the events characters who are, initially, powerless" (108). In this way, *The Poisonwood Bible* could be described as what Ansgar Nünning calls a "revisionist historical novel" (362). In her article "Where Historiographic Metafiction and Narratology Meet," Nünning says:

> Revisionist historical novels are inspired by the wish to rewrite history, particularly from the point of view of those all too long ignored by traditional historiography, and to offer alternative histories. They often do so by relying heavily on multiple internal focalization, adopting the points of view of several character-focalizers whose limited perspectives project highly subjective views of history. (363)

The Poisonwood Bible is a revisionist historical novel first because it recounts the historical period preceding and following the Congo's Independence as few other fiction works have done before.[6] Events of the historical period dealt with in *The Poisonwood Bible* such as the involvement of Western powers Belgium and the United States in the murder of the Congolese Prime

Minister Patrice Lumumba have been ignored for a long time in Western countries and have only recently been revealed to the general public.[7] Moreover, Kingsolver's novel adopts the points of view of "several character-focalizers" with limited perspectives. Indeed, the reader of *The Poisonwood Bible* gets five very distinct perspectives on the events from female characters of different ages and different personalities.

Kingsolver's novel exemplifies the *feminist* revisionist historical novel. By approaching the Congo's history from a female point of view, she offers an alternative to the mostly masculine Western fiction on the Congo. Indeed, Regelind Farn's "Colonial and Postcolonial Rewritings of Heart of Darkness," an analysis of thirty rewritings of *Heart of Darkness,* reveals that only very few of them are written by women and even fewer are narrated from a female point of view.

Nevertheless, this Western feminist revision of the Congo's history remains, like *Heart of Darkness,* a critique of the West rather than a voice for the Congolese. According to Johan Jacobs, *The Poisonwood Bible* is "more concerned with its own discursive constructedness than with the history and the political, material reality of the Congo" (116). The parallel between Nathan's oppression on the Price girls and that of the Western powers on the Congo serves Kingsolver's feminist intentions, but it reduces the complexity of the political situation in the Congo. Indeed, *The Poisonwood Bible* tends to see the historical events of the Congo in black and white, with martyrs such as Lumumba on one side, and on the other side, the American and Belgian heads of state and Mobutu as the malevolent forces, ignoring the ethnic and regional conflicts among the Congolese.

As we have seen, *Heart of Darkness* has been criticized for its "peculiar density and inaccessibility" (Straus 199). In *The Poisonwood Bible,* Kingsolver departs in many ways from Conrad's mode of writing. Not that *The Poisonwood Bible*'s language is unequivocal, given Orleanna's poetic language, the many wordplays and palindromes invented by Adah, and the malapropisms of Rachel. The realistic language of 1950s southern American teenagers ("Man alive, I am all steamed up with no place to go. When Tata Ndu comes to our house, jeez oh man" (302) clearly contrasts with Marlow's enigmatic language. In an interview, Kingsolver explains that she wants to reach the largest public possible. She says:

> It's all about accessibility. That's why I write in English as
> opposed to some sort of highfalutin English that's incompre-

hensible. I really believe that complex ideas can be put across in simple language. And a good plot never hurt anybody. It doesn't cost you in literary terms to give your readers a reason to turn a page. (Kerr 55)

In fact, Kingsolver links her vision of accessibility with her feminist intentions. As Demory notes, Kingsolver is concerned with reaching a female audience (191). In an interview, she admitted, "[My] whole life I've been reading white guy books. . . . And since I've never been a white guy, the most important stuff I have to write is going to be chick books" (DeMarr, *Barbara Kingsolver* 21).

In *The Poisonwood Bible,* Kingsolver creatively answered Straus's call for a departure from Conrad's alleged sexist "High Art" and for new artistic conventions that were able to include the female reader. Yet we might wonder if Kingsolver has not simply reversed *Heart of Darkness*'s gender vision. When looking at *The Poisonwood Bible,* Nathan's one-dimensionality may appear as reductive in contrast with the psychological development of each female Price character. Like the two Western women of *Heart of Darkness,* Nathan is only heard reported, entrapped in a world of his own, symbolizing imperialism and ignorance.

When a reader asked on Kingsolver's official Web site why she did not allow Nathan to speak for himself, Kingsolver answered: "Because of what the story is about. Some people seem to think this is a male/female issue, but that never even crossed my mind. Nathan obviously doesn't represent maleness! He represents an historical attitude." We could ironically defend Conrad in the same way by stating that "the two Western women obviously do not represent femaleness. They represent the rhetoric lying behind imperialism!" But no critics did, perhaps because Conrad's intentions in his novel are more difficult to grasp than Kingsolver's explicit political message.

When examining the alleged sexism (or racism) of *Heart of Darkness,* an essential question needs to be asked: can we assess Conrad's intentions through the words of his invented characters? In literary criticism, a distinction is generally made between the biographical author of the story (here Conrad), the narrator(s) (here the unnamed frame narrator onboard the *Nellie* and the secondary narrator, Charlie Marlow), and what is known in literary jargon as the "implied author"—that is, in Mieke Bal's terms, the "totality of meanings that can be inferred from a text" (119–20). Many critics who accuse *Heart of Darkness* of sexism or racism have considered Marlow as Conrad's alter ego and representative voice, equating the thoughts of the narrator with those of the biographical author. However, logically speaking, if Conrad wanted an objective voice for his novel, he would have chosen an omniscient and abstract narrator. Instead, he creates Marlow as a narrator who is involved in the story he tells and whose views cannot but be limited and subjective. Besides, Conrad constructs a frame tale to recount Marlow's narrative, which enables the reader to read Marlow's words at a distance from the author.

Marlow's constant use of irony also constitutes one of Conrad's methods for aesthetic distance and sense of relativity since irony creates a discrepancy between the narrator's words and their actual meaning. But it also indicates that Conrad did not want his opinion to be perceptible, since, as Farn notes, irony makes it possible "to point out problems without offering a solution or even a complete value judgment" (9). This may indeed be Conrad's aim, since he stated that "nothing is more clear than the utter insignificance of explicit statement and also its power to call attention away from things that matter in the region of art" ("Explicitness" 232). Because of the ambiguity of *Heart of Darkness,* the intentions of the implied author have never been fully grasped, which lead to varied and multiple literary responses, each trying to identify the novel with a certain ideology.

As Demory argues, the five contrasting narrative voices of *The Poisonwood Bible* initially seem to offer a greater possibility than *Heart of Darkness* for multiple truths (187–88). Whereas Marlow's narrative constitutes the bulk of the novel, and thus might appear as the most important voice, the five contrasting narratives of *The Poisonwood Bible* are more or less equal in space in the overall narrative. Each narrative voice of *The Poisonwood Bible* accounts for a distinct prototype of the possible attitudes one can have toward Western involvement in Africa. In fact, this assertion is even made explicit by Kingsolver on her official Web site:

> The four sisters and Orleanna represent five separate philosophical positions, not just in their family but also in my political examination of the world. This novel is asking, basically, "What did we do to Africa, and how do we feel about it?" . . . Orleanna is the paralyzed one here, and Rachel is "What, me worry?" Leah, Adah, and Ruth May take other positions in between, having to do with social activism, empirical analysis, and spirituality, respectively.

Héloïse Meire

The mere fact that Kingsolver explains her intentions for her novel contrasts with Conrad, who stated that he intentionally left his works of art "indefinite, suggestive, in the penumbra of initial inspiration . . ."("Explicitness" 232). But more important, her statement also reveals that the novel's heterogeneous voices represent in fact a unique authoritative narrative, that of Kingsolver herself. This authoritative narrative bears a name, assigned to the novel by its author: "political allegory." On her Web site, Kingsolver claims that indeed *The Poisonwood Bible* "is a political allegory, in which the small incidents of characters' lives shed light on larger events in our world."

In her introductory narrative, Orleanna imperatively asks the "you" she addresses to enter into the story, to become its conscience and its judge. She says:

> First picture the forest. I want you to be its conscience,
> the eyes in the trees. . . . Away down below now, single file on
> the path, comes a woman with four girls in tow, all of them
> in shirtwaist dresses. Seen from above this way, they are pale,
> doomed blossoms, bound to appeal to your sympathies. Be
> careful. Later on you'll have to decide what sympathy they
> deserve. (5)

Later in the novel, we will discover that this "you" could have different addressees (Ruth May, Africa, or the symbolic okapi), but we could argue, like Ami Regier, that this "you" must also be the personal reader of the novel (par. 3). Orleanna continues her narrative by explaining:

> You'll say I walked across Africa with my wrists unshackled,
> and now I am one more soul walking free in a white skin, wear-
> ing some thread of the stolen goods: cotton or diamonds, freedom
> at the very least, prosperity. Some of us know how we came by
> our fortune and some of us don't, but we wear it all the same.
> (9–10)

As it appears, the novel addresses a specific readership—namely, the Western reader, who is seen as directly or indirectly benefiting from Africa's exploitation. At the end of the novel, the "you" reappears as the spirit of Ruth May, and the reader then adopts the position of the mother, who seeks forgiveness for her indirect complicity in history. The child forgives the "you" and asks it to carry on. As Regier argues, this might be a request for a reader's response that goes beyond the world of the novel (par. 9). This hypothesis is quite convincing, since Kingsolver created the Bellwether Prize, which aims at promoting novels that raise readers' "social responsibility" ("Defining a Literature of Social Change").

In *Heart of Darkness,* Marlow explains that the hearers onboard the *Nellie* have to understand the "effect" of his adventure on him—namely, how his views on imperialism were shattered (35). Marlow is able to challenge the first narrator's views on imperialism, and the frame narrative seems to be structured so that the first narrator will now be able to challenge the readers' view. However, the frame narrative in *Heart of Darkness* contributes also to a sense of subjectivity and skepticism about the credibility of the narrators' words, so that in fact none of the characters seems to betray the dominant voice of the story, the implied author. In *The Poisonwood Bible,* although the Prices' narratives are more or less equal in space in the overall narrative, some voices betray Kingsolver's intentions more than others. For example, since Kingsolver's novel aims at "social responsibility," it seems difficult not to consider Leah, who represents in Kingsolver's words "social activism," as the dominant voice of the novel.

It suits Kingsolver's political as well as feminist intentions to make Leah stand out as the heroine of the novel. Indeed, Leah is the one daughter who was originally convinced of her own nation's superiority and of her father's authority, but who departs completely from both at the end of the novel. Moreover, Leah is the only Price daughter who, after the family's departure from Kilanga, stays in the Congo, marries a Congolese man, and becomes a mother. Leah can be seen as one more parallel between the lot of women and that of Africa. She symbolizes hope in the reconstruction of the Congo. She does not forget the sins of her father but tries to forgive him. Although she lives poorly in Angola, a country that has been devastated by war, she moves on and becomes involved in social projects with her Congolese husband, Anatole. The last words of *The Poisonwood Bible,* "Move on. Walk forward to the light" (614), also evoke perseverance and offer here again a contemporary counterpoint to *Heart of Darkness* and Marlow's horror. Although the Congo is still confronted with many conflicts, hopes for peace and reconstruction are huge.

To conclude, while *Heart of Darkness* reflects some nineteenth-century views on gender, *The Poisonwood Bible* may be regarded as a novel imbued with decades of feminism, which rejects this older vision. Kingsolver creatively answered the feminist call for a departure from Conrad's masculinist conventions. She has been able to include the female reader both thematically and through her narrative technique. However, her writing is clearly targeted at a Western and female public. She is not able to fully transcend gender dichotomies since her main male character is left to the same fate as women in *Heart of Darkness,* deprived of a narrative voice and relegated to delusion. Moreover, *The Poisonwood Bible* tends at times to see Africa with a sentimentalizing and Manichean eye. Nevertheless, like Joseph Conrad, she has been able to reveal some hidden "truths" about the Congolese history to the average reader. Finally, comparing *Heart of Darkness* and *The Poisonwood Bible* with the work of a Congolese author might reveal some unexpected findings on the representation of gender and African culture. A new era of Congolese writers has now emerged and Silvia Riva's book, *Nouvelle Histoire de la Littérature du Congo-Kinshasa,* which considers works written by Congolese men and women from the 1930s until nowadays, could be a helpful start for those interested in such a task.

Notes

1. *The Poisonwood Bible* is not, as Demory believed, the unique rewriting of *Heart of Darkness* narrated from a female perspective (192). For example, Farn examines Mineke Schipper's *Conrad's Rivier,* published in 1994, as a response to *Heart of Darkness* (114–220). The story is told by a female frame narrator, Hedda, and a female embedded narrator, Ellen.
2. For more information on the subject of women in the Congo, see Hunt.
3. Citations of *The Poisonwood Bible* in this essay refer to the London edition, published by Faber & Faber.
4. In order to support the argument that Marlow intends to conquer the savage woman's body, Smith quotes the famous feminist philosopher Helène Cixous in her denunciation of "[men's] phantasm of woman as 'dark continents' to penetrate and to 'pacify'" (Cixous, *The Laugh of the Medusa,* qtd. in Smith 169). Cixous herself probably refers to an utterance by Freud: "women, a dark continent," which has often been misinterpreted. By using these words, Freud was saying that women were a terra incognita, a mystery to men. Undertones perceived today in the words "dark continent" have made the metaphor an appropriate object of feminist criticism.
5. The parallel that Kingsolver draws between the exploited land and exploited women may lead some to qualify her as what is nowadays called an "ecofeminist." In their book *Ecofeminism,* Maria Mies and Vandana Shiva explain how this movement, which grew out of the feminist, peace, and ecology movements in the early 1980s, seeks to connect "the relationship of exploitative dominance

between man and nature . . . and the exploitative and oppressive relationship between men and women that prevails in most patriarchal societies . . ." (3). Kingsolver, a graduate in biology and ecology and an active supporter of human rights, clearly makes a connection in her novel between her ecologist, antipatriarchal, and pacifist beliefs.

6. There is, however, Ronan Bennett's novel, *The Catastrophist,* published in 1998, which recounts a doomed love affair just before independence in the Belgian Congo, with the rise and fall of President Lumumba as political backdrop.

7. One year after the publication of *The Poisonwood Bible,* in 1999, Ludo De Witte published *The Assassination of Lumumba.* This book sparked the 2002 Belgian parliamentary commission on the murder of Lumumba, which recognized the role of Western powers, notably Belgium, in the murder of Lumumba in 1961.

Héloïse Meire

Trauma and Memory in *Animal Dreams*

Sheryl Stevenson

The twentieth century may well be remembered as a century of historical trauma. As citizens facing the third millennium, we daily confront the unthinkable in news and television reports, in bizarre public trials, and in relentless statistics exposing rape, murder, torture, battering, and child abuse in an increasingly violent society.

—Suzette A. Henke, *Shattered Subjects*

In a 1997 review essay, "Trauma and Literary Theory," James Berger asks why psychological trauma has "become a pivotal subject connecting so many disciplines," from literary studies to historiography (569). Berger's query encompasses the question of value Geoffrey Hartman poses in a 1995 issue of *New Literary History*, focusing on trends and topics in higher education. But where Hartman asks, "What is the relevance of trauma theory for reading, or practical criticism?" (547), Berger probes possible reasons for "such interest in trauma among literary and cultural theorists" (571). One explanation is that saturated exposure to family dysfunction, violence, wars, and global disasters has created widespread awareness of the effects of traumatic events, making it "not surprising that theorists have turned to concepts of trauma as tools of . . . analysis" (Berger 572). Furthermore, both Hartman and Berger show that conceptions of trauma dovetail with other critical theories that emphasize problems of representation. As a "discourse of the unrepresentable," trauma theory attempts to deal with "the event . . . that destabilizes language" (Berger 573), an event so threatening that it provokes denial, amnesia, delayed memory, and forms of expression that, as Cathy Caruth says, are "always somehow literary"—indirect, coded, and full of gaps that are themselves

88

revealing (*Unclaimed Experience* 5). The theoretical texts that Berger examines—by Caruth, Dominick LaCapra, and Kali Tal—are part of a larger field of trauma studies, led by burgeoning research in psychology and sociology. But Berger's essay is perhaps most provocative for literary scholars in his suggestion that theory needs to be extended through study of literary representations of trauma (577). Among many works that might be designated the "literature of trauma," Barbara Kingsolver's *Animal Dreams* invites further attention, particularly as an illuminating exploration of complex relationships between trauma and memory.

Published in 1990, a decade after post-traumatic stress disorder was added to the American Psychiatric Association's official diagnostic manual, *Animal Dreams* appeared during a great surge of interest, both scholarly and popular, in trauma and its effects on memory. As Judith Lewis Herman observes in her highly influential 1992 study *Trauma and Recovery,* since traumatic experiences "overwhelm the ordinary human adaptations to life," the normal reaction to such threats, for individuals and the public at large, "is to banish them from consciousness" (1). Connecting the individual and society in her view of trauma's manifestations, Herman asserts that phenomena like the Truth and Reconciliation Commission in South Africa demonstrate that the needs of "traumatized communities" parallel those of traumatized individuals: "Remembering and telling the truth about terrible events are prerequisites both for the restoration of the social order and for the healing of individual victims."[1] Yet this return to traumatic experiences through memory conflicts with the need for self-protection, thus provoking further denial and forgetting, a catch-22 Herman calls the "dialectic of trauma" (2). Immense resistance to facing painful, disturbing knowledge can be seen in individuals who block out and then later recall traumatic memories, while acrimonious debates over recovered memories display similarly strong social resistance to dealing with experiences of trauma survivors.[2] But without the effort of remembrance and witnessing, unresolved fear, anger, and grief fester, and the avoidance of memory produces a numbed, constricted self. Kingsolver describes this outcome when explaining the genesis of *Animal Dreams:* "I wanted to write about the way that loss of memory is the loss of self, both for a culture and an individual" ("Serendipity" 3).

Animal Dreams embodies this loss in its central character, Cosima Noline (nicknamed Codi), whose story emerges through a split narrative, alternating between her first-person account and third-person narration that

Sheryl Stevenson

presents her father's perspective. Codi returns to her hometown of Grace, Arizona, in the mid-1980s, apparently because her much-loved sister, Hallie, has left the house they shared in Tucson, going to Nicaragua as an agricultural expert; in addition, their father, Homer, still practicing medicine in Grace, is showing signs of Alzheimer's. As Codi gradually reveals her persistent problems with memory, Kingsolver's dual narrative structure reinforces the symbolic doubling of the troubled daughter and her distant, disoriented father. Characterized by oscillation between numbed inability to remember and sudden overpowering floods of memory and feeling, Codi's sections of the novel constitute a crisis autobiography, uncovering the intensity of her fears and grief as she faces the possible, then actual, loss of Hallie, who is killed by U.S.-supported contras. Yet both Codi's perspective and her father's show that the present crisis elicits memories of unresolved losses in the past—the death of Codi's mother when she was three and that of a child she secretly miscarried when she was fifteen, a daughter she frequently dreams about, even as her father is also haunted by memories of this event. Homer Noline's increasingly disoriented, present-tense narrative, focusing on memories but confusing them with present interactions, has a quality of disconnected impressionism that sharply differs from Codi's retrospective account, which conveys her sense of her life through the story she tells, an order she imposes. Ironically, her father's confused thoughts reveal aspects of Codi's past that she has repressed, yet he loses his ability to bring order to his memories and impressions, and thus loses himself, a condition suggested by his lack of first-person narration. In contrast, Codi moves toward memory regained, a process that involves reconstructing her past, her place within Grace, and her identity.

By concentrating on three aspects of *Animal Dreams,* we can see how Kingsolver's novel sheds light on theories of trauma and discourses of trauma survivors. First, Codi's narrative is one of gaps, evasions, and sudden fissures of erupting emotion—an unstable discourse that resembles those of traumatized people, pulled by conflicting impulses, controlled by the need for safety. Multiple repetitions and returns are another important feature of Codi's narrative, illustrating the human compulsion to return to, and even reenact, disturbing situations. For Codi and other trauma survivors, such returns are crucial spurs to remembering the past, a process inseparable from mourning. Kingsolver's presentation of memory as dialogic emerges through a third set of devices that convey the traumatized person's need for other individuals and for community, for collective remembrance and social action.

These aspects of *Animal Dreams* reflect motifs it shares with many survivor stories—themes of safety, memory and mourning, and the struggle to reconnect with others in spite of debilitating distrust. The novel confirms Judith Herman's view that these motifs describe stages of recovery for trauma survivors (155), but Codi also dramatizes the universal character of these human needs. As a person whose disturbing experiences (unlike those of the Holocaust survivor, war veteran, or victim of incest) may not be seen as traumatic, Kingsolver's protagonist embodies an emerging view of trauma as not unusual but ordinary and frequently unrecognized (Brown 100–103; Hartman 546). *Animal Dreams* also depicts Codi as a representative figure, one whom we might call Citizen Cain, "[a] good citizen of the nation in love with forgetting" (149). Her amnesia becomes a metaphor for the widespread tendency of responsible citizens to "forget" unpleasant social realities, to become desensitized and apathetic, as in Kingsolver's chosen example, America's well-known but widely ignored financing of violence against civilians in Nicaragua. By making Codi's responses to loss and violence seem both ordinary and representative, part of a widely shared process in which memory is crucial, *Animal Dreams* highlights trauma theory's everyday implications along with its power as a tool of social analysis.

THE CATCH-22 OF SAFETY

Since traumatic experiences are defined by their "power to inspire helplessness and terror," it is apparent that providing people with safety is a first necessity, as is seen in all crisis-intervention and disaster-relief efforts, such as work with survivors of rape, large-scale accidents, and terrorist attacks (Herman 34, 159–62). A more subtle problem then arises when the need for safety causes survivors to use various psychological means to distance themselves from threatening memories and feelings (42–47). The opening chapter of Codi's narrative ("Hallie's Bones," the novel's second chapter) reveals how the dialectic of trauma—the deadlocked impulses to remember and to repress—produces an indirect, impeded disclosure. In her first three sentences, Codi defines herself by negation and implies that the real story is happening elsewhere, with Hallie as hero: "I am the sister who didn't go to war. I can only tell you my side of the story. Hallie is the one who went south, with her pickup truck and her crop-disease books and her heart dead set on a new world" (7). Mocking the classic Western whose hero rides into town and takes care of everyone's problems, Codi's first chapter describes the day she returns to Grace after fourteen years, riding into town on a Greyhound, soon to find that the orchards (and thus the economy) are dying, poisoned by the irresponsible mining company that is polluting the town's river. Belying her cowboy nickname, Codi underscores that she's no hero, mentioning that she has been in medical school but has devolved downward, to the point of dispensing remedies in an ironically debased manner: "For the last six months in Tucson I'd worked night shift at a 7-Eleven, selling beer and Alka-Seltzer to people who would have been better off home in bed" (10). Codi's mode of narration reinforces effects of her self-lacerating humor. Following her ironic description of arriving by Greyhound "like some rajah," she questions her memory of a scene she has just presented, tells how she had "lied on the bus" (saying she was "a Canadian tourist"), and abruptly feels "dragged down by emotions" she does not explain (8, 12, 13). Codi's self-undermining narrative mirrors those of traumatized people who, as Judith Herman explains, "often tell their stories in a highly emotional, contradictory, and fragmented manner which undermines their credibility and thereby serves the twin imperatives of truth-telling and secrecy" (1).

Kingsolver shows that the trauma survivor's conflicting needs for disclosure and safety are also met through language that is literary, using metaphor, analogy, and flashbacks as means of control. Thus, after describing Hallie as "dead set on a new world," Codi shifts abruptly to another time and place, perhaps in response to the threatening words "dead set":

> I stood on a battleground once too, but it was forty years
> after the fighting was all over: northern France, in 1982, in a field
> where the farmers' plow blades kept turning up the skeletons of
> cows. They were the first casualties of the German occupation.
> In the sudden quiet after the evacuation the cows had died by
> the thousands in those pastures, slowly, lowing with pain from
> unmilked udders. But now the farmers who grew sugar beets in
> those fields were blessed, they said, by the bones. (7)

This passage faces the danger to Hallie with superb indirection, echoing the chapter's title "Hallie's Bones" with a repeated image of bones and bone-fed soil that becomes one of the novel's recurring metaphors. An analogy similarly draws attention to Hallie's danger yet replaces it, shifting from the war she went to join to the vast destruction of life in World War II, affecting not only farmers (similar to Hallie with her "crop-disease books," her version of weapons) but even animals of the most harmless kind, cows whose "unmilked udders" underscore their femaleness and wasted fertility. Codi's next paragraph reveals the fragile sense of safety provided by the deflections of her thinking:

> Three years later when my sister talked about leaving Tucson to work in the cotton fields around Chinandega, where farmers were getting ambushed while they walked home with their minds on dinner, all I could think of was France. Those long, flat fields of bonefed green. Somehow we protect ourselves; it's the nearest I could come to imagining Nicaragua. Even though I know the bones in that ground aren't animal bones. (7)

Prominently displayed in the chapter's title, human bones, specifically Hallie's, emerge even under a kind of erasure, through deflection, comparison, and substitution—a perfect example of language that meets the conflicting demands of self-protection and truth-telling that constitute the dialectic of trauma.

Though personal stories of trauma survivors are especially prone to such devices, Mark Freeman's analysis of autobiographical narratives suggests that order and clarity in every life story are imposed retrospectively, with the following implication: "Perhaps . . . we ought to be paying greater attention to 'discontinuities,' 'ruptures,' 'fissures' . . ." (47). *Animal Dreams* illustrates how this approach is necessary for understanding the words of traumatized people. The end of Codi's first chapter offers a telling example, as she describes walking to the place she will stay through an orchard whose unnatural rows remind her of a vast military cemetery in northern France, showing how persistently her memory brings up what she fears in deflected, substitute images. After noting that the orchards of Grace are "full of peacocks, living more or less wild and at the mercy of coyotes but miraculously surviving in droves" (14), she seems to stumble into a kind of horrifying primal scene involving one such bird. Perceiving from a distance that a peacock is being beaten by children elicits the following sudden, fissure-like response from Codi: "I'm not the moral guardian in my family. Nobody, not my father, no one had jumped in to help when I was a child getting whacked by life, and on the meanest level of instinct I felt I had no favors to return"

Sheryl Stevenson

(15). But, prompted by what she sees as "Hallie's end of my conscience," she does try to intervene, immediately uncovering her mistake: she has disrupted a common festivity for children, the opening of a candy-filled piñata (15). Her reaction is extremely telling, but in ways she does not intend: "I felt disoriented and disgraced, a trespasser on family rites. . . . I wondered in what dim part of Grace I'd left my childhood" (16). Exemplifying the trauma survivor's tendency toward guilt and self-criticism (her "loss of self"), Codi characteristically defines herself by negation—she's "not the moral guardian," not Hallie, but instead is disGraced, cut off from the town and the Grace part of herself, her past. But if we focus on discontinuity or rupture, the eruption of words that seem to escape Codi's control, we might conclude that she has not lost touch with her past. Instead, this incident has called forth a memory that could be taken from the narratives of many incest survivors: "no one had jumped in to help when I was a child." Though these words are half-erased by Codi's shift of attention to her mistake, this passage teaches us that once we start looking at gaps, partial erasures, and sudden eruptions, these places where the narrative gets messy are prime sources for self-disclosure, as Freud long ago showed and Derrida reinforces. But because Codi's linguistic devices allow her to ignore the slip, we can also see what many analysts of survivor discourse have noted, that telling or writing the story provides a "safe space" for those who are dealing with overwhelmingly painful memories (Kuribayashi and Tharp 1).

Codi's narrative also illustrates the need of traumatized people for actual places of safety or "sanctuary," to use therapist Sandra Bloom's term, which evokes the American "sanctuary movement." This underground movement of people who provide refuge for illegal aliens escaping Latin American political terror appears prominently in Kingsolver's first novel, *The Bean Trees,* as well as in *Animal Dreams.* Codi describes the time when Hallie began to offer such protection, her action putting an end to a period Codi idealizes: "We'd had one time of perfect togetherness in our adult lives, the year we were both in college in Tucson. . . . [Then] Hallie . . . befriended some people who ran a safehouse for Central American refugees. After that we'd have strangers in our kitchen every time of night, kids scared senseless, people with all kinds of damage. Our life was never again idyllic" (35). Codi vividly recalls her contacts with traumatized refugees, such as a victim of torture whose "eyes offered out that flatness, like a zoo animal" (93), but she stresses the contrast of her reactions and Hallie's: "where pain seemed to have anesthetized me, it gave Hallie extra nerve endings"; "When Hallie

94

and I lived in Tucson, in the time of the refugees, she would stay up all night rubbing the backs of people's hands and holding their shell-shocked babies. I couldn't. I would cross my arms over my chest and go to bed" (89, 149). Hallie's need to take risks for others is expressed in attempts to provide protection, yet ironically these very efforts destroy Codi's sense of safety. Thus, after Hallie's departure for Nicaragua, the house once shared by the sisters "fell apart"; the plants die along with Codi's relationship with her boyfriend of that time (10). As *Animal Dreams* begins from moments of departure— Hallie's to Nicaragua and Codi's to Grace—the novel contextualizes Codi's individual search for safety in terms of a political movement, so that the parallel between Codi and Central American refugees highlights specific political issues and the universal need for safety. (This idea is extended with Codi's realization that industrial pollution may destroy the orchard-based economy of Grace, thus forcing longtime residents to move "to Tucson or Phoenix" for jobs, making them "refugees too" [149].) The novel's images of tormented refugees underscore the intense fear connected with place and displacement, the fragility of safety which survivors of traumatic experiences feel and convey to others. But Kingsolver especially reveals how places of safety are inherently symbolic and subjective. Hence it is clear that Codi subjectively constructs the Tucson house; whether it is "safe" or not, "home" or not, is personal for her, not even corresponding to her beloved sister's viewpoint.

In Grace, Codi's "safe house" is provided by her friend Emelina Domingos, who represents an alternative view of safety, a carnivalesque vision in which life and death, safe and unsafe, are accepted as inseparable. The second chapter of Codi's narrative encapsulates this vision. Entitled "Killing Chickens," the chapter is paired with the preceding peacock-piñata scene as Codi comes upon an actual family rite of bird killing. Yet this scene is surprisingly positive, introducing Emelina as an affectionate, capable mother of five, supervising the slaughter of roosters, showing her twin sons how to make sure that the animals feel as little pain and fear as possible. A fertile, tough-talking, down-to-earth mother watching over children "dappled with blood" (30), Emelina brilliantly embodies the carnivalesque worldview Bakhtin presents through similarly contradictory female figures, the life-giving mother who is also closely tied to death (Bakhtin 25–26). The Domingos' household is thus immediately established as a place in which safety and its opposites (violence, suffering, death) coexist. But Emelina also plays a crucial role in relation to Codi's memory. She

Sheryl Stevenson

brings up Codi's adolescent campaigns against chicken killing, and when Codi claims it was Hallie who was the caring activist, that she and Hallie are opposites ("chalk and cheese"), Emelina disputes one of Codi's basic self-constructions by insisting that her own memory is correct, that Codi was the leader and Hallie "copied [her] like a picture" (29, 31). This challenge to Codi's remembered self is the first of many cases in which her friends and family push her to move past her memory blocks and faulty self-images. As Emelina plays the role of mother and of memory for Codi, she exemplifies an attitude of open acceptance, in touch with reproduction, death, and the past—aspects of life that have long been problematic for Codi.

Furthermore, the place Emelina provides—a tiny, detached "guesthouse"—seems to fit Codi's view of herself as an orphan and outsider, while it also suggests what she seeks in her journey: "The bed had a carved headboard, painted with red enamel, and a softlooking woven spread. It was a fairytale bed. I wished I could fall down and sleep a hundred years in this little house . . ." (26). Like an exiled or enchanted princess, having found her small place of protection, Codi lies down on its "fairytale bed," and it is in this childlike space that she first allows herself to really think of Hallie: "It was frightening to speculate on specifics; I'd been rationing my thoughts about her, but now I was exhausted and my mind ran its own course. I thought of Hallie at border crossings. Men in uniforms decorated with the macho jewelry of ammunition. No, not that far. I pulled her back to Tucson, where I'd seen her last and she was still safe" (31). Unable to handle thoughts about the dangers Hallie may be encountering as she crosses literal borders and symbolic barriers of gender, Codi refuses to let her imagination go: "No, not that far" (31). So she uses her memory self-protectively, to bring her sister "back" to the last time she "was safe," to the scene where she left Codi in Tucson. Yet as she remembers this scene, having sought this memory as a safe space for her thoughts, she suddenly confronts her worst fear while remembering how she felt when Hallie was about to drive away: "I was thinking that if anything happened to her I wouldn't survive" (32). With a deflection of her thoughts from this deep fear, Codi overlays the scene of Hallie's departure with yet another memory, as she thinks of the "one time of perfect togetherness in our adult lives," the time before Hallie took in refugees (35). Through Codi's manipulations of her memories, *Animal Dreams* vividly illustrates how memory can be controlled by the need for safety. Though Emelina's safe house enables Codi to begin to deal with her fears and her past, at a much later point, more than halfway through her narrative, she writes to Hallie of the stunting effects of her fears: "I feel small and ridiculous and hemmed in on every side by the need to be safe" (200). Codi's narrative is similarly controlled and hemmed in by self-protective uses of language, because she is trapped by the catch-22 of trauma: to heal she must remember, and to remember she must feel safe, but as soon as she begins to remember, she loses her sense of safety as she faces her grief, her need to mourn.

MEMORY AS MOURNING

For traumatized people, deliberate efforts to remember are crucial to the necessary process of reconstructing their life stories, even though such memories resemble (or even trigger) involuntary flashbacks and nightmares that reenact terrifying events. Though memory blocks and a constricted, numbed awareness help ward off this painful experience, many survivors are drawn, often unconsciously, to return to the people and places associated with their traumatic past (Herman 39–40). This process of reenactment, described by Freud as the "repetition compulsion" (32), is clearly reflected in *Animal Dreams,* a novel that seems to be structured by the compulsion to return and repeat. Faced with Hallie's dangerous journey and possible loss, Codi does not simply make her own journey to the place where she experienced the traumatic losses of her mother and her child. She also returns to her high school (as a biology teacher for one school year) and eventually to her relationship with Loyd Peregrina, the man who had unknowingly impregnated her when they were high school students. While the latter relationship may seem too convenient a coincidence for some readers, Codi's attraction back to Loyd precisely fits the psychology of reenactment explained by Herman and others—the need to master a wounding experience of the past (Herman 41). In *Fiction and Repetition,* Hillis Miller suggests another way in which the returns effected through memory and reenactment can be deeply satisfying. Such repetitions can accomplish, as in Virginia Woolf's *Mrs. Dalloway,* a "raising of the dead," the return of beloved people who have been lost (Miller 178). Miller's insights concerning *Mrs. Dalloway* bring out intriguing similarities between Kingsolver's novel and Woolf's dual narrative, which features a traumatized veteran and explores the presence of the past through memory.[3] But *Fiction and Repetition* also sheds light on Kingsolver's repeated depictions of All Souls' Day, especially when Miller points out Woolf's allusion to this holiday through Richard Strauss's song "Allerseelen," which includes these lines: "One day in the year is free to the dead, / Come to my heart that I may have you again, / As once in May" (190). Even if painful, returns of the past through memory can sometimes be the only way to remain connected with those we have lost, a view expressed by a Vietnam veteran: "I do not want to take drugs for my nightmares, because I must remain a memorial to my dead friends" (qtd. in Caruth, *Trauma* vii). Codi's narrative reveals a similarly compelled, emotionally charged adherence to remembering and grieving.

The spurs to released memory and emotion in *Animal Dreams* precisely mirror those listed by Judith Herman, who suggests that repressed memories may return through "observance of holidays and special occasions," along with "viewing photographs, constructing a family tree, or visiting the site of childhood experiences."[3] One of the novel's most evocative sequences renders the powerful effect of returning to a place of great pain. After spending her second day in Grace shopping with Emelina, meeting people she does not remember, Codi describes her overcharged, blocked-off response: "Grace was a memory minefield; just going into the Baptist Grocery with Emelina had charged me with emotions and a hopelessness I couldn't name" (46). That night, dealing with the insomnia characteristic of many traumatized people, Codi goes out after midnight to try to find the road "to Doc Homer's" (47). This dreamlike scene renders the dense, obscure nature of her emotions along with a startling gap in her memory, as revealing as any slip of the tongue: "I wasn't ready to go [to Doc Homer's] yet, but I had to make sure I knew the way. I couldn't ask Emelina for directions to my own childhood home; I didn't want her to know how badly dislocated I was. I'd always had trouble recalling certain specifics of childhood, but didn't realize until now that I couldn't even recognize them at point-blank range. . . . In fact, I felt like the victim of a head injury" (47). Finally admitting that "Doc Homer's" is her "own childhood home," Codi shows that she has no idea how to find the house where she lived until she was eighteen. And when she seeks this house—secretly, in the middle of the night—she thinks instead of the field where her mother died, recalling the scene in rich, visual detail, including the stretcher "like a fragile, important package," the helicopter "sending out currents of air across the alfalfa field behind the hospital," and the "alfalfa plants show[ing] their silvery undersides in patterns that looked like waves," so that "[t]he field became the ocean I'd seen in storybooks, here in the middle of the desert, like some miracle" (48). Since Codi was "home with a babysitter" when this occurred, she accepts that this vivid memory is actually one of her many "fabrications based on stories I'd heard" (48), suggesting the self-doubts of incest survivors whose memories are denied. Yet remembering her mother's famously strong will, supposedly shown in her tenacious refusal to fly, leads Codi to see how she herself differs from Hallie in having known their mother as a "ferociously loving" presence, something Codi "tried to preserve" and be for Hallie, though feeling she "couldn't get it right" (49). This memory reestablishes a connection between her mother, herself, and Hallie that seems to enable her to find her father's house, perhaps blocked out because it lacked her mother: "I stopped suddenly in the center of the road, in the moon's bright light, with shadow trickling downhill from my heels like the water witcher's wellspring finally struck open. I'd found the right path" (50).

Codi repeatedly associates memories with imagery of water in the desert, suggesting their preciousness and life-sustaining power. Similar to therapeutic techniques for getting past trauma-based amnesia (one technique is called "flooding"), when she opens herself to remembering her father's house and her mother's death, other memories come and with them "the familiar, blunt pressure of old grief" as Codi first fully discloses her traumatic past: "Even the people who knew me well didn't know my years in Grace were peculiarly bracketed by death: I'd lost a mother and I'd lost a child" (50; cf. Herman 181–82, 184). Here the straightforward, direct syntax and repetitions emphasize Codi's double loss while the statement's parallelism ("I'd lost a mother and I'd lost a child") resembles two brackets. Codi is able to reach this difficult disclosure through trying to return to and remember the place of each loss, the house where her child was stillborn and the field where her mother died. Just as the river through Gracela Canyon is "Grace's memory of water" in times of no rain (270), so too specific places preserve Codi's past and connect her with feelings that she has defensively "bracketed" off as her "years in Grace" (50).

Like places she returns to, Codi's dreams hold memories of her past, often in a disguised form that discloses yet hides, fitting the self-protective dialectic of trauma. Judith Herman notes, "The traumatic moment becomes encoded in an abnormal form of memory, which breaks spontaneously into consciousness, both as flashbacks during waking states and as traumatic nightmares during sleep" (37). Such "dreams are unlike ordinary dreams" in that they "occur repeatedly" and "include fragments of the traumatic event in exact form . . ." (39). Herman's points are confirmed by both Codi's and Homer's narratives. In chapter 6, "The Miracle," describing the circumstances of her secret pregnancy and miscarriage, Codi tells of recurring

Sheryl Stevenson

dreams that have continued to bring her daughter back to her: "In one of the dreams I run along the creek bank looking among the boulders. They are large and white, and the creek is flooded, just roaring, and I know I've left a baby out there" (51). Though at this point Codi apparently does not remember the night of her miscarriage, Homer's memories reveal the extent to which her dream includes fragments of memory. In one of his flashbacks, to a time when he was secretly aware that his daughter was about six months pregnant, Homer observes that she locks herself in the bathroom for hours and then leaves the house with a "small bundle in her arms" (140). Mirroring her secrecy, he follows her to the dry riverbed where she buries the child: "Round volcanic boulders flank her, their surfaces glowing like skin in the moonlight. She is going down to the same dry river where they nearly drowned ten years ago, in the flood" (140). Homer's narrative shows that Codi's dreams and even her waking thoughts about finding her baby in water (221) reflect her buried memories of where she left her child. But his memories also suggest a reason for one of her most prominent memory gaps—her inability to recall her childhood attempt, with Hallie, to save a litter of motherless coyote pups, abandoned in a burrow above the river that flooded, nearly drowning the girls along with the similarly orphaned animals. Though Homer, Emelina, and Hallie each recall this incident (19–21, 77, 121), said by Emelina to be "famous" (77), for Codi it remains blocked out until more than halfway through the novel (191), undoubtedly because of the riverbed's association with her lost child. Most strikingly, Codi needs the people who have shared her life, especially her father, in order to recover more of their past and see it differently—to remember the night she lost her child, to understand that Homer tried to help, and to see through Loyd and her father that the baby was not just hers and not just her loss (332). The novel's dialogic narrative structure, separating Homer's memories from Codi's dreams and reflections, vividly conveys how reconstructing the past is a dialogic process, requiring an interplay of incomplete perspectives.

Thoughts of Codi's child keep returning, both to her and to her father, suggesting that traumatic memories indeed have the "frozen," repetitive quality Herman describes, causing them to be repeated until the individual can reconceptualize and thus rewrite the past, seeing it within new frameworks of meaning (Herman 37, 41). *Animal Dreams* shows how this process might occur through place, as new places enable Codi to think about her child within different contexts. This mode of healing can be seen when Loyd takes Codi to Kinishba, an eight-hundred-year-old Pueblo structure with "more than two hundred rooms—a village under one roof" that provides a vision of interconnected life, as its stones fit together naturally, looking "like cells under a microscope" (128, 129). When Codi notes the thick walls, Loyd tells her, "The walls are graveyards. When a baby died, they'd mortar its bones into the wall" to keep it "near the family" (128). This attitude of seeing the dead as a natural part of one's daily life is one that Codi moves toward, as she shifts from its opposite, thoughts of the unnatural rows of military graves in distant Europe, to scenes of unique, creatively decorated family graves, lovingly tended on All Souls' Day, as children play among their dead ancestors, so that the families of Grace seem "lush as plants, with bones in the ground for roots" (165). Similar words capture Codi's new sense of life springing up amid death when she and Loyd drive through snowy mountains in December and find "lush plants thriving" near a stream fed by hot springs, reminding Codi of her dreams of finding her child, miraculously alive: "I wondered if perhaps I was, after all, in one of my strange dreams, and whether I would soon be looking under the foliage beside the stream for my lost baby" (221). In these new places, Codi's familiar memories are re-placed, as she forms new associations with her dead loved ones.

Among Codi's many comments about memory, one of the most provocative is that "[m]emory runs along deep, fixed channels in the brain" (269), a metaphor she develops by describing the river as "Grace's memory of water" (270). This metaphor is richly suggestive, implying the utter necessity of memory while also pointing toward research that has shown traumatic memories are deeply imprinted and thus especially fixed (Herman 38–39). Codi's description also resembles Susan Griffin's imagery in *Woman and Nature:* "We say everything comes back. And you cannot divert the river from the riverbed. We say every act has its consequences. That this place has been shaped by the river, and that the shape of this place tells the river where to go" (186). Griffin conveys, as Codi says in *Animal Dreams,* that "the land has a memory," though Codi offers a different example: "The lakes and the rivers are still hanging on to the DDT and every other insult we ever gave them" (255). Griffin's river that cannot be diverted particularly coincides with the view of Grace's older women, who steadfastly oppose the mining company's attempt to divert the river away from the town, a place so "shaped by the river" that it would no longer exist without its water. But although Codi's metaphors evoke key insights, they do not fully describe how memory works, since for both Homer and Codi memories do not stay in fixed channels. In fact, Homer's disordered memories frequently show his mind skipping channels, making poetic, true connections between times and people by mixing them up. Though Codi's memory is not as disordered or creative as her father's, the novel shows that dialogic interactions with others enable Codi to recover previously repressed memories, discard false ideas, and reinterpret her own identity. Hence, for example, once she discovers that her father has lied about their family's not being from Grace, she remembers her past differently, rewriting herself in a more positive way as a child who was watched over by "fifty mothers" (the women of Grace [311, 328]), not a No-line but a Nolina, a Gracela descendant and also, Roberta Rubenstein notes, a hardy desert plant, "capable . . . of surviving for years between flowerings" (15). As she revises her identity, from "victim" to "survivor," Codi decidedly confirms narrative therapy's central tenet—that neither the past nor one's self is fixed, that "[s]elf is a perpetually rewritten story."⁵ But since those around Codi—her father, Emelina, Loyd, and the women of Grace—play an instrumental role in spurring her memories and new self-knowledge, *Animal Dreams* adds this crucial emphasis: that it takes a town to raise a child, to resurrect her memories, to help her grieve and heal.

ONLY RECONNECT

> My heart is moved by all I cannot save:
> so much has been destroyed
> I have to cast my lot with those
> who age after age, perversely,
> with no extraordinary power,
> reconstitute the world.
> —Adrienne Rich, "Natural Resources"

Since overwhelming experiences of violence and loss produce feelings of helplessness, distrust, isolation, and despair, relationships with others are both essential and difficult for traumatized people. Recovering "a sense of control, connection, and meaning" is problematic in any case, but is especially so when the trauma is hidden or given little recognition (Herman 33, 188). Too often, the survivor avoids speaking about and grieving for the loss, whether it is an unborn child or her own innocence and trust. As Codi unfolds her feelings about her secret pregnancy and miscarriage—starting with adolescent shame and fear, later compounded by grief and anger—she exemplifies the pressures that silence those who feel their experience cannot be shared. A society alarmed by the impact of unresolved trauma (seen, for example, in cycles of violence in families) needs to recognize the role of community and culture for those like Codi, overwhelmed by the awareness that "so much has been destroyed" (Rich 172). People surrounding the survivor can help create the sense of security necessary to risk memory and relationship; communities can also offer rituals and gatherings for collective mourning. But further, according to Judith Herman, "the breach between the traumatized person and the community" requires not just "public acknowledgement of the traumatic event," but also "some form of community action" (70), as Rich suggests in the choice to "cast [her] lot with those" joined through generations of struggle. *Animal Dreams* illuminates how communities and cultural influences can enable traumatized people to connect with their past and with other people, thus finding value in their lives, however much has been destroyed or lost.

One way the novel presents such influences is through prominent depictions of rituals. Psychiatrist Marten deVries highlights the importance of rituals for individuals and communities affected by traumatic events. He notes that both long-established ceremonies and informal gatherings at a symbolic place—a church, tree, or schoolyard—can help reconnect individuals as a community, reestablishing their sense of being part of the social order and "life cycle."[6] *Animal Dreams* precisely renders this effect of rituals by focusing on Codi's relationships to others during three celebrations of All Souls' Day. As Rubenstein observes (14), these events structure the novel, occurring in chapter 1, chapter 14 (a midpoint), and chapter 28 (the final chapter). Beginning with Homer's memory of the last All Souls' festivities he allowed for his daughters, these three chapters suggest that Codi is deeply drawn to the yearly rite because it expresses ties with community and ancestors that her father has denied and effaced, but which she finally recovers. The novel's last chapter, "Day of All Souls," conveys in its title the inclusiveness of relationships Codi has sought. The chapter depicts November 2, 1989, more than two years after the story's main events, a day that reveals how Codi—pregnant and tending her father's grave among those of the other Nolinas—has become fully reconnected with her community and the cycle of generations (the novel's twenty-eight chapters structurally reinforce the impression that she is part of something larger, a female fertility cycle). But this "particular day in 1989" is also chosen by Codi for her return to her mother's death site, with the woman who took her secretly to witness that departure (339). Thus Codi ends her narrative with a long-denied, long-cherished memory, and her new understanding of it: "This is what I remember: Viola is holding my hand. . . . I can see my mother there, a small white bundle with nothing left, and I can see that it isn't a tragedy we're watching, really. Just a finished life" (342). Through the novel's final words, describing how the helicopter, "empty and bright, . . . rises like a soul" (342), Kingsolver suggests that Codi's participation with others in rituals of memory and mourning enables her to release her grief for her mother, as though she can finally heed her dream about carrying her fully grown daughter and hearing Hallie say, "Let her go. Let go. She'll rise" (301).

While revealing the power of traditional holidays and customs, *Animal Dreams* shows that unconventional rites are also sometimes necessary for traumatized people, especially for those who have experienced losses that are "invisible" or that "rupture the ordinary sequence of generations" (Herman 188), as is the case with Codi's secret miscarriage and her loss of a twenty-nine-year-old sister. Codi also speaks for many whose loved ones have died in ways that make their bodies unrecoverable: " . . . I kept coming back to this: we had no body. I wanted to have a funeral for Hallie, but I was at a loss. I knew the remains should not have been important, but in a funeral the body gives the grieving a place to focus their eyes" (324). Like those affected by the Oklahoma City bombing, for whom the "Survivor Tree" became a symbol and gathering place, Codi tries to find a miraculously thriving tree (one that the people of Grace call a "semilla besada—the seed that got kissed" [324, 49]) where the community can meet to remember Hallie.[7] Though the informally created memorial rite has many rough edges, other people's mementos of Hallie's childhood enable Codi to experience the powerful grief she feared would be "unbearable" (327; cf. Herman 188, 195). Furthermore, in an unconscious reenactment of the night of her miscarriage, Codi leaves the memorial gathering "alone," to bury the bundle of mementos wrapped in a black wool afghan, which replicates the black sweater (her mother's) she had chosen for her daughter's burial (328, 139). Homer's perspective blends the two times (331), though it is clear that Codi replaces an earlier act of secret hiding with a ritual of mourning that includes her father and allows her to "let go" of both her daughters, an idea reinforced when she tells Homer that they "gave . . . Hallie" to the world (333). As Rubenstein points out, this "ritual reburial of her lost child" allows Codi "to lay to rest—and to reconnect with—the spirits of others she has lost" (17). The scene ends with Homer's confused perception that both his daughters are present, but in contrast to previous passages in which his strong love for them and for his wife seemed a painful burden that "trapped" them all (98), the final moment of his narrative suggests that Codi's rite of mourning has also made it possible for him to release his grief: "He understands for the first time in his life that love weighs nothing. Oh God, his girls are as light as birds" (335).

Through repeated image patterns, Kingsolver connects Codi with her mother, sister, and daughter: they are like birds but also like seeds; they "rise" but also go back to the earth, a carnivalesque image suggesting the cycle of life inseparable from death (Bakhtin 21, 24–25). Embodied in many forms of culture, including rituals and works of art, a vision of interconnected life is crucial to Codi, her father, and others paralyzed by loss, violence, and despair. Ursula Le Guin sees this sense of "relatedness" as central to *Animal Dreams*—indeed, she holds that the novel "belongs to a new fiction of relationship, aesthetically rich and of great political and spiritual significance and power" (8). Kingsolver develops this vision through several memorable devices. The most striking is use of multiples, as in the networks of women who hold the town together: Codi's "fifty mothers"; the town's founding Gracela sisters, also called "the great-grandmothers"; and the many Grace women (including Codi's mother) named Althea, such as those Codi refers to collectively as "the Altheas," who operate the town's popular restaurant (265). The novel's title and sixteen of its twenty-eight chapter titles foreground plural words: "Pictures," "Mistakes," "Endangered Places," "The Souls of Beasts," and so on. *Animal Dreams* also features two sets of twins and two sets of drowned coyote pups, a doubling that underscores the story's basic pairing, that of Codi and Hallie, whom the reader sees are very much alike (as Emelina says) rather than being the opposites Codi projects. In addition, ties between the opening and closing chapter titles create the impression of a circle, with the last chapter title, "Day of All Souls," being a one-word variation of the first, "Night of All Souls"; similarly, the penultimate chapter, "Human Remains," connects with the second, "Hallie's Bones." Numerous repetitions of the novel's beginning, along with images of return, characterize the last four chapters, starting with Codi's return to earth (and Grace) in chapter 25 and culminating with her second pregnancy and signs of plant life returning to Grace's poisoned and badly irrigated lands. Overall, the novel's repetitions form a cyclical structure that encapsulates Codi's many reconnections—with herself and her past, her community and the earth—as she comes to feel the sense of belonging and responsibility fundamentally necessary for those who have been isolated and anesthetized by trauma.

Codi reaches this point, in part, through another cultural influence: she has been drawn into collective action as she finds she cannot separate herself from large-scale social conflicts affecting Grace and Nicaragua. Aware that her tax dollars are financing the contras (262), Codi's deeply ingrained sense that she is her sister's keeper conflicts with her Cain-like disavowal of social responsibility. The two major threats that spur her involvement converge as painfully realistic details of the letter-writing campaign to obtain Hallie's release are interwoven with colorful vignettes showing the Stitch and Bitch Club's successful efforts to release Grace from the mining company's hold (270–72, 273–77; cf. 261–67, 313–17). Through this pervasive doubling, *Animal Dreams* links the problems in two sites of struggle, and these mirroring depictions (with their contrasting outcomes) reinforce key ideas about collective action. The most important of these ideas closely resemble what Sharon Welch has called "a feminist ethic of risk," in which "[a]ction begins in the face of overwhelming loss" and "[t]he fundamental risk . . . is the decision to care and to act although there are no guarantees of success" (67, 68). Needing to learn "how to live without guarantees, without safety" (298), Codi searches Hallie's letters and is struck by her sister's sense that she is "doing the only thing [she] can live with"; she is "not Saving Nicaragua," and even knowing that her side in the war may fail does not matter so much as the "daily work" that does some good (299). The same ethos underpins the Stitch and Bitch Club, Grace's older women who feel they have no other choice than to try to stop the mining company. When union-style demonstrations fail, they turn to their domestic skills, making peacock piñatas that draw attention to Grace's plight, even though they know that "a piñata" probably will not "stop a multinational corporation."[8]

Though at first self-defeated by her crippling sense of failure, Codi is compelled into action by threats to those she cares about—her students, her town, and her family. Before returning to Grace, she has taken after her father, dwelling on personal failures as a healer, just as Homer recalls his helplessness when Codi was pregnant, her resemblance to his wife (who died from complications of childbirth) paralyzing him with the sense of his family as "a web of women dead and alive, with himself at the center like a spider."[9] In contrast, Codi as a teacher is galvanized by her feelings, as pregnancy among her students, like the damage done to the local river, brings out her crusading zeal and gift for vivid explanation, traits she shares with Hallie. Hence, in the aftermath of the novel's crises, after Hallie has been killed and the mining company defeated, Codi, like many trauma survivors, finds that drawing upon what she has witnessed and learned in order to educate others gives her a sense of hope and purpose, a "survivor mission" (Herman 207–11). When she describes her goals for her students—that they will develop "a cultural memory" and "be custodians of the earth" (332)—it is clear that she becomes able to survive her sister's death by fusing her own mission with Hallie's. She thus feels that Hallie lives through her: "Everything we'd been I was now" (328).

Like many survivor discourses, *Animal Dreams* ends with a sense of affirmation, emphasizing resolution, continuity, new life, and the next generation. Especially resembling *The Color Purple* with its controversial "happy ending," Kingsolver's novels have been criticized for their optimism, perceived by some readers as an evasion of difficult issues (see Comer, Ryan). However, such a charge seems to overlook that the small battles for Grace and for Codi's soul are won in the context of a greater war in which thousands of civilians were killed, and Codi's efforts make no discernible difference. Moreover, the violence against Hallie is not forgotten in the novel's conclusion, since Codi is able to speak about what was done to her sister only a few chapters from the end.[10] But *Animal Dreams* does conclude with Codi's growth and recommitment to life, literally embodied in her pregnancy. Why this emphasis on hope? One reason offered by Kingsolver's writings is that the turn toward hope is true to life, as she shows based on her close involvement with a failed mining strike and her personal experiences of violence and loss.[11] Audre Lorde speaks for Kingsolver and many others when she asserts that hope and meaningful action are necessities for survival, just as "[d]espair and isolation are [the] greatest internal enemies" (126; cf. 80). Though a natural defense and a mode of healing, commitment to social action also constitutes, for survivors, a compelling ethical choice. Hence, along with others who have felt the impact of violence or who write about effects of trauma, Kingsolver moves from describing individual recovery to setting forth responsibilities of citizens and communities. If what occurs in Grace is "such an American story" and Codi is a "good citizen" of a numbed, disengaged nation (240, 149), then *Animal Dreams* prescribes what American citizens need—commitment to individual and collective remembrance, to acts of memory that are inseparable from risk, mourning, and social involvement.

Notes

Many thanks to my colleague Daryl Palmer, a generous reader whose suggestions promote not only revision but new understanding. I also wish to thank Laura Cameron for invaluable research assistance.

1. Herman, 242–43. For other studies that examine parallels between individuals and communities or societies affected by psychological trauma, see Erikson, deVries, and Bloom.

2. Herman, 242–47. Among numerous texts dealing with the recovered memory debate, see Armstrong's spirited contribution, Haaken, and two recent collections of scholarly viewpoints, that of Williams and Banyard, and Appelbaum et al.

3. See also DeMeester's analysis of *Mrs. Dalloway* for a provocative and cogent argument presenting connections between modern literature and psychological trauma.

4. Herman 185. For examples of how such activities bring back Codi's repressed memories, see passages depicting All Souls' Day (159–60, 164–65, 342) and her discovery of her father's photographs showing that she and Hallie had the pale eyes of infants descended from the Gracelas (284), knowledge that reconstructs her family tree.

5. In "From Victim to Survivor," Warner and Feltey illuminate the process of identity reconstruction for trauma survivors; Kingsolver similarly writes of the need to move from "casualty to survivor" in "Stone Soup" 139. See Bruner, "The 'Remembered' Self" (53), for the idea that self is "perpetually rewritten." Cf. Bruner's "The Narrative Construction" and also Freedman and Combs (34–35).

6. For deVries's comments on symbolic places, see p. 410. Along with discussing potentially positive effects of culture for traumatized individuals and groups, deVries also offers equally significant ideas about the growth of "negative social forms" (such as gangs) among the traumatized when traditional culture is weak (407–8).

7. For a description of the "Survivor Tree" as a symbol and a site of informal rituals, see Daugherty (510–11). It is significant that Codi cannot find the specific semilla besada that she remembers, which for her symbolizes Hallie; instead she sees that "[e]very tree in the orchard looked blessed" (324), suggesting that she needs to relinquish her tendency to set Hallie apart and thus devalue herself and others.

8. *Animal Dreams* 266. Grace's older women show the union's influence in their clothes (a steelworkers T-shirt), meetings, and strategies for opposing the mining company (see 175, 179). As Kingsolver notes, *Animal Dreams* in many ways draws upon *Holding the Line,* her nonfiction account of women's roles in the 1983 Arizona mining strike. See Kingsolver's 1996 introduction to *Holding the Line* (xiv); also see Swartz (74–75).

9. *Animal Dreams* 98. For a discussion of the "wounded healer" that sheds light on Codi's and Homer's struggles, see Palgi and Dorban, who analyze the vulnerability of doctors, stemming from the necessity of facing inevitable failures to heal.

10. *Animal Dreams* 316–17. At the opposite pole from critics of Kingsolver's optimism, one survivor of child abuse rejected *Animal Dreams* because of the violence it depicts, leading Kingsolver to explain her criteria for "commit[ing] an act of violence in the written word"; see "Careful" (255), an essay that speaks to many people's concerns about evaluating representations of violence in culture.

11. For the "lesson [of] hope" Kingsolver derived from observing women in the mining strike, see *Holding the Line* (xxiii). The first and last essays of *High Tide in Tucson,* providing a conceptual frame for that collection, present hope as a basic impulse of survival; the essays reflect Kingsolver's scientific training as well as her experience of violent assault and miscarriage. Also see her comments on writing as a rape survivor (Perry 163).

Sheryl Stevenson

"Hemmed In": Place, Disability, and Maternity in *Animal Dreams* and *The Poisonwood Bible*

Breyan Strickler

I t is hard to ignore the plight of Adah Price, Barbara Kingsolver's disabled protagonist in *The Poisonwood Bible,* who embraces her disability as normal and uses the biases of our culture to subvert that culture's obsession with purity and wholeness. Indeed, given Adah's spirit of subversion, she might serve as the poster child for disability studies as she reimagines the context of her disability, as critics such as Sheryl Stevenson, Steven Fox, Jenny Bangsund, and Feroza Jussawalla have demonstrated. However, disability comes in a number of guises in Kingsolver's work—physical as well as mental—and occurs in a number of rhetorical patterns. For example, Codi Noline's identity in *Animal Dreams* centers squarely around the traumas of the death of her mother and a possible infanticide, resulting in a mental disability akin to post-traumatic stress disorder. In *Animal Dreams,* the rhetoric constructing disability plays on our culture's assumptions about pregnancy and birth as monstrous, even obscene, prefiguring similar rhetorical patterns of Adah in *The Poisonwood Bible,* published just a year later. In Adah's case, however, the rhetorical transformation moves from loss toward a rhetoric of maternity figured as disability (rather than away from it, as we see in Codi's case), suggesting that Adah's character stagnates rather than develops. Yet, given the plethora of birth images in the latter half of *The Poisonwood Bible,* Adah's character does grow, finding freedom in the same kind of monstrous rhetoric and maternal trauma from which Codi strives to separate herself. In fact, Codi too ultimately comes to terms with her own identity only by embracing this monstrous rhetoric of maternal trauma.

ADAH

In Book 1: Genesis, Adah Price wryly regales us with the story of her disability and her identity, describing the "fetal mishap" that occurred between her twin sister, Leah, and herself in the womb: "we were inside the womb together dum-de-dum when Leah suddenly turned and declared, Adah you are just too slow. I am taking all the nourishment here and going on ahead. She grew strong as I grew weak. (Yes! Jesus loves me!) And so it came to pass, in the Eden of our mother's womb, I was cannibalized by my sister" (34). Her "condition," as Adah calls it, refers to "the cessation of motion" in half her body, but doctors assured her "exhausted" mother that she "might possibly someday learn to read" (34). This in itself indicates our culture's tendency toward a slippery slope based on the seen: the physically retarded must also be mentally retarded. However, Adah is a "gifted" child and describes herself as "hemmed-in" by her body's disability (56). Adah uses her culture's attitude toward disability to help her build a clearly defined identity: she retreats into the "many advantages" of silence, because "[w]hen you do not speak, other people presume you to be deaf or feeble-minded and promptly make a show of their own limitations" (34).

Adah's position makes her acutely aware of another medical fallacy: the infallibility of physicians. Adah rejects the physicians' pronouncements of mental incapacity while "claim[ing]" her physical difference, an idea set out by disability studies theorist Rosemarie Garland Thomson (23). In the African village of Kilanga, Adah discovers that a disabled body does not connote imperfection. For disability studies theorists—and for Adah—the disabled body must be liberated from the confinements of the medical field and the quest for a cure, thus allowing the "disabled" a social identity that exists and is empowered in a number of areas. What path, then, would liberation take? Steven Fox suggests that "Adah's dysfunctions are completely socially marked. When she redefines herself as unique and worthy, the stigma of her disability vanish[es]" (412). Yet this is not the case. Even though Adah finds a happy ending in Atlanta as a physician, its foundation rests on her being cured. Thus, she remains subject to the medicalization of her body.

Upon her return to the United States as an adult, Adah learns that her limp is mental—she is not necessarily physically disabled. Yet the doctors' declaration of her disabled identity at birth has "hemmed" her in as much as any physical disability. She voices the lament of many disabled when "cure" is thrust upon them: "I was unprepared to accept that my whole sense of

Adah was founded on a misunderstanding between my body and my brain" (439). Having lived only in the domain of medicine, "cured" patients lose the only identity they have known.

This depiction reflects Foucault's place of "confinement"—in fact, Adah describes her experience even outdoors back in America as a "peculiar confinement"—something the field of disability studies also addresses (Kingsolver, *Poisonwood Bible* 411). For Foucault, "confinement" referred to the exercise of power to label a group as abnormal. In *Madness and Civilization,* Foucault describes the confinement of the insane in the Hopital General in Paris as a measure used not for the safety of its patients but rather to mark the patients as deviant, both morally and economically. The abnormal could not function in the rest of society, particularly in terms of economic productivity, and were thus marked and controlled through the gaze—by literally being observed—and deemed rehabilitated if they could reverse their lack of economic success—their lack of normalcy—and become economically productive members of society. Foucault charts similar patterns of confinement in his treatises on the rise of the clinic and hospital, where illness and disability are marked as the inability to participate in an economically productive capacity in society. Disability studies seeks to complicate the confinement of a medicalized understanding of disability with a social and political model of disability. Rather than simply defining disability as a "lack"—"a lack of normalcy," the product of which is not useful to society but a waste of a good body—this sociopolitical view defines "disability" as a way of interpreting human differences. In other words, this critical perspective considers "disability" as a process of thinking about bodies and minds rather than as something that is wrong with bodies or minds.

While on the surface Adah seems cured—both physically and mentally—and seems to embrace her disability, the rhetoric framing her identity actually vacillates between different kinds of disability over the course of the novel: initially, she negotiates a rhetoric of "lack" and absence; during her time in the African village of Kilanga, Adah's rhetoric of disability is empowering and "balanced," as the villagers see disability as a normal state of affairs; and finally, upon her return to the United States, the American Adah, liberated from her physical disability, shifts to another kind of disability rhetoric—that of the female, monstrous, pregnant body—that works metaphorically as she labors to give birth to a complex new identity that takes into account her new place in America, her career as a physician, and her life as a physically "perfect" woman.

In fact, this last rhetorical pattern is remarkably similar to that of Codi Noline, the protagonist of another Kingsolver novel called *Animal Dreams*. As a pregnant teenager, Codi deprived herself and her fetus of food, resulting in the premature stillbirth of her daughter and years of psychological struggle that is only healed when Codi embraces her past and accepts the imperfect, mentally disabled, hybridized history of her life. Healing occurs for both women when they free themselves from the confines of medical discourse through a process of deconstruction akin to rebirth, and monstrous in its own way. The language of birth merges with the language of the monstrous in both characters, resulting not in a more clearly defined sense of identity but in more clearly seen possibilities for growth and change.

THE THREE PHASES OF ADAH

On the surface, place and context offer Adah two distinct identities. As a young girl in America, Adah relies on the assumption that she will go unnoticed because disabilities are ignored or unseen. Thus Adah's perception of herself is phrased in negatives: Adah "unpasses her judgments [on Kilanga]; I am the one who does not speak" (32); "I do not walk fast or well" (33); "Leah and Adah began our life as images mirror perfect. . . . But I am lame gallimaufry and she remains perfect" (34); she retreats into silence and "keep[s] [her] thoughts to [her]self" (34); she reverses words and whole sentences into palindromes; she "sets [her]self apart" (35). However, when the missionary family arrives in the Congolese village of Kilanga, Adah meets other physically imperfect people who nevertheless are valued as contributing and important members of their society. For the first time, Adah is welcomed as an asset to a culture. "Here," Adah observes, "bodily damage is more or less considered to be a by-product of living, not a disgrace. In the way of the body and other people's judgment I enjoy a benign approval in Kilanga that I have never, ever known in Bethlehem, Georgia" (72). However, she does not enjoy access to power in Africa. This marks the first transition in the rhetorical construction of Adah's identities. Adah recognizes that identity in America is governed by pathology, or more precisely, the absence of pathology. Yet in Kilanga, pathology is not privileged; rather, pathology is but one component of a complex identity that has little bearing on one's social worth.

For Adah, then, place sets the stage for very different constructions of identity. In America, Adah's identity is constructed around a rhetoric of

Breyan Strickler

lack that breeds other dichotomies: if Adah accepts a cure, she can become a productive member of society; if she rejects a cure, she will remain a burden to society. This juxtaposition mirrors other juxtapositions, particularly in terms of place. When Adah recognizes the power of place in determining her worth—when she enjoys that approval in the African village of Kilanga that she did not enjoy in the city of Bethlehem, Georgia, in America—Adah also introduces a juxtaposition of America and Africa—of city and jungle village. In America, the city, with its well-defined system of classification, categorizes Adah immediately, failing to recognize her potential outside the confinement of her illness. In Kilanga, however, Adah's identity is not so easily pegged, and she exercises a freedom she does not have in America.

This dichotomy is obvious, as is Kingsolver's critique of this either/or fallacy, particularly when Adah is read in contrast to her sister, Rachel. Rachel longs for the comforts of a city (and spends most of the book re-creating a city life in the jungle). In Rachel's first chapter, she complains that "already I was heavy-hearted in my soul for the flush commodes and machine washed clothes and other simple things in life I have took for granite" (23). Given Rachel's ignorance and the tongue-in-cheek dialogue errors Kingsolver ascribes to Rachel, it would seem Kingsolver derides all things Western and commodified. Freedom, it would seem, is found in a rejection of the kinds of attitudes Rachel exhibits.

This is reinforced by Kingsolver's depictions of place in the novel. Like Adah's character, place is perceived in terms of medical discourse and pathology, divorced from a more natural identity where pathology is an integral part of creation. Instead, the American city is depicted as a truly alien landscape, one of "neutral-smelling air," disorienting in its conflagration of "color and orchestrated metal movement" (411), and resembling a crime scene, where the human is cast as a perpetrator who "slink[s] back" to the scene and is "presumed insane" (407). Relationships, too, are governed by the discourse of pathology: neighbors diagnose your cultural standing, and you "took [that] diagnosis well," without question (496). Unlike the Congolese jungle and the village of Kilanga, where her sense of self found "power in the balance," where "we are our injuries, as much as we are our successes," the American city preserves unnatural dichotomies such as a distinction between urban and natural that carried over into ideas about identity (496). For Adah, there is no power to be had in American cities unless she defines—and limits—herself according to her pathologies.

"Hemmed In"

The lack of dependence on dichotomies in the Congolese jungle encourages Adah to recognize that one's sense of self must be fluid in order to live with the world around it:

> [M]untu does not mean exactly the same as person, though, because it describes a living person, a dead one, or someone not yet born. *Muntu* persists through all those conditions unchanged. The Bantu speak of 'self' as a vision residing inside, peering out through the eyeholes of the body, waiting for whatever happens next . . . *muntu* itself cannot die. . . . In that other, long-ago place, America, I was a failed combination of too-weak body and overstrong will. But in Congo I am those things perfectly united: *Adah*. (343)

The concept of a lack of integration between—or lack of a willingness to integrate—the powers of the natural world with the powers of the human world seems illogical to the Congolese, and an act of destruction rather than creation. Indeed, this way of knowing destroys human relationships, and Anatole, Leah's African husband and Adah's brother-in-law, cannot grasp the point of such a discourse.

Leah tries to explain how American cities are organized, and why they must be separated from the natural world to maintain their structure. She cries out in some exasperation that "[i]t's not like here. Everything's farther apart. People live in big towns and cities. . . ." Anatole responds using the logic and rhetoric of integration, saying, "If everyone lived in a city they could never grow enough food." Leah counters:

> Oh, they do that out in the country. In big, big fields. The farmers grow it, then they put it on big trucks and take it all to the city, where people buy it from the store." The store isn't "a bit like the market. It's a great big house kind of thing, with bright lights and all these shelves inside. It's open every day, and just one person sells all the different things.
>
> Anatole: "One farmer has so many things?"
>
> Leah: "A storekeeper buys it from the farmers, and sells it to the city people."
>
> Anatole: "And so you don't even know whose fields this food came from? That sounds terrible. It could be poisoned! . . ."

Leah: "In Congo, it seems the land owns the people."
Anatole: "You must find the Congo a very uncooperative
place." (283–84)

Kingsolver, however, complicates the dichotomy between America and
Africa, jungle and city, that we have seen so far by having Adah find a kind
of refuge in the American city. She becomes a success, gaining acceptance
into medical school and a powerful, lucrative career. There she meets "an
upstart neurologist" who suggests that the physical disability that has been
the basis of so much of her self-definition might be a "great lifelong false-
hood." She explains that "[i]n his opinion, an injury to the brain occurring
as early as mine should have no lasting effects on physical mobility . . . my
dragging right side is merely holding on to a habit it learned in infancy. . . .
I scoffed at him, of course. I was unprepared to accept that my whole sense
of *Adah* was founded on a misunderstanding between my body and my
brain" (439). Although possibly free from disability, Adah wonders "[w]ill I
lose myself entirely if I lose my limp" (441). She is "losing [her] slant" (439)
and must undertake the labor of reconfiguring her sense of self (441). The
new, successful identity is an American identity—one that shuns visible disability and promotes monetary success and dedication to logic, all of which
describe American attitudes toward medicine.

Even though Adah is a product of both her American and Congo experiences, when she centers her identity solely around finding a cure, we see
that the ambivalence of Africa loses its power over her, and she finds refuge
only in the American city, where disease and madness are looked upon with
distaste and she is actively encouraged to make medical discourse the center
of her life. The American city becomes the place of "the good Dr. Price, seeing straight. Conceding to be in [her] right mind" (493), signaling Adah's
transition into a third rhetorical pattern. Caught in the trap of an either/
or fallacy, Adah's "right mind" still leaves her with an absence to grapple
with—the rejection of the power she felt in Kilanga where her body was easily accepted.

From a Western perspective, it would seem that Adah has found power
in America. Adah is cured, and she has a successful career within the medical field. Furthermore, the same character who praised the "balance" of
Kilanga now praises her urban environment, which we have been taught to
see as part of a dichotomy that results in confinement. For the first time in
this very long novel, a character, Anatole, acknowledges the natural in the

midst of the city: the "pigeons roosting in the eaves of the Atlanta's Public Library" (441). The irony of this passage is underscored by Anatole's acute perception of realities in the United States. These pigeons become food for the "bums who inhabit the street corners of Atlanta"—a group whose plight is largely ignored by the city's other inhabitants but who have a certain kind of freedom that Anatole and Adah both appreciate (441). This somewhat grisly image also indicates a shift in Adah's rhetoric, a shift that allows for a more complex understanding of the city and pathology as well as her sense of self.

Up until this image, Adah's identity has oscillated between confinement and liberation: in both worlds she is empowered in some aspects but at the same time forced to repress significant elements of her identity. Continuing to defy rigid definition—and indeed cannibalizing parts of her Kilanga identity in her new life in America—Adah's rhetoric in the last third of the novel becomes that of the maternal and monstrous body as she undergoes a third self-metamorphosis, and in this way Kingsolver complicates not only her well-known environmental views but also Adah's character. In the same chapter—the chapter that begins "I am losing my slant"—Adah undertakes her rebirth in America (439). Through a series of procedures to trick the mind into learning how to walk, Adah becomes a "grown-up baby" (439). In fact, she makes a point of clarifying that she was not "learning it all over again but for the first time, apparently, since Mother claims I did none of these things as a baby" (440). Adah's work in the neonatal wards mirrors her own newly emerging life and the doubts that go with it. Using monstrous rhetoric, Adah ponders the lives of "three tiny creatures whose lungs struggled like the flat, useless wings of butterflies prematurely emerged," and considers whether or not these "damaged children" might not be better off laid to rest at "the base of [their] own pine tree" (442–43).

The following chapters show a new rhetoric that subverts the dichotomies typically used to describe both place and identity in America. Adah's last chapter at first suggests that her new life is lived at the expense of her old one: "Along with my split-body drag I lost my ability to read in the old way. . . . the mirror image poems erase themselves half-formed in my mind" (492). And Adah misses that old body, assuming that because "there is no good name for my gift, . . . it died without a proper ceremony" (493). This is not entirely true, however. Adah is intensely aware of all her abilities, as her language indicates. The disabled and monstrous body allows for a fluid perception of identity that helps Adah merge with Ada of the palindromes—the

Breyan Strickler

identities of America and Congo. Instead of being threatened by hybridiza-tion, Adah is "abled" by the very nature of her "disability." Indeed, Adah's medicalized identity is a paradox—her limp is all in her mind. Thus Adah constantly evades definition and epitomizes the "specter of the hybrid, and the notion of difference as not outside power, but pressuring along its bor-ders, from within" (Morris 85; Lai 16). In other words, there is no identifi-able place of difference; it is already within the body. Adah accomplishes the re-creation of herself using a combination of rhetorics: not surprisingly, that includes a vision of birth that is traumatic and monstrous, as well as cannibalistic, but nevertheless productive and liberatory.

Unexpectedly, Kingsolver gives the power of reimagining the city—typ-ically understood in environmental circles to be a place of confinement that valorizes the normal—to the character who has the least amount of power in that culture: the disabled, pathologized, female. In effect, disability wedges open cracks in the city's facade through which nature is reincorporated into a definition of the city. Adah's "disjunct[ion]" between health and dis-ease opens up opportunities for balance that are invisible to more "perfect" people, but she accomplishes this only through the use of some grotesque, monstrous—even cannibalistic—birth images.

THE MONSTROUS PREGNANT BODY AND THE CANNIBAL

Linking the monstrous with the feminine is not new. Feminist philosopher Rosemary Betterton relies on Rosi Braidotti's understanding of the pregnant body as a paradox or site of contestation, suggesting that "the monstrous helps organize structures of difference" (Betterton 82). Braidotti explains that images of pregnancy are often linked to an "unstable, potentially sick subject, vulnerable to uncontrollable emotions" that must be confined (Betterton 83; Braidotti 149). The connections between Foucault's ideas about confinement and labor and the rhetoric of pregnancy are obvious: pregnancy is patholo-gized and confined by medical discourse. Indeed, women enter into "their confinement" in the latter months of pregnancy. Women are deemed overly emotional and unstable—abnormal and, therefore, monstrous—during pregnancy. And women are "delivered" of their babies and their instability through "labor"—they are rehabilitated by virtue of work.

However, for Braidotti the threat of pregnancy—its monstrosity—is also its "promise" (Braidotti 150). The "monster is a process without a stable

object" (Betterton 83; Braidotti 150). Betterton's study of artistic representations of the pregnant body shows us that the "embodied pregnant woman,
like the monster, . . . destabilizes the concept of the singular self, threatening to spill over the boundaries of the unified subject," creating the
opportunities for new growth that we see in the development of Adah's
character (85).

In American culture, the monstrous is located on the outside, strengthening the boundaries of an identity because of its threat. Thus the idea of the
normal is reinforced by defining the deviations from normal very clearly.
The Adah of the first part of the novel—the antithesis of her whole and pure
twin—will remain on the outside in American culture, functioning to reinforce norms. Drawing on Claude Levi-Strauss and Eric Cheyfitz, sociologist
Zygmunt Bauman argues that the ways in which this Other is disposed of
fall into two broad categories. The first reflects an anthropoemic society that
"vomits" or expels the enemy, promoting societal rifts that establish "absolute and irrevocable" boundaries between Self and Other (Bauman132). This
type of social organization is prevalent in the modern age and is the compulsion behind Adah's agreement to finding a cure.

Yet, as we see in Adah's case, another system of organization exists: an
"anthropophagic" (meaning cannibalistic) relationship with the Other in
which they "eat their enemies" (Bauman 131). Indeed, Adah intimately connects the idea of cannibalization to her identity, describing her hemiplegia
as a result of her being "cannibalized by my sister" (34). Although this seems
to be a negative at first, over the course of the novel we see that this cannibalistic relationship between Self and Other reflects a continuous dialectic
between "unity and difference, separation and reunion" that deconstructs
the "anthropoemic way of constituting the Other and coping"—of metaphorically 'vomiting' those we define as others into specified places such
as asylums—with the rigid boundaries that this form of social functioning
mandates (132).

The cannibalism of the anthropophagic society can, then, be "more pro-
ductively read as a symbol of the permeability, or instability, of such boundaries" (Guest 2). In *Cannibalism and the Boundaries of Cultural Identity*,
Kristen Guest suggests that "the discourse of cannibalism persistently gives
voices to the diverse marginal groups it is supposed to silence and questions
dominant ideologies it is evoked to support" (3). Using Maggie Kilgour's
seminal study as the focal point for her work, Guest points out that canni-

balism "depends upon and enforces an absolute division between inside and outside," yet at the same time, the act "dissolve[es] the structure it appears to produce" (Kilgour 4).

This theory is particularly relevant to Adah's development because cannibalism is linked to female power (Goldman 168). However, men often fear the "inarticulate powers vested in those who are a source of disorder" (Douglas 100). Thus powerful women are labeled as monstrous. The link between the monstrous or the deformed and the cannibal in an anthropophagic society is crucial in reevaluating the power the monster holds. Men fear being colonized or eaten up by this portion of society, and so they repress them by confining their social identities within the realms of medicine, where they can be institutionalized or rehabilitated, thus removing them from their access to power. Difference becomes part of an insidious process of erasure, often in the guise of treatment (J. Epstein 104). Consequently, the disabled female character might display a reinhabitory effort that reinvokes the power consolidated in the marginalized voices of entities that transgress the absolute boundaries of patriarchal control (Buell, *Writing for an Endangered World* 108). The power of women such as Adah comes from their awareness of the utility of permeable barriers. The transmission of their knowledge, then, gives voice to other ways of knowing and experiencing the world that have hitherto been suppressed.

The invocation of this, however, is not always a pretty sight. In *The Poisonwood Bible*, Adah struggles with the source of her Congolese power and its linkages to dirt. Her mother's grief at the death of her youngest daughter sends her, literally, back to the earth. And Adah resents this new discourse of power that so contradicts the Western understanding of disability. Somewhat horrified, she watches the mothers—her mother included—grieve for their dead children as they "crawl forward on their hands and knees, trying to eat the dirt from their babies' fresh graves" (413). Bemoaning her fate as a woman who must find her power in grief, in dirt, and in disability, she asks "how could I, the village idiot, be ashamed of her? I somewhat enjoyed the company of her madness, and certainly I understood it. But Mother wanted to consume me like food" (409).

Kingsolver draws attention to the aspects of the individual that contemporary culture habitually isolates through the construction of social taboos—aspects such as body waste and disabilities that deviate from the norm. These are not something to be shunted off to one side, where they fester and grow in an atmosphere of darkness and fear; rather, these things should be reincorporated into our society, using them to feed other aspects of society. This is a complex vision of the maternal and disability—one that embraces hybridity and oscillates between confinement and liberation so as to create healing by deconstructing boundaries. Indeed, Kingsolver relies on disability and cannibalism rhetoric in the construction of many of her female protagonists, particularly Codi Noline in *Animal Dreams*.

CODI NOLINE

Dealing with a physical pregnancy, Codi's character allows us to see the rhetoric of the monstrous at work in a more literal way than Adah's character does. Like Adah, Codi's identity is founded on lack: her mother died after the birth of Codi's sister; her father, the physician of the small town of Grace, New Mexico, regiments his daughters' lives and seems emotionally absent, spending most of his time documenting pregnancies and births— in particular the odd genetic pattern of Grace's blue-eyed Hispanic babies; Codi becomes pregnant as a teenager and miscarries; Codi's sister, her only close connection, leaves her to work in Nicaragua; Codi's relationship with her boyfriend, Carlo, is based on the promise of no relationship—"No strings" (105); Codi describes herself early on as "emptied-out and singing with echoes, unrecognizable to myself" (9); "I don't look like who I am" (8); her life "had no mission beyond personal survival; it was nothing like Hallie's" (107). Throughout *Animal Dreams,* Codi wrestles with a mental disability largely brought on by a sense of abandonment (as a result of the death of her mother) and the trauma of her pregnancy and the stillbirth (or, some might argue, the infanticide) of her daughter: she abandons her career as a physician as a result of symptoms that would suggest post-traumatic stress disorder (PTSD), and thereafter avoids emotional contact and struggles with a crippled sense of her own worth. The disorder manifests itself with an obsession with appearing normal on the outside, to the point that the reader notices an obsession with her looks that seems at odds with her personality. Perhaps this obsession stems from the trauma of her pregnancy, which Codi hid even from her sister and father by refusing to eat and wearing baggier clothing. Even years after her miscarriage, Codi believes her "future was mapped in negatives" (149).

While Gill Rye's 2006 article on the body in childbirth does not address *Animal Dreams* specifically, Rye's arguments can easily be applied to Codi's character. Rye suggests that infanticide narratives are actually narratives that "critique family relations" and "literalize" the mother's "own abuse by [her own] unloving mother" (100). In Codi's case, we have an absent mother and a distant father, Doc Homer. Homer himself confesses to his lack of participation numerous times: he dreams that he rescued the girls from a flood early in the novel, but upon waking realizes that he has no memory of the event because "he wasn't able to go to them. There is no memory because he wasn't there" (20). Most shocking is chapter 10—a chapter of just two pages detailing Doc Homer's absence as both father and physician from Codi's pregnancy, despite the fact that he recognizes the signs of pregnancy in his daughter. The brevity of the passage mirrors his lack of "participation" that Codi notes just two chapters before (73). Doc Homer "has no idea what he can say. . . . He lies mute," and while we sympathize with his inability to find a way to deal with the event, we see this as abandonment bordering on abuse (98). In fact, like Adah Price, Doc Homer seems "hemmed in" by medical discourse—able to label but unable to act.

On top of this loss is the loss of Codi's child. As a result of the trauma of birth, Rye explains, the "protagonist's subjectivity has been fundamentally damaged. . . . In trauma discourse, trauma entails a loss of the self, but is at the same time an event that guarantees the subject—the trauma subject—as 'witness, testifier, survivor'" (Rye 101, 103). Thus, as Sheryl Stevenson suggests in her article "Trauma and Memory in *Animal Dreams*," Codi's narrative is broken up into first and third person accounts that witness the abuse (88–89). I quote Codi's early account of her miscarriage in full, as it demonstrates the rhetoric of lack associated with disability as well as the traumatic effects the event had on her identity:

> I was fifteen years old, two years younger than my own child would be now. I didn't think of it in those terms: losing a baby. At first it was nothing like a baby I held inside me, only a small impossible secret. Slowly it grew to a force as strong and untouchable as thunder. I would be loved absolutely. But even in the last months I never quite pictured the whole infant I might have someday held in my arms; that picture came later. The human fact of it was gone before I knew it. But evidently that word "lost" was somewhere in my mind because I've had thousands of dreams of losing—of literally misplacing—a baby. (51)

. . . He never knew what he'd spawned, much less when it died. . . . I couldn't help but think sometimes of escape: the thing inside me turning to blood of its own accord, its bones liquefying, leaking out. And then one evening my savage wish was granted. . . . I kept quiet, first to protect her [her sister Hallie] from the knowledge of terrible things, and later to protect myself from that rock-solid element she came to own. That moral advantage.

It *divided* me from the people I knew, then and later, but in broader human terms I don't pretend that it sets me apart in any great way. A miscarriage is a natural and common event. All told, probably more women have lost a child from this world than haven't. Most don't mention it, and they go on from day to day as if it hadn't happened, and so people imagine that a woman in this situation never really knew or loved what she had. (52–53; emphasis mine)

Codi's identity, like Adah's identity, is initially based on a dichotomy or division. And, as we see in the construction of Adah's identity, Codi also struggles with paradox. The "impossible secret" was not only the knowledge of the child, but also her role in the death of that child, and this is the seed of the trauma that results in PTSD-like symptoms that Codi struggles with throughout the rest of the novel (51–53).

The accounts of Codi's pregnancy and miscarriage—and hence her identity (as these events shape her)—are, like the accounts of Adah's identity, hemmed in by this idea of lack that is common in medical discourse. The rhetoric of the medical discourse in *Animal Dreams* depicts Codi's pregnancy as monstrous or unnatural, connecting it with rhetorical patterns typically seen in depictions of disability. Doc Homer offers us another account of Codi's miscarriage from the perspective of medical practitioner as well as parent, in which we see both the monstrous and the confined:

She's in the fifth or sixth month, from the look of her, although Codi was always too thin and now is dangerously thin, and so skillful at disguising it with her clothes he can only tell by other signs. The deepened pigmentation under her eyes and across the bridge of her nose, for one thing, is identical to the mask of preg-

> nancy Alice wore both times, first with Codi, then with Hallie. It
> stuns him. . . . He can't help feeling he has damaged them all, just
> by linking them together. His family is web of women dead and
> alive, with himself at the center like a spider, driven by different
> instincts. He lies mute, hearing only in the tactile way that a spi-
> der hears, touching the threads of the web with long extended
> fingertips and listening. Listening for trapped life. (98)

Note that the image of being trapped occurs again, just as Adah's rhetoric
in the first half of *The Poisonwood Bible* revolves around a sense of being
hemmed in or confined. This passage also draws attention to the monstrous
as Homer describes the "damage" he has done to the women in the family,
a family described using arachnoid language.

The rhetoric of maternity as a traumatic disability—something to be
confined and hidden—controls not only Codi but, clearly, Doc Homer, the
physician who presided at the birth of many of Grace's inhabitants. In fact,
it even impacts his hobbies. Doc Homer photographs things that appear to
be something they are not—"clouds that looked like animals, landscapes
that looked like clouds" (69-70), " a clump of five saguaro cacti" that resembles a hand (70), "men who look like stones" (72) . His penchant for visual
deception echoes the language of Codi's identity that is initialized as a series
of negatives—of how she should not be perceived. More startling, however,
is the perspective he has on one photo he was not happy with: "He sees now
that the problem isn't in the development; the initial conception was a mistake" (142). One wonders if this is how he feels about his daughter.

This sense of wrongness, so typical of the rhetoric of disability critiqued
by disability studies theorists, controls much of his discourse, including his
relationship with his daughter. Rather than showing concern in a typical
fatherly fashion, Doc Homer assumes the role of detached observer and cli-
nician, relying on the privilege of sight, as he watches Codi's ordeal:

> The house is dark. Her curtain of hair falls as she leans out, look
> ing down toward the kitchen. She comes out. The small bundle
> in her arms she carries in the curl of her upper body, her spine
> hunched like a dowager's, as if this black sweater weighed as much
> as herself. When he understands what she has, he puts his knuckle
> to his mouth to keep from making a sound. . . . She has reached

> the spot where the rock bank gives over to the gravel and silt
> of the river bed. . . . He sees how deeply it would hurt her if she
> understood what he knows: that his *observations* have stolen the
> secrets she chose not to tell. She is a child with the dignity of an
> old woman. . . . He can't know who she has buried down there,
> but he can mark the place for her. At least he can do that. To save
> it from the animals. (141–42; emphasis mine)

Despite the pain he feels for his daughter, Homer does not transgress the bounds of this discourse, continuing to describe pregnancy using the language of shame and secrecy, along with a bias toward sight and an abhorrence of illness or disfigurement.

One can see this prejudice at work in portrayals of Codi's body. Unlike Adah, Codi can hide her disability—her changing pregnant body—from her father and sister, remaining tall and slim by "passively refus[ing] food a thousand times" (153). Thus when Codi kills her fetus through starvation, we remain sympathetic to this protagonist: throughout the rest of the novel the "crime" is labeled a miscarriage, the fault lies with the father's abandonment of his daughter, and the reader eagerly follows the story of Codi's romance with Loyd. It is more difficult, however, to love Adah Price. Her disability marks her as an Other, and this is reflected in her personality.

Nevertheless, Codi is disabled in a way that Adah Price is not. Codi's narratives in *Animal Dreams* are birth stories—literally and metaphorically—stories that, as Tess Cosslett argues in *Women Writing Birth* (1994), "offer a sense of both individual and collective agency" (Rye 94). As a result of telling her birth story, we see Codi develop a strong sense of self that allows for the creation of healthy relationships, a sympathetic audience, and the establishment of a sense of place in the town of Grace, New Mexico. Indeed, as she heals herself, she heals the town. The theme of loss extends even to the construction of the town, as Codi explains to Loyd that we are "a nation of amnesiacs, proceeding as if there were no other day but today. Assuming the land could also forget what had been done to it" (240–41). Again, Codi dwells on our amnesia just a few chapters later, saying, "People can forget, and forget, and forget, but the land has a memory" (255). We forget because we cannot *see* the changes, and it takes a science experiment and a microscope to see absence: the missing biotic life of the river (109–10). Codi's birth stories make visible what we refuse to see, both in terms of her own identity and the health of the town. We see in Codi's stories the relationship between place and identity and how place can reclaim memory and create new perspectives on identity. Ultimately, Codi was deemed to be an asset to Grace: she tells Homer, "Did you know I'm a good science teacher? The kids and the teachers all voted. They say I'm spirited" (332). She has taught the people of Grace how to have "a cultural memory. . . . I want them to be custodians of the earth" (332), thus reclaiming memories that have been hidden or lost completely. I emphasize, though, that Codi's happy ending comes at the expense of a traumatic birth written in the language of the monstrous. Again, the cannibal is linked to female power and "gives voices to the diverse marginal groups it is supposed to silence and questions dominant ideologies it is evoked to support" (Guest 3).

Here we see most clearly Kingsolver's maternal rhetoric of the city—an oscillation between confinement and liberation where the child is "delivered" from the body as if the woman seeks to be free from the monstrosity—the unnaturalness—of maternity. Kingsolver's complex vision of the maternal body and the maternal space, one where the two themes—confinement and deliverance—work together rather than against each other, creates a new vision of the city, one both natural and unnatural. In this hybridity, we see the monstrous as a necessary component of healing. In the tradition of the anthropophagic society—the society of the cannibal—Codi is reincorporated into Grace and uses her experiences to feed other aspects of society. Codi, the former exile, finds the way to save the town from the poisons of the mining corporation. We see between Codi and the town the cannibalistic relationship between Self and Other that we saw in Adah's character: theirs is a continuous dialectic between "unity and difference, separation and reunion" that deconstructs the "anthropoemic way of constituting the Other and coping" with the rigid boundaries that this form of social functioning mandates (132; Cheyfitz).

DISABILITY AND THE CITY

Kingsolver's female heroes in these two novels are not the typical heroes one sees in contemporary American fiction, particularly fiction with an environmental theme. The primary characters of Thomas Pynchon, Cathy Acker, and Don DeLillo's novels, to name just a few contemporary American authors who address similar environmental themes, are usually male, relying on battle rhetoric as they wage a war against a bodiless corporate force in an urban and decaying jungle. Indeed, ecocritic Lawrence Buell has categorized these books as examples of "toxic fiction." Instead, Kingsolver portrays a reinhabitory effort at work in the depiction of contemporary urban environments. Australian critic Margaret Henderson observes that inner-city spaces are no longer solely the setting for novels about decay and waste or "personal growth and experimentation, or political awareness." Rather, these beautiful and natural city-spaces "are potentially emancipatory and feminine spaces" because they do not recognize the boundaries that separate nature from city, woman from man, abled from disabled (79). Henderson describes these novels, which usually have female, disabled protagonists, as grunge fiction.

Ultimately, these characters give birth to a discourse that embraces permeability and hybridity. Reading the urban through disability studies leads us to recognize the city not only as a place of violence, where people compete in the concrete jungle, but also as a feminine, healing, and domestic space that promotes permeable borders. In so doing, it invites a postcolonial reading that allows a "city" to be a "process" rather than a static space—a process for reimagining the nature/culture schism. In both *The Poisonwood Bible* and *Animal Dreams,* the city-space is reimagined as a *wild* space, to use Gary Snyder's term, embracing a variety of identities, and offering freedom and wildness—a different way of being "abled" and "healed"—to its inhabitants.

Breyan Strickler

Part 2
Social
Justice

"Give Me Your Hand": Accessibility, Commitment, and the Challenge of Cliché in Kingsolver's Poetry

Meagan Evans

Barbara Kingsolver is not known for her poetry. Her novels are popular and her essays frequently anthologized, but when her poetry is mentioned at all, which is not often, it is considered either a kind of index to her better-known work or a window opening onto a more intimate view of the personal life and political commitments of the author. Marie Jean DeMarr, in *Barbara Kingsolver: A Critical Companion*, explains that in *Another America/Otra América*, Kingsolver's single published collection of poetry, Kingsolver "speaks . . . often in her own voice, of many of the concerns which underlie her novels" (39). DeMarr further describes the poems in the collection:

> Politically, their stance is clearly on the side of the oppressed, or the "other" Americans who are treated cruelly by the U.S. government or the established power structure. . . . Kingsolver makes no apology for her leftist and feminist stances, but she has no need to do so, as the collection of poems cannot be mistaken for being anything but a very personal statement. (40)

Kingsolver herself, in an interview published in *Backtalk: Women Writers Speak Out*, calls the poems "personal" and "intimate" and says they are her "moments of truth" and that "the poems are little steam vents on the pressure cooker" (Perry 162). This pressure cooker, it seems, is the American political landscape, and Kingsolver's poems, with Spanish translations on facing pages, are meant to be accessible "little stories" that "describe personal and national violations and praise individual acts of heroism in the name of justice" (144). But there is more to these poems than "little stories." Kingsolver's personal, intimate, moments of truth are also complex negotiations of competing political and aesthetic commitments. A closer look at the supposedly transparent language of these poems, especially their double-edged use of the cliché, reveals useful strategies for maintaining the skepticism about the relationship between language and truth that is vital to effective social criticism without sacrificing the accessibility and openness that are so important to Kingsolver's project.

As explicitly political poems intended to be accessible to a wide audience, these poems claim a rare place in American poetry, and reactions to the political aims of *Another America/Otra América* have been mixed. As Kingsolver notes in a 1993 interview with "Poets and Writers," "Since the 1950s McCarthy era, we've been told that art and politics should live in different houses, and we've accepted that verdict on the whole. Artists are supposed to roll over and play dead; we're not supposed to be social critics" (Pence 18). But Kingsolver's collection of poems, like her novels, refuses to roll over; the poems are critical of American foreign and domestic policy, gender politics, education, racism, and xenophobia. Though many of Kingsolver's interviewers and reviewers praise her political stance in *Another America/Otra América,* reviewer Lorraine Elena Roses asks, "Can lyrical poetry bear the weight of politics?" (19).

Roses praises the collection's efforts to bridge the "North-South gap—political, economic, and cultural..." (19). These poems often blur the lines of division and reach across them: in "Justicia" Kingsolver compares housewives in McAllen, Texas, to the "Bolsheviks" of Managua (17), and in "In Exile," which is presumably dedicated to translator Rebeca Cartes, Kingsolver acknowledges "[t]hese mountains I love / are knuckles / of a fist / that holds your dreams to the ground" (29). But Roses does not seem to believe that this poetic solidarity can work. She calls the poems a "sanctuaried space" and implies that their vision is narrow. She dismisses them as poems that "will appeal primarily to those who seek to commemorate and mark political occasions" (19). It seems likely that Roses is not alone in her estimation of Kingsolver's poems as naive in their claims to accessibility and political vitality. Indeed, despite the popularity of her novels and essays, the poems have been largely ignored.

But the battle over American poetry (if we can be allowed such dramatic phrasing) is being fought out at just the crossroads of politics and poetry at which Kingsolver and others situate her work. There are many who

Meagan Evans

wonder, along with Roses, if lyric poetry can bear the weight of politics. If the lyric creates a sense of isolation and timelessness, if it is the form of self-knowledge and quiet epiphany, how can its individualized voice be at the service of the polis? How can utterances that are supposed to transcend time and circumstance be used for protest or material betterment? Poets have lived uneasily in the Republic, at least since Plato, and many writers are uncomfortable with poetry that has an agenda or is committed to a particular political cause, either because poetry is unequal to the cause or because the cause is unequal to the demands of art. For others, such reservations about politics in poetry are the result of a "McCarthyite chill," an overly academic attitude toward poetry, or an apolitical postmodern stylizing that has bankrupted poetry's cultural cache (Randall xi). Margaret Randall, in her foreword to *Another America/Otra América*, cites Kingsolver as the "keeper of the faith" of an almost extinct American poetry, passed down from Adrienne Rich and Alice Walker, that claims the power of political relevance and still believes that poetry can change the world. Many readers and writers of poetry believe that poetry can only be revitalized in America if it speaks directly to and about the personal and political lives of its readers, and they laud poetry like Kingsolver's or the work of *Poets Against the War* that is directly, unflinchingly, literally political.[1]

But, even amongst those who share the feeling that art can and should be political, there are deep divisions about *how* art can best do so. For some, Kingsolver's plain-spoken, personal style cannot possibly be on "the side of the oppressed." In fact, for many, accessible "little stories" cannot be called poetry at all. For poet-critics from Edgar Allen Poe to Ron Silliman, poetry is marked by, even defined by, its distance from plain-spokenness.

The case for poetry as an art that necessarily foregrounds the opacity and slipperiness of language (rather than using it as a transparent and accessible vehicle for meaning) is made most profoundly by theorists like Roman Jakobson. Basing his understanding of the workings of literary language on the discoveries of structuralist linguistics, Jakobson claims that the function of poetic language is to prevent the ossification of language into unquestionable and ostensibly natural forms.[2] It does this by radically reordering the forms of language. Jakobson explains in "Linguistics and Poetics" that "poeticalness is not a supplementation of discourse with rhetorical adornment, but a total reevaluation of the discourse and of all its components whatsoever" (93). Without this poeticity, which "makes the word felt as word," Jakobson claims that "the sign becomes automatized. Activity comes to a halt, and the awareness of reality dies out" ("What Is Poetry?" 378). Thus, when Kingsolver claims to be making political realities accessible to her readers by speaking plainly in her poems and telling them personal stories of rage and disenfranchisement, the supposed transparency of her language only makes possible what Jakobson would call a fetishization of the word, a fetishization that makes language a tool of oppression, no matter what it is used to say.

Supporters of politically committed poetry have rejected the claims of theorists like Jakobson as overly formalistic and politically detached. Yet, Theodor Adorno, whom one could hardly call apolitical, seems to have had Jakobson's worries about the "fetishization of the word" in mind when he wrote his influential critique of the politically committed work of art in "Commitment." Adorno does not claim that art should avoid the difficult intersection of politics and poetry. He agrees that art should be political. But he denies in the strongest of terms that art should do so by making a direct political statement. In response to those who, like Brecht and Sartre, would make the forms of art into a mouthpiece for political or philosophical programs, Adorno claims, "It is not the office of art to spotlight alternatives, but to resist *by its form alone* the course of the world, which permanently puts a pistol to men's heads" (180; emphasis mine). Adorno's case for autonomous art as more truly and usefully political than committed art refers specifically to the modernist moment, but his arguments are influential in establishing for subsequent writers that nonreferential writing is, "by its form alone," a more meaningful resistance to the systems of power than Kingsolver's direct confrontation of racism, sexism, and imperialism in *Another America/ Otra América.* Though Kingsolver's poems claim to unite the alienated and dissolve the border between official America and its Others, their realistic, narrative style could be said to, ultimately, allow the kind of thinking that reifies and naturalizes the differences that separate America from Otra (Other) America. As Adorno puts it, " . . . hostility to anything alien or alienating can accommodate itself much more easily to literary realism of any provenance, even if it proclaims itself critical or socialist, than to works which swear allegiance to no political slogans . . ." (179).

Thus, though Kingsolver speaks out directly against hostility to the alien and unfamiliar, her realistic style can be said to accommodate the very hostility she wishes to undermine. In "Waiting for the Invasion," for instance, the speaker derides those in her childhood hometown who believed that the Russians might come and blow up their water towers: "someone, believe this, painted the towers black / hoping to save us" (15). This belief is an emblem for the larger beliefs in a dangerous enemy outside the borders, the narrative that is used as a justification for fearfulness and violence. But the poem calls this a false narrative: "No one slipped through a lake of night sky / in search of our secret towers. / No one. I know this now, but some believed / and believing still, prepare the massacre" (15). The poem is invested in questioning the fear of the alien, invading Other and in revealing the violent uses to which that fear is put. It links belief in narratives of otherness to violence and fear, and it challenges its readers to be unbelievers. And yet, formally, it requires them to *be* believers. "Someone, *believe this,* painted the towers black . . ." (15; emphasis mine). The reader is not, ultimately, asked to question the *processes* of narrative that can make children live in fear of Russian planes that never come, but only asked to question one certain narrative and believe another. The power of storytelling, the fetishization of the believable word, is left intact. For Adorno, and for many poets, critics, and readers who doubt the usefulness of overtly political art like Kingsolver's, "[t]he notion of a 'message' in art, even when politically radical, already contains an accommodation to the world: the stance of the lecturer conceals a clandestine entente with the listeners, who could only be rescued from deception by refusing it" (193). This accommodation is inherent, for Adorno, in art that relies on a "lying positivism of meaning" (191). Thus, poetry that seems to assume a transparency of language, a believable word, can only ratify ideology, even where it seeks to unmake it.

But if the "stance of the lecturer" is not available to the politically radical, what are the options for an artist like Kingsolver who wishes to claim a disruptive politics for poetry? The answer, for some, has been a dive into ambiguity, aleatory writing processes, formal experimentation, antisyntactic structures, and other techniques for estranging and defetishizing language. Poets connected to the L=A=N=G=U=A=G=E school, for example, have claimed that their antinarrative and antigrammatical poetics are inherently and democratically political.[3] In short, lines such as

> potato used well part well
> at often parting being no action
> but into gold shirks
> rosy good shook
> into tug water

what else but brief spout forth
each time I embellish degrees
one step of reading and another
text in patches cigarette. . . . (Hejinian pt. 8)

are forces of resistance because they make the word, in Jakobson's terms, radically "felt as word." But these poetic strategies are, in turn, accused of being elitist, escapist, and even fascist evasions of real political struggle.[4] Adorno, even as he outlines the failure of "committed" art, warns of literature that becomes too aesthetically autonomous, or work that is "merely itself, and no other thing." Thus, if poems set out to challenge the ideology out of which they are written there are two ways they can fail:

> The type of literature that, in accordance with the tenets
> of commitments but also with the demands of philistine moral-
> ism, exists for man, betrays him by traducing that which could
> help him, if only it did not strike a pose of helping him. But any
> literature which therefore concludes that it can be a law unto
> itself, and exist only for itself, degenerates into ideology no less.
> (Adorno 193)

For Adorno, then, political poetry should be *formally* political but assiduously avoid the solipsism that marks the purely formal work of art.

Kingsolver's poetry, in its reach for accessibility, has clear formal allegiances with the kind of poetry that, for Adorno and Jakobson, is unpoetic and politically ineffective in its claims to transparency and in its linguistic reinscription of the rule of law it claims to transgress. However, a closer look at the negotiations of familiarity and estrangement in Kingsolver's poetry will reveal that *Another America/Otra América* is not as easily situated on one side of the committed/autonomous divide.

On first reading, the poems in *Another America/Otra América* are direct and plain-spoken and have a clear "message." Their syntax is easily parsed. They are written almost entirely in complete sentences, using, for the most part, conventional imagery and unambiguous metaphor. They can be paraphrased and their meanings are accessible: rape is an invasion, American openness to immigrants is a lie used to exploit them, replacing the humanities with technology impoverishes our schools. Whether or not one believes the accessibility of these poems to be politically useful, it seems right that

Meagan Evans

Kingsolver calls them "little true stories about things that have happened to me, and people close to me, and things I have witnessed that have made me feel strongly" (Pence 18–19). Kingsolver is certainly invested in realism, but these poems are not as transparently accessible as they seem. Though they do not, on the sentence level, make the "word felt as word," they can still be said to avail themselves of a kind of Jakobsonian poeticity that makes it possible to read in Kingsolver a poetic ambiguity that belies her claims to accessibility and transparency. As Paul De Man explains in "Semiology and Rhetoric" and "Resistance to Theory," poeticity is not confined to the purely grammatical or semiotic level of the sign, but can also work its disruptive magic on the level of the figure. Ambiguous or paradoxical figures of speech, like the rhetorical question that is both question and answer, can reveal even more profoundly the disjunction between word and thing than a grammatical recognition of the arbitrary nature of the relationship between signifier and signified ("Semiology" 9–10). "Tropes, unlike grammar," says De Man, "pertain primordially to language" ("Resistance" 15). To focus exclusively on grammatical poeticity leaves much of what language does, its rhetorical and emotional figures, unread (13–16). But pulling back the lens from the "word as word" to figures of speech reveals a tropological disruptiveness in the poetic strategies of *Another America/Otra América*.

The dominant tropes that Kingsolver uses to attain poeticity, to foreground the workings of language, are set idiomatic expressions, or clichés. Ruth Amossy's work is especially useful for understanding the possible effects of cliché on readers of literature. In her article "The Cliché in the Reading Process," she explains that the cliché is "common property" that is felt as both "familiar" and, because of its appearance in a literary text, "radically foreign" (34–35). Amossy divides this familiarity and foreignness into two axes of effects that a cliché may produce; she identifies the functions of clichés that are "passively registered" and those that are "critically perceived." The functions of the passively registered cliché (or the set expression that is so familiar as to be invisible) create ease of emotional and rhetorical identification and the sense of transparency and solidarity; the critically perceived cliché (or the familiar expression that has been estranged by its literary context) can create complicity between the text and the reader by foregrounding group membership through a commonly held language and can expose the triteness of public opinion. As Amossy puts it, the passively registered cliché "as the bearer of a stereotyped meaning . . . presents a picture conforming to the reader's conception of what is real," and the critically perceivable cliché "convinces the reader of the gap between discourse and Truth and between discourse and the real" (36–38).

Let us consider a short lyric from *Another America/Otra América* that is representative of Kingsolver's use of the cliché.

REFUGE

For Juana, raped by immigration officers
and deported
Give me your hand,
he will tell you. *Reach*
across seasons of barbed wire
and desert. Use the last
of your hunger
to reach me. I will
take your hand.
Take it.

First
he will spread it
fingers from palm,
to look inside,
see it offers nothing.

Then
with a sharp blade
sever it.

The rest he throws back
to the sea of your
blood brothers.
But he will keep your hand,
clean, preserved in a glass case
under lights:
Proof
he will say
Of the great desirability
Of my country. (21)

Meagan Evans

The operative cliché in this poem is "Give me your hand." Though the reader has already been warned by the dedication that this poem is not likely to be a celebration of the American dream, the phrase "Give me your hand" is a set expression linked with amity, trust, and offers of aid that evokes the promise of American sanctuary to the weary and oppressed. It is a phrase that is familiar, comfortable, and understandable. It accomplishes the purposes of the passively registered cliché: establishing identification and emotional solidarity.

Though Kingsolver is clearly questioning the truth of that outstretched hand and the solidarity it implies, she does not question the cliché "I will take your hand" by saying, "But he will not take your hand." That kind of negation would leave the cliché itself intact; it would question whether the promise of the hand was fulfilled, but it would not question the form of the promise itself. But the poem does not let the reader rest long in the passively received cliché. Instead, the poem estranges the familiarity of the phrase and reveals its falseness by affirming it and literalizing it, making it a concrete demand. The "he" (who almost stands in for the border itself) reaches for "your" hand and "he will keep it," a grisly souvenir. This is the critically perceived cliché; it takes language that would normally be passed over and makes it legible in a new way. But, instead of merely revealing the "triteness" of common wisdom and ordinary language that Amossy notes, it reveals the threat of what lies beneath the official story, the "they say" of what America is. The poem recognizes the seduction of cliché, of familiar phrases like "Give me your hand," and its power comes from revealing the danger of trusting in the self-evidence of the symbols of nation.

But if Kingsolver questions the transparent working of common phrases, if she wants to undermine the passive reception of language to reveal the dangerous truths it can conceal, then why does she focus on accessibility? If these poems are meant to estrange their readers from the "they say" and to unhome our homespun phrases, then why do they seem to trust ordinary homely syntax and leave the sentence, largely, unbroken?

Audience, for Kingsolver, is indissolubly tied to her political commitments. Kingsolver has something to say, and she wants it to be comprehensible. "As Kingsolver admits, these are narrative poems, written to be accessible to mainstream readers. She talks about accessibility being one of her 'prime movers,' because she writes for and about the kind of people she grew up with, not just the 'acutely educated'" (Pence 20). Her poems are meant to include readers who might be excluded by or impatient with the kind of formal experimentation that often characterizes what Adorno would call autonomous art. And so, in *Another America/Otra América,* Kingsolver must perform a difficult balancing act. She invites her readers in with homey words, but she cannot let them remain comfortable; she must not simply tell them what they want to hear. In a sense, her poems, by using ordinary language and familiar narratives, also say, "Give me your hand," but their estrangement of that language and those narratives says, "Now let me show you what you've used it for." Her politics depend on accessibility to a wide audience, but her politics also depend on profoundly questioning accessibility itself.

In "This House I Cannot Leave," one of the two poems in *Another America/Otra América* that treats Kingsolver's rape, accessibility and estrangement are not only formal elements but also central themes. The poem describes and laments the destruction of homeliness even as it depends on a similarly destructive invasion and disruption:

THIS HOUSE I CANNOT LEAVE

My friend describes the burglar:
how he touched her clothes, passed through rooms
leaving himself there,
        staining the space
between walls, a thing she can see.

She doesn't care what he took, only
that he has driven her out, she can't
stay in this house
she loved, scraped the colors of four families
from the walls and painted with her own,
and planted things.
She is leaving fruit trees behind.

She will sell, get out, maybe
another neighborhood.
        People say
Get over it. The market isn't good. They advise
that she think about cash to mortgage
and the fruit trees

But the trees have stopped growing for her.

I offer no advice.
I tell her I know, she will leave. I am thinking
of the man who broke and entered

me.

    Of the years it took to be home again
in this house I cannot leave. (37)

Here again a cliché is central to Kingsolver's negotiations. The phrase "broke and entered" is the hinge on which the poem turns, both in its shifting subject matter and in its multifaceted relationship with accessibility and comfort. When we read "the man who broke and entered" the first time, it refers to the thief who entered the house of the speaker's friend. But in the next strophe, composed of the single pronoun "me," the poem takes a sharp turn and "the man who broke and entered" becomes the rapist, the one who unhomes the speaker's body with his invasion. "Breaking and entering" names the crime; the same name is given to countless crimes, their differences obscured. It is easy, conventional, official language; it is the passively received cliché that establishes a sense of comprehensibility to what has happened. But when that name is given to another crime, the crime of rape, suddenly the easy, obscuring phrase becomes a revealing phrase, making the rape immediate and perceivable. The realities of what it means to break and enter a home and to break and enter a woman's body are both revealed in this turn of phrase that relies, first, on our passive reception of the set expression and then on the foreignness of it, its critical reception in its new context. When it becomes the speaker who is broken and entered, the phrase "broke and entered" is no longer hospitable in the same way. It has been changed, irrevocably, by its poetic estrangement.

    As a poet Kingsolver can, in a sense, be allied with "the man / who broke and entered." She breaks into homely language, clichés and set phrases, and makes them foreign, marks them with poeticity, changes their former hospitableness into something uncomfortable. Her poetry has passed through the ordinary language she uses, leaving traces of itself there. "If no word which enters a literary work ever wholly frees itself from its meanings in ordinary speech, so no literary work . . . leaves these meanings unaltered, as they were outside it" (Adorno 178). But Kingsolver cannot be entirely aligned with the one who breaks and enters. Her poetry works by invading and unhoming, but it is also concerned with the process of healing after invasion and with pragmatic responses to violence. This insistence on moving forward from disruption is, perhaps, one reason she does not avail herself of the word-level strategies for estrangement championed by Jakobson and why syntax and sentence structure remain largely transparent. She may break open clichés and make the users of ordinary language uncomfortable, as she does in both "Refuge" and "This House I Cannot Leave," but she also recognizes that ordinary language is where her readers must live; it is the house they cannot leave.

Therefore, though some of the poems in this collection reveal the danger of trusting clichés, others must reaffirm the usefulness and beauty of ordinary language. In "Possession," the familiar phrase "Never let me down" is given new life as both a declaration of need and a celebration of a gift given:

POSSESSION

The things I wish for are:
A color. A forest.
The devil and ice in my mouth.
Everything
that can't be owned.
A leopard, a life, a kiss.
You
Never let me down.
To know that you have wanted me too
is as good as the deed of trust. (75)

Syntactically, "You / Never let me down" is a statement of fact. The speaker addresses a person who has never let her down. But, by its inclusion in a list of the speaker's desires, "Never let me down" is also a request, another thing the speaker wishes for. This is reinforced by the capitalization across the enjambed line, which does not occur elsewhere in the poem or in the collection. The capitalization of "Never" signals the separation of the line from the "You" that proceeds it, making both "You" and "Never let me down" discrete parts of the list of things wished for, as well as a sentence in their own right. The speaker thus simultaneously wishes that the "you" will never let her down and has been granted that wish. This double existence in desire and satisfaction of desire is an elegant and succinct evocation of love, and it is achieved through affirming and expanding the usefulness of ordinary language, rather than undermining it.

Though many of the poems in *Another America/Otra América* work by estranging ordinary language and the cultural narratives that employ it, the collection ends on an affirmation of the power of a familiar, seemingly sentimental phrase: "you have your mother's eyes." The poem "Your Mother's Eyes" is addressed to Maura Lopez, whose mother was raped while in prison for "painting walls" (115). Maura's mother, Lesbia, chose to give birth to Maura and to see the world hopefully: "even the men in boots were treated with kindness" (115). Maura may look like her mother, but she has her mother's eyes in a deeper sense; she has eyes that can see hope for a new beginning even amid violence and hate. The cliché, shared and ordinary, is shown to be a source of meaningfulness and hope, as well as a tool for deceit. Kingsolver must not make language seem so accessible that she allows it to be a tool for the naturalization of the evils she wishes to undo, but she cannot estrange it so deeply that it is not meaningful and useful. Thus, the cliché is central to Kingsolver's poetic strategies because it allows the insistence on the "gap between discourse and Truth" and a simultaneous emotional identification with language that is "common property" (Amossy 35–36).

This same politically motivated balancing of accessibility with estrangement can be read in Kingsolver's choice to publish her single volume of poetry bilingually. Each poem is faced by Rebeca Cartes's Spanish translations, and the title of the book is printed in both Spanish and English on the book's cover. On the one hand, the decision to include translations in Spanish is clearly, explicitly political. These poems are about bridging the gaps between "America" and its "Otra," and these gaps are often widened by language. Kingsolver explains that the purpose of the translations is to make the poems accessible to as many Americans, both English and Spanish speaking, as possible. She says, when asked why she chose to publish *Another America/Otra América* in English and Spanish, "I feel that it's appropriate that a book that's about these other Americas besides the one on *Dallas* be accessible to the citizens of that other America. In Tucson about a third of the people speak Spanish at home, so that's the world that I'm accustomed to. . . . I enjoyed the increased accessibility" (Perry 162). Translation, then, seems to be a tool for making the meaning of Kingsolver's poems accessible to the greatest number. But, if we consider Walter Benjamin's "Task of the Translator," it is possible to see, again, the balancing act between the accessibility Kingsolver claims and the estrangement that is also central to her project.

Benjamin stridently rejects that the task of the translator is to serve the reader by making work accessible to her that she cannot read in the original language. Instead, he claims that the purpose of translation is to reveal the larger workings of language itself. Instead of revealing the superficial kinship of languages by reproducing, as faithfully as possible, the form and content of literary work (the more traditional conception of translation and one that seems to drive Cartes's translations of Kingsolver's poems), Benjamin claims that "translation is only a somewhat provisional way of coming to terms with the *foreignness* of language" (75; emphasis mine). Translation disassociates word from object and reveals the higher functioning of Language, rather than mere languages. It makes language foreign and uncomfortable, revealing where it does not fit with the things and meanings toward which it intends. If this is so, then Kingsolver's use of translation is ambiguous in its relationship to accessibility. Like her clichés, which are both familiar and estranging, the translations with which each of her poems is juxtaposed do double duty. In accordance with Kingsolver's political commitments, they invite both English- and Spanish-speaking readers into her work, but, in accordance with the politics of poeticity, they also insist on the disjunction between word and thing. Like the phrases "give me your hand" and "broke and entered," the translations make readers comfortable while also moving beyond that comfort into a formal disruption that questions the transparency it relies on.

The disruptiveness of translation on the transparency of language is especially noticeable because these poems rely so heavily on idiomatic phrases. Almost every poem in *Another America/Otra América* can be said to use, in some way, a set expression or cliché. But phrases like "let the chips fall where they may," "that's a plus," "what it is you can hold a candle to," "cut our losses," and "never let me down," while they are so common as to be almost invisible in English, simply cannot be literally rendered in Spanish. For the bilingual reader, these phrases signal the incommensurateness of languages and of cultures. Despite the gesture of solidarity inherent in translation, there is also an embedded inscription of difference, a revelation of where the trusted phrases of English are separated from the self-evidence of their truth. Like the turns within each poem that question the truth of homespun phrasing and "they say" aphorisms, the choice to face each poem with a translation also reminds us that language, however welcoming and accessible, is not entirely to be trusted.

Another America/Otra América, as poetry that makes political claims, performs a difficult balancing act. These poems are poised, as are all political poems, between Adorno's two types of failure: the "lying positivism of meaning," which ratifies and naturalizes the cultural apparati it seeks to undo, and the solipsism of completely self-referential autonomy. Kingsolver's politics do not permit her to err on the side of artistic autonomy; she certainly avoids the temptations of a purely self-referential formalism. But neither do her politics permit her to unquestionably employ language as a transparent medium. Instead, through her double-edged use of the cliché, she makes her poetry accessible while simultaneously availing herself of the powers of estrangement and ambiguity that more formally experimental writers claim as the truly disruptive power of the poetic. At their least effective, Kingsolver's poems seem to be decorating political rhetoric with poetics. Sugaring the pill. But, at their best, these poems draw a kind of third way for the poet who would disrupt the narratives of her culture. The tensions of this task, to both hold out a hand to the reader and slap them awake with it, to be both home and invader, are the tensions of all poetry. But for a political poet like Kingsolver the stakes are high, and the wire must be drawn especially taut if her readers are to use it to cross over the borders she has stretched it between.

Notes

1. A series of anthologies that collects antiwar poetry from around the world in response to the U.S. invasion of Iraq.
2. Building on the work of Ferdinand de Saussure, Emile Benveniste investigates the significance of the autonomy of language from reference: "That such a system of symbols [language] exists reveals to us one of the essential facts—perhaps the most profound—about the human condition; that there is no natural, immediate, and direct relationship between man and the world or between man and man. An intermediary is necessary . . ." (26).
3. See especially Steve Benson and George Hartley.
4. See Emmanuel Levinas, especially "Ethics as First Philosophy."

Wild Indians: Kingsolver's Representation of Native America

Robin Cohen

Writing about an ethnic group other than one's own is always fraught with hazards; when Barbara Kingsolver wrote of a white woman adopting a Native American child in *The Bean Trees* and *Pigs in Heaven,* she addressed what may be the most controversial subject in Native America today, adoption "off the reservation." For example, in Sherman Alexie's *Indian Killer,* the account of a Native American child taken without the consent of his birth mother and delivered by helicopter to his white adoptive parents reads like a scene from *Apocalypse Now:* "Suddenly this is a war. The jumpsuit man holds John close to his chest as the helicopter rises. The helicopter gunman locks and loads, strafes the reservation with explosive shells. Indians hit the ground, drive their cars off roads, dive under flimsy kitchen tables" (6). Alexie's surreal scene dramatizes Native America's horrified response to the very real "devastation of Indian cultures by social workers who, misunderstanding Indian cultures, plucked thousands of children from reservations and placed them with non-Indian families" (Thomas). According to B. J. Jones, litigation director for Dakota Plains Legal Services and author of the American Bar Association's legal manual *The Indian Child Welfare Act Handbook,*

> Before 1978, as many as 25 to 35 percent of the Indian children in certain states were removed from their homes and placed in non-Indian homes. . . . In Minnesota, for example, an average of one of every four Indian children younger than age one was removed from his or her Indian home and adopted by a non-Indian couple.

A number of these children were taken from their homes
simply because a paternalistic state system failed to recognize traditional Indian culture and expected Indian families to conform to non-Indian ways. (quoted in Thomas)

Such removals affected not only individual families but also entire tribes;
childrearing in most Native American groups is a communal activity, the
tribe one big extended family. Removal of 25 to 35 percent of the community's children, who were then assimilated into white society and lost to
the tribe forever, was as devastating as an epidemic; Marc Mannes, of the
Children's Bureau of the U.S. Department of Health and Human Services,
refers to these actions as "a form of cultural genocide" (Thomas). In response to tribal outrage, Congress enacted the Indian Child Welfare Act of
1978, which gives a child's tribe the right to be involved in custody decisions
and allows parents and tribe to request that the tribe's court be given juris-
diction in such adoption cases. In *Pigs in Heaven,* Cherokee tribal lawyer
Annawake Fourkiller explains to Alice the tribe's history (the Trail of Tears,
Indian boarding schools) and its objections to adoption of Indian children
by outsiders: "We've been through a holocaust as devastating as what happened to the Jews, and we need to keep what's left of our family together"
(291). The history of the events leading up to the Indian Child Welfare Act of
1978 support Annawake's account; she does not overstate the case.

Some critics, both Native and non-Native, have described Kingsolver's
treatment of the issue in *The Bean Trees* as ignorant of Native American communities. Indeed, Kingsolver herself recognized that she had not dealt with
the moral issues. Interviewer Karen Karbo reports, "Ms. Kingsolver recalled
that she began to form the architecture of the story [for *Pigs in Heaven*] when
she realized it had been set up in her first novel, *The Bean Trees.*" She quotes
Kingsolver: "I conceived of the idea for *Pigs in Heaven* as I watched Native
American children being adopted by outsiders. . . . I had the option and the
obligation to deal with the issue because the moral question was completely
ignored in the first book" (Karbo).

Yet critics have described Kingsolver's resolution of the adoption in *Pigs
in Heaven,* in which Taylor's white mother marries Turtle's Cherokee grandfather, and Taylor and the tribe agree that Turtle will remain with Taylor
for most of the year but spend summers on the reservation with her grandparents, as naive and utopian. Kathleen Godfrey writes, "as she [Kingsolver]

Robin Cohen

tries to correct misconceptions about Native peoples, she slips into the problematic trope of playing Indian" (270). Similarly, Kristina Fagan writes that *Pigs in Heaven* enacts "the fantasy of becoming indigenous, or 'going Indian,' [which] reflects a longing to be confidently at home on the North American continent" (251).[1]

Considered in light of Kingsolver's treatment of Native American characters, cultures, and issues in the larger body of her work, however, this problematic adoption may be somewhat utopian as charged (the characters themselves seem skeptical of the convenient romance), but it is not naive. Rather, I would suggest that it is part of a thoughtful attempt to suggest the need for a hybrid society, favoring feminine and tribal forms of community over the lone masculine individualist of conventional Western literature, offering new definitions of kinship and family. The adoption is part of a larger pattern in which Kingsolver engages other stereotypes such as the universal Cherokee grandmother, Indian Country as wasteland, the alcoholic Indian, and so forth, in order to deconstruct them. In incidents ranging from the minor to the more consequential, Kingsolver exposes the racism embedded in the very language and culture of mainstream America and suggests an alternative.

For example, Lou Ann (*Bean Trees*) remembers a schoolchild's mnemonic for spelling "arithmetic": "A red Indian thought he might eat tobacco in church" (121). After blurting it out, she remembers Turtle's heritage and says, "No offense to anyone present, about the Indian" (121). The language of racism is so pervasive that even nonracist Lou Ann inadvertently uses it.

Another example of racist language comes from an unexpected source. In *Animal Dreams,* when Codi surprises her Apache boyfriend, Loyd, with a picnic lunch, he responds, "That's mighty white of you" (121). Codi thinks, "I didn't know what to make of that. It was something people said, but usually when they said it both people were white" (121). We understand Codi's confusion. Is Loyd using the term ironically? He is otherwise straightforward, so irony would be out of character. Does he mean it literally—that white people always think they have to provide food? Again, such sarcasm seems out of character. Or has the use of the word "white" as a synonym for "good" or "decent" become so pervasive that even Loyd, a man conscious of and proud of his Native American heritage, can use the term without thinking? The latter seems the most likely, but like Codi, the reader cannot be sure what to make of it. And Kingsolver clearly chose to leave it ambiguous, to raise such questions without answering them.

148

Perhaps less innocent is Virgie Mae Parsons's referring to Turtle: "And is this naked creature one of theirs? She looks like a little wild Indian" (141). This seems like more than a slip of the tongue. After all, the same Virgie Mae later reacts to Estevan's account of his Chinese employer who speaks no English by muttering, "Before you know it the whole world will be here jibbering and jabbering till we won't know it's America. . . . They ought to stay put in their own dirt, not come here taking up jobs" (143). Though Taylor takes an immediate dislike to Virgie, the two older women (Virgie and Edna) eventually become her close friends and loving babysitters for "wild Indian" Turtle. Virgie's ethnocentrism, though initially causing both Taylor and the reader to see her negatively, seems more a knee-jerk reaction or an attitude unthinkingly received from society around her rather than a carefully considered belief. Contrary to first impressions, we later see a "kinder, gentler" Virgie. Through this reversal, Kingsolver makes the point that even decent people can unthinkingly perpetuate racism.

Similarly, Taylor's (and Alice's) claim to "head rights" (membership in the Cherokee tribe) initially seems like just one more dubious claim to the universal Cherokee ancestor. Zora Neale Hurston wryly comments on the desire for exotic ancestors manifested by claims of an Indian grandmother —often an "Indian princess" (though no such hereditary royalty exists in Native American cultures). More specifically, Hurston notes, "From the number of her children, one is forced to the conclusion that that Pocahontas wasn't so poky, after all" (147). Such claims do seem motivated by the desire to "play Indian"; such people are often described as members of the "Wannabe Tribe."

However, on arriving in Oklahoma, Taylor muses, "I had to laugh, really. All my life, Mama had talked about the Cherokee Nation as our ace in the hole. She'd had an old grandpa that was full-blooded Cherokee. . . . Mama would say, 'If we run out of luck we can always go live on the Cherokee Nation" (18). But Taylor is appalled by the flatness and barrenness of the part of Oklahoma that she initially encounters and the apparent poverty of its residents: "Of course, if she had ever been there she would have known it was not a place you'd ever go to live without some kind of lethal weapon aimed at your hind end" (18). This place is clearly less desirable than Pittman County, Kentucky, the place she is escaping. Her ace in the hole, her safety net, dissolves in thin air. Yet when she returns and visits the beautiful Lake o' the Cherokees, she discovers that her first impression was false: "Lake o' the Cherokees was a place where you could imagine God might live. There were enough trees" (275). Each perception is accurate in its own way. Like so many other elements in Kingsolver's works, things are seldom as they first appear; things are seldom simply black or white. The Cherokee Nation is a place of great poverty, but also a place of great beauty, a home to the derelicts Taylor encounters on her first visit, but also a place of great community and family ties.

Her perception of the place shifts yet again in *Pigs in Heaven*. When attorney Annawake Fourkiller sees Taylor and Turtle on the *Oprah Winfrey Show* and determines that the adoption is illegal, the strong mother-daughter bond that has formed over the past three years is threatened. Taylor takes Turtle "on the lam," and the Cherokee Nation becomes something to run *from*, not *to*, no longer a refuge but a threat. In a reversal of years of Native American children being forcibly removed from their families, either to attend boarding schools (and assimilate into white society) or to be adopted by outsiders, the Cherokee Nation threatens Taylor, a white woman, with the loss of her child.

This reversal forces non-Native readers to empathize with the tribe in a new way. The circumstances of Taylor's acquiring Turtle—the signs of physical and sexual abuse, the desperation of the woman (Turtle's aunt) who puts the child in Taylor's car—tend to make the reader more sympathetic to Taylor's claim on the child, at least initially. And, indirectly, the pain that Esperanza and Estevan experience at the kidnapping of their child encourages the reader to sympathize with the parent's loss (*Bean Trees*). But other circumstances direct the reader's sympathy to the tribe.

The account of the removal of Annawake's brother Gabe and problems with his adoptive family is certainly moving. In her letter to Jax, Annawake describes how their mother was institutionalized when Annawake was ten years old. Her older brothers were sent to their father and she stayed with her Uncle Ledger. But her twin brother was adopted by a white family: "Probably the social workers knew a couple who wanted a little boy—something as simple as that" (154). His frustrations with not fitting in at school and the insensitivity of his adopted family led him to rebel; Annawake tells Jax, "When he was fifteen, he was accessory to an armed robbery in Corpus Christi. Now I only know where he is when he's in prison" (155). And Cash Stillwater, Turtle's birth grandfather who wants custody, is a sympathetic character. He tells Alice that one of his daughters, Turtle's birth mother, was killed in a car accident. His other daughter, who ran off with "a no-count boy to Tulsa" (319) gave away her niece (his granddaughter) to a stranger (Taylor). Having lost his wife, his daughter, and his granddaughter all in the same year was more than he could bear.

Paradoxically, by vicariously experiencing Taylor's fear of losing her adoptive daughter, the reader more fully understands the loss experienced by Turtle's birth family and the tribe. Through reversals and variations on a theme, Kingsolver demonstrates the complexity of the adoption issue from the perspective of the child, of the tribe, and of the adoptive parent.

Kingsolver repeatedly sets up stereotypes only to dismantle them and creates expectations only to reverse them. Even in her earlier work, *Animal Dreams,* we see this in the character Loyd Peregrina. He is introduced to us as a *"real* Apache, and the kind of handsome you could see coming down the road like bad news" (53). He was such a heavy drinker in high school that Codi is "frankly surprised to hear he is still alive" fifteen years later (53). He was the father of Codi's miscarried baby, but "he never knew what he'd spawned, much less when it died" (53). Codi is sure that he will not remember her since they only dated for one month and for Loyd "it was one in a hundred, he was a senior and ran around with everybody" (53). So Loyd, attractive and popular, seems the stereotypical drunken Indian, a "love 'em and leave 'em" kind of guy. Codi learns that he raises fighting cocks, a trait that adds to the image of Loyd as being cold-hearted, perhaps something of a savage.

But as Codi becomes reacquainted with the adult Loyd, she finds him much different than the boy she remembers. He has long since ceased to be a heavy drinker, and he is a hard worker and solid citizen. Far from having forgotten her, he apologizes for "being a jerk" in high school (134). Codi finds Loyd to be thoughtful and philosophical, in contrast to her well-educated, well-to-do former boyfriend. While discussing the nature of dreams, animal and human, with Loyd, she thinks, "Carlo wouldn't have paid the slightest attention to a conversation like this; he'd be thinking about whatever men think about, how much gas is left in the tank" (135). She even learns that Loyd is only half Apache, a nomadic tribe with a wild reputation; his mother is Pueblo, a group thought to be more peaceful, stable, and home loving.

When Loyd takes her to a cock fight, she sees that Loyd is a gifted bird handler: "The physical relationship between Loyd and his rooster transcended winning or losing" (194). But she is still appalled by the spectacle. She is upset not by the blood or even by the animal's death, but rather by people enjoying it as sport: "What I believe is that humans should have more heart than that. I can't feel good about people making a spectator sport out of puncture wounds and internal hemorrhage" (196). Once Loyd understands her feelings, he voluntarily gives up cockfighting. (Later, Codi learns that Inez, Loyd's mother, also disapproves of the sport. Codi realizes that Loyd gave up cockfighting for his mother as well as for her and finds his desire to please Inez endearing.) Loyd shatters any image of brutality that Codi—or the reader—may have had. Not bound by a macho refusal to "give in" to a woman, Loyd deeply cares about what Inez and Codi think of him and wants to please them, even though doing so means giving up something he treasures. It is also significant that cockfighting was something he learned from his Apache father. In agreeing to give up the sport, he chooses the feminine nonviolent values of his girlfriend and of his home-loving Pueblo mother.

In "Kingsolver's Anti-Western," Naomi Jacobs notes that Loyd is a blend of the domestic and the wild, of modern and traditional; his Native American affinity for home is a counterpart to Codi's restlessness. Critics have complained that Kingsolver idealizes Native Americans. But Loyd is more than an imaginary ideal; he is the model for a new man, transcending ethnicity, for a new age and a better world. Although his Native American spirituality and worldview contribute important traits for this new man, these traits are not essentially or exclusively Native American. We can see this by comparing Loyd to Jax, Taylor's non-Native boyfriend in *Pigs in Heaven*. Jax has many of the same qualities as Loyd; he is sensitive, supportive, and accepting of Taylor's independence. And in the same novel, Cash Stillwater, a more mature model for the new man, breaks the stereotype of the uncommunicative, domestically helpless male (a stereotype that crosses racial and ethnic boundaries). Alice marvels that conversation with Cash is easy and abundant, and when he brings her breakfast in bed, "She feels she has died and gone to the Planet of Men Who Cook" (316). All three men are part of Kingsolver's larger project, described by Jacobs: "Dismantling one set of myths, Kingsolver begins to construct another, based in an optimistic vision of a cooperative and sustainable multicultural community in which men and women work together toward common goals." This project transcends the desire to "go Native" that critics allege, and involves reconsidering constructs of gender, ethnicity, and the most basic structures of society.

Catherine Himmelwright observes that when characters "go Indian" in traditional Westerns men adopt the *physical* traits of the Indian, such as hunting skill. But Kingsolver's female protagonists adopt Native American *spiritual* attributes (36). For example, the rootless Codi learns to value home and history. The fiercely independent Taylor and Alice Greer both learn to value community and choose to create their own extended families. And both Greer women learn to value the absence of materialism on the Cherokee reservation. They stop seeing what the Cherokee do not have and learn to see what they do have: strong morals based on concern for the welfare of others. Rather than escaping to some imagined site of regression, Kingsolver's characters move forward to a newly constructed hybrid society that rejects the violence and greed of modern capitalist America and embraces a whole new set of gender-neutral values.

In traditional Westerns, "going Indian" always fails, always ends tragically. Though such works act out white desire to return to an imagined Eden, such a conclusion is never truly possible. For example, in *Dances with Wolves*, the ultimate "going Indian" fantasy, Dunbar sets off at movie's end to try to save the Lakota by interceding with his fellow whites. But we see the inexorable progress of the cavalry and know that he will fail. We know American history, and we know the end of this story; though quaint, the idyllic Native oneness with nature must inevitably give way to the forces of progress, industrialization, and capitalism. These forces cannot be stopped and, once advanced, cannot be reversed, according to the standard story. Thus, Native people are cast as a vanishing race of noble savages. But Kingsolver goes beyond this nostalgic yearning for the impossible and looks toward a new social paradigm. Maureen Ryan, in "Barbara Kingsolver's Lowfat Fiction," charges that Kingsolver's novels are "too pat, too nice"—politically correct yet conservative. But the paradigm shift that her works collectively advocate is radical, even revolutionary. Kingsolver suggests that Native American values are not necessarily impossible in a modern world. In *Animal Dreams*, she demonstrates that environmental devastation can be reversed and, given the chance, the earth can heal itself. In *Pigs in Heaven*, she suggests that people can heal, as well. Though Annawake mourns her brother Gabe as lost, her Uncle Ledger helps her to see that she could go after him and bring him back. In Kingsolver's new paradigm, such changes can be wrought through the will and efforts of a harmonious community.

Despite Kathleen Godfrey's claim that Kingsolver's works are "populated by 'cuddly, colorful' Native characters," Kingsolver's portrayal of Native America is nuanced and balanced (272). Yes, "quirky Boma Mellowbug, teenage boys who love their grandmothers, and gentle Andy Rainbelt, the

Robin Cohen

wise social worker" (Godfrey 272) may qualify as cute and cuddly at one end of the spectrum, but such characters are balanced at the other end of the spectrum by the hard-drinking teenaged Loyd, by Annawake's absent father and alcoholic mother, by Turtle's aunt and her abusive boyfriend. Kingsolver shows us the complex context of alcoholism, poverty, broken families, and despair that produces such troubled people. Most of Kingsolver's Native characters, such as Annawake and the adult Loyd, fall in the middle of the two extremes. They are personally and professionally successful, complex, sometimes prickly, and far more than Godfrey's "cuddly, colorful" stereotypes.

When Annawake explains the tribe's communal approach to childrearing, Alice asks, "So with all this love going around, how does it happen that somebody walks up to my daughter's parked car one night and gives a baby away?" (236). Annawake explains the consequences of forced assimilation:

> God knows why. . . . What's happened to us is that our chain of caretaking got interrupted. My mom's generation. . . . Federal law put them in boarding school. Cut off their hair, taught them English, taught them to love Jesus, and made them spend their entire childhoods in a dormitory. They got to see their people maybe twice a year. Family has always been our highest value, but that generation of kids never learned how to be in a family. The past got broken off. (*Pigs in Heaven* 236)

People such as Annawake, Sugar, and Cash in *Pigs in Heaven,* and Loyd in *Animal Dreams,* reconnect with that past, finding redemption for themselves and for the community.

Though readers may come away from these novels with a predominantly sunny view of Native America, the hardships and negatives are far from invisible in Kingsolver's representation. While riding in Cash's truck, Alice asks him why his former boss, who was something of a "wannabe" (a white person who wants to be Indian), committed suicide. Cash answers, "'I think he was depressed about the Indians being all gone. . . . He should have come down here and had a look.' They pass a ragged little shack with a ragged little birdhouse on a post beside it, and Alice thinks; Then he would have taken the pills and shot himself too" (264).

It is difficult to see Kingsolver's resolutions as "too pat, too happy." These novels are as much about loss as they are about happy resolutions. In *The Bean Trees,* Estevan and Esperanza have little hope of ever seeing their daughter again. *Pigs in Heaven* is about compromise; everyone wins something, but everyone also loses something. When Taylor first hears the court's decision, she "takes her first breath of the too-thin air of the rest of her life—a life of sharing Turtle with strangers" (350). Taylor later thinks,

> [She] understands she has lost something she won't get back. Cash Stillwater is Turtle's legal guardian. No matter what.
>
> Taylor can still remember the day when she first understood she'd received the absolute power of motherhood—that force that makes everyone else step back and agree that she knows what's best for Turtle. It scared her to death. But giving it up now makes her feel infinitely small and alone. She can't even count her losses yet; her heart is an empty canyon. . . . (352–53)

Animal Dreams ends with Codi happily with Loyd, pregnant with his child, and the land recovering from the mining company's abuses, but Codi loses her father and her sister. This is not a fairy-tale world of "happily ever after"; it is a real world where, as Loyd notes, everyone dies.

Kristina Fagan criticizes Kingsolver for "sidestepping" the "big issues" in *Pigs in Heaven* and reassuring readers "that all ethical and cultural conflicts that the book lays out can be solved by individual acts of love. . . . despite its emphasis on the importance of community the novel is resolved by individualization. Its resolution is so unusual and so particular that it does not offer a feasible approach to either interracial adoption or the broader issue of community versus individual interests" (260). I would argue the opposite; the adoption settlement that works so well in the interest of Turtle without depriving Taylor of her relationship with her adopted daughter would not be possible without the presence and support of the community. Kingsolver's argument is not the facile one of "love conquers all," nor is the joint custody arrangement just a sort of "deus ex machina" to rescue the characters from an irresolvable situation. Rather, it is a part of her larger message that American culture must change in fundamental ways.

What would Kingsolver's new America look like? For one thing, it would be less materialistic. Children would not be ridiculed for their lack of possessions. There would be no room for Barbie dolls, human or plastic. Conversation would be valued over television. People would have a closer relationship to nature and more respect for the environment.

Robin Cohen

There would be no room for organized religion as we know it. Kingsolver certainly approves of churches that shelter refugees (as in *The Bean Trees*) and activist clergy (such as the nun who befriended Hallie in *Animal Dreams*). But the church would no longer serve to enforce assimilation or to colonize people, as Annawake describes the Indian Boarding Schools' use of Christianity to achieve their goals. The ideal of separation of church and state would be realized in this new America.

Gender roles would be redefined. The Hardbine family in *The Bean Trees* are victims of the traditional male role run amok. The abusive father created a troubled son, Newt, who ultimately broke down under the pressure and attempted to kill his wife before killing himself. Loyd, Estevan, Jax, and Cash all reject the paternalism that is just as destructive for men as for women. These new men are communicative, able to show emotion, and unafraid of commitment. Some of them can even cook. Women are strong, smart, and can perform traditionally male roles such as being auto mechanics or lawyers. Yet they can choose to be mothers in a land where children and those who nurture them are valued.

Ethnicity would be reconstructed. Difference would be valued rather than feared or scorned. Apache/Pueblo Loyd could marry white Codi (whose ethnicity as a member of the Noline/Nolina family is not entirely clear) without raising an eyebrow. Southerner Lou Ann could date Cameron John, a black man (*The Bean Trees*). Skin color would not be cause for rejection. We would value and preserve unique cultural practices.

Family would be valued, and families would be more fluid constructs. Currently, the demands of careers take offspring thousands of miles from home, and extended families live at great distances. Kingsolver does not seem to suggest that this should end, although many characters such as Codi and Annawake come home in her works, and Taylor and Alice reconnect and strengthen their bond. Rather, Kingsolver's characters construct their own families. Taylor realizes that Lou Ann, Dwayne Ray, and Mattie are her family; she defines family as "the people you won't let go of for anything" (339).

But the most important characteristic of the new America that Kingsolver suggests would be the demise of rugged individualism and the rise of community. Although strong individuals are admirable in Kingsolver's work, they ultimately find that they cannot function without a supportive community. Taylor needs her family, both blood and adopted, as well as the help of the Cherokee Nation to raise Turtle. Codi needs her fifty mothers, the women of Grace who loved and supported her as a child, as well as the Stitch and Bitch Club. Alice needs Cash, Sugar, Letty, and the communal power of the stomp dance.

All of these characteristics of the new paradigm for a new America are exemplified to some extent by Native American culture and characters, but none so much as the value of community. When Annawake Fourkiller tells Jax the story of the greedy boys who turned into pigs, she muses, "I had a hundred and one childhood myths, and they all added up more or less to 'Do right by your people'" (*Pigs in Heaven* 91). When she asks Jax for his, he replies, "Oh, you know, I heard the usual American thing. If you're industrious and have clean thoughts you will grow up to be vice president of Motorola" (91). Annawake summarizes, "Do right by yourself" (91). When Kingsolver's characters try to "do right" by themselves, they fail. Taylor cannot support Turtle; Codi cannot find her own identity. Pittman is a terrible place to live because it has no sense of community. The Cherokee Nation, on the other hand, is like heaven because people feel connected to each other. They watch out for each other. In what is perhaps Kingsolver's biggest reversal, what is best for the group winds up being what is best for the individual.

Note

1. The issue of whites playing Indian has been addressed in greater depth by Philip Deloria in *Playing Indian;* by Robert Baird in his essay, "Going Indian: Discovery, Adoption, and Renaming toward a 'True American' from *Deerslayer* to *Dances with Wolves*" (in *Dressing in Feathers,* edited by S. Elizabeth Bird); and by Louis Owens in "Apocalypse at the Two-Socks Hop: Dancing with the Vanishing American" (in *Mixedblood Messages: Literature, Film, Family, Place).*

Robin Cohen

The White Imagination at Work in *Pigs in Heaven*

Jeanne Sokolowski

*Here I was, faced with the impossible choice of keeping perma-
nently quiet or perpetuating ruthless violence.*

—Harold Fromm

*While I started out to learn about Indians, I ended up preoccupied
with a problem of my own.*

—Jane Tompkins

Though Barbara Kingsolver's novel *The Poisonwood Bible*
(1998) is the one work in her oeuvre that critics and reviewers recognize as overtly postcolonial, Kingsolver's
interest in internal colonization dates back to her novel *Pigs
in Heaven* (1993). Postcolonial critic Jenny Sharpe has written
about the intersection of postcolonial studies and global multiculturalism, noting how the multiculturalism of the 1960s
and 1970s drew upon the "anticolonial writings of Third World
liberation movements to suggest . . . the disenfranchisement
of racial minorities" as a mode of contemporary colonization (114). This "internal colonization" model allowed minorities to separate the experience of European immigrants
from slaves and the conquered (114). The critical investigation into modes of neocolonialism reflects the persistence of
colonial attitudes and policies. However, as scholars such as
Toni Morrison in *Playing in the Dark* and Anne Anlin Cheng
in *The Melancholy of Race* remind us, the impact of racism,
colonialism, and imperialism is perpetuated not only in the
psyches of their victims but also in the ongoing guilt of the
oppressors. Morrison's proposition for examining the Afri-
canist presence in the writing of white authors involves
"avert[ing] the critical gaze from the racial object to the

racial subject; from the described and imagined to the describers and imaginers" (90); this redirection also characterizes my strategy for approaching Kingsolver's representation of Native American characters. Kingsolver's novel *Pigs in Heaven* demonstrates how educated Anglo writers and thinkers struggle with the legacy of colonialism, racism, and prejudice in the United States. The problem *Pigs in Heaven* addresses is how to proceed in a nation permeated with these memories and, in the eyes of many Native Americans, including novelist and critic Louis Owens, still engaged in a colonialist project. As Owens states in his essay, "As If an Indian Were Really an Indian: Native American Voices and Postcolonial Theory," America never became *post-colonial*; even today, he writes, the "indigenous inhabitants of North American can stand anywhere on the continent and look in every direction at a home usurped and colonized by strangers" (14–15). Kingsolver's novel deals with the adoption of Native American children outside of the tribe, a practice that elicits from some accusations of neocolonialism and that underscores the difficulty of forging a collective future that neither punishes white Americans for the sins of their fathers nor deepens the gulf between ethnic and racial groups in the United States. Kingsolver enters this difficult territory in which she challenges herself, and her readers, to imagine the future of white-Native relations. For Euro-American authors, the choice between keeping quiet or perpetuating the problem, to paraphrase Harold Fromm, can fail to satisfy; Kingsolver's choice to confront this aspect of life in America deserves recognition as an honest attempt at coming to terms with American history.

By approaching the question of how the white imagination functions in *Pigs in Heaven,* I am suggesting that Kingsolver's fictional treatment of cross-racial adoption evokes the American government's treatment of Native people and demonstrates how the colonial experience in the American context continues to affect those who were colonized while also influencing the colonizer, tracing the colonial legacy to its contemporary manifestations.[1] The plot of the novel is this: Taylor Greer takes her adopted Cherokee daughter, Turtle, to Hoover Dam, where Turtle alerts her mother that she has seen a man (the mentally disabled Lucky Buster) fall into the spillway. He is rescued and Turtle's role wins her a spot on the Oprah Winfrey show, where the mother-daughter duo are spotted by Cherokee lawyer Annawake Fourkiller, who suspects that the adoption was not on the up-and-up. Fourkiller, particularly sensitive to the issue of external adoption of Indian children because of the fate of her twin brother, Gabriel, tracks down Taylor and confronts her. Taylor responds by taking Turtle and fleeing Arizona, leaving her boyfriend, Jax, behind. Meanwhile, Taylor's mother, Alice, is having problems of her own: upon hearing of Taylor's plight, she finds this a good excuse to leave her TV-obsessed husband, Harlan, and joins Taylor and Turtle on the road. When Alice finally learns more about Annawake Fourkiller's position on adoption and her history of loss, she decides to journey to Cherokee country in Oklahoma, reuniting while there with her cousin, Sugar, who has married into the tribe. In the meantime, Turtle's grandfather, Cash, has returned to Heaven, Oklahoma, from Wyoming, and contacts Annawake about finding Turtle. Annawake hatches a plan to play matchmaker between Cash and Alice, who has learned from Sugar that they have Cherokee blood, enough to legally enroll in the nation. Taylor ends up in Seattle with Turtle, but, finding herself unable to care for Turtle without a support network, finally agrees to bring Turtle to Heaven, where she is reunited with her grandfather. In the conclusion of the novel, Cash is granted legal guardianship, but with the understanding that he and Taylor will work out custody arrangements so that Turtle can live with Taylor while spending summers on the reservation.

The plot impels me, a white female reader, to ask myself how I am called upon by Kingsolver to identify with the characters presented, and to what end. I conclude that Kingsolver's characterization of the relationship between Taylor Greer, her adopted daughter, Turtle, and members of the Cherokee tribe allows readers, particularly non-Native readers, to imagine the range of positions possible in contemporary interactions between whites and Native Americans. The novel challenges Anglo readers to acknowledge the history of genocide and displacement endured by Native populations; to view the dramatic consequences of the government's policy of paternalism on Native families and communities; and to consider how post-paternalist policies, specifically those that insist on greater Native self-sufficiency, foreground some of the most significant differences between Native American and Anglo-American concepts of citizenship and civic identity. The body of the narrative endeavors to capture the tension between Anglo and Native perspectives, and in doing so forces Anglo readers to consider their attitudes and preconceptions. Taylor's character exemplifies the psychological discomfort for Anglos (and, by extension, Anglo readers) wrought by direct confrontation with Native Americans about the past, and the implications for present-day relations between the two groups. Her decision to flee her

160

home with Turtle rather than engage directly with Annawake demonstrates how avoidance may ease that angst, but only temporarily. Though the conclusion of the novel undermines these challenges to the reader by too easily reconciling the differences between the mind-sets of Taylor and Annawake, Taylor's character serves as a mirror for non-Native readers to explore vicariously these issues through the shifts in Taylor's thinking and perspectives.

In a multination state like the United States, a sense of solidarity is often difficult to achieve, as Will Kymlicka has pointed out in his work on multicultural citizenship. One of the obstacles to national identity formation in such places is national history; as Kymlicka notes, the "people and events which spark pride amongst the majority nation often generate a sense of betrayal amongst the national minority" (182). As a result, history becomes a source of contention rather than a means of solidifying national identity. In a (post)colonial context,[2] in which the experience of colonization continues to affect not just those colonized, but the colonizers as well, forgetting the past becomes, as Ernst Renan wrote in 1882, "a crucial factor in the creation of a nation" ("What Is a Nation?"). A (post)colonial reading strategy is one that takes these facts into account and identifies the places in the text where the narrative reflects the legacy of a colonial past: in Kingsolver's case, her attempts to wrestle with the ethics of representing cross-cultural relations and cross-racial adoptions within the historical context of the American government's policies toward Native Americans and the contemporary attitudes that are the result of this history. Though a segment of (post)colonial theorists deny the validity of identifying the United States as (post)colonial (given its current neocolonial status), the United States presents an opportunity for testing the applicability of (post)colonial theory to cases that are not clear-cut. The goals of (post)colonial studies also dovetail with the challenges facing liberal theorists, which Will Kymlicka articulates as the challenge "to identify the sources of unity" in multination states (185). John Rawls's answer to this problem is the claim that such a source lies within a mutual understanding of justice.

Kingsolver's comments on her motivation for writing *Pigs in Heaven* demonstrate her interest in the question of justice, as does the publication of her nonfiction work, *Holding the Line: Women in the Great Arizona Mine Strike of 1983*. The publication of *Pigs in Heaven* followed that of *The Bean Trees*, which details the handover of Turtle to Taylor and her subsequently illegal adoption. About her imperative to write *Pigs in Heaven*, Kingsolver

Jeanne Sokolowski

has stated, "I had *the option and the obligation* to deal with the issue because the moral question was completely ignored in the first book" (Perry 165; emphasis mine). This explanation broaches the ethical question of fictionalizing a cross-racial adoption as beneficial to both parties, without considering how this act would be viewed by the Native community, as well as toward Kingsolver's position as *able to speak* and publish about these issues. As a popular, white writer, Kingsolver enjoys a kind of privilege in writing about this topic that Native writers may not, but I think most readers will recognize and respect her interest in facing the challenge of writing about "the places where disparate points of view rub together" ("The Spaces Between" 154).[3] As Ella Shohat has argued, elements of culture "must be analyzed not only in terms of who represents but also in terms of who is being represented, for what purpose, at which historical moment, for which location, using which strategies, and in what tone of address" (173). Kingsolver denies that one needs certain "genetic or cultural credentials" to write about other cultures, particularly as the focus of this particular story is the point where "the reservation child come[s] into the place where I live" ("The Spaces Between" 155).

Kathleen Godfrey's assessment of the novel in her essay "Barbara Kingsolver's Cherokee Nation: Problems of Representation in *Pigs in Heaven*," acknowledges Kingsolver's attempts to represent Native American characters speaking for themselves, but she also details the "authorial and rhetorical practices which commodify, ritualize, and idealize the Cherokee" (259). Therefore, according to Godfrey, the novel "require[s] little adjustment on the part of Anglo readers"; rather, they will finish it "feeling as though they had visited an 'authentic' piece of Indian country—without examining their own relationship to racism and stereotypes" (272). Godfrey's insightful reading of the novel, including her discussion of the commodification of Indian culture, however, underestimates the way in which Kingsolver actually sets up the plot to lead readers through variations on commonly held attitudes toward Native Americans. Readers who recognize that these encounters reflect cultural attitudes but not necessarily reality may emerge from the reading experience with a greater appreciation of the inadequacy of overgeneralization and mythologizing. Kingsolver's success in her attempt at this type of discursive disruption hinges upon the reader's ability to view the development of the characters and the changes in their attitudes toward the situation. Through an analysis of several dramatic moments in the novel, I want to argue that the novel does pose challenges to the typical Anglo viewpoint. These moments feature encounters between Annawake Fourkiller and significant figures in Turtle's life: Taylor, Jax, and Alice. The first of these occurs when Annawake visits Taylor after seeing her on *Oprah;* the second after Taylor's flight, when Annawake returns and finds Jax alone; the next, as Alice meets Annawake on the reservation in Oklahoma; and, finally, when Taylor and Annawake come face to face again in Cherokee Country, an event which leads to the Tribal Council meeting that concludes the book.

ON THE WARPATH

In the chapter entitled "A More Perfect Union," Annawake Fourkiller journeys to Arizona, having convinced her boss, Franklin Turnbo, of the value of visiting Taylor Greer and investigating Turtle's adoption. Kingsolver cleverly merges two clichés: that of the Indian on horseback going "on the warpath" and of the idealistic knight on a white horse, fighting on the side of what is right. The chapter title is an ironic take on the seeming impossibility of reconciling the points of view of cultures in conflict, represented here by Taylor and Annawake. The individualism of white America suggested by Taylor's emphasis on what is best for Turtle flies in the face of Annawake's concern for the tribe and its future, embodied by the children. The conversation between the two also demonstrates the refusal of Anglo America to recognize the persistence of racism in contemporary society and the need for cooperation and dialogue. As Taylor puts it, "'my home doesn't have anything to do with your tragedy'" (75). This chapter also highlights the difficulties in cross-cultural interaction, brought about in part because of legal systems that are coeval. Taylor's thoughts rush to the Constitution and its purpose in protecting the rights of citizens; she is unable or unwilling to recognize, despite Annawake's attempts to inform her, that the Constitution has not "prevent[ed] terrible unfairness" for all citizens equally (77). Annawake, for her part, gives primacy to the legal system of the Cherokee Nation, and her approach to the situation similarly fails to acknowledge Taylor's position. Though Annawake frames the motivation for her visit in terms of a "friendly meeting of the minds," the two parties involved are unable to find common ground for discussion or negotiation (77).

Taylor responds to this confrontation with the intelligent and powerful lawyer by deciding to pull up stakes and leave Tucson with Turtle. In a reversal of her behavior in *The Bean Trees,* in which Taylor's decision to leave rural Kentucky frees her from being trapped by a small-time, small-town life, Taylor's taking to the road in *Pigs in Heaven* imprisons her in a cycle of guilt and insecurity about her relationship to Turtle and to the Native American community.

CULTURAL RELATIVITY, OR THE GEOMETRY OF INTERESTS

The second encounter—between Annawake and Taylor's boyfriend, Jax— occurs in the subsequent chapter, "The Pigs in Heaven," which refers to the Cherokee story behind one of the constellations, known as the Pleiades to Jax. This chapter stages another dialogue between "unlike minds," though Jax shows himself more willing to listen objectively to Annawake's argu- ment. Both Jax and Annawake draw on stereotypes to negotiate the encoun- ter, though with a subtle difference: Annawake's experience with white cul- ture allows her to more dispassionately assess Jax and his situation, while Jax's thinking leads in the direction of idealization of Native Americans. Jax rather self-consciously epitomizes what Jane Tompkins has characterized as the tendency of white Americans to indulge in "narcissistic fantasies of freedom and adventure, of a life lived closer to nature and to spirit" when thinking about Native Americans (60).

Choosing to look at Kingsolver's work through the lens of (post)colonial theory forces us to ask the larger question, What *is* the "position of white or 'first-world' writers within postcolonial critique," as Geoffrey Sanborn que- ries in his reassessment of Herman Melville. And, more to the point here, what are the limits to or obstacles evident within these white critiques (xiii)? Sanborn articulates his theory in *The Sign of the Cannibal: Melville and the Making of a Postcolonial Reader,* stating that white writers like Melville have a distinct function, which is to register the "dynamics of anxiety and men- ace in the colonial encounter" (xiii). Sanborn refers to Gareth Griffiths, who has argued that the "discursive disruption" indigenous groups wish to reg- ister is broadened and deepened through the work of like-minded white writers (xiii). Sanborn, however, qualifies his argument by noting, with a nod to Ernesto Laclau, that certain "conditions of possibility" must be pres- ent.[4] In short, these critiques and disruptions can only occur when an area of representation is characterized by significant ambiguity; that ambiguity opens up a space in which a writer can walk us through a series of possible explanations or representations with the goal not of reaching a "correct" interpretation, but of allowing the reader to "experience the tension between . . . competing perceptions" of a group (xiv).

Melville's writing, of course, was contemporaneous with the imperial projects of the United States in the South Pacific and elsewhere. Kingsolver, on the other hand, writing *Pigs in Heaven* in 1993, faced the challenge of dealing with the persistence of the colonial legacy on Native Americans and Anglo-Americans alike. In this case, old stereotypes of Native Americans as violent and bloodthirsty, as likely to scalp their enemies and/or steal their horses, form a palimpsest with more contemporary images such as the drunken, shiftless Native American incapable of taking care of him or herself, let alone a child. Kingsolver's novel, like those of Melville, registers Anglo-American thinking and suspicion through a spectrum of positions while also creating a reading experience that forces Anglo readers into confronting the tension between their own thinking—ignorant at best and prejudicial at worst—and their complicity in creating a world in which Native Americans so easily fall into victimhood.

Upon first seeing Annawake, Jax's connection of her appearance to a "visitation" (80) takes a page from Tompkins, pointing to the common association of Native American culture with spirituality and "new age" lifestyles. Similarly, Annawake's interaction with Jax reminds the reader that Anglo culture is often seen as synonymous with material and financial security. Upon looking closely at the living conditions and listening to the story of Jax's family, she comments that she "'used to think all you needed was white skin to have an easy life'" (81). Annawake here gestures toward a critical reflection on the stereotypes that each group uses to interact with one another; Jax's response suggests the extent to which romanticism and idealizing of Native American culture is tied into Anglo thinking, noting his past desires to actually be Indian (81). Furthermore, when Jax speaks his comments are heavily littered with references to Anglo American culture, including white authors such as John Steinbeck and white actors such as James Dean. If the overwhelmingly "white" cast that Jax includes in his discussion of American culture seems natural to Anglo readers, Annawake's narration of an alternative story to explain the existence of the constellation known as the Pleiades disrupts the Anglo reader's complacency in accepting American culture as homogenous and monolithic. The difference in cultural mythologies that Jax notes leads him to conclude that the two stories, their messages, and, by extension, the values and ethics of the two groups are incompatible, that there is "no point of intersection" between the two (89). Annawake, however, clings to the hope that Jax can serve as an intermediary, a function he serves by relating Annawake's perspective to Taylor and Alice in chapter 14, "Fiat."

That chapter includes the letter written from Annawake to Jax that attempts to explain her perspective by using the personal and local to combat and complement the stereotypes and generalizations that proved so unsuccessful for them during their first meeting. The story of Annawake's twin brother, Gabe, his adoption off the reservation, and his fate (incarceration) help to convince Alice to travel to Oklahoma to talk to Annawake personally and find out the other side of the story (174).

HELP IS NOT A DIRTY WORD IN HEAVEN

The novel's theme, as noted before, is developed through a series of encounters between Annawake and the other characters. The first two encounters, with Taylor and Jax, fail to resolve anything because both of those characters conceive of independence and self-sufficiency as inherently valuable. Annawake's meeting with Alice, in the chapter "Welcome to Heaven," deliberately places the predominant perspective on social citizenship and welfare—the perspective that undergirds fundamental Anglo-American history, politics, and legal decisions—against a conception of citizenship and community that reconfigures aid, assistance, and interdependency as fundamental elements of survival.

Postpaternalist policies, specifically those that insist on greater Native self-sufficiency, foreground some of the most significant differences between Native American and Anglo-American concepts of citizenship and civic identity. Contemporary scholarship on citizenship posits three categories: civil citizenship (individual freedoms and civil rights); political citizenship (the right to vote and hold political office); and social citizenship (the equalization of economic and social standards). Social rights comprise a range of benefits, from public education, welfare, health care, mental health care, public parks and facilities, to child care, child welfare, tax breaks, and farm aid. While crises over the first two categories have for the most part abated, social citizenship still offers a challenge to contemporary societies. Nancy Fraser and Linda Gordon argue that the idea of a welfare state has been denigrated by the trend to define social rights in terms of "charity," in opposition to the rhetoric of "contract rights" that are premised on the abstract ideal of independent, equal citizens. Receiving aid, consequently, is stigmatized, and rather than an aura of dignity surrounding the idea of receiving one's (due) social rights, there is an aura of shame. The conversation between Annawake and Alice, during which the two women discuss poverty, economic dependence, and the responsibility of a community to its neediest members, reveals the divergent attitudes of white Americans and Native Americans toward the subject of social citizenship. The ethic of charity that Kingsolver suggests as critical to Native American identity conflicts with the Horatio Alger myth of individual effort and social mobility that Taylor's colleague Kevin references in the preceding chapter, "Skid Row." Though Annawake's meeting with Alice is from the beginning less antagonistic than those with Taylor and Jax, Alice's opinions still originate from within an individualistic neoliberal perspective. As Kathleen Godfrey has noted, Alice's thinking and understanding are fundamentally altered through her time in Heaven (270), but at this moment in the narrative, she has not yet seen enough to make her change her mind and feels that the inability of either party to articulate her position to the other is a fundamental failure of language, a position with which Annawake apparently concurs (232).

Annawake and Alice meet twice more, both times at the houseboat that belongs to Annawake's uncle, Ledger, the local medicine man; these meetings demonstrate the grip of racial notions of identity on the white imagination. Following a trip to the Cherokee Heritage Center, Alice, who has located her grandmother's name on the Dawes Rolls, discusses the implications of this discovery with Annawake. Though Annawake clearly states that enrollment and participation in Cherokee tribal life is open, she also differentiates between the legal and cultural definitions of Cherokee identity. Annawake's concern for Turtle stems from her phenotypical appearance as "Indian," as opposed to the lighter skin that both Alice and Taylor apparently possess. (Though Taylor's hair is described as long and straight, and the makeup artist on *Oprah* notes what "great cheekbones" (47) Taylor has, it is clear that she appears "white.") The opposing assumptions in operation for the two parties emerge forcefully in this conversation: for Annawake, the subject is really the future, whereas for Alice (and Taylor), it is the present. Annawake cannot see Alice (or Taylor) in terms of their potential for *becoming* Cherokee because of their age and their past; her thinking about Turtle is (as Godfrey and others have pointed out) centered less around Turtle's identity as a little girl and more around her future identity as Cherokee. Though the novel contains a character—the lawyer Franklin Turnbo—who represents the potential for those with Indian blood raised off-reservation to become "born-again Indian," the possibility that Turtle could be helped by drawing her mother and grandmother into Cherokee culture seems to go unconsidered (63). Perhaps this logical flaw in the novel tells us less about Cherokee culture than about the failure of the white imagination. Kingsolver's plot does not develop in this way because, despite what Sugar articulates about the ease in which Cherokee identity is assumed, Anglo-Americans believe that phenotype trumps all other factors.[5] The novel suggests that children can be molded, but that you cannot come to an ethnic or racial identity later in life.

The third private meeting between Alice and Annawake occurs when Alice realizes Annawake's role in engineering the budding romance between her and Cash, another instance of how Anglo and Native attitudes toward "help" differ. After tracking Annawake down in order to express her anger at what she perceives of as interfering in private matters of the heart, Alice accepts Annawake's admission of guilt and also her statement that she had done so on a whim. The conversation concludes with a second telling of the "pigs in heaven" story—a significant point. Why does Kingsolver, an experienced writer working with a nationally recognized publishing house, include a second telling of the story at the risk of sounding repetitious? The retelling contains a twist: this version adds a part of the story that Annawake perhaps suppressed the first time around (when telling it to Jax), suggesting that the characters in this story—regardless of racial or ethnic identification—are changing their thought processes. In this version, the mothers "grab[bed] their sons by their tails, and . . . begged the spirits to bring them back" (314). In trying to reconcile the difference between the Cherokee story about the six stars that form the constellation and the Western belief that there are seven stars, the stories merge and Annawake alters the story to account for the new perspective. The fact that the story is told a slightly different way at different times and to different audiences also reflects, to Kingsolver's credit, a sensitivity to and familiarity with the dynamism that characterizes oral cultures. Annawake, who throughout the novel has been fighting for the letter of the law, much like the mothers in the story—without duly considering the full consequences—finally opens herself up to compromise, wondering if the seven stars could possibly be "'the Six Pigs in Heaven, and the one mother who wouldn't let go'" (314). By providing a retelling of the "Pigs in Heaven" story, Kingsolver gestures toward the multiplicity of narrative truth.

THE SHOWDOWN AT THE OK LAW OFFICE

The final encounter I want to discuss occurs very close to the end of the book, when Annawake and Taylor finally meet face-to-face once more for the "showdown." Yet Annawake's voice is strangely silent here: she reads from a court decision (*Mississippi Band of Choctaw vs. Holyfield*), but states that her voice is not the important one, and that Child Welfare Services will make the decision. Annawake's silence is part of a larger pattern in this scene: Taylor, too, is less vocal than usual. When told of Cash's account of the chronology of Turtle's early years, concluding with her transfer to a "stranger in a bar north of Oklahoma City," Taylor responds that she "'can't say anything about that'" (317). Cash, likewise, sits silent in the corner of the office for a large portion of the scene. When Taylor addresses Cash directly, it is to ask about Turtle's personality, and, in particular, her speech. The final, and most difficult, speeches of the meeting involve a mutual admission of guilt: Cash, that he did not immediately go to Tulsa to claim the child, and Taylor, that she has been struggling financially to provide for Turtle (320). To Taylor's revelation, Annawake reacts with surprise but "no words" (320). The scene offers a model of receptivity in its description of characters that choose to listen rather than to speak, in marked contrast to the manifestoes, accusations, defenses, gossip, and speculation that characterize the bulk of the novel.

CONCLUSION AND COMPROMISE

In "Mission Impossible: Introducing Postcolonial Studies in the U.S. Academy," Henry Schwarz looks at (post)colonial studies as a way to investigate both uneven power relations and encounters with the Other. Schwarz describes (post)colonial studies' approach as one that "questions the violence that has often accompanied cultural interaction . . . as well as . . . provide(s) alternate models of accommodation or getting along" (5). He also acknowledges that suspicion of (post)colonial studies exists, on the grounds that it is the "bad faith effort of Western scholarship to atone for its sins of knowledge production in the service of imperialism" (6). Kingsolver seems aware of the slippery ground she occupies in co-opting Native American issues such as adoption for her own profit; her narrative emphasis on negotiation and compromise signal her awareness of the history of violence that publication of her novel threatens to perpetuate. The novel's conclusion is the culmination of the motif of compromise that permeates the book. The novel's beginning, middle, and end include places, people, and events that reference historical examples of the rigors of achieving a successful compromise and the negative consequences of a failure to reach compromise.

By opening the novel with the trip to Hoover Dam, Kingsolver establishes the key debates the narrative will negotiate, including displacement, compromise, power, and community. As a cultural artifact (and entry on the National Registry of Historic Places), Hoover Dam and the history of its construction stand for the larger national project of westward expansion, Manifest Destiny, and taming of the wilderness. When the anthropologist M. R. Harrington received funding to undertake a dig at the current site of the Hoover Dam in Nevada, he unearthed remnants of a Lost City, Pueblo Grande de Nevada. The Pueblo Indians and another group, termed the Basket-Makers, both established settlements there; what Harrington found was, as Wallace Stegner phrases it, "one cultural level on top of another, Early Pueblo sitting on Post-Basket-maker" (52). It was the Lost City that was almost completely submerged under water when Hoover Dam was built; the Lost City now lies under Lake Mead. To begin with, the construction of the Hoover Dam project required negotiations between representatives from the various western states regarding what percentage of the Colorado River's water would be allocated to which location. Herbert Hoover served as the government spokesman and helped draft the Colorado River Compact, also known as the Hoover Compromise, the official document that detailed how much water Colorado, Nevada, Arizona, and California would have access to ("Colorado River Compact"). Hoover's success at this difficult task, and his continued interest in and involvement with the dam's construction, resulted in the naming of the dam after him.[6] By opening the novel at a site that evokes the successful merger of two cultures (the Pueblo and Basket-Weavers), Kingsolver uses history as a model for the present and foreshadows the uplifting ending of the novel. The fact that the dam (and other projects of westward expansion) displaced Indian communities, however, complicates this otherwise rosy picture.

The second allusion to the history of compromise in this nation comes with the naming of the white store owner in Jackson Hole, right outside of Grand Teton National Park, as Crittenden. As a Kentucky-born writer, Kingsolver is quite likely familiar with John Crittenden, whose name is attached to various streets in Louisville. Crittenden served as a senator of Kentucky, and in 1860 the Senate selected him to work on the so-called Committee of Thirteen to attempt to avert war between the states. Crittenden helped author the Crittenden Compromise, which sought to avoid the necessity of war between the North and South by proposing several Constitutional amendments. The document opens by observing the extreme tension between the North and South and offering the compromise as a way of restoring the "peace and good-will which ought to prevail between all the citizens of the United States."[7] As with the material history of the Hoover Dam, Kingsolver's reference to the historical past here underscores the nation's continual need for individuals willing to take a broader, nonpartisan view of current events in order to offer solutions that protect the welfare of both sides. Alice herself becomes a kind of Crittenden figure in the novel. Having forged a bond with members of the Cherokee Nation, she works to facilitate Taylor's arrival in Heaven, Oklahoma.

The final compromise, of course, is the most explicit: the resolution to the problem of Turtle's legal guardianship and care that ends the novel. The conclusion of *Pigs in Heaven* does seem contrived and unnatural, in that the manipulated relationship between Alice and Cash offers an overly convenient resolution to the legal and ethical conundrum faced by the parties involved. The conclusion reverses how white readers understand guardianship and caretaking. In most divorce proceedings, custody is usually awarded to the party who will spend the most time with the child, and the other parent receives (less substantial) visitation rights. Joint or shared custody, of course, allows for both parents to spend roughly equivalent amounts of time with the child. Though Taylor and Cash's case is not that of a divorce, similar language is used. Annawake announces the tribe's decision to "go ahead and give Cash Stillwater legal guardianship of Turtle Stillwater, with the recommendation that Taylor Greer has shared custody" (338). However, when Annawake goes into more detail, it becomes clear that the "shared custody" is not equal; rather, Annawake refers to a case in Utah where the Navaho tribe "allowed the child to spend the school year with the adoptive family and summers with her grandparents on the reservation" (338–

39). She then continues to clarify that the tribe will "require the guardians to come up with a plan fairly soon that places Turtle here on the Nation at least three months out of the year" (339). This conclusion lets Anglo readers off the hook, in that they are not forced to confront the reality that legal precedent suggests the strong possibility that a woman in Taylor's situation would lose custody of a child like Turtle completely, given Cash's existence and his desire to care for Turtle. Kingsolver raises this possibility during an early conversation between Annawake and Franklin, in which Annawake cites the Supreme Court case recently decided in a tribe's favor. The illegality of Taylor's actions invalidates the adoption, but that would have occurred anyway, given Cherokee law. In the end, Taylor's life will be improved by the expanded network of help; Loretta Murrey notes that Taylor fits into the stereotype of the American loner and reads the novel as a lesson in the impossibility of raising a child without the help of a community. The opening of the novel—in which Taylor and Turtle save Lucky Buster—foreshadows Taylor's struggle with accepting the fact that she cannot raise and care for (or protect) her child alone. The way in which the community rescues Taylor is what Godfrey objects to, I suspect, in asserting that Anglo readers face little need for a readjustment of their thinking in reading the novel.

While I remain unsatisfied with the resolution of the novel, I cannot quite reconcile my reaction to *Pigs in Heaven* with the conclusions that Godfrey draws. The conclusion does mitigate the criminality of Taylor's behavior with Turtle's illegal adoption, and seemingly advocates the ends justifying the means, but readers cannot fail to note the dynamism of Taylor's character. The changes in her thinking throughout the course of the novel illustrate how many points there are on the spectrum of white-Native relations; Taylor's character offers a model for readers in that she reflects on and learns from each experience and trial, albeit not always immediately, and this growth cannot escape the reader's attention.

Additionally, I suspect that readers are capable of both empathizing with Taylor's plight and experiencing some shock that her reaction is to pull up stakes and leave Arizona to avoid the consequences of her actions. The centrality of movement and transience in the novel and the self-imposed exile Taylor experiences alert the reader to the role of place in the novel. An ironic reversal of the colonial power relations in America that resulted in the displacement of Indians occurs with Taylor's departure and is emphasized by later discussions between Annawake and Alice about the Trail of Tears.

According to Ashcroft, Griffiths, and Tiffin in *The Empire Writes Back,* the relationship between identity and place represents a special crisis of colonialism. The resolution of *Pigs in Heaven*—in which Turtle is returned to the reservation for a minimum of three months out of the year—fits into both a (post)colonial framework and into Kingsolver's vision of the importance of community, place, and belonging. Taylor's guilt, cognizant as she is that her conscience is not completely clear about the circumstances surrounding Turtle's adoption, manifests itself in this decision to uproot, an act of individual will in typically American style that reflects exactly the kind of imaginative flight from reality that Kingsolver's novel works—albeit with mixed success—to critique.

Notes

I would like to thank Priscilla Leder and Wes Berry for their helpful comments on early versions of this essay.

1. By using the term the "white imagination," I am condensing the two elements of the subtitle of Toni Morrison's book *Playing in the Dark: Whiteness and the Literary Imagination* to suggest an imagination that is influenced by American culture, history, and law to view race relations in a particular way, a way that impedes deconstructing the idea of race.

2. In my choice to put parentheses around "post" in "postcolonial," I follow Native American literary critic Chadwick Allen, who adopts this strategy in *Blood Narrative: Indigenous Identity in American Indian and Maori Literary and Activist Texts* in order to "emphasize the irony of an often-asserted post-colonial situation (where the hyphenated "post-"implies "beyond") that is never quite one for indigenous minorities" (8).

3. While it is true that both Leslie Marmon Silko and Sherman Alexie have written books that foreground adoption issues (*Garden in the Dunes* and *Indian Killer,* respectively), it is also worthwhile to note that both of them had established themselves with other, more palatable, publications first. Moreover, *Indian Killer* reads as an over-the-top spoof on the murder-mystery genre, and Alexie's critique of external adoption is thus more easily overlooked.

4. Ernesto Laclau and Chantal Mouffe argue, in *Hegemony and Socialist Strategy,* against a Kantian view of meaning as permanently rooted in human consciousness, asserting instead that meaning is based on conditions of possibility, which include political and economic factors, and that meaning is heavily reliant on its context within a particular discursive system. It is this last point that Sanborn deploys for his argument on Melville: that there was sufficient ambiguity within nineteenth-century discourses of cannibalism to allow Melville to position and advance his view of third world colonial cultures and peoples.

Jeanne Sokolowski

5. For an interesting discussion of the role of phenotype in creating Cherokee identity, see Circe Sturm's *Blood Politics: Race, Culture, and Identity in the Cherokee Nation of Oklahoma*. Sturm investigates the symbolic significance of blood in Cherokee identity but also posits the importance of other categories, including phenotype, social behavior, language, religion, and community residence/participation.

6. But not without controversy. The dam was originally to be named Hoover Dam, following a tradition of naming dams after the president in office during the construction and also acknowledging the role Hoover played in facilitating the signing of the Colorado River Compact (also known as the Hoover Compromise) in 1922. However, Hoover lost his bid for reelection, and when Roosevelt entered office, his newly appointed secretary of the interior, Harold Ickes, renamed it the Boulder Dam in all official correspondence and promotional materials. In 1947, after Roosevelt's death and Ickes's retirement, the name was changed back to Hoover Dam by Truman (Whisenhunt 120–21).

7. In short, the Crittenden Compromise suggested that slavery be abolished in the North but recognized as existing in the South and that the institution be allowed to continue without interference from Congress. The compromise, which came after four states had already seceded from the Union, failed mainly because it refused to recognize the objections to slavery and sought to reinstate the status quo as unproblematic. John Crittenden's two sons eventually fought as generals on opposite sides of the Civil War.

Imagined Geographies

Kristin J. Jacobson

Pittman, Kentucky, one of the settings for my novel, The Bean
Trees, is a very real place of the kind that can't be found on a map.
—Barbara Kingsolver, "Dialogue"

W hether the protagonists in Barbara Kingsolver's novels are leaving or returning home, their travels carefully situate them within real histories and political
geographies. Their journeys also often carry them through
and to imaginary locations. Kingsolver's decision to locate
so much of her realist fiction in invented locales has put her
literary and political reputation on the line. Scholars such
as Krista Comer, Kathleen Godfrey, and Diane Kunz con-
demn Kingsolver's fictional sites. For example, Comer faults
the "fantasy topography" (147) of Grace, Arizona, in *Animal
Dreams* for its "deracinated...deregionalized" (142) and con-
summately "ahistorical" plot (148). Building from cultural
geographer David Harvey's conception of "spatiotemporal
utopianism," this essay maps an alternative understanding
of the political efficacy of Kingsolver's controversial imagined geographies.

The analysis that follows confirms that Kingsolver's geopolitics are by no means perfect; however, Harvey's work
on utopian space helps us see how these imperfect fictional
locations grounded in present realities still provide important guides to finding approaches, if not solutions, to current
social inequities. As seen in much speculative fiction, the
fictional locales in Kingsolver's realist, political novels construct imagined, hopeful geographies that challenge the
reader to envision alternative realities. I specifically focus on
the invented locations found in three of Kingsolver's novels:

The Bean Trees, Animal Dreams, and *The Poisonwood Bible*. Much of *The Bean Trees* takes place in a fictionalized section of Tucson, Arizona. *Animal Dreams* is also set in the Southwest, in the made-up town of Grace, Arizona. Finally, significant sections of *The Poisonwood Bible* take place in an invented Congolese village. Kingsolver's landscapes, as Amanda Cockrell points out, mark and transform her characters (3). Likewise, rather than produce roadblocks to America's political consciousness, the settings' unreality is key to their political aims to mark and transform the reader.

THEORIZING PLACE: KINGSOLVER'S PROBLEMATIC AND PROMISING FICTIONAL LOCALES

The predicaments involved in the presentation of fictional locales, especially those located in the American West, are clearly articulated by Krista Comer in *Landscapes of the New West: Gender and Geography in Contemporary Women's Writing* and by Kathleen Godfrey in her article "Barbara Kingsolver's Cherokee Nation: Problems of Representation in *Pigs in Heaven*."[1] According to Comer, the uncritical "wilderness plot" found in Kingsolver's fiction "usually contains the following: a love of wide-open, 'wild' spaces; a penchant for the mystical, which is also the 'natural,' American Indian; the suggestion of redemptive possibility; a disavowal of the industrial or technological; and representations of woman as nature" (127). Describing *Animal Dreams* as a story "that could happen anywhere in the United States," Comer condemns the novel's presentation of the Southwest: "Spanish names and a paganized Catholic-American Indian ritual" mark the novel's stereotypical Southwest location (142, 143). As a result, Comer suggests that the rural "utopic and pastoral impulse available in the wilderness plot . . . [cause] the tale's progressive politics [to] implode" (149). Godfrey also argues, "Kingsolver's depiction is undercut by authorial and rhetorical practices which commodify, ritualize and idealize the Cherokee" (259). Writing about *The Poisonwood Bible*, Kimberly Koza similarly maintains the African setting and characters provide little more than local color (287–88): "Africa seems to function as a backdrop for working out essentially American concerns" (293). Given Africa's colonial histories—not to mention its present relationship with the United States—situating Africa as white women's Other produces a menacing geography.

Kristin J. Jacobson

Clearly at stake in scholars' condemnations of Kingsolver's fictional and frequently utopian settings is more than whether places like Grace, Arizona, can be located on a map. After all, while Grace, Arizona—as Kingsolver points out in *Animal Dreams*' "Author's Note"—is imaginary, the novel specifically refers to Grace's proximity to Tucson, Arizona, and Las Cruces, New Mexico. The characters' travels as well as other geographic hints locate Grace in Arizona's Catalina Mountain Range. In fact, we know that the New Mexico border is "thirty miles to the east" (57). Such geographic boundaries are not what shape scholars' objections. The presentation of the regions' cultural geographies, especially the representation of indigenous cultures, forms the debate's parameters. Both Comer and Godfrey, for instance, censure Kingsolver by linking her idealized landscapes to commodified and exoticized representations of the Southwest.[2] Additionally, Koza's claim that *The Poisonwood Bible* is primarily a novel about America, not the Congo, follows an apparent pattern of cultural appropriation begun in her earlier novels. The fact that only the white American Price women have narrative voices in the novel seems to further Koza's argument. Such fictionalized geographies at best turn indigenous cultures into local color, perpetuating hurtful, ugly stereotypes.

There are, nevertheless, compelling arguments that Kingsolver's fiction plots more than appropriated and stereotypical local color. The nature of Kingsolver's problematic and promising local geographies can be understood more fully when we look closely at the novel's spatial plots. My understanding of local space's "promise and predicament" builds from Arif Dirlik's essay "The Global in the Local." Dirlik characterizes the local as "a site both of promise and predicament" and focuses on "the local as a site of resistance and liberation" (22). Kingsolver's novels place the fictional local environment in dialogue with real national and global politics. For instance, in *The Bean Trees* the protagonist Taylor moves from the imaginary town of Pittman, Kentucky, to a fictional sanctuary for Central American refugees located in a phony Tucson district called Roosevelt Park. Grace, Arizona, the imagined setting in *Animal Dreams,* also connects a fictionalized local setting with real global concerns. Patti Capel Swartz explains Grace's struggles are not purely invented but hold many similarities with the Phelps-Dodge Arizona mining strike Kingsolver describes in her nonfiction study *Holding the Line* (Swartz 74). A band of women utilizing local knowledge and resources to beat big Capital has real precedent: "Kingsolver's early reporting of that strike that grew into a book of oral history, analysis, and

178

reporting explains much of the background information that appears in *Animal Dreams*" (Swartz 74). Furthermore, *Animal Dreams* is dedicated to Ben Linder, an Oregon engineering student who was shot by Contras while working in Nicaragua during the 1980s.

We also see connections between the fictional locale and the real global in *The Poisonwood Bible*. In *The Poisonwood Bible* the missionary Price family moves from the real community of Bethlehem, Georgia, to an imaginary rural village (Kilanga) in the Belgian Congo. (There are two cities named Bethlehem in Georgia: one located in Barrow County and another in Union.) The novel connects the Price family's American housekeeping practices with Patrice Lumumba's assassination, sharpening the connections between everyday domestic life and transnational politics. Therefore, we can begin to see that despite the fact that the local community is often an imaginary place in Kingsolver's novels, the fictional local home cannot easily be dislocated from the real global milieu.

In each of these examples from Kingsolver's novels, the global, historical backdrop—whether it is Central America or the Belgian Congo—shapes the fictional local geopolitics and vice versa. Kingsolver plots the real global alongside the fictional local domestic story as a means to situate the narratives politically and historically. From this imaginative place the fiction attempts to theorize routes out of conventional patterns. Thus, one of the significant consequences of these imaginary locales is the ability to envision a home that is specifically located within its geopolitical environment—even if it cannot be positioned by global satellites—while simultaneously crafting an imaginary geography that challenges the reader to envision alternative realities. In short, these fictional locales present what cultural geographer David Harvey calls "spatiotemporal utopias."

Spatiotemporal utopian spaces, according to Harvey, allow us to "conduct a 'thought experiment' in which we imagine how it is to be (and think) in a different situation. It says that by changing our situatedness (materially or mentally) we can change our vision of the world. But it also tells us how hard the practical work will be to get from where we are to some other situation like that" (238). Such spaces are utopian in the sense that they are literally "no place," but they are still grounded in material realities and informed by history. Utopia, derived from two Greek words, *ou* (not) and *topos* (place), literally translates as "not place" or no place. A utopia, in this sense, is a place that does not exist. Nicholas Spencer describes a similar concept, "critical space," in *After Utopia: The Rise of Critical Space in Twentieth-Century American Fiction:* "'Critical space' refers to fictionalizations of spatiality that identify, analyze, oppose, and imagine alternatives to the forms of social domination implemented by American capitalism" (10). Like the twentieth-century novels Spencer studies, Kingsolver's fiction crafts critical spaces that "imagine alternatives to . . . social domination" (Spencer 10).

Kingsolver herself articulates the idea of spatiotemporal utopias or critical space in response to a reader's question about her fictional town Pittman, Kentucky, in *The Bean Trees.* Kingsolver explains:

> Pittman, Kentucky, one of the settings for my novel, *The Bean Trees,* is a very real place of the kind that can't be found on a map. Its character and people are consistent with what you'd find in any number of small towns in the east-central part of Kentucky, including the one where I grew up. . . . So yes, Virginia, there is a Pittman, Kentucky. It exists in your heart and your imagination. So long as its truth sustains you from one page to the next, while a new way of looking at the world settles in beside your own, it's true enough. ("Dialogue")

Kingsolver addresses two key components of spatiotemporal utopias in this statement: first, she underscores a grounding in historical and present realities and, second, she addresses the ability of such critically imagined spaces to provide the reader with new, different ways of constructing reality.

The novel provides an ideal place to experiment with critical space. Of note, Harvey cites the novel as one of the key sites for such development: "The novel, as an exploration of possible worlds . . . has now become the primary site for the exploration of utopian sentiments and sensibilities" (189). Also of note, according to Harvey, is the large number of women writers doing such work (189). For Harvey, the spatiotemporal utopian novel "holds out the tantalizing prospect of an inner connection between actual historical-geographical transformations (understood with all the power that a properly constituted historical-geographical materialism can command) and the utopian design of an alternative spatiotemporal dynamics to that which we now experience" (191). Thus, the novel's ability to be grounded in but not limited by reality makes it an ideal form for this type of experimentation. While Harvey restricts his discussion to obviously utopian or speculative fictions such as Kim Stanley Robinson's trilogy about the settlement of Mars, the more 'realist utopian' fiction by Kingsolver also applies. Her fictional locations work as spatiotemporal utopias because they allow the writer to imagine and the reader to experience alternative realities. These spaces, furthermore, play a foundational role in understanding and evaluating her fiction's aesthetics and politics.

Aesthetically, it makes sense to read Kingsolver's novels as a blend of at least three genres. In addition to invoking a critical form of utopian fiction, Kingsolver's novels combine the didactic traditions of the domestic and political novels.[3] These realist traditions share the political goal of transforming the reader. Both traditions frequently rely on sentiment to achieve their aim to reform the reader. Kingsolver blends the domestic novel's focus on the domestic sphere with the political novel's activist stance. She describes her troubling of these generic boundaries in her essay "Knowing Our Place": "I write about the likes of liberty, equality, and world peace, on an extremely domestic scale" (37). The focus on local home-spaces as the primary site for Kingsolver's construction of fictional places is also significant to understanding their transformative aims and merits. Feminist geography in particular helps analyze the home in a global context.

Feminist geographers—such as Doreen Massey in "A Place Called Home"—argue the home is a frame of reference that concepts such as "transnational" or "globalization" do not elicit clearly or sometimes even outright ignore. Kingsolver's fictional locales, conversely, emphasize the global domestic sphere. They exemplify James Clifford's term "translocal," which he defines in *Routes: Travel and Translation in the Late Twentieth Century*. Linda McDowell summarizes Clifford's "new conceptualization of place" as "places where the 'culture' is a complex articulation of 'local and global processes in relational, non-teleological ways'" (209). McDowell goes on to explain, "key concepts used to refer to translocal culture and identities include hybridity, diasporic identity and cultural translation" (210). Kingsolver's fiction engages the "translocal" home and redefines conventional American domesticity's boundaries by explicitly and self-consciously locating home within national and global political contexts. These domestic sites also often highlight hybridity and mobility and serve as points of cultural negotiation and translation.

The Poisonwood Bible best illustrates Kingsolver's translocal domestic politics. The novel consciously deconstructs the traditional, supposed boundary between domestic and worldly affairs, or the notion of "separate spheres." The novel translates the connections between "masculine" domestic politics at the national and international levels and "feminine" domestic acts at the local scale. Unlike Kingsolver's earlier novels, *The Poisonwood Bible* relies on conventionally gendered space; the fictional spaces in *The Poisonwood Bible* are largely composed of a feminine domestic sphere and a masculine public sphere.[4] *The Poisonwood Bible*'s fictional domestic locales, however, do reshape our notions about how such frequently gendered spaces function and relate. One striking example occurs at the beginning of book 4, "Bel and the Serpent," where the mother Orleanna Price reflects on the 1960 political uprising in the Congo. This passage in the novel features translocal links between various levels of domestic politics.[5]

In this passage, Orleanna compares President Eisenhower's "household" to the world (320). International affairs become domestic concerns in this metaphor. A mention of Lumumba's "house arrest" quickly follows (320). Here the house becomes a literal prison, inverting home's traditional definition as a safe haven from the outside world. In the very next paragraph Orleanna refers to President Eisenhower's photograph that keeps her company in the kitchen house by providing "a beacon from home, reminding me of our purpose" (320). With another reference to Lumumba's "prison house in Léopoldville," we can see Orleanna's kitchen house is a prison as well. Enjoyable places, after all, usually do not require "a beacon from home." Furthermore, the beacon from America—an image of the president—reminds Orleanna of her "purpose." Her homemaking abroad in Africa connects her to the White House and its foreign policy. The rapid succession of homes concludes with a brief description of "household employees from the night shift on their way home to the shantytown margins of the city" (321). This final image brings *home* the economic gulf between poor household employees and rich home-owning employers.

More than deconstructive play highlighting domestic terminology's shifting and transient meanings, this passage challenges the firm division between the (masculine) public and (feminine) private spheres. The passage underscores that the "politics of home" engage local and national realms—and it questions American roles in such processes. While this passage does not necessarily challenge how space is gendered, it does question the local domestic sphere's alleged isolation from global and national events. As Homi Bhabha writes in regard to feminist criticism, this passage "results in redrawing the domestic space as the space of the normalizing, pastoralizing, and individuating techniques of modern power and police: the personal-*is*-the-political;

the world-*in*-the-home" (11). The homes Orleanna's daughters construct further demonstrate the connections between the personal and the political, especially in terms specific to white American women and globalization.

Nevertheless, as Diane Kunz points out in her essay "White Men in Africa: On Barbara Kingsolver's *The Poisonwood Bible*," the reader will not finish *The Poisonwood Bible* with an encyclopedic knowledge of the human rights violations and America's dirty dealings in the Congo. Koza concurs, "And at times her portrayal of the Congo becomes essentialized in the figure of a long-suffering, enduring Africa. As these examples suggest, Kingsolver's shift to polemic in the second part of the novel often leads her to generalize and, at times, to oversimplify historical complexities" (288). One might say readers will not get the 'real' story from this fictional location. Echoing elements of Comer's dismissal of *Animal Dreams*, Kunz argues the presentation of African and American relations demands greater complexity than the "simple morality play" Kingsolver presents in her novel (Kunz 287). She writes, "Pity the poor historian" because s/he, unlike the novelist, is bound by "Von Ranke's injunction to tell it like it really was" (Kunz 296). Telling it "like it really was," however, may not be Kingsolver's primary objective.

The choice to locate her stories in fictional locations reserves and emphasizes the unique space for fiction's truth. Imaginary geographies self-consciously emphasize fiction's manipulation of reality. Such fictional places engage the uncanny—something simultaneously strikingly correct and yet strange, unfamiliar. They represent *unheimlich,* a figurative and sometimes literal unhousing of the protagonist and reader's stable, known sense of the local sphere. Kingsolver's decision to set so much of her fiction in invented locations emphasizes her aim to engage reality while imagining a place's potential. Kingsolver's focus on Anglo protagonists, furthermore, simultaneously centers white experience and works—through her uncanny translocal settings—to decenter white privilege. Translocal space engages, complicates, and "updates a long tradition of Anglos who document and describe tribal peoples and cultures for personal gain" (Godfrey 265). Godfrey, however, argues Kingsolver's "reformist stance" is ultimately compromised due to "[h]er continuation of this tradition. . . . Their [her novels'] perpetuation of the mythic West belies their political engagement with Western issues" (265). While Godfrey and Comer maintain that Kingsolver uncritically "recycles" (to borrow Rosemary Marangoly George's terminology) these colonial story-telling practices, scholars such as Naomi Jacobs and Roberta

Rubenstein suggest that Kingsolver reinvents ritual and myth in politically productive ways.

Whether articulated by Harvey or Kingsolver, the engagement with what Harvey terms "spaces of hope" frequently meets skepticism, if not outright cynicism. Our academic and political climate often confers especially skeptical and critical analysis upon theories of optimism, hope, and community. The term "utopian," furthermore, is often considered pejorative, synonymous with unrealistic ideals and naïveté. As a result, I cannot stress enough the spatiotemporal aspect of Harvey's (and Kingsolver's) conception of "spaces of hope." This is the notion Kingsolver explains in terms of *fictional truth* that results in "a new way of looking at the world [that] settles in beside your own" (Kingsolver, "Dialogue"). There is much promise as well as predicament in these local spaces of hope. Along these lines, Deborah Clarke, referencing Jane Tompkins's work, invokes Kingsolver's sentimental politics while tempering such readings with the ways "Taylor is also forced to confront the limits of female empowerment" in *The Bean Trees* (122). Taylor's optimistic geography is fictional but not without material limitations.

IMAGINING PLACE: SKEPTICAL READINGS OF KINGSOLVER'S UTOPIAN LOCALES

In Kingsolver's case, skepticism is warranted. For example, in the problematic *Bean Trees* the protagonist Taylor forms an unconventional family whose neocolonial ramifications the author herself admits she was not fully aware of until after the novel's publication. Taylor's search for and construction of home in *The Bean Trees* is implicated in the civil rights of illegal aliens and Native Americans. Her family reflects international and national concerns. The thorny narrative involves an illegally adopted Native American child. In brief, during Taylor's travels West a woman shoves her dead sister's Native American child into Taylor's car (17–19). Telling Taylor to take the child, the woman says, "There isn't nobody knows it's alive, or cares" (18). Before Taylor can protest, she finds herself alone with the child. Deciding to take the child for the night and figure out what she should do, she goes to a hotel. While giving the child a bath, Taylor discovers the child has been horribly abused (22–23). At this point Taylor decides to keep the child, who she names Turtle. The illegal adoption mars the novel's critical cultural geography. As Mary Jean DeMarr points out, "People living in the

184

Southwest are familiar with cases of well-meaning white families adopting Native American infants who are later wanted back by their tribes" (94). Contemporary Native American writers such as Sherman Alexie and Leslie Marmon Silko focus on the stealing of Native children in their respective novels *Indian Killer* (1996) and *Gardens in the Dunes* (1999).

After publication of *The Bean Trees* Kingsolver admits,

> I realized with embarrassment that I had completely neglected a whole moral area when I wrote about this Native American kid being swept off the reservation and raised by a very loving white mother. It was something I hadn't thought about, and I felt I needed to make that right in another book. Otherwise I don't think I would want to write a sequel. I would just start from scratch. (Perry 165)

Turtle's "adoption" becomes the main focus of *Pigs in Heaven,* the unplanned sequel to *The Bean Trees.* Kingsolver apologizes for her uncritical reproduction of this colonial narrative by writing another novel; however, *The Bean Trees*'s ability to get published and its popularity arguably speak louder than Kingsolver's acts of contrition.

While she does not name Kingsolver directly, Leslie Marmon Silko characterizes and chastises this novel as a significant uncritical reproduction of white privilege in her essay "Books: Notes on Mixtec and Maya Screenfolds, Picture Books of Preconquest Mexico." Silko writes,

> Books were and still are weapons in the ongoing struggle for the Americas. Only a few years ago, a best-selling novelist breathed new life into old racist stereotypes with a portrayal of the Cherokee reservation people as pitiful drunks and child abusers whose children are better off with any white woman who comes along. Such sentiments soothe the collective conscience of white America. The subtext of such stereotypical portrayals is: Take the children, take the land; these Indians are in no condition to have such precious possessions. (155)

Silko's remarks reminds us of the need to examine carefully the idealized narratives our fictions tell and the ways in which white privilege spins an innocuous dream for some and an ongoing nightmare for others. The egregious errors committed by *The Bean Trees* pose serious questions about its specific political efficacy and the role fictional locales generally play in further whitewashing narratives.

While racist errors in her early fiction undermine her progressive political goals, these novels still accomplish important political work. Kingsolver's *The Bean Trees* and *Pigs in Heaven* follow Taylor Greer's travels from rural Kentucky to the outskirts of Tucson, Arizona—along the way bridging the geographical as well as cultural distances between the Appalachian South and Greater America. In other words, this South-to-West movement in Kingsolver's Western writing makes it a prime candidate for the examination of what José E. Limón calls in *American Encounters* "a set of 'unsuspected relationships' between the U.S. South and Greater Mexico" (9). In fact, Kingsolver's oeuvre expands such "unsuspected relationships" and covers territory best described as Greater America.[6] Kingsolver's Greater America articulates both fictional and real "imagined communities," revealing surprising geopolitical relationships.[7] Kingsolver's novels transcend or defy real state and national boundaries, connecting the United States with Africa, for instance. Her translocal Greater America attempts to envision local settings where cultures collide in ways not always predicated on violence.

The Bean Trees and *Pigs in Heaven* attempt to map such positive cross-cultural communities that reflect contemporary Greater America. For instance, the topography of Roosevelt Park in *The Bean Trees*—like Grace, Arizona, in *Animal Dreams*—is fictional. Unlike Grace, however, Roosevelt Park is urban and more culturally diverse. Jesus Is Lord Used Tires, a tire repair shop/sanctuary for Central American refugees, sits just around the corner from a Chinese grocery (30). The porn shop Fanny Heaven hunkers between the tire shop and grocery. Lou Ann, a Kentucky native married to local Mexican American Angel Ruiz, lives in one of the houses across the street from the market and city park. Lou Ann keeps a clip file of Hispanic bank presidents to show her racist family back home that "[i]n Tucson . . . there were so many Mexicans that people didn't think of them as a foreign race. They were doctors, bank clerks, TV personalities, and even owned hotels" (27). Traveling from rural Appalachian (and fictional) Pittman, Kentucky, the spunky protagonist Taylor Greer arrives with her "adopted" daughter Turtle, a Cherokee Indian girl, at the crossroads of America. Taylor's interactions with two Guatemalan refugees, furthermore, stress the Greater American connections. While the hodge-podge of characters and cultures seem a bit fantastic, Roosevelt Park is not the cultural backwaters of commodified multiculturalism. The subplot between Taylor and the Guatemalan refugees Estevan and Esperanza is a case in point. While there are moments, just as in *Animal Dreams,* where these characters need to be and perhaps should be better developed, this text, which is primarily about Taylor and Turtle's relationship, educates a largely unaware American reading public about the plight of indigenous peoples in South and Central America.

Estevan and Esperanza's specific tragedy involves their daughter, Ismene. Estevan explains that she was kidnapped and her uncles and two friends were murdered in a raid. The uncles and friends along with Estevan were all members of the teachers' union. Estevan clarifies: "'Esperanza and I knew the names of twenty other union members,' he said. 'The teachers' union did not have open meetings. We worked in cells, and communicated by message. . . . In Guatemala, you are careful. If you want to change some thing you can find yourself dead . . . '" (136). Instead of bargaining for their daughter with the names of the other union members, Estevan and Esperanza flee the country. Turtle reminds them of their lost daughter. When Taylor fears that she may lose Turtle because she did not legally adopt her, Estevan and Esperanza agree to help. Taylor, in turn, helps smuggle them to another sanctuary in the United States when immigration threatens to deport Estevan and Esperanza back to Guatemala.

Estevan and Esperanza's lack of legal papers to document their need for exile in the United States parallels Turtle's story. As Mattie, the owner of Jesus Is Lord Used Tires, explains to Taylor, "Their own say-so is no good; they have to have hard proof. Pictures and documents . . . [however]. When people run for their lives they frequently neglect to bring along their file cabinets of evidence" (159). Thus it is not surprising that Estevan and Esperanza agree to pose as Cherokee parents giving up their child to Taylor for adoption. Mr. Jonas Wilford Armistead and Mrs. Cleary at the clerk's office in Oklahoma City, Oklahoma, are none the wiser; the shared brown skin seemingly provides enough evidence: "Even though they were practically standing on it, Mr. Armistead and Mrs. Cleary seemed to think of 'tribal land' as some distant, vaguely civilized country. . . . It was enough that I [Taylor], a proven citizen with a Social Security card, was willing to swear on pain of I-don't-know-what (and sign documents to that effect) that they were all who they said they were" (214). Taylor's documented citizenship seems enough to make here a suitable parent. Ironically, Kingsolver consciously uses white privilege against the system to obtain the illegal adoption in this passage, and yet the novel still fails to consider fully the implications of Taylor's guardianship of the Native American child.

The story's sentimental, utopian, and political plot encourages readers to consider their views of illegal aliens, the role of the American government abroad, and the definition of family. The formal scene of giving away "their" daughter to Taylor proves to be a "catharsis" for Estevan and Esperanza, helping them deal with the loss of their real daughter (220). The catharsis produced by Turtle's fake adoption and the formation of Taylor and Turtle as a stable family unit fulfills the conclusion preferred by the conventional domestic novel. Significantly, in this regard, Taylor and Turtle end *The Bean Trees* by going home to Lou Ann. While the women are not lesbians, their compassionate relationship exhibits both commitment and affection. Their redesigned family structure is as inventive and hopeful as the joint custody agreement at the conclusion of *Pigs in Heaven*.

The Bean Trees's optimism continues in *Pigs in Heaven*. The novel's resolution to the conflict between individual (represented by Taylor) and community needs (represented by the Cherokee Nation), as Gioia Woods points out, sent reviewers in a frenzy, splintering them into the two camps: "Some critics appreciated Kingsolver's clear vision, while others felt the author relied on a pat formula of sentimental political correctness" (Woods). In simple terms, the narrative resolves Turtle's disputed guardianship by making Cash Stillwater, Turtle's biological grandfather, her legal guardian. But that is not the whole council decision. The recommendation includes shared custody for Taylor. Cash at this point is also engaged to Taylor's mother, Alice Greer. Like the ending of Shakespeare's *Twelfth Night,* the characters end up in fortuitous pairs. Fiercely independent Taylor finds love with the cowboy Jax, and Alice, who said, "I don't want another husband that's glued to his everloving TV set," is set to marry Cash after he publicly shoots his TV (340). The Native American lawyer, Annawake, is not paired off; however, she is not Malvolio in the end seeking revenge. When Annawake's brother suggests that all she needs in her life to make her happy is a man, Annawake retorts, "men are just not necessarily always the solution" (333). The novel suggests implicitly that her "solution" is to continue to work for the Cherokee Nation on difficult cases like Turtle's custody hearing, fighting to devise viable resolutions to no-win situations.

As Ralph E. Rodriguez argues in his essay "*Men with Guns:* The Story John Sayles Can't Tell," some stories can be valuable for simply making people better aware of the multifaceted politics that surround them—even if the cost of this recognition demands exclusions and simplifications. Rodriguez writes, "It is disappointing that this film fails to implicate the United States for its role in shattering the lives of innumerable Latin Americans. But this failure doesn't vitiate the power of the story Sayles does tell. . . . While *Men With Guns* won't necessarily help the noninitiate know where to direct their anger, it can't help but outrage them, and that's a start" (172–73). Rodriguez examines the productive and problematic aspects of this local text and its global connections. Along these same lines, at least readers will leave *The Bean Trees* and *Pigs in Heaven* having confronted some of the issues involved in cross-racial adoption, particularly for Native Americans. Similarly, readers who perhaps could not locate the Belgian Congo or Guatemala on a map will hopefully leave the imaginary terrain of Kilanga or Roosevelt Park with a more translocal consciousness, connecting and coming to a better understanding of the ways in which our local domestic activities have global implications.

The utopian nature of *Animal Dreams* also opens it to criticism. Linking idealized landscapes to commodified and exoticized representations of the Southwest, Comer describes the novel's "flight from *urban* history" (Comer 151): "By manufacturing an artificial and rural place against which to test ecofeminist politics, *Animal Dreams* drafts environmental policy for areas that are distant from most southwesterners' actual homes" (Comer 148). Surely, the rural Grace, Arizona, is *like no place* on earth. Pushing on the sense of utopia as a "no place," we can also read Grace as an example of what Harvey terms "spatiotemporal utopianism": a "dialectical utopianism—that is rooted in our present possibilities at the same time as it points towards different trajectories of human uneven geographical development" (196). Grace does not exist, but Kingsolver tries to ground this no place in present material conditions.

Emphasizing Grace's productive features figures a rural Southwest utopia that imagines and represents the local as a burgeoning place—a region seeped in the processes of recovering and remembering the past, coping with the present as well envisioning a hopeful future. As Meredith Sue Willis writes in "Barbara Kingsolver, Moving On," the local in *Animal Dreams* is not ultimately an escape from reality:

> . . . this is a novel that is in some sense a dream of how a poor
> community might, and sometimes does, join together to take

control of its future. . . . This kind of idealization, unlike the love
affairs in some popular fiction, is not an escape from reality but
a fictional consideration of what people really want—in a lover,
in a community—no small thing in our disenfranchised and
frightening era. (83)

Willis suggests, like Harvey, that idealized representations of nature and communities do not have to be regarded as dangerous flights from geopolitical realities. In fact, they are needed maps for our contemporary culture. Like speculative fiction, Willis implies, *Animal Dreams* explores the question "what if?"

Simplicity also figures into the analysis of Kingsolver's fictional sites. Scholars express frustration with the narratives' simplicity. Faulting *Animal Dreams* for its uncomplicated depiction of environmental problems, Comer writes: "In Grace, the good guys and the bad guys, the environmental battle lines themselves, are simple. It's a 'poor folks against Capital' econarrative, with feminist nuance and primitivist flavor" (148). More often than not in the real world the battle lines between "good" and "evil" are not so clearly discernable. As a novel attempting to appeal to a mass audience while simultaneously juggling at least four central plot lines, however, something must give. Amidst Codi's search for her roots, Hallie's struggle in Nicaragua, and Doc Homer's (Codi's and Hallie's father) advancing Alzheimer's, Grace's environmental struggle is unapologetically painted in broad strokes. Additionally, Kingsolver's conservative rhetoric allows her to "set up explicit goals and . . . to reach these goals by direct precept and example" (Guth 30). Conservative, black or white rhetorical practices have the advantage and predicament of not dealing with shades of gray.

While the eco-politics in Kingsolver's early novels are crafted in simplified terms, other important themes are fleshed out in more complex and intricate ways. Dreams, memory, history, and myth saturate *Animal Dreams* and complicate our understanding of the econarrative. For example, the protagonist Codi does not remember her childhood, and she has problems distinguishing her dreams from events that really happened. Early in the novel she admits: "This is my problem—I clearly remember things I haven't seen, sometimes things that never happened. And draw a blank on the things I've lived through" (48). Juxtaposed against her 'amnesia' is her father's progressing Alzheimer's. Additionally, Doc Homer has the unusual hobby of making "photographs of things that didn't look like what they actually were.

He had hundreds: clouds that looked like animals, landscapes that looked like clouds" (69–70). Codi interprets his art in relation to memory and history: "All his photographs begin in his memory. That is the point. He might be the only man on earth who can photograph the past" (138). Additionally, from these local, personal examples emerges a larger, national forgetting: "That's the great American disease, we forget," says Codi (316). This palimpsest of history and memory questions stable, traditional notions of history and reality.

Addressing other themes like history and memory well does not excuse the more simplistic econarrative present in *Animal Dreams;* however, thinking about the ways in which history and memory impinge on the econarrative complicates our interpretation of it. Additionally, when our reading of Grace's local landscape seriously considers a non-Western framework on its own terms, with its own viable traditions, our understanding of Grace's spatiotemporal utopianism enters a discrete context, a different way to understand wilderness. In doing so, we do not fly from (Western) history but rather engage with another historical and cultural context, albeit not the dominant one. Discussing the feminine landscape in Leslie Marmon Silko's *Ceremony,* Paul Gunn Allen summarizes a non-Western "wilderness plot": "We are the land. To the best of my understanding, that is the fundamental idea that permeates American Indian life; the land (Mother) and the people (mothers) are the same. . . . The land is not really a place, separate from ourselves, where we act out the drama of our isolate destinies" (127–28). Instead of locating Grace within dominant history, what happens if we imagine this place as engaged with and representative of an alternative locale and history? Sheryl Stevenson, Roberta Rubenstein, and Naomi Jacobs all emphasize myth and ritual's significance to *Animal Dreams.* In view of this alternative understanding, Grace, Arizona, maintains spatiotemporal specificity while simultaneously offering a different, albeit sometimes simplified, version of reality. Yet faced with a Western history of idealized wilderness—a history implicated in the exploitation of the Southwest—what value, if any, could such utopian or mythical space serve?

The value of spatiotemporal utopian spaces, according to David Harvey, is that they allow us "to conduct a 'thought experiment'" (238). In this light, while Grace represents a rural Arizona town—an environment apart, as Comer reminds us, from the local experiences of most southwesterners— the narrative still holds imaginary potential, especially when we consider that Grace is not isolated completely from the urban or global. For example, the subplot of Hallie's activist work in Nicaragua—to paraphrase Codi—brings *home* the TV disasters that Americans so quickly forget (316). Jacobs clarifies, "Dismantling one set of myths, Kingsolver begins to construct another, based in an optimistic vision of a cooperative and sustainable multicultural community in which men and women work together toward common goals" (par. 16). While Kingsolver's optimism is sometimes credited with her popular success, it has not earned her universal acclaim.

We also see the ambivalent "promise and predicament" of these optimistic spaces in the initial chapters Codi narrates in *Animal Dreams* (Dirlik 22). In the second chapter, Codi nostalgically describes Grace's timelessness. Returning home after a fourteen-year absence, she describes the dearth of urban geography: "Grace hadn't yet entered the era of parking meters, for example. There were iron rings mortared into the block wall of the courthouse where a person could tie a horse" (11). Codi is also responsible for the description of Grace that Comer holds up as quintessentially "classic" local color of the worst sort (Comer 143). In this passage, Codi waxes eloquent about Grace's "shamelessly unpolluted sky" and of "houses . . . built in no big hurry back when labor was taken for granted" (8). Such passages highlight the local's predicament as a site that can be nostalgically produced in the service of a global economy that profits from the existence of untrammeled wilderness. Still, consider Grace's potential as a place *named* a "reprieve," or "temporary immunity or exemption" ("Grace" def. 6). This special and blessed space *zones* hope.

Of note, in this same chapter during her first nostalgic trip through town Codi mistakes a piñata for a real peacock, going so far as to yell at the children to stop killing the bird before she realizes her mistake (15). As the closing scene of the second chapter, this passage calls into question Codi's previous romanticized observations about Grace, especially after it is revealed the town's river is polluted. Additionally, strategic passages that critique southwestern kitsch like the lobby of the Las Cruces Holiday Inn also distinguish Grace from the commodified southwestern environment: "The bar was done up in this madly cheerful south-of-the-border décor. . . . It was somebody's idea of what Old Mexico would look like if you didn't have to take poverty into account" (68). Cracks about the "Barrio Volvo" and "gentrified adobe neighborhoods" found in cities like Tucson divide—or at least attempt to divide—Grace from commodified locations (263).

When Codi's powers of observation improve within a few days, moreover, she realizes Grace has changed, shaped by external and internal economic forces: "Drinking establishments had proliferated in Grace since my day. The mine had closed in the interim, of course; bars and economic duress are common fellow travelers" (57). Grace has a dark underbelly as well. And when Codi and her high school biology class discover the town's river supply has been poisoned—endangering Grace's fruit orchards—big money threatens the only remaining local means of production. Grace's skies may appear clear, but hidden toxins abound. The passages mark Codi's developing powers of observation. The reader is brought through this changed perception of the local geography with Codi.

Our understanding and evaluation of Grace is not only impacted by the story's engagement with history and the environment; racial relations also play key roles in the construction of place. The seemingly ahistorical and oversimplified econarratives get connected with the purportedly abecedarian ways in which *Animal Dreams* deals with race and ethnicity (Comer 149). Without a doubt, race relations in Grace are ideal: "By the time people elsewhere were waking up to such ideas as busing, everyone in Grace had pretty much given up on claiming a superior pedigree" (57). In fact, the sisterhood Codi uncovers and eventually cultivates in Grace is literal. As it turns out, the women in the novel are all related, able to trace their roots back to a family of eight Spanish sisters. As mentioned previously, one of the subplots in the novel is Codi's recovery of her roots. When she returns home, she believes she is returning to a place where she has always been an outsider—someone different who moved to Grace with her family from Illinois. The recovery of Codi's family and ethnic heritage—her connection to the Gracela sisters who traveled from Spain to the Arizona territory to marry gold miners—unearths a local history everyone who knew about it actively repressed.

As it turns out, one of the Gracela sisters married into the wrong family and "produced a legacy of trash—that was my father's family" (260). Codi's mother defies her family by marrying Doc Homer, a descendant of this family from the wrong side of the tracks, and leaving Grace. Eventually, however, Codi's family returns, but Grace's other families do not publicly recognize their connections. Codi—prior to discovering her family's Spanish roots—believes she is Anglo. She is culturally Anglo. Discussing land use practices with Loyd, Codi's Apache-Navajo-Pueblo boyfriend, Codi says, "The way they tell it to us Anglos, God put the earth here for us to use, westward-ho. Like a special little playground" (240). Her perception of herself as an Anglo is her own, however, not the community's; they know her ethnic roots.

A key problem with the narrative of Codi's roots and the town's history is that it does not complicate the notion of *"puro"* Spanish blood and the decision to trace Grace's history through Spain: when Codi discovers her heritage, she exclaims, "We're *puro*" (284). In my research, I was unable to find information about the practice of Spanish women coming to the Arizona territory as brides. This story sounds more like the *puro* Spanish "fantasy heritage" historians such as Carey McWilliams discuss regarding status within the Hispanic community. In this light, the Gracela story offers *puro* local color to the discovering-one's-roots story. The portrayal of Loyd Peregrina is often equally problematic for the ways it sometimes relies on Native American stereotypes: "Loyd lay with his head propped on his elbow. . . . With his finger he traced concentric circles around my breasts, and triangles on my abdomen, as if warpainting me for some ceremonial mission" (130). As the above examples illustrate, the depiction of ethnicity is not the novel's strongest feature.

However, as Meredith Sue Willis points out, "We are in an imaginary world here but one that is neither stupid nor innocent" (86). The roots Codi finds in Grace, Arizona, are real and deep—grounded in the region's folk culture. Where Comer labels Kingsolver's use of rituals and folklore "exotica" (Comer 144), Raymund A. Paredes, writing about *Bless Me, Ultima* in his article "Contemporary Mexican-American Literature, 1960–Present," offers another lens in which to read geographies infused with myth and ritual: "Like other Mexican-American writers, Anaya creates a distinctive cultural ambience primarily through the use of folklore. (The language of *Bless Me, Ultima,* except for an occasional word or phrase, is conventional English)" (1109). Authors like Pam Houston, Sandra Cisneros, and Louise Erdrich, on the other hand, "[refuse] emplotment by the wilderness ideal . . . [which] grows from [their] interest in representing women and female desire in nonexotic or mystical terms" (Comer 193). Myth quickly seems to become a naughty word in some critical vocabulary. And while I agree mythic or fictional geographies can create dangerous discursive terrain—crossing the line between folklore and stereotypical local color—I am reluctant to throw these elements out with the contaminated depictions of the Southwest. In the words of Oscar Wilde, "A map of the world that does not include Utopia is not even worth glancing at" (par. 24). We need contemporary myths and utopian maps.

The critical tendency to spurn the invocation of mythical or spiritual place is not limited to Kingsolver's fiction. Geoffrey Bent, for instance, claims that Toni Morrison in *Paradise* "undermines her talent for characterization by making the protagonist a place for a piece of real estate to have a personality" (Bent 149). Bent, along with other reviewers, especially takes issue with *Paradise*'s magical elements. His criticism also could have easily been addressed to *Beloved* and its haunted house. Bent hypothesizes that the reason so many contemporary novels rely on magic is because "Magic gives the homeliest of settings a spiritual aura, while also affording the author a convenient means of realigning the drama when needed (a *dues ex machina* in a world without *Deus*)" (147). Do spiritual or utopian, unreal geographies necessarily render a novel's politics problematic? Morrison's spiritual geographies—like Kingsolver's fictional locations at their best—historicize and bring home the "racial project" of moving "the job of unmattering race away from pathetic yearning, and futile desire; away from an impossible future or an irretrievable and probably nonexistent Eden to a manageable, doable, modern human activity" (Morrison, "Home" 3–4). When geopolitically situated, these fictional spaces provide real maps or "thought experiments" that can help theorize solutions to geopolitical inequalities. Patricia McKee, for example, explains that Morrison's spatial politics in *Paradise* work to "replace" or "refill" space (205). While McKee insists *Paradise* "resist[s] utopian constructions," her description of the novel's spatial politics follows Harvey's conception of a utopianism grounded in space and time. Situated mythic or spiritual geographies can provide necessary "spaces of hope."

Kingsolver does not craft every representation "right," but she is critically engaged and responsible for the representations of people and cultures she creates. For example, Kingsolver's public admission of her first novel's mistakes and the decision to write another novel to try to mend those errors took courage and integrity. Kingsolver also established the Bellwether Prize, which "supports 'a Literature of Social Change'" ("About Barbara"). Thus, while fictional reality can often be an escape, it can also be a means to experience reality differently, to try out another reality that can impact our real lives for the better. The story Kingsolver does tell critiques American exceptionalism. Through the process of reading her novels, American exceptionalism becomes a misnomer or false landmark in the text's and hopefully the reader's cultural geography. Readers, like Taylor, consider for the first time terms like "illegal alien" and its implications. As Taylor says, "A human being can be good or bad or right or wrong, maybe. But how can you say a person is illegal?" (*Bean Trees* 195). Making readers better aware of their own location in and means of navigating the world is a start—a start that does not cancel the novel's political consciousness or its fictional representation of reality.

One scene in particular from *The Poisonwood Bible* self-consciously underscores Kingsolver's thinking about fictional locations. When the Price women in *The Poisonwood Bible* attempt to return to Kilanga in the novel's final chapter, they cannot cross the border, and a local merchant tells them no such village exists, challenging what they thought they knew (540–42). In this scene the merchant may simply be trying to protect the village from outsiders. Additionally, geographies shift frequently in the novel, reflecting the current forces in power. One of the Price women, Leah, explains,

> You can't go to Léopoldville now, or to Stanleyville, Coquilhat- ville, or Elisabethville. The names of all those conquerors (and their ladies) have been erased from our map. For that matter you can't even go to the Congo; it's Zaire. We repeat these words as if we're trying to memorize a false identity: I live in Kinshasa, Zaire. The places we've always used to position ourselves are suddenly unfamiliar—cities, villages, even rivers. (445)

Leah emphasizes the premature nature of the name changes that "erase" colonialism and colonial history: they feel "false." She also emphasizes how her environment has been made strange by these sociopolitical changes. Perhaps, in this light, their old village's name changed, too.

When Leah presses the woman in the market the woman unflinchingly insists, "There is no such village. The road doesn't go past Bulungu. There is only a very thick jungle there, where the men go to make charcoal. She is quite sure. There has never been any village on the road past Bulungu" (542). Novelistically, the passage functions to remind readers that Kilanga, the village where the Price family lived, is not a real place. The merchant's curious claim perplexes and forces the reader and the characters to question truth's construction in the novel. Does her saying the town does not exist make it so? The merchant's remarks especially require the reader to contemplate the reality of the narrative. If this place does not exist, what do we make of the characters' experiences? This process of distancing the reader and, in this instance, the characters, from home—from a stable sense of one's past and location—highlights fictional geographies' uncanny role. This imaginary geography self-consciously emphasizes fiction's manipulation of realty, representing the *unheimlich*—or the figurative and sometimes literal unhousing of the protagonists and reader's stable sense of the local.

CONCLUSIONS: IMAGINED GEOGRAPHIES FOR A GREATER AMERICA

Kingsolver's fiction maps alternative geographies in both politically successful and unsuccessful ways. When successful, her fiction raises awareness about a variety of political issues in a wide range of readers. *Pigs in Heaven,* for instance, is available in Spanish, and *"The Bean Trees* has been published in more than sixty-five countries around the world" ("Barbara Kingsolver"). Barbara Kingsolver's official HarperCollins Web site, furthermore, boasts that *The Bean Trees* is available in a low-cost, mass-market format and can be found in local grocery checkout lines and drugstores ("Update"). In fact, Kingsolver describes her writing as a negotiation between university instructors and her relatives: "I have a commitment to accessibility. I believe in plot. I want an English professor to understand the symbolism while at the same time I want one of my relatives—who's never read anything but the Sears catalogue—to read my books" (See 47). If poets truly are, as Percy Bysshe Shelley writes in "A Defense of Poetry," the "unacknowledged legislators of the world," the poet and fiction writer Kingsolver aims to carry on this tradition. She maintains it is her job to, "[w]ell, to change the world. . . . It's like absolute heresy for an artist to say that. That's why I say it" (Epstein 37). Her imagined geographies play key aesthetic and political roles in accomplishing this goal.

Kingsolver's critics remind us of the necessity to be critical of utopian-fictional geographies, especially when they do not fully consider material and historical realities. David Harvey recognizes that those who imagine or otherwise engage in utopian constructions of space must eventually confront material realities: "Any contemporary struggle to envision a reconstruction of the social process has to confront the problem of how to overthrow the structures (both physical and institutional) that the free market has itself produced as relatively permanent features of our world" (186). Kingsolver's imagined geographies consciously confront the status quo—even as they sometimes unwittingly reproduce it. Harvey also stresses that to navigate material reality we need utopian maps based in spatiotemporal realities. Kingsolver actively produces such maps. A reluctance to value her utopian narratives may stem from their failure to reveal consistently white privilege's machinations. Those fault lines represent key, but not the only, aspects of Kingsolver's fictional geographies and fictional locales' place and value more broadly in American literature.

The clear and present danger that comes with a dearth of imagined geographies is a rampant cynicism that can envision no way out. Some suburban fiction epitomizes this trap, such as John Updike's *Rabbit Redux* (1971), with its cynical protagonist, Harry Angstrom. This perspective often rationalizes uneven geographic development and its consequences as a kind of natural selection, or simply the way things are. A lack of fictional utopian spaces creates a void. Thus, spatiotemporal utopian representations remain not only politically viable but also important visions in "our disenfranchised and frightening era" (Willis 83). Kingsolver's frequent use of imagined geographies prompts critical recognition and analysis of fictional space in American literature. She joins several major American authors who utilize fictional geographies. William Faulkner's Yoknapatawpha County perhaps represents American literature's most well-known fictional geography. Contemporary writers joining this tradition include Toni Morrison and Louise Erdrich. Locations near or in the fictional town of Argus, North Dakota, provide the setting for much of Erdrich's fiction. Morrison developed two fictional all-black towns in *Paradise,* Haven and Ruby, Oklahoma. For better and sometimes for worse and hopefully for richer, not poorer, understanding, Kingsolver participates in the project of constructing imaginary places.

Alongside the consideration of Kingsolver's historical and cultural accuracy, we need to examine how the idea of place—a shifting geography across time in the novels—changes the characters' and readers' worldviews. Rooted in time and space but imaginative and utopian all the same, Kingsolver's fictional American geographies at their best are "hope fulfilled, transcending outworn concepts of race, gender, and nation, and restricted versions of sexuality for better forms of social struggle toward the pure relationship" (Limón 213). They are "a symbolic prelude to an eventual resolution" (213). By creating critically imagined places Kingsolver aims to change her reader's mental map, the internal geography of the heart. As Joseph R. Urgo writes about Faulkner's Yoknapatawpha, Kingsolver's fictional geographies "may be less a place than a perspective, less significant for mapping a landscape than for mapping a mode of consciousness" (639). Fictional geographies visualize for the reader the ways in which history, geography, and identity converge. Kingsolver's specific fictional locations attempt to join the fractured consciousnesses of Greater America and map a series of utopian but certainly not perfect places with real histories, cultures, and ethics.

Notes

1. See Comer 124–31.
2. For an overview of texts considered feminist utopian writing, see Anne Cranny-Francis's chapter "Feminist Utopias" in *Feminist Fiction: Feminist Uses of Generic Fiction* (1990). This chapter contains a brief overview of the history of this genre.
3. Kingsolver is known for crafting spunky, independent women that challenge women's traditional gender roles and women's place within the domestic sphere: for example, Taylor Greer (*The Bean Trees* and *Pigs in Heaven*), Codi Noline (*Animal Dreams*), Leah Price (*The Poisonwood Bible*), and Deanna (*Prodigal Summer*).
4. See *The Poisonwood Bible* 317–24, esp. 320–21.
5. Limón gets the term from Américo Paredes. In Limón's introduction: "I am following the lead of Américo Paredes (and not for the first time), who coined the term Greater Mexico to refer to 'all the areas inhabited by people of a Mexican culture—not only within the present limits of the Republic of Mexico but in the United States as well—in a cultural rather than a political sense'" (215n1).
6. I wish to invoke the practice of "remapping American studies." See Limón and José David Saldívar (*Border Matters: Remapping American Cultural Studies*).

Kristin J. Jacobson

Earthbound Rhetoric and Praxis: Authentic Patriotism in a Time of Abstractions

Wes Berry

Bespectacled, wearing faded jeans and a purple T-shirt, holding a basket of tomatoes, Barbara Kingsolver stands with her two daughters and husband. The youngest daughter holds a wire basket of eggs; the oldest daughter, a basket of peppers; the husband, three huge vegetables that resemble onions. The arms and hands of the middle-aged parents reveal a musculature sculpted by physical labor. This image decorating the dust jacket of Kingsolver's newest book, *Animal, Vegetable, Miracle: A Year of Food Life,* recalls Thomas Jefferson's democratic ideal: a self-sufficient and independent household economy, representing a nation in which authentic freedom and independence grows from the land and from the stewards who farm it. Although Jefferson's ideal has fallen apart in the United States, with less than 1 percent of approximately 300 million people currently engaged in agriculture, revolutionaries like the Kingsolver-Hopp family are gradually reconstructing Jefferson's agrarian ideal by growing their own food, building support for small-scale independent farmers, and promoting local food economies. In the dust-jacket photo, Barbara Kingsolver stands in the foreground as an icon of successful motherhood, accompanied by her family, each member appearing healthy and hardworking. This is the kind of image politicians and preachers have in mind when they talk about "family values." It is therefore surprising that Bernard Goldberg, in his book *100 People Who Are Screwing Up America,* lists Kingsolver at #73. How can an advocate of environmental justice, human rights, and sustainable living who practices what she preaches—donating royalties from her book *Small Wonder* to Physicians for Social Responsibility, Habitat for Humanity, Environmental Defense, and Heifer International—earn a spot on a list that includes voices of intolerance like white supremacist David Duke, slipping in ahead of Kingsolver at position #66?

Goldberg's stated reason for listing Kingsolver involves her "America bashing" in an op-ed piece published in the *San Francisco Chronicle* on 25 September 2001. In this newspaper article, Kingsolver critiques patriotic sentiment in the United States following the demolition of the World Trade Center towers two weeks earlier. Feeling uneasy that her daughter's school prompted students to wear red, white, and blue as a sign of solidarity, Kingsolver questions the gesture, fearing that her taxes and children are being enlisted to answer death with more death. Goldberg calls Kingsolver's dissent "a kind of knee-jerk paranoia about a dark and dangerous America that is way too common among her kind" (106). By "her kind," Goldberg is referring to what he calls "today's cultural-elite liberals" who he describes as "snooty, snobby know-it-alls, who have gotten angrier and angrier in recent years and who think they're not only smarter, but also *better* than everyone else, especially everyone else who lives in a 'Red State'" (x). Using generic labels like "liberal" and "conservative" to describe the political divide in the United States does not adequately illustrate the complexities of individual people. Nevertheless, it seems plausible that Kingsolver appears on Goldberg's list because her "liberal" ideals offend his "conservative" ones. Such an explanation relies on the popular dualisms embedded in our religious and political language—body/soul, earth/heaven, black/white, Muslim/Christian, red state/blue state—and is therefore ultimately reductive and unsatisfactory. The schism between the political right and left is difficult to ignore in this conflict, however; and thus I want to understand better why the right views Kingsolver with such suspicion.[1] By evaluating the rhetorical strategies Kingsolver employs in her essays, one sees more clearly why Goldberg and other people who define "patriotism" as devotion to an abstraction (a flag, a political organization) feel challenged by Kingsolver's brand of dissent. More to the point, Kingsolver appropriates and revises so-called conservative values in order to put forth her own ideas about what patriotism and democracy should look like. For example, Kingsolver applies the language and imagery of religion—for a while now the purview of voters on the conservative right—to the process of natural selection, thereby challenging those who view evolution as antithetical to divine Creationism. Furthermore, she presents a model of good citizenship that rejects the concept of acquisition as an indicator of growth in favor of the nonacquisitive and self-sufficient individualism of Henry David Thoreau; and she redefines patriotism as loyalty to a particular place rather than as slavish devotion to an abstraction. In short, Kingsolver threatens Goldberg and his cronies because of the ways in which she revises and redefines concepts dear to the political right in favor of her own vision, which is arguably just as much in the American grain as theirs.

In 1974, Ezra Taft Benson, an outspoken Christian leader who served as U.S. secretary of agriculture during Eisenhower's administration, published *God, Family, Country: Our Three Great Loyalties,* encapsulating in his title the patriotic imperative evoked by these three words. Likewise, in the country song "God, Family and Country," Craig Morgan sings about a member of the "Greatest Generation" who fought for his country in a time when "[t]here was no gray, only black and white," a man who knew the difference between wrong and right "'Cause he had God, Family, and Country." Kingsolver addresses each of these concepts in her writing, often challenging the traditional dualistic sentiments attached to them, which in part explains why an American apologist like Goldberg finds her dissent offensive.

For example, religious conservatives may take offense at how Kingsolver borrows sacred language to describe commonplace things, like food, breaking the "spiritual" out of the abstract by grounding it in earthly life. In the foreword to Norman Wirzba's essay collection *The Essential Agrarian Reader,* Kingsolver calls agrarian living—"the decision to attend to the health of one's habitat and food chain"—a "spiritual choice," extending the "spiritual" beyond the sacred texts and the church house to the actual living world (xvii). In *Animal, Vegetable, Miracle,* she points out that while our culture accepts religious reasons for accepting or declining certain foods—for instance, the rabbi who refuses to eat pork—we have not yet accepted spiritual and moral reasons for refusing food whose production and transport wastes energy, poisons agricultural workers, and destroys the land. "Is it such a stretch," she asks, "to make moral choices about food based on the global consequences of its production and transport? In a country where 5 percent of the world's population glugs down a quarter of all the fuel, also belching out that much of the world's waste and pollution, we've apparently made big choices about consumption. They could be up for review" (67–68). Furthermore, Kingsolver uses the Christian term "Promised Land" to describe rich earth in the southeastern United States (6) and applies the word "hallelujah"—in Christian use, "Praise the Lord"—to the emergence of food from the earth at springtime: "Every religious tradition from the northern hemisphere honors some form of April hallelujah," she writes, "for this is the season of exquisite redemption" (341). She adds: "Our personal hallelujah was the return of good, fresh food." Is this blasphemous? When Christians sing, "I am bound for the promised land," they are not singing about rural Virginia; skimming through a Protestant hymnal, one observes that "hallelujahs" are reserved for Christ, God, and Heaven. We see in Kingsolver's critique her desire to reclaim "spiritual practice" from worshipers whose primary focus is on the afterlife, to reestablish connections between worship and work, the sentient world, the living earth.

Not just a rhetorician, Kingsolver extends her preference for the tactile over the abstract to her family's daily life, in the form of earthly praxis. For example, she explains in *Animal, Vegetable, Miracle* how she taught her daughter, not yet four years old, the scientific story of dinosaur life and extinction on earth, about "the millions and millions of years, the seaweeds and jellyfish and rabbits" that have birthed and changed over time—what Kingsolver calls "a fine creation story, a sort of quantifiable miracle" (334). The evolutionary explanation for life on earth is a quantifiable miracle because scientists have learned to create a natural history time line through carbon dating. Fossils from those ancient seaweeds and fishes have been found in Midwestern states, like Indiana, dating back to a time when what we call North America was covered by seawater. They are on display at the Field Museum in Chicago, in a permanent exhibit called "The Evolving Planet," where one can also view fossil skeletons of the short-faced bear (a giant bear from the Ice Age whose skeleton dates back to 12,000 years ago, found in Indiana), enormous beavers, colossal dinosaurs, and the much smaller skeleton of "Lucy," an early hominid that scientists date back to approximately 3.2 million years ago. What a challenge it is to square this fossil record, a quantifiable miracle, with the biblical creation story—even when we have the biblical Flood to explain the existence of sea creatures embedded in terrestrial stone. By using the words "quantifiable miracle," Kingsolver calls to mind another miracle of creation—the virgin birth—which in contrast to the fossil record cannot be counted or measured.

Moreover, attaching religious metaphors to her family's ecologically sensible eating praxis, Kingsolver again breaks the binaries of worship/work and spirit/body that dominate conventional Christian doctrine. Explaining the joys and fellowship of buying produce at a local farmer's market one

April morning, Kingsolver notes that "something *like* religion" was working for her family as they "search[ed] for a new way to eat" that reduced fossil fuel consumption and supported their local economy. Kingsolver invokes religion here because, she explains, "it can take something on the order of religion to invoke new, more conscious behaviors" (38). The "something *like* religion" working on her family, however, is of the body instead of the soul (the number one emphasis of many Christian churches). By blurring a familiar category of dualistic language—worship/work—Kingsolver upturns conventional ideals associated with the concepts. For another example of this blurring of the sacred and secular, consider Kingsolver's chapter title "Waiting for Asparagus," seemingly a spin on Samuel Beckett's modern drama *Waiting for Godot,* which casts two men who do not seem to have much to do except talk while waiting around for the mysterious Godot, a scenario that conjures images of human beings waiting for the Second Coming. For modernists like Beckett, human existence lacks a definitive purpose without religious ritual. A famous example of this spiritual dearth is revealed in the modernist poem "The Love Song of J. Alfred Prufrock," in which the lonely Prufrock wanders a dingy city, ostensibly lacking a real purpose of existence, taking toast and tea and attending fancy parties, or as Prufrock puts it, measuring out his life with coffee spoons. Kingsolver echoes Eliot, noting, "I've measured my years by asparagus," in the same chapter that she revises Beckett's title (29). I believe Kingsolver invokes the Modernists because, as previously noted, a primary concern of these writers is how humankind loses its purpose in the twentieth century as people's faith in God is shattered by the atrocities of modern warfare and the alternative explanations of the universe offered by science. Kingsolver, on the other hand, keeps a type of faith, suggesting that growing vegetables like asparagus has provided for her a spiritual experience, as illustrated by her use of religious language, highlighted here for emphasis:

> *I believe in vegetables* in general and [asparagus] in particular. Gardeners are widely known and mocked for this sort of fanaticism. But *other people fast or walk long pilgrimages to honor the spirit of what they believe* makes our world whole and lovely. If we gardeners can, *in the same spirit,* put our heels to the shovel, *kneel* before a trench holding tender roots, and then wait three years for an edible *incarnation* of the spring

equinox, *who's to make the call between ridiculous and rever-
ent?* (29; emphasis mine)

Kingsolver puts her faith in things seen and, ultimately, tasted: the quantifiable miracle of creation illustrated by the fossil record, the glorious incarna-
tion of asparagus emerging from the soil in the spring.

As Kingsolver's unorthodox use of religious language and teaching of
evolution may threaten religious fundamentalists, her stance on what constitutes family values may upset social conservatives because she supports
family structures that move beyond the "traditional" family unit, defined
by many Americans as a nuclear unit consisting of mother, father, and children—a stance, by the way, that threatens the economic status quo of the
United States. The primary characters on the television shows *Leave It to
Beaver* and *The Adventures of Ozzie and Harriet* represent famous examples
of nuclear families and old-fashioned American values. As Goldberg describes *Ozzie and Harriet* in his book—admitting that the show was quite
boring at times—the show depicted a simpler life: "No divorces. No mis-
tresses. No single mothers. No babies born out of wedlock. No drugs. No
racial trouble at school. No racial anything, for that matter. No sadness. The
parents never even argued" (13). Without naming names, Kingsolver argues
with those who criticize family structures that lie outside the "Family of
Dolls" ideal, especially those who are critical of divorced people, in her essay
"Stone Soup" from *High Tide in Tucson* (1995). Kingsolver testifies from experience that divorce is not easy, comparing it to cutting off a gangrenous
leg, but insists that divorce is a necessary alternative to staying in a miser-
able marriage. She criticizes the "policy gatekeepers who coined the phrase
'family values' [who] have steadfastly ignored the desperation of too-small
families, and since 1979 have steadily reduced the amount of financial support available to a single parent" (141). We should, Kingsolver insists, embrace types of families that have become "facts of our time," including those
reshaped by divorce and remarriage, those supported by single parents and
gay parents, and other types of blended families (140).

Moreover, those who value "unlimited economic growth" above all
other measures of success may take issue with Kingsolver's support of extensive kinship/friendship circles, because since World War II the economic status quo of the dominant culture has depended on isolated family
units to power American commerce. In "Stone Soup," Kingsolver claims that
"[t]he sooner we can let go the fairy tale of families functioning perfectly in

isolation, the better we might embrace the relief of community" (144). Here, I think, we can unravel another reason why Kingsolver's vision may make the political right uncomfortable, and that is because she challenges much of what Americans hold dear, including the freedom to consume endlessly, to have unlimited production and ever-increasing profits for stockholders, and to be, of course, the world's number one superpower—a position necessitated by our endless consumption of material goods and fossils fuels required to produce and ship these goods to us. What does this economic talk have to do with Kingsolver's support of extensive community-based family structures? Foremost, a traditional nuclear family disconnected from community responsibilities provides a mobile labor force for American industry. When the breadwinner's job calls for relocation, a nuclear family does not have to worry about what to do with numerous kinfolk, as does the multi-generational family that, Kingsolver notes, was much more prominent in America during the 1930s–40s (142). Furthermore, numerous families living in isolated units spur the economy, for each family unit needs shelter and food and desires transportation and entertainment—boosting the construction sector and the production of automobiles, televisions, home computers, and lawn mowers (few post–World War II suburban homeowners in America, I dare say, *share* a lawnmower). All this production and consumption increases the government coffers with accumulated personal income taxes and sales taxes, allowing the government to increase military spending, which increases the possibility of sending American troops and technologies to fight wars in distant places, which—at least with the wars in the Middle East of the past twenty years—has secured more cheap petroleum to power American commerce. Thus, when Kingsolver encourages us to abandon the "neat family model constructed to service the Baby Boomer economy" and instead to "embrace the relief of community," she goes against the status quo of American commerce for the past half century (144). No wonder a conservative social critic like Goldberg dislikes Kingsolver. She criticizes free-market economics but defends divorce and supports gay parentage.

In addition to critiquing mainstream conceptions of God and family, Kingsolver also revises ideas of patriotism, or unquestioned love of country—what some defend as the "American way of life"—criticizing unfettered American commerce and offering as an alternative a voluntary simplicity in the independent tradition of Thoreau. In her foreword to *The Essential Agrarian Reader*, Kingsolver describes the currently fashionable American way of life as "an aggressive consumer culture devoted to the sustained effort of inventing and engorging people's wants" (xiii). She points out the hypocrisy of "politicians who support purely market-driven economics, which favor immediate corporate gratification over long-term responsibility, [who] also express loud concern about the morals of our nation's children and their poor capacity for self-restraint" (xvi). In other words, some free-market ideologues who want unlimited economic growth in a world of limited resources simultaneously bemoan the unlimited desires of youth —a glaring mixed message. In a speech titled "The Press under a Free Government," U.S. President Calvin Coolidge once said "the chief business of the American people is business." This statement has been revised to one of the most recognizable sound bites on American life: "The business of America is business," a sentiment that needs little explanation when viewed in context of the high-octane commerce of the Unites States since World War II. Kingsolver's vision of the good life throws a wrench into the engine of American commerce. To be certain, *Animal, Vegetable, Miracle*, the home-economics memoir Kingsolver coauthored with Steven L. Hopp (her husband) and Camille Kingsolver (her older daughter) reads like a guidebook for personal independence and self-sufficiency, a model of how to remove one's household economy from the electrical grid and to withdraw one's support of the United States' "Grossest" National Product—salesmanship. (In *Small Wonder*, Kingsolver points out how multinational corporations spend, on average, over one hundred dollars per year in advertising for every human on the planet [11–12]). Observing how much time Americans invest at their jobs, Kingsolver writes that "overwork actually has major cachet in a society whose holy trinity is efficiency, productivity, and material acquisition"; complaining about being overworked, she quips, "is the modern equivalent of public prayer" (*Animal* 308). Rather than buy into this "religion" of excessive work and material acquisition—defining "work" as "tasks that are stressful and externally judged, which the worker heartily longs to do less of"—Kingsolver prefers to "[s]ign . . . up on the list of those who won't maximize their earnings through a life of professionally focused ninety-hour weeks" (308). Much like her literary predecessor Thoreau, Kingsolver reveals the pleasures of the dictum: "Simplify, simplify, simplify!"—a sentiment that is, I think, un-American for those who believe that "[t]he business of America is business." Planning for her fiftieth birthday party, Kingsolver asked for no presents, noting that "[t]he stuff-acquisition curve of my life has long since peaked and lately turned into a campaign against accumulation"

(106). Describing her own family as "a household of mixed spiritual back-grounds," Kingsolver notes that "some of the major holidays are not ours, including any that commands its faithful to buy stuff nobody needs" (285). Such Scroogey Christmas spirit could certainly offend the CEOs of major corporations who reap large profits during holiday seasons.

Kingsolver's family opposes powerful corporations and the destructive absentee global economy by producing most of their own food or buying it from local farmers: a small-scale but vital dissent to an "American way of life" that depends upon corporations to satisfy wants and needs, a system of commerce grown increasingly destructive of places and people as the scale of technology and distance from producer to consumer has increased. Kingsolver's family withdraws from the absentee economy that, in the words of Kentucky writer Wendell Berry, is essentially destructive:

> Almost the whole landscape of this country—from the exhausted cotton fields of the plantation South to the eroding wheatlands of the Palouse, from the strip mines of Appalachia to the clear-cuts of the Pacific slope—is in the power of an absentee economy, once national and now increasingly international, that is without limit in its greed and without mercy in its exploitation of land and people. Between the prosperity of this vast centralizing economy and the prosperity of any local economy or locality, there is now a radical disconnection. The accounting that measures the wealth of corporations, great banks, and national treasuries takes no measure of the civic or economic or natural health of places like Port Royal, Kentucky . . . and it does not intend to do so. (8)

Kingsolver, in many ways a literary scion of Wendell Berry, addresses the dangers of this big absentee economy in the title essay of *Small Wonder,* where she reflects upon the great disparity of wealth between the haves and have-nots, between the Middle East and the West. She calls the global corporate economy "Goliath," noting that in recent history (the 1990s) "the combined sales of the world's ten largest corporations exceeded the gross national product of the world's hundred smallest countries *put together,* and the gap is growing" (13). An inevitable result of such disparity of material wealth, Kingsolver claims, is that "hungry souls and angry hands rise up against the amoral giant, and ever-higher walls of armaments are required to keep them at bay" (13). In her essay "Saying Grace," Kingsolver criticizes American hubris, especially our propensity for indulgent waste and our lack of compassion for people who live outside the political borders of the United States, and connects this prideful ignorance to the terrorist attacks of 11 September 2001. She expresses embarrassment for our "prideful wastefulness," our "noisy, celebratory appetite for unnecessary things, and our vast carelessness regarding their manufacture and disposal" (25), and notes that after 9/11 some sales people "rushed to convince us in ads printed across waving flags that it was our duty even in wartime, *especially* in wartime, to get out and buy those cars and shoes. We were asked not to think very much about the other side of the world, where, night after night, we were waging a costly war in a land whose people could not dream of owning cars or in some cases even shoes" (25). One means of quietly opposing such "prideful wastefulness" is voluntary simplicity—a notion so radical to contemporary Americans (who are bewildered that Amish people actually choose to live without television and computers) that this lifestyle could rightly be called "civil disobedience."

As an alternative to jingoistic patriotism—uncritical flag waving and conducting business as usual—Kingsolver explores authentic patriotism: caring for a particular place and its creatures. She addresses the antipatriotism charges leveled against her in "Small Wonder," saying, "I find it insufferable to bear silent witness to the flesh-and-bone devastations of war, and bitterly painful to be cast sometimes as a traitor to the homeland I love, simply because I raise questions. I find myself in a strange niche, reviled by some compatriots because I can't praise war as the best answer, and reviled everywhere else because my nation does" (18). As an alternative to symbolic patriotism, or nationalism, Kingsolver offers an alternative patriotism that, in the end, may help save us from our own destructive tendencies. For example, she critiques the unhealthy eating habits of Americans, asking of her country people: "Oh, America the Beautiful, where are our standards [of healthy, delicious food]? How did Europeans . . . somehow hoard the market share of the Beautiful?" She notes how much more particular Europeans are about their foodways—how much more demanding of freshness and high quality—getting "their favorite ham from Parma, Italy, along with a favorite cheese, knowing these foods are linked in an ancient connection the farmers have crafted between the milk and the hogs. Oh. We [Americans] were thinking Parmesan meant, not 'coming from Parma,' but 'coming from a green shaker can.' Did they kick us out for bad taste?" (4). As I read these lines, I imagine critics like Goldberg accusing Kingsolver of cultural elitism and America bashing, and I am reminded of the "freedom fries" episode of the recent past, where Americans took a stand against French opposition to the American invasion of Iraq by changing the "french" in "french fries" to "freedom." Kingsolver, pondering American bad taste and gluttony, notes that the "all-you-can-eat buffet is an alien concern to the French," who, "[o]wing to certain rules about taste and civility . . . seem to know when enough is enough" (16). Explaining that her French friends puzzle over why Americans eat so much "scary food," Kingsolver asks, "Why do we? Where are *our* ingrained rules of taste and civility, our ancient treaties between our human cravings and the particular fat of our land?" What Kingsolver wants for and from her fellow Americans is a reevaluation of our foodways, a transformation of the way we eat, from a long-distance food system propped up by loads of petroleum and processed corn to a local food system grounded in place-specific foodways that make use of in-season produce grown with care by farmers who care about nutrition and taste. Her words, therefore, are *pro*-American because embedded within Kingsolver's critique is a love of American land and people. She wants us to be healthy—a health that will be nourished by eating fresh local food grown by farmers who care about soil health and water quality. This love for places—including the human and more-than-human inhabitants who live there—is authentic patriotism because that is what patriotism is: love of country—rivers, farms, communities. The kind of patriotism valued by Goldberg, in contrast, is a love for *America,* a political abstraction that exists through a nexus of symbols (the flag), myths ("the land of opportunity," "rags to riches"), written texts (Bill of Rights), and to a great extent a shared language. These symbols, however, are subject to change, as are the written texts and language. The land, however, remains, or at least will remain for a lot longer than various political entities. Authentic patriotism cares for one's place—for the human and other-than-human species that dwell there, including, of course, the soil, water, and air—and careful tending to a place requires settled inhabitants shaped by a limited geography.

Many people living in the country called the United States sincerely believe that the "American way of life" is the world's greatest, and these are the people who will be most put off by Kingsolver's "America bashing." One could instead call Kingsolver's dissent "a necessary corrective to centralized power" or "a check on gross consumerism" or "a critique of American exceptionalism." If most people in the United States thought critically about our country's war waging and wasteful consumption, as Kingsolver does, then perhaps we would not be facing a *trillion* dollar war debt, massive casualties of war, the destruction of our homelands by clear-cutting and mountain-top removal mining, and climate disruptions linked to fossil-fueled global warming. In the "Final Word" of *100 People Who Are Screwing Up America,* Goldberg claims that what ordinary Americans really want is "a little more appreciation for the values that most of us—liberals as well as conservatives, Democrats as well as Republicans—used to take for granted: civility, mutual respect, a semblance of decency and yes . . . a little old-fashioned love of country, too" (304). I actually agree with Goldberg here, although I think we interpret "love of country" differently. For Goldberg, it means loving the abstract political entity "the U.S.A." Authentic patriotism, however, involves caring for one's local communities—a place and all of its life forms: soil, water, trees, humans—and taking a stand against those who would destroy them. Peacefully removing oneself from the destructive global economy and supporting one's local economy, as Kingsolver outlines in *Animal, Vegetable, Miracle,* is one means of modeling such patriotism, or love of country.[2] In closing, Kingsolver's sane, thoughtful social criticism and familial efforts to foster durable local economies offer more constructive ways to achieve health in our homelands than does nationalistic flag waving.

Notes

1. As Patti Capel Swartz notes, Kingsolver's political causes are varied and, some would say, leftist: "Environmental issues connected with our use of the earth, United States policy in Central America, the sanctuary movement, treatment of and beliefs of Native American people, discrimination against Hispanic or Latino/Latina Americans, family relationships, women's control of their own lives, and people organizing in order to create a community in which action is possible are themes of all of Kingsolver's work" (65).

2. Other writers join Kingsolver in this opposition to the destructive global economy. Wendell Berry, for instance—mentor for many environmental writers like Kingsolver and Bill McKibben, who dedicates his recent *Deep Economy: The Wealth of Communities and the Durable Future* to Berry—sounds much like Kingsolver (or rather she sounds like him) when he advocates a "quiet secession by which people find the practical means and the strength of spirit to remove themselves from an economy that is exploiting them and destroying their homeland. The great, greedy, indifferent national and international economy is killing rural America, just as it is killing America's cities—it is killing our country. . . . All true patriots must find ways of opposing it" (17–18).

Wes Berry

Part 3
Ecology

Remembering Our Ecological Place: Environmental Engagement in Kingsolver's Nonfiction

Christine Cusick

I believe the purpose of art is not to photocopy life but distill it, learn from it, improve on it, embroider tiny disjunct pieces of it into something insightful and entirely new.
—"The Not-So-Deadly Sin"

Through these words, Barbara Kingsolver maps a process of observation, inscription, evolution, and ultimately creation. The same story might be told of a seed's transformation to plant, to bud, to flower, the culmination, Kingsolver beautifully reminds us, that is "the plant's way of making love" ("Knowing Our Place" 38). In this simple gesture, Kingsolver distills for us the poetry of science, a union that might do well to guide us in our current historic moment of environmental crisis, a crisis that calls us to honor our origins, to remember our stories, and to become reacquainted with our biological communities.

Barbara Kingsolver's writing has generated provocative conversations about its recurring themes of community, place, and memory. Scholars such as Magali Cornier Michael study the "diversity within deliberately constructed familial communities" in *The Bean Trees* and *Pigs in Heaven* (73), while Rinda West, regarding the character of Codi in *Animal Dreams*, argues "we see that many problems are rooted in an absence of memory. . . . People forget, but 'the land has a memory' and it holds in the earth the scars of human thoughtlessness" (154). Kingsolver's fiction thoughtfully anticipates the collective power of created worlds, and while her fiction receives due critical attention for its social commentary, Kingsolver also achieves this effect in her nonfiction. Through her narrative engagement with memory, story, and place, Kingsolver offers an environmental ethic of bioregionalism, ultimately suggesting that when humans begin to understand their place within an evolving biological context, their actions will move toward the sustenance of and care for their human and nonhuman communities.

In "Postcards from the Imaginary Mom" from *High Tide in Tucson*, Kingsolver describes "the masses of nonfiction scholars [as writers] whose subject matter is more vital than it is sexy" (163). Although her comments are not self-referencing, Kingsolver's nonfiction addresses a subject that is indeed vital: human relationship to nonhuman nature. Her literary inscriptions are successful not only because of her artistic sensibilities but also because of her empirical skills of perception as a trained evolutionary biologist. In this way, her nonfiction uncovers the value and need for an interdisciplinary meeting of literature and science, a meeting that both activists and scholars alike are increasingly aware of as crucial for our current state of environmental crisis.

Assuming the complementary voices of science and literary writer, Kingsolver is of course in good company. Rachel Carson is perhaps the most formidable nonfiction voice of the twentieth century to teach us about our biological place using both scientific and poetic language. In the expressive prose of *Silent Spring*, which remains one of the most revolutionary works of environmental science, Carson integrates references to Medea of Greek mythology, the Grimm fairytales, and Robert Frost's metaphorical paths, subtly revealing how literature might inform science writing to render meaning. And although Kingsolver admires both Thoreau and Darwin as "unabashedly . . . scientific and literary," she seems particularly humble about her own interdisciplinary path: "For all the years I studied and worked as a scientist, I wrote poems in the margins of my chemistry texts and field notebooks. But I never identified myself as a poet, not even to myself" ("Confessions of a Reluctant Rock Goddess" 131). And yet, Kingsolver esteems historical thinkers who have taught us through their successful union of these spheres: "Henry David Thoreau, Darwin's contemporary . . . brought to his work an expansive poetic sensibility" ("The Forest in the Seeds" 237). Kingsolver's own writing successfully interweaves these sensibilities without undermining either perspective. She remarks that Thoreau "understood that the scientist and the science are inseparable, and he insinuated himself into his observations in a way that modern science writers, we virtuosos of the passive voice, have been trained carefully to forsake" (239). Like Thoreau, she treads such depths, understanding that her perceptions of place breathe the same air as her lungs and walk the same soil as her predecessors. In this way, her work responds to a desperate need of our historical moment to reacquaint human life with the physical and conceptual places and processes that sustain and nurture it.

Neil Evernden contends that because of recent scientific discoveries of ecology and cellular biology, humans more fully comprehend the extent to which "there is no such thing as an individual, only an individual-in-context, individual . . . defined by place" (103). Evernden, a natural scientist, continues to argue that science alone is insufficient for conservation: "environmentalism involves the perception of values, and values are the coin of the arts" (103). In the field of literary scholarship, the emergence and growth of ecocritical studies is perhaps the most hopeful enactment of interdisciplinary engagement to confront environmental crisis. Camps of scientists and poets have been preaching to their own choirs, but with too little impact on the wider masses that remain unaware, or unconvinced, of how and why as citizens of this earth we should care about the ecological sustainability of our daily choices and impulses. Through their accessible explanations of ecological processes, Kingsolver's narratives examine how humans are individually and collectively wed to place. If there is ever to be a practical application of ecocritical scholarship, if it is ever to effect change, it must, as Kingsolver's essays do, be unafraid to embrace and listen to the lessons of science.

The scholarship of ecocritic Glen Love is indeed a call for such praxis, recognizing that "[w]e have to keep finding out what it means to be human. And the key to this new awareness is the life sciences" (6). Tearing down the long divisive notions that the sciences are antithetical to the humanities, Love reminds us, and Kingsolver enacts for us, that to more fully understand our humanity we must more fully understand our biology. Kingsolver's nonfiction offers us a paradigmatic example of how narrative discourse can achieve this union and perhaps even nourish the mindful citizenship of its ready listeners willing to take her words to the earth.

Central to Kingsolver's invitation to environmental engagement is her framework of memory. Her essay "Memory Place," for example, begins with lush descriptions of a spring morning drive down the deep and winding roads of the Kentucky woods. The silence of the front seat is broken with what she describes as her daughter's sigh and childlike "poetic logic": "'This reminds me of the place I always like to think about'" (170). This narrative intrusion reminds the reader that the literary translation of the deep forest is rooted in Kingsolver's immediate experience, in this instance her role as a mother. At the same time, as the prose unfolds, Kingsolver sketches her present moment against memories of familial play in these woods:

> My brother and sister and I would hoist cane fishing poles over
> our shoulders, as if we intended to make ourselves useful, and
> head out to spend a Saturday doing nothing of the kind. We
> haunted places we called the Crawdad Creek, the Downy Woods
> (for downy woodpeckers and also for milkweed fluff), and—
> thrillingly, because we'd once found big bones there—Dead
> Horse Draw. ("The Memory Place" 170–71)

Through their active play, Kingsolver and her siblings gave story to their woods, unknowingly participating in the ancient ritual of place-lore that we find in the native tribal cultures of North America as well as in the Celtic inscriptions of *dinnseanchas,* a place-naming identified by natural features and by human interaction with these topographies, what J. F. Foster calls a "venerable if patchy folk natural history," that for centuries have connected humans to their landscapes through local story (43).

Moreover, Kingsolver's recollections in this essay concern something less tangible than active play and events. Her memory is also of emotive states, a learned appreciation that is nourished by her patience for seasonal returns and remembrance of what will come:

> Then we waited again for spring, even more impatiently than we
> waited for Christmas, because its gifts were more abundant . . .
> and somehow seemed more exclusively *ours.* I can't imagine that
> any discovery I ever make, in the rest of my life, will give me the
> same electric thrill I felt when I first found little righteous Jack in
> his crimson-curtained pulpit poking up from the base of a rotted
> log. ("The Memory Place" 171)

The "gifts" that Kingsolver refers to belonged to her and her siblings; they were "more exclusively ours," because of her timed investment in their arrival and in their passing. This is not a proprietary arrangement, however. These places were theirs not because of an arbitrary legal contract but rather because of an organic biological contract of physical and emotional sustenance. Ultimately, from the child's perspective this place was *theirs* because they gave story to it and it, in turn, contributed to the possibilities of these stories through a symbiosis of human, place, and memory. Considered within the larger context of Kingsolver's work, nonfiction essays that carefully insinuate a biologist's acuity, this childhood awe is not without consequence. Such wonder leads her into a mature appreciation for an inheritance of the land's sustenance.

The narrative inscriptions in this example are not mere gestures of nostalgia. Her record and reflection contribute to an evolving ethic for how she proceeds in the world: "[I]t was the experience of nature, with its powerful lessons in static change and predictable surprise. Much of what I know about life, and almost everything I believe about the way I want to live, was formed in those woods" ("The Memory Place" 171). In the case of these "lessons" of what to predict, they are only possible because of such "experience," experience that is made meaningful because she returns to this place; as a child she returns season after season, recalling what should come, and as an adult she returns through memory and through the eyes of her daughter. Nature is didactic only to the extent that we acknowledge our communal participation in the movements of the natural processes. The learned patterns of her home woods are formative tools that nurture and sustain Kingsolver, even in their physical absence. These are her literal and figurative roots in place. And so the memory is an active presence in her place identity: "In times of acute worry or insomnia or physical pain, when I close my eyes and bring to mind the place I always like to think about, it looks like the woods in Kentucky" ("The Memory Place" 171). Ultimately, Kingsolver's childhood play taught her to rely upon the physical actors of her experience, to see place not as mere context but as a character in the script of her life story.

Even in this comfort, however, Kingsolver's turn to her identity source is not a naive one; she understands that while the place might be fixed in memory, what these woods "look like" is quickly changing, and because of her evolving connection with this place, these changes matter to her. As the essay evolves, so too does Kingsolver's ecological discourse on the Kentucky landscape of Horse Lick Creek. Though this waterway has "won enough points for beauty and biological diversity to be named a 'wild river,'" Kingsolver gives voice to its threatened viability ("The Memory Place" 172):

> Nobody, and everybody, around here would say that Horse Lick
> Creek is special. . . . In addition to the wild turkeys, the valley
> holds less conspicuous riches: limestone cliffs and caves that
> shelter insectivorous bats, . . . fast water where many species
> of rare mussels hold on for their lives. All of this habitat is
> threatened by abandoned strip mines, herbicide and pesticide
> use, and literally anything that muddies the water. So earthy and
> simple a thing as *mud* might not seem hazardous, but in fact it
> is; fine silt clogs the gills of filter-feeding mussels, asphyxiates
> them, and this in turn starves out the organisms that depend on
> the filter feeders. ("The Memory Place" 173–74)

Moving from personal narrative to ecological explication, the essay juxta-poses human story with land story, in both cases illuminating unanticipated value. Just as sibling play acquires new worth in the moments of adulthood struggle, humans acknowledge the land's riches when it is in its most vulnerable state. With attention to the geological detail and native dwellers of Horse Lick Creek, Kingsolver gives voice to a biological explanation of its ecological fragility. She illustrates for the reader that this place and its dangers are not always what they might seem, for the threats come not just in foreign pesticides and objects, but also in the mere redirection of seemingly harmless mud; the cruelest consequence of human apathy in fact brings the earth to turn upon itself.

In the same way, Kingsolver brings the reader's attention to the challenge of confronting these violations. Situating humans' earthly presence, Kingsolver ultimately locates the potential for healing in local thought and action:

> But when human encroachment alters the quality of a place that
> has supported life in its particular way for millions of years, the
> result is death, sure and multifarious. The mussels of Horse Lick
> evolved in clear streams, not muddy ones, and so some of the
> worst offenders here are not giant mining conglomerates but
> cattle or local travelers who stir up daily mudstorms. . . . Saving
> this little slice of life on earth—like most—will take not just
> legislation, but change at the level of the pickup truck. ("The
> Memory Place" 174)

Christine Cusick

This passage is careful not to simplify the process of endangerment. It is not the case that the threatened mussels were healthy in clear waters and now are harmed in muddy ones. Kingsolver writes that these mussels "evolved in clear streams." Theirs is not a static existence that is suddenly pushed into change because of human action, and yet now, because of muddied waters, an impossible adaptation is being asked of these mussels. Such impossibility suggests a disconcerting imbalance. In this one passage, human agency is both humbled and pronounced.

Even in our temporal smallness, our actions yield a tremendous power that must be acknowledged and surrendered at the level of the individual. As our national history of civil rights reminds us, such change is perhaps the more daunting task, particularly when, as is the case with many environmental decisions, economic survival is at stake:

> Poverty rarely brings out the most generous human impulses, especially when it comes to environmental matters. Ask a hungry West African about the evils of deforestation, or an unemployed Oregon logger about the endangered spotted owl, and you'll get just about the same answer: I can't afford to think about that right now. ("The Memory Place" 174)

Kingsolver incisively acknowledges the global predicament of these choices, giving story to a challenging and painful dilemma, that of human nature's immediate economic dependency on land use. Despite the comparatively short histories of human habitation that create this use and need of the land, the consequences are cogent, often allowing humans to conclude that we must choose between short-term economic stability and long-term environmental sustainability. This binary thinking brings environmental activism to a standstill because it perpetuates false divisions of human sustenance. What we cannot afford, it turns out, is to understand the earth's wellness as separate from the economic decisions that place the short-term interests of human markets over long-term interests of biological health. Any solution to debates on land use that relies on the compartmentalization of land and labor for its rationale will ultimately fail. What this also means is that we must be honest with ourselves about distinguishing between the economies that sustain us and those that appease us. Hunger and convenience are not equal considerations.

In telling the story of this small community of Horse Lick, Kingsolver draws our eye to the choices we make about which places warrant our investment. Too often, voices of the environmental movement privilege the most remote, the most exotic and extreme of our landscapes. In so doing, activists risk neglecting the voiceless communities of both human and nonhuman nature, an omission that the environmental justice movement works carefully to heal:

> We point to our wildest lands—the Amazon rain forests, the
> Arctic tundra—to inspire humans with the mighty grace of what
> we haven't yet wrecked. Those places have a power that speaks
> for itself that seems to throw its own grandeur as a curse on the
> defiler. . . . But Jackson County, Kentucky, is nobody's idea of
> wilderness. I wonder. . . . Who will complain, besides the mute
> mussels and secretive bats, if we muddy Horse Lick Creek. ("The
> Memory Place" 174–75)

As if in answer to her wondering, the essay unravels the local histories of this area. The family life of Polly and Tom Milt Lakes, for instance, invites a consideration of those who would complain, who would care, a story made more pronounced by her visit to the Lakes family cemetery, "where seventy or more seasons of rain have eroded the intentions of permanent remembrance" ("The Memory Place" 175). This faded word against stone is this land's first whisper of vulnerability. The lives had passed, but "the place itself seems relatively unaltered—at least at first glance" ("The Memory Place" 175). Continuing farther along the road, she observes: "The pollution here is noticeable. Upstream we passed wildcat strip mines, bulldozed flats, and many fords where the road passes through the creek" ("The Memory Place" 176). The disruption of this land comes in the form of development decisions, but it also comes in the ordinariness of the human traveler's path. Kingsolver is again assigning agency to the local and individual decisions that map the land's fate through daily routine.

Kingsolver also connects such ruin to a changed agricultural relationship to the land cycles and to the consequences of human habit:

> When Tom Milt and Polly Lakes farmed and hunted this land,
> their lives were ruled by an economy that included powerful

obligations to the future. If the land eroded badly, or the turkeys were all killed in one season, they and their children would not survive. ("The Memory Place" 177)

The mere magnitude of the American expanse permits us to postpone the inevitable consequences of our decisions; removing our agriculture and land dependent economies from our homes allows disinterested development to persist in the wake of excessive consumption. The turn from the local to the global may delay recognition of these inevitabilities, but their eminence remains. Without a sense of obligation that comes from our attachment to immediate communities, this delay will still lead to our demise.

This changed dependence on the land, however, is about more than just economic separation from our source; it is essentially about "a failure of love for the land" as more than commodity, a love that is cultivated not by economy but by a willed remembrance of *all* that it teaches us ("The Memory Place" 177). A "new question in the environmentalist's canon, it seems to me, is this one: who will love the *imperfect* lands, the fragments of backyard desert paradise, the creek that runs between farms?" ("The Memory Place" 180). This is indeed the question that is at the center of bioregional thinking. "One might argue that it's a waste of finite resources to preserve and try to repair a place as tame as Horse Lick Creek. I wouldn't. I would say that our love for our natural home has to go beyond finite, into the boundless" ("The Memory Place" 180). While there is inherent value in knowing that true wilderness exists, the reality is that most humans have not intimately experienced the vast places so often associated with environmentalism and thus have not learned from them in the same way that they have learned from their own backyards. Our imaginative spaces begin with our own places of origin, our own locale, however these places might change with time and need, and however aesthetically unimpressive they may appear to the human eye that has been conditioned to equate grandness with value. Kingsolver invites us to see the value and force of our local habitat for the intricacies of our connection to it. By weaving together stories about a family car ride, recollection of her own childhood romps, detailed observation of current ecological processes, and the possibility for change, Kingsolver reminds us that this connection is a tapestry of childhood, motherhood, science, and legislation. It can never be just one of these. Memories of the "place [we] like to think about" teach us this, because they are never apart from the past or the present that they negotiate. This is why and how Horse Lick gains new importance, not just for the characters of this essay, but now, because of the essay, for the reader as well.

Kingsolver's narrative return to her home place recurs throughout her nonfiction. Even while recognizing and appreciating her formed home in the desert land of Arizona, she simultaneously relies on her native landscape of Kentucky. In response to this settled life in the desert, she writes in "High Tide in Tucson":

> And yet I never cease to long in my bones for what I left behind. I open my eyes on every new day expecting that a creek will run through my backyard under broad-leafed maples. . . . Behind the howl of coyotes, I'm listening for meadowlarks. (6)

The topographical specificity of her home landscape and its wildlife summons her imaginative expectation. And yet, Kingsolver's individual memory of her local origin quickly melts into its larger context: "No creek runs here, but I'm still listening to secret tides, living as if I belonged to an earlier place: not Kentucky, necessarily, but a welcoming earth and a human family. A forest. A species" ("High Tide in Tucson" 7). Kingsolver understands her place in a biotic community through the lens of the Kentucky forest, suggesting that while we may "long" in our "bones" for our places of origin, they are only the starting points from which we envision our role in the larger narratives of ecological interconnection. For Kingsolver, this place is beside a running creek while for her neighbor in the Tucson desert land it might be the settling sand. Whether it is a riverbed, a prairie horizon, or a sea salted wind, there are fragments of place the ready listener can rely on to reveal a larger biological habitat. This turn is purposeful in Kingsolver's nonfiction and is the very convergence upon which she synthesizes her eye as a scientist with that of a literary voice.

Kingsolver's remembrance of a personal sense of place is described in emotional terms, but it is also situated in physical, bodily terms of primal connection. Her consistent return to biological origin is intricately informed by her attunement to evolutionary biology. She writes in "High Tide in Tucson": "What does it mean, anyway, to be an animal in human clothing? We carry around these big brains of ours like the crown jewels, but mostly I find that millions of years of evolution have prepared me for one thing only: to follow internal rhythms" (8). In their articulation of the emotional sensibilities that shape human relationship, Kingsolver's essays simultaneously articulate the biology, the animal nature of human beings that exceeds the capacity for rational thought, which we so often privilege as our salvation. Glen Love argues that in such recognition lies the value and import of ecocritical study: "Although I recognize that our perceptions of nature are necessarily human constructed, these constructions are also, necessarily, the product of a brain and physiology that have evolved in close relationship to nature" (8). In this context, we might understand Kingsolver's internal rhythms as both literal and figurative. Such confluence is a powerful example of how the life sciences effectively teach us "what it means to be human" (Love 6).

Through her nonlinear movement between personal and public, human and nonhuman, Kingsolver's nonfiction communicates this awareness in a way that appropriately positions the human story within the larger diachronic landscape of evolution.[1] In so doing, her reflections on human behavior and proclivity are grounded not merely in her literary insight, but also in her biological understanding of human animal instinct. The power of these reflections is that seemingly ordinary events inspire their creation. Observing the quirky behavior of her daughter's pet hermit crab, Buster, Kingsolver writes: "Like Buster, we are creatures of inexplicable cravings. Thinking isn't everything. . . . I can laugh at my Rhodesian Ridgeback as she furtively sniffs the houseplants for a place to bury bones, and circles to beat down the grass before lying on my kitchen floor. But she and I are exactly the same kind of hairpin" ("High Tide in Tucson" 8). An understanding of these affinities, however, demands that human perception is guided by an understanding of the past, by a collective memory of what it is to exist as a being whose decisions are at the very least influenced by biological forces that may or may not fit their immediate contexts. The canine's instinct is to find rest only after spinning circles in an effort to turn tile into earth. This behavior reaches into the depths of an entrenched memory of how to claim the earth as a participant in a pack's survival. And while in the context of domestication such seemingly comical behavior risks violating rational order, from an evolutionary perspective it is a cogent reminder of a biological past that witnesses a comparatively fleeting present. By extension, this analogy suggests that if we as humans limit our explorations of self, of community, to our rational capacities, we will undoubtedly fall short in figuring out not only who we are but also how we will survive.

While Kingsolver points to the peculiar behaviors that propel us through our ordinary days, she also risks considering the darker implications of being a part of such a lattice:

> It's easy to speculate and hard to prove, ever, that genes control our behaviors. Yet we are persistently, excruciatingly adept at many things that seem no more useful to modern life than the tracking of tides in a desert. At recognizing insider/outsider status, for example, starting with white vs. black and grading straight into distinctions so fine as to baffle the bystander—Serb and Bosnian, Hutu and Tutsi, Crip and Blood. ("High Tide in Tucson" 8–9)

In this passage, Kingsolver asks us to confront the dismal human capacity for purposeful division, thus dissipating naive assumptions: human place within an evolutionary context should not be idealized as a peaceful balance. There are base and annihilating consequences for survival: "Deference to the physical superlative, a preference for the scent of our own clan: a thousand anachronisms dance down the strands of our DNA from a hidebound tribal past, guiding us toward the glories of survival, and some vainglories as well" ("High Tide in Tucson" 9). Acknowledgment of our place within the web of evolutionary feat must embrace even the darkest of the incongruities of human action and reaction.

However, Kingsolver does not fall into a simplified determinism; rather, she uses physical imagery of control to remind us of our agency: "If we resent being bound by these ropes, the best hope is to seize them out like snakes, by the throat, look them in the eye and own up to their venom" ("High Tide in Tucson" 9). In this image, we assert agency through recognition of our animal natures. The ropes that we resent so much are alive, and we must scavenge them, "like snakes," clench this life at its source, confronting its power and grotesqueness. The only thing more destructive than these ropes, according to Kingsolver, is the human inclination to neglect, or worse, deny them. We "rarely do" seize them as Kingsolver admonishes, making us the "silly egghead of a species that we are" ("High Tide in Tucson" 9). Humans willfully forget these ropes because we resist ourselves as animal beings, a resistance that diminishes the potential of individual and collective memory to sustain human existence, and that is rooted in and perpetuated by modern alienation from nonhuman nature.

Christine Cusick

Environmental philosophers and biologists alike have effectively challenged this cultural construction of nature as Other. And yet, while cultural theorists, literary critics included, might claim to recognize that humans are, as Emerson would argue, part and particle of nonhuman nature, there is a dearth of explorations of our animal natures. There are even fewer studies that explore how both the natural sciences and the humanities can illuminate these natures for a fuller understanding of ecological interaction. Kingsolver's nonfiction offers us both a subject for such study and an articulation of it:

> It's starting to look as if the most shameful tradition of Western
> civilization is our need to deny we are animals. . . . Air, water,
> earth, and fire—so much of our own element so vastly contam-
> inated, we endanger our own future. Apparently we never owned
> the place after all. Like every other animal, we're locked into our
> niche: the mercury in the ocean, the pesticides on the soybean
> fields, all come home to our breastfed babies. ("High Tide in
> Tucson" 10)

This passage offers a narrative unwinding from our global to our local place. Braiding personal story into a reflection on comprehensive consequence, Kingsolver's testimony thoughtfully reintroduces humans into their biological homes, reminding us of our implication in environmental degradation. Human denial of biological origin has led to illusions of human ownership and control of place. The prospect of such control is nebulous at best; the paradox of such power suggests that our potential for damage is ultimately as great as the ties that connect us to place.

Kingsolver's careful recognition that there are also other influences on human action and will, however, grants her position authority. Assessing the controversial though well-respected claims for genetic determinism of renowned biologist E. O. Wilson, for example, she writes: "In seeking biological explanations Wilson provided almost no direct evidence for genetic control (as there is almost none to be found). . . . He ignored other levels of pressure—the social, material, and economic contexts—that influence decision making in the enormously flexible human brain" ("Semper Fi" 73). Human beings' evolutionary connection to the land is not exclusively biological; what we learn from a truly integrated understanding of natural history is that it is simultanously connected to cultural histories. By positioning personal memory of place against intellectual scientific explorations, Kingsolver's nonfiction enacts such integration, thereby emphasizing nature as both connected to and more than social constructions.

But even E. O. Wilson would argue that "human advance is determined not by reason alone but by emotions peculiar to our species" and the more intimately attuned we are to our emotional realities the more fully we will engage with our biological ones: "Humanity is part of nature, a species that evolved among other species. The more closely we identify ourselves with the rest of life, the more quickly we will be able to discover the sources of human sensibility" (Wilson 203). Kingsolver's nonfiction brings the reader to reflections on such identification, specifically to how humans dwell as part of the natural world through the memory of personal story. She also demonstrates, however, the way larger scripts of memory inform her personal experience. Kent Ryden suggests that when humans ask for stories we are essentially asking for "memory over the land" (54). Ryden's words imply an implicit connection between story, recollection, and the land. The materiality of this connection, however, manifests itself in the very processes of memory that enable the relations between person and place: "The notion of sense of place would be impossible without memory, the recollection of personal history grounded in a particular landscape or set of landscapes. Anything that awakens such memories or keeps them alive . . . can be understood as an expression of sense of place" (Ryden 75)

Ryden's sense of an awakening suggests that recognition of ourselves as a part of a place, whether it is in Horse Lick Creek or rural Bosnia, cannot be separated from memory. Memory, both individual and collective, relies on narrative connection. Personal attachment to and knowledge of place, one's bioregional identity, occurs through the invocation of and return to memory.

In a similar way, if science is to illuminate the paths that connect human and nonhuman nature, it too must negotiate the present through the lens of the past. Kingsolver's nonfiction does not merely tell us about such biological and cultural filters, it uses them to explicate her attachment to place. This explication is mindfully articulated in her response to the Heard Museum, a center of Native American heritage. Kingsolver writes: "It tells an extraordinary tale of human landscapes cradled and shaped by physical ones" ("The Spaces Between" 151). Kingsolver's maternal language describes human stories "cradled" by the land, thus reinforcing her ethics of place as relying on ecological dependence and emotional affection. This nurturance, however, is not an essentialist feminization: neither of the land nor of woman's inclination to care for it.[2] Rather, it is a humble recognition that humans exist in the arms of and because of our physical expanse. Without recognition of both of these landscapes, the "change at the level of the pick-up truck" will continue to slip from our grasp.

This persuasive discourse gains life in Kingsolver's essays through story and, more specifically, through a narrative articulation of the processes of memory.[3] In his incisively lyrical essay "Landscape and Narrative," Barry Lopez distinguishes between what he names our "external" and "internal" landscapes. The former of these, he writes "is the one we see—not only the line and color of the land and its shading at different times of the day, but also its plants and animals in season, its weather, its geology, the record of its climate and evolution" (64). Kingsolver is keenly aware of such seasonal rhythms and nuances in her nonfiction essays, engaging these details not as mere context but as participant in the narrative. In "Knowing Our Place" from *Small Wonder*, Kingsolver describes her family's summer dwelling in southern Appalachia, calling attention to variations on a day's rainfall:

> We pace the floorboards of its porch while rain pummels the
> tin roof and slides off the steeply pitched eaves in a limpid sheet.
> I love this rain; my soul hankers for it. Through a curtain of
> it I watch the tulip poplars grow. When it stops, I listen to the
> woodblock concerto of dripping leaves and the first indignant
> Carolina wrens reclaiming their damp territories. (32)

Kingsolver is unafraid to acknowledge her emotional need for these surroundings, in all their record of home and in all their climatic lushness. The fluidity of these lines captures a sensorial immersion into the rhythms of this place, holding still this moment, but also gesturing toward a pervasive movement: the birth of the poplars, the arrival of the wrens. Beginning with a familial collective "we," moving to the personal "I," the narrative ends with a turn to all life native to the moment and its fruition.

As the essay unfolds, Kingsolver's tactile and olfactory details invite the reader to feel the wetness of the ground, to smell the age of its crops. Such descriptions reinforce the truth that this is a place with a history, with seasons, and that to capture a moment is to necessarily be a part of this past: "My daughters hazard the damp grass to go hunt box turtles and crayfish, or climb into the barn loft to inhale the scent of decades-old tobacco. That particular dusty sweetness, among all other odors that exist, invokes the most reliable nostalgia for my childhood" ("Knowing Our Place" 32). The beautiful spontaneity of child play is set against the mnemonic sequences of its place, and it is through this stitching that Kingsolver's exterior landscape is wed to an interior one. Human use of the land, in the form of youthful scavenges and agrarian commerce, helps to create and shape this story in potent ways, just as sensory details connect places and inform narratives of memory. Lopez defines this dialogue of internal and external landscapes as a "kind of projection within a person of a part of the exterior landscape. Relationships in the exterior landscape include those that are named and discernible . . . and others that are uncodified or ineffable. . . . That these relationships have purpose and order . . . is a tenant of evolution" (65). For this moment of Kingsolver's essay, the evolutionary phenomenon is as seemingly simple as a generational passing on of place, and yet as Lopez's words remind us, this culmination is indeed purposeful, perhaps *because* of our evolution. Is teaching our young *how* to allow the contours of the woods into our stories of play and imagination any different than a bird teaching its young where to find berries or how to find a winter path to a faraway place? Our "human sensibility," as Wilson called it, may in fact be particular to our species, but it is no less a part of our animal beings that rely on relationship and community.

Both Lopez and Kingsolver see story as an extension of this purpose. Lopez writes: "The purpose of storytelling is to achieve harmony between the two landscapes, to use all the elements of story . . . in a harmonious way to reproduce the harmony of the land in the individual's interior" (68). The purpose is also to further engender storytelling as rooted in nonhuman nature, and Kingsolver sees such communion with place as a path to ecological understanding:

> Whether we are leaving it or coming into it, it's *here* that matters,
> it is place. Whether we understand where we are or don't, that
> is the story: To be *here* or not to be. Storytelling is as old as our
> need to remember where the water is, where the food grows,
> where we find our courage for the hunt. It's as persistent as our
> desire to teach our children how to live in this place that we have
> known longer than they have. ("Knowing Our Place" 40)

Regardless of how we choose to "be" in place, the narrative impulse endures; the move toward story abides as instinctually as thirst to drink, as parent to pedagogy.

Christine Cusick

By moving from personal memory of place to a broader discussion of human evolution, Kingsolver articulates this reverence for the embeddedness of story and place as the impetus for environmental engagement. Even if the stories tell of human failure to honor earthly origins, biological inevitabilities will not yield:

> Protecting the land that once provided us with our genesis may turn out to be the only real story there is for us. The land *still* provides our genesis, however we might like to forget that our food comes from dank, muddy earth, that the oxygen in our lungs was recently inside a leaf. ("Knowing Our Place" 39)

Kingsolver's ear for the dialogue of natural rhythms, for the shared oxygen of a breath, reveals a biologist's sensibility. Her descriptions of place are not merely metaphorical. She weds science to human perception and in so doing moves the reader's eye to the "bronze-eyed possibility of lives that are not our own" ("Knowing Our Place" 40). Ultimately, this is how the life sciences teach us what it means to be human. Once we understand the sustenance of our existence, the biological roots of our stories, we can no longer responsibly choose to exist on the margins of our communities.

In her essay "Losing Home," Melissa Holbrook Pierson perceptively observes "home is physical before it can be metaphorical. It is also personal while being collective." Through their narrative mapping of Kingsolver's place, her nonfiction essays in *High Tide in Tucson* and *Small Wonder* astutely enact an epistemology that recognizes these layers of home. If we come to know our localities with these prescriptions in mind, we are moved to act differently not just in how we exist in our own isolated lives, but also how we engage with our local communities. Anthropologists Pamela Stewart and Andrew Strathern argue that field study reveals to ethnographers that "perceptions of and values attached to landscape encode values and fix memories to places that become sites of historical identity," thus making the landscape a certain "codification of history itself" (1). Such processes of value invite us to reconsider the limitations of our cultural prescriptions for these landscapes, limitations that may only be overcome through a rediscovery of the physical over the metaphorical.

At one level, these connections seem intuitive, not in need of uncovering, and yet within an increasingly profit-driven globalization that in its most sordid and ironic form denies relationship, and devalues communal threads, the seeming simplicity of the story beguiles the listening ear. The values of knowing and dwelling in place that Kingsolver communicates so clearly in *High Tide in Tucson* and *Small Wonder* come to labored fruition in her most recent book *Animal, Vegetable, Miracle: A Year of Food Life*. This study seems to implicitly demonstrate the environmental engagement for which *High Tide in Tucson* and *Small Wonder* have prepared Kingsolver. A memoir narrative created in the company of her family, *Animal, Vegetable, Miracle* documents what it means to know and understand the most vital source of our sustenance—our food. She remarks that this project is about the "adventure of realigning ourselves with our food chain" (6). And yet this journey is steadily understood through the lens of its global importance: "Isn't ignorance of our food sources causing problems as diverse as over-dependence on petroleum, and an epidemic of diet-related diseases?" she asks as she inscribes her rationale (*Animal* 9). Attention to the personal, to the local, is the first integral gesture toward a global social consciousness. The resulting text records how one family learns to understand this web by living within the resources of their farm and their local community. In this way, it is a document of bioregional living.

Understood within the context of Kingsolver's earlier nonfiction, *Animal, Vegetable, Miracle* enacts the consequences of a personal biological and emotional investment in place origin. Kingsolver understands the tangibility of this connection when she describes a food culture as a presence that "arises out of a place, a soil, a climate, a history, a temperament, a collective sense of belonging" and as "an affinity between people and the land that feeds them" (17, 20). The collective sense of belonging and the affinity that Kingsolver attributes to a food culture is only possible through a narrative engagement with what the land was and is. This is why the most recent study tells a familial story of agricultural science and culture.

In response to what Kingsolver calls the loss of our "intuitive sense of agricultural basics," the project suggests that without such empathy, our investment in place falters (*Animal* 9). Humans nurture this investment, or at the very least begin to understand its need, through knowledge of food origins and conscious preparation; cooking, as Kingsolver describes it, is "good citizenship" (130). Using the collaborative narratives of her husband and daughters to record food processes, the memoir reminds us of the economies of sustainability, bringing their tactile growth into the most intimate corners of the authors' kitchen.[4] Through form and content, the book reminds us that we learn good citizenship at the most local of unions, in our

Christine Cusick

families, in our homes, in our towns, in knowing our place as an evolving origin.

At the core of Kingsolver's nonfiction essays is the notion that if unchecked, alienation from our evolutionary biology can lull us into a dangerous and presumptive apathy. In *High Tide in Tucson* and *Small Wonder*, she achieves this through hopeful narratives that use story to connect her own histories to their nonhuman homes, while in *Animal, Vegetable, Miracle* she more consciously invites her local communities into this narrative. In all of her nonfiction, hope lies in the persistent human desire to find a connection to land. Ruminating about the addictive quality of gardening, Kingsolver reflects that it is "probably mixed up with our DNA. Agriculture is the oldest, most continuous livelihood in which humans have engaged . . . the first activity that gave us enough prosperity to stay in one place, form complex social groups, tell our stories" (178). Conventional wisdom teaches us about the value of these stories, about the need to listen to one another, to ask about how we get along in our minds, our families, our communities. And yet what we seem to have forgotten is that the fiber of these stories is bound to our relationship with the land.

Academics are beginning to give new energy to this relationship, in part because of ecological criticism, and in part because our current environmental crisis confronts us with this reality in ways that are more immediate than ever before.[5] This immediacy does not undermine the reality that any polemical crisis affords a choice; we must choose how we will respond to the present story of the land, whether we will act toward union or alienation. This is a long-spun dilemma in a new form; it was the choice of Coleridge's ancient mariner, and now it is ours.

In Virginia Woolf's autobiographical *A Sketch of the Past* she describes a revelatory moment in a St. Ives garden: "I was looking at a plant with a spread of leaves; and it seemed suddenly plain that the flower itself was a part of the earth; that a ring enclosed what was the flower; and that was the real flower; part earth; part flower" (71). Woolf ultimately attributes this moment to her existential and earthly place: "It proves that one's life is not confined to one's body and what one says and does; one is living all the time in relation to certain background rods or conceptions" (73). Is it possible that the contours of a flowerbed, perhaps the most local of life processes we can nurture, could contain and prescribe such evolutionary meaning? Is that as far as we need to look for our map of how to proceed? Our current environmental crisis is inarguably daunting, and perhaps we do not know for certain if our vegetable gardens or our canvas grocery bags or our community recycling initiatives will give us the time we seek or change the course of our earthly story. But for now, just beyond our windowpane, there is still a seed resting in the moist soil beneath a rainstorm, and if we choose to embrace its scientific promise of dependence, in time, Kingsolver reminds us, it will teach us how to love more than ourselves.

Notes

1. Scholars such as Christopher Manes would argue that such perspective is needed: "It is no exaggeration to say that as a cultural phenomenon, as opposed to a scientific discourse, evolutionary theory has been absorbed by the *scala naturae* and strategically used to justify humanity's domination of nature. Evolution is often represented graphically as a procession of life forms moving left to right, starting with single-celled organisms . . . up to "Man," the apparent zenith of evolution . . ." (23).

2. Sherilyn MacGregor's *Beyond Mothering Earth: Ecological Citizenship and the Politics of Care,* in which she calls for a "project of feminist ecological citizenship," offers an integral discussion of this distinction, moving ecofeminism into "non-essentialist" activism (6).

3. Nicola King argues that "identity, or a sense of self, is constructed by and through narrative," but that "it is not only the *content* of memories, experiences and stories which construct a sense of identity: the concept of the self which is constructed in these narratives is also dependent upon assumptions about the function and process of memory and the kind of access it gives us to the past" (2–3). The assumption that rightfully seems to imbue Kingsolver's writing is that this memory relies on an understanding of place.

4. The economic sustainability of the local food movement earns the attention of prominent environmentalists such as Bill McKibben, who in *Deep Economy* argues that "local economies would demand fewer resources and cause less ecological disruption . . . they would allow us to find a better balance between the individual and the community" (105).

5. Daniela Koleva, a sociologist of culture and oral history, remarks on this phenomenon in the context of her research project "Experienced History," which invoked a life history method to record human experience of historical events in present-day Bulgaria. She writes: "we did not originally aim to include the theme of the environment, or to account for the formation and development of environmental consciousness . . . ," but "the constant reappearance of various aspects of environment in autobiographical narratives without the asking of specific questions is evidence of how deep is our consciousness of our environment" (63).

Christine Cusick

Contingency, Cultivation, and Choice: The Garden Ethic in *Prodigal Summer*

Priscilla Leder

B arbara Kingsolver responds to a reader's question about
how to read her most recent novel, *Prodigal Summer:*
"I'd ask you to read slowly; this is the most challenging book I've ever given my readers. . . . My agenda is to lure
you into thinking about whole systems, not just individual
parts. . . . Notice the sentence that begins and ends the book:
'Solitude is only a human presumption'" ("FAQ"). The novel
brings to life the Appalachian ecosystem of Zebulon mountain and creates its own system by interweaving three stories of people enmeshed in systems of their own—the ranger
who tends the mountain and the hunter who invades it; a
chestnut breeder and an apple farmer, aging neighbors who
quarrel about propriety and pesticides; and an entomologist
struggling to adjust to life as a farmer's widow. All of these
characters presume themselves to be solitary in some sense,
yet each emerges from solitude as the story unfolds.

Kingsolver believes her American audience is unaccus-
tomed to thinking in terms of systems. "The story asks for
a broader grasp of connections and interdependencies than
is usual in our culture" ("FAQ"). Readers who meet the
novel's challenge to think systemically are ready to ponder
the other sentence that begins and ends *Prodigal Summer:*
"Every choice is a world made new for the chosen" (1, 444).
As Kingsolver's characters move from solitude toward connection, as biological creatures and as conscious, thinking
beings, they demonstrate the difficulty and the necessity of
choices made in and through an awareness of "whole
systems."

Peter Wenz maintains that *Prodigal Summer* expresses
the "land ethic" articulated by Aldo Leopold in *A Sand
County Almanac.* A land ethic, Leopold declared, "changes

the role of Homo sapiens from conqueror of the land-community to plain member and citizen of it. It implies respect for his fellow-members, and also respect for the community as such" (204). Wenz demonstrates in detail the correspondences between Kingsolver's systems and Leopold's land community. With the similarities established, Wenz goes on to compare the two works as environmental rhetoric and finds *Prodigal Summer* more effective. "Because readers often assimilate views more easily when associating those views with identifiable people and personalities, Kingsolver's exposition of environmental conflicts has a pedagogical advantage over Leopold's" (122)

Wenz sees character as an effective means to lure the reader into thinking about systems, but some reviewers of *Prodigal Summer* focus on people and personalities while criticizing the lessons they present. For instance, Jeff Giles of *Newsweek* finds the ending "suddenly and unexpectedly touching" but complains that the "fierce-minded female characters" who "stand in for the author" are "almost always smart and right" in the mini-lectures they deliver to the men (82). Reviews by Paul Gray and Jennifer Schuessler offer similar criticisms, finding the characters engaging but their message too heavy-handed. Reviewers such as these have the wrong approach, according to Kingsolver: "Several reviewers have completely missed what the book is about, because they paid no attention to anything beyond the human plot on the shallowest level. This novel is not exclusively—or even mainly—about humans" ("FAQ").

Writers of short reviews like those cited above may lack the space or the inclination to focus on anything other than "the human plot on the shallowest level." But even the thoughtful readers that Kingsolver hopes to foster through her suggestions will understandably identify with the human characters—that's how people read novels, after all. By reading "the human plot" beyond "the shallowest level" to examine how those characters think and act within that system, readers can learn to consider their own actions. As the novel unfolds, the characters learn and develop through delicate, nuanced negotiations—with each other, between their own biology and their consciousness, and between themselves and their environment, making new worlds with every choice.

To better understand the distinction between a superficial emphasis on the human plot and an understanding of that plot as a narrative of characters making considered choices in and through their connection to the system, we can examine the work's much-discussed emphasis on sexuality. Each of the three interwoven plots incorporates the teeming fecundity of the Appalachian summer: The chestnut farmer Garnett Walker experiences a dream about his neighbor Nannie Rawley "so real that he'd awakened plagued with the condition he hadn't known for years," despite both his animosity toward her and their ages—she seventy-five and he pushing eighty (368). The widowed Lusa Landowski's erotic dreams feature a giant moth, and, like a moth, she attracts the men of her late husband's family through the power of pheromones. Deanna Wolfe, the solitary ranger who guards and maintains Zebulon Mountain, enjoys an intense summer-long affair with the hunter Eddie Bondo despite their differences. Kingsolver describes that relationship in glowing detail, evoking a snide comparison with "romance novels at the grocery store" from one reviewer and a pained reference to "overabundant detail" from the *National Catholic Reporter* (Charles 20; MacEoin 19). Though their perspectives obviously differ, both reviewers see the eroticism of *Prodigal Summer* in the context of the insistent depictions of sexuality that have come to pervade our culture. Perhaps partly in response to comments like those, Kingsolver acknowledges the difficulty of depicting sexuality in a cultural climate in which the "language of coition has been stolen . . . divvied up like chips in a poker game among the sides of pornography, consumerism, and the medical profession" ("Taming" 225). In such a climate, reviewers may have seen more of what they see so often and overlooked her efforts to reclaim that language.

In the essay "Taming the Beast with Two Backs," Kingsolver comments humorously and insightfully on her search for a language to describe the beast, to "tell of its terror and beauty" (227). She undertook that search with self-conscious care because she had never depicted sex explicitly. "In my previous books," she notes, "I mostly wrote about sex by means of the space-break" (222). But sex was integral to the subject matter of *Prodigal Summer,* "the biological exigencies of human life," so the characters not only engage themselves with reproduction—breeding apples, chestnuts, and goats—but also experience the exigencies of their own biology (227). The elderly neighbors face the painful joints and diminished hearing and eyesight that come with aging; the widowed Lusa feels the longings of the mateless and rediscovers the power of hormones through the return of her monthly cycle; Deanna experiences her first sex with Eddie as "the body's decision, a body with no more choice of its natural history than an orchid has" (24).

Perhaps because of comparisons like this, and/or because their decision making is often not detailed, Linda Wagner-Martin describes the characters of *Prodigal Summer* as "strangely volitionless human beings" (117). Though Kingsolver does stress the force of biology within and upon them, their actions more often serve to illustrate how consciousness and experience shape that force. Reacting to E. O. Wilson's assertion that almost all human characteristics are biologically based, Kingsolver applauds him "for trying to bring humans back into the fold of nature," but faults him for ignoring other factors "that influence decision making in the enormously flexible human brain" ("Semper Fi" 72, 73). Though securely in the fold of nature, the characters of *Prodigal Summer* must exercise their flexible brains; even Deanna's "body's decision" has been prefaced by a conscious one, as she invites Eddie to spend the night in her cabin.

Similarly, in proposing to go dancing with her nineteen-year-old nephew Rickie, Lusa questions the assumption that "'dancing's basically just the warm-up act.'" "'[T]hat's probably true for most animals. Insects do that, birds do, even some mammals. But we've got great big brains, you and me. I think we could distinguish a courtship ritual from the act itself. Don't you?'" (418). Though bodies cannot choose their "natural history"— the needs and urges common to mammals—they do create contexts for and assign meanings to the expression of those needs and urges. *Prodigal Summer* is, significantly, "about humans" because it explores the process through which humans create contexts and assign meanings. Its characters participate in biological systems both within and outside of themselves; every choice makes both a new individual and a new world—for the chooser as well as the chosen—in ways that are not always predictable.

Kingsolver's triple plot underscores the ways in which individuals interact within a system, altering and influencing each other in myriad and sometimes unexpected ways. Each plot features a single species referred to in its title—[Luna] "Moth Love," "Predators" [coyotes], and "Old Chestnuts," but all three species figure in each plot. For example, all of the characters encounter a coyote at some point in the narrative, and the coyote's ramblings, in fact the very presence of coyotes in this region at all, illustrate the sometimes unpredictable variation in biological systems and the complex interconnections among species.

The characters not only experience and interact with the living species that surround them; they also discuss the nature of that interaction, invoking scientific principles to elucidate it. In each plot, one character carefully explains to another how the relationship between species in a system can be characterized as a pyramid incorporating layers of predators and prey. According to the "Volterra Principle," predators reproduce more slowly than the species they prey upon, and, as Nannie tells Garnett, "'that works out right in nature because one predator [insect] eats a world of pest bugs in its life. The plant eaters have to go faster just to hold their ground. They're in balance with each other'" (275). This balance holds all the way up the pyramid to the carnivores, like the coyote, who form its apex. Human actions, such as killing coyotes or spraying with broad-spectrum insecticides that kill predator insects along with prey, disrupt this balance, allowing prey such as rabbits or plant-eating insects to reproduce unchecked. Through her characters, Kingsolver cautions against such practices, choices that remake worlds in destructive ways and, ironically, fail to achieve their intended results.

Articulations of the Volterra principle appear and reappear in *Prodigal Summer* just as do the three focal species. The characters illustrate the principle with concrete examples, but it is actually a mathematical formula that describes relationships between predators and prey. Thus, that most human of artifacts, an abstract mathematical principle, performs the same narrative function and recurs in the same cycle as moths, coyotes, and chestnut trees, along with other human artifacts such as a pair of green brocade easy chairs. This intermingling of products of nature and of the human mind parallels the lives of the characters—the interactions between their "big brains" and the biological processes within and around them. It also reflects the reality that humans can never encounter a natural world untouched by their own presence, not only because our actions have altered that world but also because, as Michael Pollan points out in "The Idea of a Garden," "we know nature only through the screen of our metaphors" (227). *Prodigal Summer,* a book that is "not about humans" implicitly acknowledges this reality, and the experiences of the characters reveal it.

Pollan distinguishes between the "wilderness ethic," which sees humans as distinct from nature, and the "garden ethic," which acknowledges the inescapable reality of the human presence in nature. The wilderness ethic grows out of "the sense that nature undisturbed displays a miraculous order and balance, something the human world can only dream about" (214). Though this concept incorporates a reverence for nature, it also generates a false either/or which allows us to do anything we want with whatever

238

is *not* wilderness. Thus, Pollan points out, "Americans have done an admirable job of drawing lines around certain sacred areas (we did invent the wilderness area) and a terrible job of managing the rest of our land" (223). Based on a simple either/or (the kind of absolute distinction so prevalent in today's political climate), the wilderness ethic is easily followed: anything outside the lines can be exploited for maximum profit.

Following a garden ethic demands more thought, in part because conscientious gardeners must adapt to place. The good gardener must also be "in control of his appetites, solicitous of nature, self-conscious and responsible, mindful of the past and future, and at ease with the fundamental ambiguity of his predicament—which is that though he lives in nature, he is no longer strictly *of* nature" (232). In other words, gardeners must react responsibly to individual situations, aware always that "every choice is a world made new for the chosen." Through the experiences of her protagonists, Kingsolver shows both the limitations of the wilderness ethic and the constant vigilance, analogous to the interaction between "big brain" and biology, necessary to maintain a garden (or its larger version, a farm) responsibly.

On the mountain which she has undertaken to maintain as pristine wilderness, the ranger Deanna Wolfe imagines herself alone among thousands of living species and the ghosts of the extinct species whose loss she mourns. But she cannot maintain her solitude inviolate any more than she (or anyone else) can know exactly where the wilderness area ends and the Widener farm begins. Her encounter with the hunter Eddie Bondo not only ends her solitude but also compels her to accept the inevitable interaction of humans and nature.

"Predators," the title of the sections describing Deanna's relationship with Eddie and her resulting pregnancy, conflates the two of them with all of the predatory animals on the mountain, especially the coyotes that he intends to hunt and she observes and protects. More than once, she feels herself watched by a creature who could be either Eddie or a coyote (67). Both forest creatures given to solitary ramblings, Deanna and Eddie resemble one another like the competing predators of the same species described by one of the Volterra equations. Similarly, the spontaneity and intensity of their sexual encounter makes them seem like predators in a sexual sense, out for immediate gratification.

Deanna resents her own needs even as she gratifies them; Eddie's presence in her mind and on the mountain violates her hard-won sense of solitary autonomy. She tells him she despises him for "me wanting you to come back," revealing her inner turmoil through her awkward expression (99). And she resents his discovery of her favorite shelter in a huge old hollow chestnut tree, insisting "'That's my place!'" and stubbornly denying his reasonable assertion that "'a few other people might have run across it'" since "'[i]t's been lying there about a hundred years'" (95). Her sense of ownership of the tree (and the mountain itself) contradicts the idea of wilderness as open and variable, just as her resentment of Eddie contradicts her attachment to him. According to Pollan, the notion of absolute possession of territory is simply the complement of the idea of the pristine, bounded wilderness (223). Deanna's sense that the forest is hers grows out of her belief that her efforts can keep it inviolate.

To keep the mountain and herself inviolate, she must maintain her image of Eddie as a threatening, competing predator and ignore other aspects of his character and their relationship. After his departure she regrets that "she'd made no dent, had never altered his heart to make room in it for a coyote" (432). With this conclusion, she ignores the change that she herself has brought about through interaction: neither Deanna nor the reader knows Eddie's heart, but he has altered his behavior and given space to coyotes. From the beginning, he tells her, he has accepted a tacit "deal" that he will not hunt the coyote family on Zebulon Mountain (181). And instead of roaming the countryside annihilating other coyotes, he spends his time assisting Deanna, "bringing armloads of firewood like bouquets" (180). His only kill in the novel is a tom turkey that he shoots to provide her with protein because he thinks she looks "peaked."

This restrained predator differs considerably from the bounty hunters who compete to see who can kill the most coyotes in forty hours, described in "The Ultimate Survivor," Mike Finkel's essay on coyotes and coyote hunting that Kingsolver drew upon for *Prodigal Summer*. Eddie's willingness to adapt, even to read Deanna's thesis, which argues that coyotes should not be killed because they maintain a healthy balance between predators and prey, raises the possibility that responsible interaction with the natural world can grow out of the mutual education of human beings. In *Prodigal Summer*, according to Patrick D. Murphy, "male and female characters learn from each other, articulate ideas to each other, and engage in verbal and sensuous dialogues with each other and the interanimating world in which they grow ..." (202). Though Deanna clings to her idea of the mountain as pristine and

Eddie continues to hate coyotes because they kill livestock, their many dialogues demonstrate the kind of negotiation necessary to arrive at reasoned, responsible interaction between people and with the natural world. After all, both are farmers at heart.

The productive resolution of their dialogue occurs not literally but symbolically with Deanna's pregnancy, raising the possibility that future generations might grow to be good gardeners. No longer solitary, she writes to Nannie Rawley: "'I'll be coming down from the mountain this fall . . . when it starts to get cold. It looks like I'll be bringing somebody with me'" (391). With a child, she can neither stay on the mountain nor maintain the illusion that she is only a respectful observer of the natural cycles unfolding around her. No longer just a student of biology, she is now subject to its laws. Further, she must help her child become not a coyote but a reasoning human being mindful of his/her place in the natural world, even though she has never liked teaching. Deanna's acceptance of her new existence as a gardener remains implicit in her letter to Nannie, and some of her experiences on the mountain reveal the limitations of her vision of herself as solitary in the wilderness, accepting and observing all of its actions.

Over their turkey feast, Deanna and Eddie agree that "living takes life." In other words, death, including violent death, is vital to the natural cycle. Eddie imagines himself participating in that cycle by killing coyotes; Deana believes that humans should not interfere with that cycle—but should simply observe and respect it. But she finds herself protesting it hours later when she discovers that the blacksnake that has been living in the roof of her cabin has eaten the fledgling phoebe birds nested on her porch. "*But not the babies,* she cried in her mind. *Not these; they were mine*" (329). Her cry prefigures the pregnancy of which she is not yet aware, and, like the pregnancy, it reveals the impossibility of the kind of detachment to which Deanna aspires.

Significantly, she has always had difficulty with another destructive manifestation of nature—thunderstorms terrify her. After Eddie departs, unaware of what he has left behind, Deanna endures a hurricane. Panicked as the solid trees around her cabin bend and break, she remains "unaware that she was holding her braid in her teeth and both hands protectively over her abdomen. Unaware that she would never again be herself alone—that *solitude* was the faultiest of human presumptions" (434). She attempts to stem panic by counting the logs in the wall and realizes that the stack of interlocked trunks that composes her cabin is stronger than any single falling tree. "*Shelter,* was what dawned on her as she stared" (435). Though Deanna thinks of them as "fallen," she knows the trees have been felled by humans years before. More important, the interlocking design is the product of human ingenuity. Though she will always cherish and preserve the natural world, she can no longer imagine herself solitary in it; rather, she must acknowledge the action of humans, including herself, upon and within that world.

The cabin that shelters Deanna was built by a "'[g]uy named Walker, Garnett something Walker. There was this whole line of them, all with the same name. Kind of like land barons in this area, a hundred years ago'" (173). "Old Chestnuts," another of the three plots of *Prodigal Summer*, features the last Garnett Walker, now close to eighty. His modest farm all that remains of the Walker holdings, the retired vocational agriculture teacher occupies himself with the effort to breed a strain of chestnuts resistant to blight. However, he retains some of the attitudes of his land baron ancestors: though he cherishes the nature he knows, he regards it as his to possess and control. Kingsolver introduces him with an image that embodies his point of view: "The grass-covered root cellar [built by his father and grandfather] still bulged from the hillside, the two windows in its fieldstone face staring out of the hill like eyes. . . . Every morning of his life, Garnett had saluted the old man in the hillside with the ivy beard . . . and the forelock of fescue hanging over his brow" (49). Garnett's gesture acknowledges the old man's power—his salute conveys respect, but at the same time the face literally and figuratively reflects his own, suggesting the god he both resembles and worships.

Writing to Nannie, Garnett sets forth his view that we are to "think of ourselves as keepers and guardians of the earth, as God instructed us to do. . . . 'So God created man in his *own* image: . . . and God blessed them and said to them, "Be fruitful and multiply, and replenish the earth, and subdue it!"'" (186). For Garnett, man's dominion over nature is bound up with his creation in God's image. Thus, his arguments with Nannie often insist on the importance of proper, dignified human behavior, the absolute dominion of reason over body, along with the primacy of man over nature. If humans do not have such God-given dominion, he maintains, then we have no definite responsibility to nature: it is not "our duty to set free the salamanders, any more than it is the salamander's place to swim up to the state prison . . . and liberate the criminals . . ." (186). Garnett thinks in the kinds of absolutes that underlie what Pollan calls the wilderness ethic. Whether one reveres nature as an autonomous entity, as Deanna does, or as a manifestation of God, as Garnett does, "[f]or many of us, nature is a last bastion of certainty; wilderness [is] something beyond the reach of history and accident" (Pollan 218). That certainty not only comforts but also relieves us of the obligation to choose how we will deal with the natural world.

Garnett does make choices—laboring to preserve the mighty chestnut trees but annihilating insects with Sevin. In nature, as in his own life, he cherishes the godly image that he struggles to maintain and protect. Kingsolver's depictions of the personal aspects of that struggle reveal the reflexive, and consequently limiting, quality of Garnett's interactions with his own biology and the natural world of which it is a part. In one episode, his first reaction to an unusual heaviness in his left leg is embarrassment, then terror that he might be having a stroke. Injured dignity gives way to vulnerability—if he is not in control, he feels helpless, but an investigation might have revealed that a snapping turtle has attached itself to his boot. His thoughts about the turtle unwittingly reveal himself: "Poor thing, thought Garnett, to have to commit yourself so hard to one moment of poor judgment" (89). Another passage reveals that he has endured episodes of vertigo for twenty years without consulting a doctor because, as he explains it, "'At first I thought it must be something awful gone wrong inside my head. . . . then I didn't want to know'" (340). With "something awful gone wrong," he is no longer whole or adequate, something he does not want to contemplate. He also thinks of the dizziness as a "curse," perhaps a manifestation of God's disfavor, which reduces him to less than godly status.

From Nannie Rawley, Garnett learns an exercise that eliminates his dizziness, and his interactions with her begin to penetrate his carefully maintained sense of his godlike dominion over himself and the world around him. In a final comic incident, he becomes obsessed with a mysterious man he observes leaning on Nannie's fence. When the man does not leave for two days, Garnett takes a shotgun and goes to confront him. On closer inspection, "everything about him appear[s] unnatural," and Garnett realizes that "[h]e'd been jealous of a scarecrow" (423). By creating a scarecrow, a farmer like Nannie makes a modest attempt to control nature by placing a human image in it. Garnett and those who think like him project a human image, God, onto nature in order to assert dominion over it. But, Kingsolver gently suggests, that image is as flaccid and blank as the scarecrow. "But of course there was no face" (423). Garnett's mistake, like the projection of an anthropomorphic God onto nature, results from his refusal to see himself as vulnerable by consenting to cataract surgery. "The less he could see of this world . . . , the better" (396). His attitude, like his limited vision, isolates him, but when Nannie sees the shotgun and asks about it, he manages to admit his folly. "'I didn't care for the way [the scarecrow] was looking at you in your short pants'" (427). Once again, human interaction leads to productive change: touched as well as amused, Nannie embraces him, and, like Deanna, he begins to lose his illusion of solitude.

Deanna and Garnett maintained illusions of solitude based on the visions of nature as a self-contained absolute that Pollan identifies with the wilderness ethic. Lusa, in contrast, manifests the attitude of a gardener from the beginning; significantly, she has dreamed of becoming a farmer since childhood (35). The gardener, according to Pollan, "accepts contingency" and "doesn't spend a lot of time worrying about whether he has a god-given right to change nature," though s/he also "respects and nurtures" it (226, 228). Married only a year, Lusa has not yet adapted to life on a farm and as part of a large extended family when her husband Cole's death in a truck accident confronts her with an overwhelming contingency. As she copes with his absence by gradually turning her love and her energy to the farm and the family, her experiences illustrate the sensitivity and thought necessary to be a good gardener—to respect nature's systems while acknowledging the reality of human needs.

When two of Lusa's brothers-in-law inform her that they intend to plant tobacco on the farm she has inherited from her husband, their family farm, her personal gardener's ethic prompts her to balk, even after they point out the near-impossibility of making a profit on any other crop. To her sister-in-law, she acknowledges the difficulty of her position even as she defends it: "I'm being stupid, I guess. Farm economics, what do I know? But half the world's starving, Jewel, we're sitting on some of the richest dirt on this planet, and I'm going to grow *drugs* instead of food? I feel like a hypocrite. I nagged Cole to quit smoking every day of our marriage" (122). As she continues to weigh her own profit against her concern for the health of others, the tobacco sets she needs to plant the crop become unavailable, and the decision is no longer hers to make. Thus, readers participate in the process of deliberation by reading arguments for and against raising tobacco; in the absence of a decision from Lusa, they must make their own decisions or continue to deliberate. Through this and other episodes in which characters take major decisions "off camera," Kingsolver engages readers in the deliberative process.

Readers also participate as Kingsolver details the process through which Lusa discovers a crop for her first year of farming. According to Pollan, an "ethic based on the garden would give local answers," and Lusa finds her answer in the goats many local families have left over from ill-considered 4-H projects undertaken years before (225). The goats constitute a solution for Lusa (though not for the locals) because she knows of a market for them, but she makes the connection between product and market through a conversation with her seventeen-year-old nephew Rickie. The saving solution emerges through Lusa's openness and willingness to engage Rickie in the kind of mutually educational dialogue that, in Kingsolver's work in general and in *Prodigal Summer* in particular, leads characters to an understanding of themselves and of their relationship with the natural world.

When Lusa reveals that the fresh milk from the cow she is milking does not agree with her, the conversation turns to nationality and religion. Rickie has heard from his mother and aunt that Lusa is "one of those other Christianities" and expresses surprise when she describes the religious traditions she has encountered through her Palestinian mother and her Polish Jewish father (151). "'I thought people who didn't believe in God just mostly worshipped the devil and stuff'" (153). Taken aback by his ignorance, she considers abandoning the conversation. "This was her cue, surely, to shrug this boy off and shoo him home. But then what? Wait for Cole to explain her to this family?" (153). She could, of course, give up on the family as well as on the conversation. But her ability to adapt prompts her to try to lift "the burden of her aloneness" by relating to the family even though she seems foreign to them. Throughout Kingsolver's works, families are made as well as born, and adoption becomes a form of adaptation. Lusa survives by cultivating the soil in which she finds herself.

Lusa explains the "other Christianities," pointing out that Jews, Moslems, and Christians worship the same god. When the talk turns to "other Christmases," she describes the goat feasts of Id-al-Fitr and Id-al-Adha, and Rickie remarks that he would not eat goat even though he's raised two. As Lusa begins to imagine goats on her farm, she interrupts herself: "She walked over and took the [cigarette] pack from him. 'Can I try this?'" (157). She attributes her surprising gesture first to depression—"'I can't even get excited about seeing thirty, to tell you the truth'"—and then to a kind of solidarity "'if tobacco's the lifeblood of this county, I should support the project'" (157–58). By lighting the first cigarette of her life, she also embraces her vulnerability, to death and to the family, and returns to Rickie some of the authority she has established by her vastly superior knowledge. After an interval in which Lusa learns about Cole's sisters and imagines the young Cole through Rickie, he asserts that authority by returning the subject to goats and informing her that neighbors will give her their unwanted goats. By opening herself to her immediate environment and drawing on her own resources, she strikes on a productive idea. She will raise organic kids that a Palestinian cousin, a New York butcher, can sell for traditional feasts. Her willingness to talk to Rickie, despite their differences, creates the soil in which a solution can bloom. "He was listening to her carefully. It made her listen more carefully to herself" (165).

Goats prove a practical solution for Lusa's farm: the locals readily give her their unwanted animals, and her overgrown pasture provides excellent fodder. But for environmentally conscious people like Lusa, Kingsolver herself, and certainly some of Kingsolver's readers, raising animals for slaughter can seem morally problematic. Lusa tells her niece Crys, "my vegetarian friends [have] . . . informed me I'm a sellout" (356). She categorizes them and their criticism of her with "Uncle Joel," a brother-in-law who feels that she is "throwing the place away" through her refusal to plant tobacco (356). This juxtaposition of the two attitudes reveals the underlying similarity that Pollan condemns in the wilderness ethic. Uncle Joel believes nature should be exploited for profit; the vegetarian friends believe that nature must be left absolutely alone.

In "Lily's Chickens," a thought-provoking essay on the ethics of food production and consumption, Kingsolver questions rigid edicts on what should and should not be consumed. Acknowledging that she and her family eat "some animals," she deconstructs the notion that "it's a sin to eat anything with a face," pointing out that the "[b]utterflies and bees and locusts" killed, along with the wildlife killed or displaced to raise (even organic) vegetables, all have faces (119). Rather, Kingsolver limits meat consumption because it can be wasteful of resources. "A pound of cow or hog flesh costs about ten pounds of plant matter to produce" (119). Lusa's farm uses resources economically, however, since her goats feed on an otherwise unused pasture, and her garden and trees produce ample vegetable food for her and some of the family as well. In addition, *Prodigal Summer* associates the consumption of animals with rituals that link humans to nature by commemorating their place in the natural cycle.

When Lusa and Rickie sight a coyote, she refuses his offer to go home for a rifle and to seek out and kill the intruder. When he reminds her of the threat to her goats, she responds with a story:

> "In Palestine, where my people came from, . . . they had this
> tradition of sacrificing goats. To God, theoretically, but I think
> probably they ate them after the ceremony. . . . They'd always let
> one goat escape and run off into the desert. The scapegoat. It was
> supposed to be carrying off all their sins and mistakes from that
> year. . . . I'm not such a perfect farmer that I can kill a coyote for
> the one kid it might take from me. There are other ways I could
> lose a goat through my own stupidity. And I'm not about to kill
> myself." (413)

The explanation likens the coyote's actions to Lusa's and thus implies the reverse: If predators behave like humans, humans may play their part in the natural system by behaving like predators and eating whatever they can assimilate. Also, the story equates nature's contingencies with human error, contradicting the assumption of human dominion over nature. We cannot exert absolute control over ourselves or over our world.

The reference to religious tradition evokes the feasts where the goats will be consumed. In the case of Id-al-Fitr, which concludes the month of Ramadan, the personal sacrifice of fasting parallels the ancient sacrifice of goats and commemorates the deprivation that nature can impose and that humans must accept. Even the consumption itself implicitly acknowledges human vulnerability to nature by invoking gratitude for its blessings. In that context, Lusa's earlier comment to Rickie that "'the deal on religion between Mom and Dad was that we'd skip the guilt-and-punishment stuff and celebrate the holidays. Feasts, basically'" becomes more than frivolous (153). For environmentally conscious people such as Kingsolver, feasts constitute genuine worship because, in feasting, we participate in the natural cycle even as we consciously contemplate our place in it. In "Lily's Chickens," Kingsolver identifies her family's food ethic as "along the lines of a religion" (112). In this mindful spirit, the consumption of meat is acceptable and even appropriate.

Priscilla Leder

Lusa's goats will enable her to maintain the farm, and they represent the conscientious interaction with the natural world manifested by Kingsolver's food ethic, which encompasses far more than the appropriate eating of animals. Kingsolver notes the waste involved in the consumption of "food that's been seeded, fertilized, harvested, processed, and packaged in grossly energy-expensive ways and then shipped, often refrigerated, for so many miles it might as well be green cheese from the moon" ("Lily's Chickens" 114). Lusa avoids such waste by cultivating her extensive and varied vegetable garden, much of it planted by Cole, and canning the products of this particularly fecund summer. "'Between this and my chickens,'" she tells her sister-in-law Jewel, "'I may not have to go to Kroger's again until next summer'" (375).

Lusa's gardening and canning represent the quintessence of the garden ethic, working with nature to sustain life at its most basic and to please the higher sensibilities as well. "'I swear,'" Jewel affirms, "this is *pretty*. It looks like a woman's garden, some way. It doesn't look like other people's gardens'" (375). The garden's beauty comes from contrasts that reflect Lusa's background: she has planted fava beans, eggplant, and peppers along with the more conventional corn and carrots. Human variety and ingenuity produce the garden's multiple satisfactions. Lusa's prodigious canning efforts preserve those satisfactions for months to come; the filled jars of fruits and vegetables have a beauty of their own and represent the judicious application of human knowledge to nature. "She should put in something acidic to lower the pH. . . . would vinegar work? She added one tablespoon, a wild guess" (119). A few minutes later, Jewel confirms the rightness of Lusa's guess. "'Do you put a dash of vinegar in it, or not? Oh good, you did, I can smell it'" (121). Her question initially makes Lusa the authority ("do you put . . . ?"), but her next comment implies that she knows what to do and confirms that Lusa has done it.

The politics of this farmhouse kitchen demand the kind of delicacy Jewel displays, for Lusa now owns the space in which Jewel's mother and sisters have cooked all their lives, and some of the family resent her and what they consider to be her foreignness. Through a series of interactions involving gardening and canning, Jewel and Lusa gradually forge a bond that becomes the basis for Lusa's acceptance by the family. As they fulfill fundamental human needs by preparing and preserving food, they also address their own needs. Lusa needs company in her grief; Jewel needs help with her children, who, like Lusa, seem strange to the rest of the family. Acknowledging those needs suggests ways to assuage them: Lusa cannot imagine spending her "'nothing of a life in this kitchen cooking for nobody.'" Jewel replies, "'I wish you'd make a pie for my kids once in a while. When I come home from work I'm so tired, I practically feed them hog slop on a bun'" (114–15). This exchange foreshadows the larger problem and solution that unfold with the narrative: Jewel is dying of cancer, and Lusa eventually offers to adopt her children, not only out of regard for Jewel but also out of affection for them and for their eccentricities.

Lusa's generosity earns her the respect of the family, along with her hard work. "She knew . . . that the family had begun to talk about how hard she worked with her hands. They seemed to respect her use of tools" (440). In addition to connecting her to her late husband's family, maintaining the farm gives Lusa an identity that feels like a birthright. She begins to think, as she tells Rickie, that Cole "'wasn't supposed to be [her] whole life,'" but rather a "doorway" to herself. She imagines that self as a "landholder. Not just a mortgage holder, not just burdened, but also blessed with a piece of the world's trust. The condition forbidden to her zayda's people for more than a thousand years" (412, 413). A legal document such as a mortgage cannot fully convey that trust; it must be earned through such homely human efforts as blanching carrots and vaccinating goats.

Lusa's developing sense of the meaning of ownership helps her to understand the family's concern about the farm and her possession of it. Only late in the narrative does she learn that their concern arises not out of personal animosity toward her but out of fear that she will remarry and the farm will pass out of the family. Living daily among the family's possessions, the evidence of the years of human effort that have earned them the landholder's trust, she comprehends the nature of their attachment and crafts a solution: she not only adopts the children but also makes them the heirs of the farm. Living there with her, they in turn can work their way into true ownership, as their ancestors did before them.

For Lusa, and for Kingsolver, true landholdership is never absolute possession: "This was still the Widener farm, but the woods were no longer the Widener woods, Lusa explained. They were nobody's" (439). The natural world cannot be possessed or bounded, and mindful farmers and gardeners must accept uncertainty and contingency even as they continue to act within and upon that world. Similarly, the ending of the novel requires readers to accept uncertainty and contingency in the lives of the characters. Though they all begin to lose their illusions of solitude, their futures, like next year's crop on the Widener farm, remain in question. Still attached to "the impalpable thread . . . pulling mate to mate," Lusa may find another man; Deanna's child may want a father; Garrett and Nannie's aging bodies may fail them (444). By inviting readers to speculate, Kingsolver reminds us again of the delicate, nuanced negotiations—with each other, between biology and consciousness, and between ourselves and our environment—that make for responsible action, making new worlds for chosen and chooser alike.

Celebrating a Lively Earth: Children, Nature, and the Role of Mentors in *Prodigal Summer*

Susan Hanson

Recalling childhood adventures with her brother and sister, during which they caught crawfish with their bare hands and studied birds whose names they had yet to learn, Barbara Kingsolver writes, "Much of what I know about life, and almost everything I believe about the way I want to live, was formed in those [Kentucky] woods" ("The Memory Place" 171). That Kingsolver would evolve into a fierce but poetic advocate for the natural world—a "nature writer," if you will—is not surprising. As Gary Nabhan and Stephen Trimble observe in their preface to *The Geography of Childhood,* "Many naturalists start their journeys on ditchbanks, in empty lots—in any open space just beyond the backyard fence" (xiii). Further, Trimble writes in "A Land of One's Own," "The earth allows children to be themselves, to be active rather than passive, to take control of their play, their time, their imaginations" (64). In such environments, Trimble argues, girls in particular find an independence they might otherwise never know (64–67).

More recent scholarship—Nabhan and Trimble published their work on this topic in the mid-1990s—supports these observations. As psychologists and educators Richard Louve, David Sobel, and Louise Chawla argue, a connection to nature in childhood not only shapes values and identity, but it also engenders a creative spirit. Moreover, they contend, children who have the opportunity to explore and play outdoors—even if it is in a city or in the "nearby nature" of their own backyard—develop trust, confidence, and security in who they are. In his most recent book, *Childhood and Nature,* David Sobel shares part of a letter from his twenty-year-old daughter that illustrates this point: "This connection to the earth, which is everywhere and always nurturing, is one of the greatest gifts I have ever received; it allows me to feel at home any-where I plant my feet in the soil and hug the trees and helps me to find soli-tude and peace within myself and the world around me" (57).

That Sobel's daughter was able to write such a letter is testimony to the fact that she grew up with a father who knew how to pay attention to and value the world around him. In short, she had a good mentor. As Barry Lopez explains in his essay "Children in the Woods," the role of such a men-tor is not merely to *instruct*; it is to *go with* and to guide. "The quickest door to open in the woods for a child," he writes, "is the one that leads to the smallest room, by knowing the name each thing is called. The door that leads to the cathedral is marked by a hesitancy to speak at all, rather to en-courage by example a sharpness of the senses" (572).

Transferring these observations to a literary setting, the ecocritic finds no shortage of writers whose childhood experiences in nature have shaped their work. An obvious case in point is the late Rachel Carson, author of *Silent Spring,* as well as a series of more lyrical natural histories that include *The Sea Around Us.* "If I had influence with the good fairy who is supposed to preside over the christening of all children," she wrote in 1956, "I should ask that her gift to each child in the world be a sense of wonder so indestruc-tible that it would last throughout life . . ." (Carson 54). Carson herself grew up as such a child, one of whom biographer Linda Lear writes, "Her acuity of observation and her eye for detail were shaped on [her] childhood outings" (16). In short, long before she became an icon of the modern environmental movement, Rachel Carson was a curious child at play, hunting for fossils on the banks of the Allegheny River and observing the habits of birds. Her mentor during this time was her mother, who passed on her own love of na-ture and supported Rachel's desire to explore the woods around their farm-house. Carson, in turn, would later serve as mentor to her grandnephew Roger, whom she adopted following his mother's death. Encouraged by Roger's delight—even as a toddler—in watching the marine life in the rocky tide pools below her house in Maine, Carson was convinced that a child's innate sense of wonder requires faithful cultivation in order to stay alive; "he needs the companionship of at least one adult who can share it, redis-covering with him the joy, excitement and mystery of the world we live in" (Carson, *Sense of Wonder* 55).

Barbara Kingsolver's introduction to nature was strikingly similar to Carson's. Brought up in rural Kentucky, Kingsolver was allowed the free-

dom to experience the land firsthand, to locate herself among rocks and rivers and all manner of living things. As a consequence, she developed a passionate attachment to that land, a connection that has shaped both her character and her work. "The values I longed to give my children—honesty, cooperativeness, thrift, m233
ental curiosity, physical competence—were intrinsic to my agrarian child-hood, where the community organized itself around a sustained effort of meeting people's needs," she notes in her foreword to *The Essential Agrarian Reader* (xii). One might say that she longed to give her "literary children" the same set of ideals, all of which were born of her early encounters with the natural world.

Lest her readers imagine that such formative experiences can occur only in pristine or spectacular environments, Kingsolver admits that the place where she grew up "wasn't a true wilderness . . . but a landscape possessed by hunters and farmers" ("The Memory Place" 175). Neither was it home to any rare or exotic species. "The hayfields beyond these woods, the hawk cir-cling against a mackerel sky, the voices of frogs, the smells of mud and leaf mold, these things place me square in the middle of all my childhood mem-ories," writes Kingsolver (178). Nevertheless, she knows that even these ob-vious phenomena routinely go unnoticed by inattentive passersby. What those who fail to see such everyday wonders never have, Kingsolver says, is the experience of awe. "My parents taught me this," she recalls, "to gasp, and feel lucky. They gave me the gift of making mountains out of nature's ex-quisite molehills. The day I captured a giant, luminescent green luna moth, they carried on as if it were the Hope diamond I'd discovered hanging on a shred of hickory bark" (179). Years later, Kingsolver would have the op-portunity to share a similar moment with her own daughter, Camille. Hav-ing returned to southeastern Kentucky to visit the Horse Lick Creek Bio-reserve, Kingsolver took the child exploring along the creek bank, where together they hunted for mussels and crayfish holes. "I recognize, exactly, Camille's wide-eyed thrill when we discover a trail of deer tracks in the soft mud among bird-foot violets," she writes in "The Memory Place." "She kneels to examine a cluster of fern fiddleheads the size of her own fist, and is startled by a mourning cloak butterfly. . . . Now I realize they are fairly or-dinary members of eastern woodland fauna and flora, but I still feel lucky and even virtuous—a gifted observer—when I see them" (178). Kingsolver never uses the word "mentor," but it is clear that this is what she has been to her daughters as they have navigated the natural world, and it is what her parents were to her. Beyond the promise of food and shelter, she writes, she was guaranteed "the run of several hundred acres of farm and wild Kentucky hills, the right to make a pet of anything nonvenomous, and a captive audience for theatrical projects" ("Civil Disobedience at Breakfast" 92). What she hopes to do for her own children, Kingsolver notes, are many of those things that her parents did for her: "Laugh, sing out loud, celebrate without cease the good luck of getting set down here on a lively earth" (91). *Joy*—in a word, that is what she desires for her daughters.

Playing a role similar to that of Kingsolver's parents, as well as the adult Kingsolver herself, is the character Lusa Landowski in the novel *Prodigal Summer*. A lepidopterist who gives up the academic life to move to her new husband's home in Appalachia, Lusa struggles without success to fit into the tightly knit Widener family. Though her husband, Cole, has inherited the largest share of the family's farm, he and Lusa are surrounded by one-acre parcels owned by his five sisters, all of whom see his new wife as "a dire outsider from the other side of the mountains, from *Lexington*." Well aware of the family's resentment of her, Lusa feels "marooned" physically and emotionally (33). If her choice of profession were not enough, Lusa's ethnic background—Palestinian mother, eastern European Jewish father—makes her truly "other" in her husband's rural community. Lusa is without status, except as Cole's wife; even though she had kept her own name when she married, "it hadn't mattered: everyone called her Mrs. Widener, as if there were no Lusa at all" (40).

> "Your sisters haven't learned my name yet," she complains
> to Cole at one point during a fight.
> "Lusa, come on," he responds.
> "You ask them. I'll give you ten dollars if one of them gets
> it right—the whole thing. Lusa Maluf Landowski. They make a
> show of not being able to remember it. You think I'm kidding?
> Lois evidently told Oda Black my maiden name was Zucchini."
> (39–40)

Ironically, Lusa feels included by the family only after Cole's unexpected death, at which point she begins to focus less on his sisters' acceptance of her and more on keeping the family farm productive and intact. Although the townspeople expect her to leave Zebulon County following the funeral, Lusa is torn; on one hand, she welcomes the freedom to return to her former life, but on the other, she wants to assume her rightful place as owner and manager of the farm. Resolution of this dilemma comes through a dream in which she is visited by a man/moth who speaks her name and claims to have known her "always." In the erotic scene that follows, the creature's confidence and strength somehow migrate into Lusa. When she awakes at dawn, she discovers a "day of her own" in which the previous night's "tangle of work and choices" is gone. What her strange visitor had attempted to tell her, she realizes, is that "words [are] not the whole truth. What she'd loved was here, and still might be, if she could find her way to it" (80). To the surprise of Cole's family, Lusa resolves to stay. Nature, in the form of the man/moth who knows her *by name,* has restored her sense of identity, as well as her courage and her faith in her own imagination.

The surprising apparition of the man/moth recalls an exchange that occurs early in Lusa and Cole's relationship, a time that was both intensely sensual and nurturing, an affirmation of Lusa's identity as scientist and lover. Noting that he "made love like a farmer," Kingsolver writes that Cole "had a fine intelligence for the physical that drove him toward her earthy scents, seeking out with his furred mouth her soft, damp places, turning her like fresh earth toward the glory of new growth." It was only through his eyes that Lusa was finally able to see herself as "voluptuous." Pleased by his interest in the details of "moth love," Lusa concludes, "He could only love sex more if he had antennae the shape of feathers, like a moth, for combing the air around her, and elaborately branched coremata he could evert from his abdomen for the purpose of calling back to her with his own scent" (37). Later, when the man/moth comes to her, it is exactly in this guise. It is not his image that she recognizes, but the sound of his voice, and his scent. "*This is how moths speak to each other,*" Lusa realizes. "*The wrong words are impossible when there are no words*" (79). Transformed into the object of her life's passion, the luna moth, Cole continues to nurture Lusa at the most intimate level.

As she grows more self-assured, Lusa feels herself easing into a better relationship with Cole's sister Jewel, who is also without a husband, hers having left her four years before. This connection, in turn, results in Lusa's getting to know Jewel's two children, ten-year-old Crys and five-year-old Lowell. When the brother and sister are introduced to the reader, however, they are referred to simply as "the kids," like Lusa before them, they are nameless, their only identity coming from their relationship with their mother. Ironically, it is due to Lusa's observations that the reader initially mistakes Crys for a boy: the "older child" enters Lusa's kitchen "carrying a box of canning jars on *his* head" (109; emphasis mine). Shortly thereafter, Lusa frowns when she hears Jewel reprimanding one of the children, who has accidentally broken a jar on her back porch: "[Lusa] couldn't see Jewel or the kids but could hear a smack and a wail. 'That is no way to treat your little brother,' she heard. 'You keep this up and you're wearing a dress tomorrow. I mean it!'" (119). Later, Lusa is plainly confused when Jewel remarks, "*She's* going to be my death, if I don't kill *her* first" (120; emphasis mine). Noting Lusa's expression, Jewel laughs off the mistake. "'You thought she was a boy. You and everybody else. When she started kindergarten, the teacher refused to let her go to the girls' bathroom until I rushed down there with her birth certificate'" (120). With her gender in question, thanks to her androgynous name—"Chris"—and her tomboy-ish behavior and looks, Crys lacks any clear identity until Lusa begins mirroring a positive image back to her a bit later in the story.

Perceived as a misfit, Jewel's "crazy mixed-up daughter" is more than a source of worry for her mother (120). As Jewel reveals,

"She's about half the reason why Shel left. He blamed me—oh, Lord, did he blame me. He said I was making her a little homo by letting her wear jeans and cut her hair like that. And maybe he was right. But it wasn't my idea. I'd like to have seen *him* try and get her into a dress. That's what I told him: *You* try putting panty hose on a tomcat!" (121)

Admitting that she sees herself in the young girl, Lusa comes to her defense, saying, "'Jewel, she's just a tomboy. I was exactly like that at her age. . . . You should've seen me. I skinned my knees and caught bugs and wanted to be a farmer when I grew up. . . . Maybe it's not really about trying to act like a boy,' she hazarded cautiously, 'but just her way of trying to be herself'" (121–22). Outdoors, while Lusa and Jewel talk, "Lowell and Crys [orbit] the barnyard in their dark, soaked clothes, laughing and galloping on a pair of invisible horses, traveling in circles through the infinite downpour as if time for them [has] stopped, or not yet started" (127). The freedom they feel in this moment is almost palpable. Outside the house, where they are warned not to break anything—and then scolded when they do—the brother and sister experience the sense of timelessness that accompanies what writer Diane Ackerman calls "deep play." "Swept up in the deepest states of play," she writes, "one feels balanced, creative, focused" (17). Immersed in the "infinite downpour," Lowell and Crys are free to be the children they are. Once again, nature is the catalyst for self-actualization, for claiming one's identity.

Ultimately, Lusa will learn what the rest of the family already knows— that Jewel has terminal cancer. Toward the end, when it is clear that Jewel is actively dying, Lusa hesitantly expresses her desire to adopt the children. "'I love Crys and I love Lowell,'" Lusa tells her. "'Lowell's easy, he's a heart stealer, and Crys and I are two peas in a pod.'" To her surprise, Jewel readily agrees. Lusa is able to make the claim that she and Crys are "two peas in a pod" because she has been the girl's friend and mentor for many months (380–81). Surprised by the child's lack of knowledge about the natural world, Lusa had undertaken to fill the gaps in her education.

On one of Crys's early visits to the farm, for example, Lusa takes her on an insect-collecting excursion, during which Crys is treated to her first up-close look at a grasshopper. "'*Whoa!*'" the ten-year-old exclaims when Lusa extends one of the creature's green wings. It is a gasp of wonder. When Lusa captures a katydid, Crys is even more amazed. "'You never saw a katydid before?'" Lusa asks her. The child responds by shaking her head and admitting, "'I thought katydids was some'n *big*. A big old whopper bird or some'n.'" Lusa is shocked by Crys's response. "How could rural kids grow up so ignorant of their world?" she wonders. "Their parents gave them Game Boys and TVs that spewed out cityscapes of cops and pretty lawyers, but they couldn't show them a katydid" (296–97). Through such exchanges as this, Lusa little by little wins over her initially hostile niece, tapping the child's inborn curiosity and thereby increasing her sense of belonging and self-esteem. Crys may be woefully unschooled in the ways of nature, but with each discovery she makes, the more relaxed and contented she becomes. "For the first time since she'd planted herself fiercely on Lusa's driveway that morning," Kingsolver writes, "[Crys] sounded clear and transparent, like a child. Like the crystal she was" (298). In the course of their conversation about bugs, Lusa speaks to Crys with an unfamiliar forthrightness: She admits uncertainty about whether Jewell will live or die. She honors Crys's feelings about her "Ain't" Lois, who has maliciously chopped up the child's favorite corduroys for rags. And she gives Crys a new understanding of her name. It is not just jewelry, or

258

jewry, as Crys calls it, a "stupid thing." Rather, as Lusa explains, "It's a kind of rock. Hard, sharp, and shiny" (298). It is a thing of substance and weight. Her mother may have believed that "Crystal" was not a fitting name for her unfeminine child, but in proclaiming it beautiful *and* appropriate, Lusa in effect saves Crys from anonymity. Like the man/moth who calls Lusa by name, thereby helping her emerge from despair over her husband's death, the sight of the katydid opens a door for Crys.

Considered from an ecocritical perspective, Kingsolver is illustrating through both Lusa and Crys the way nature can empower and liberate the individual. In Lusa's case, it is her willingness to lose herself in her intimate encounter with the man/moth that gives her renewed energy; for Crys, life comes with Lusa's invitation—and permission—to experience the natural world with awe. "Wonder heals through an alchemy of mind," Diane Ackerman writes, referring to "the tonic value of reacquainting ourselves with nature's charms, the charms we fell in love with when we were children, when nature was a kingdom of wonder, play, self-discovery, and freedom" (156–57).

Just as Barbara Kingsolver and Rachel Carson experienced the natural world in similar ways as children, they both came to the task of "speaking a word for nature," as Thoreau put it, via the study of biology. "I can go through a trip without ever noticing the names of streets but I note the lunar moths and kinds of trees, because that's my training," Kingsolver told an interviewer in 2001. "It's almost my religion. I grew up in a natural setting, in that interface between farms and wilderness. That's where I learned to love life" (Brace 17). Having grown up relating to the land in a protective and intimate way, both writers carried with them into adulthood the curiosity and wonder of which Carson spoke, and both found a way to translate their scientific knowledge into poetic prose. Whether decrying the environmental consequences of strip-mining and overconsumption, as Kingsolver does, or the dangers of pesticide use, as in Carson's case, each has been impelled by her earliest experiences in nature to come to its defense. The result is a body of work that not only conveys delight in the physical world but also challenges readers to treat the Earth with respect. In different ways, both ask the question that Kingsolver voices at the end of "The Memory Place": "who will love the *imperfect* lands, the fragments of backyard paradise, the creek that runs between farms? In our passion to protect the last remnants of virgin wilderness, shall we surrender everything else in exchange?" (180).

Susan Hanson

Motivating people to care for "the imperfect lands" is no easy task, but in returning to the words of Rachel Carson, we find a place to begin: with wonder. It is doubtful that such a capacity can be taught, but as illustrated by Lusa in *Prodigal Summer,* it can certainly be modeled. Carson intuitively knew this, and now eco-psychologists and educators are discovering it as well: If we want to produce adults who lead lives of healthy reciprocity with the earth, we must stir their natural human desire to gravitate toward life—what biologist E. O. Wilson calls "biophilia."

Written off as child's play, the experience of wandering through the woods or watching birds or simply digging in the dirt is essential for the developing human mind. Through venturing farther and farther into the world—even if that world is the vacant lot next door or the ditch behind the house—the child not only gains a sense of autonomy and competence, but he or she also develops an implicit trust in that world, a trust that nurtures creativity and feeds a nascent hunger to learn more. As Carson put it,

> for the child, and for the parent seeking to guide him, it is not half so important to know as to *feel.* If facts are the seeds that later produce knowledge and wisdom, then the emotions and the impressions of the senses are the fertile soil in which the seeds must grow. The years of early childhood are the time to prepare the soil. . . . It is more important to pave the way for the child to want to know than to put him on a diet of facts he is not ready to assimilate. (56)

Through direct experience with the natural world, the fortunate child will ultimately discern that he or she truly *belongs,* and it is out of this sense of belonging, of feeling at home in the world, that the child will come to love and care for that world.

Only in the last decade has it become clear that conventional methods of teaching children to be environmentally aware are doing more damage than good. According to David Sobel, project director with the Antioch New England Institute, much of what young students hear in the classroom results in detachment from the natural world rather than identification with it. "They hear the story of the murder of [environmental] activist Chico Mendez and watch videos about the plight of indigenous forest people displaced by logging and exploration for oil," he writes in "Beyond Ecophobia." "They learn that between the end of morning recess and the beginning of lunch, more than 10,000 acres of rainforest will be cut down, making way for fast food 'hamburgerable' cattle." In burdening children with problems they can do nothing about, parents and teachers are in effect encouraging a paralyzing fear—"a fear of ecological problems and the natural world. Fear of oil spills, rainforest destruction, whale hunting, acid rain, the ozone hole, and Lyme disease. Fear of just being outside." A more effective alternative, Sobel argues, is the nurture of wonder and awe, of the innate human desire to draw closer to living things, to "gasp" in sheer delight. Environmental educator Louise Chawla of Kentucky State University agrees. Following up on a study by R. Thomas Tanner, professor of environmental studies at Iowa State, Chawla considered the two questions that had driven his research: "What motivates people to take action to protect the environment?" and "When people explain the sources of their commitment to action, how much credit do they give to childhood learning?" A great deal, Chawla discovered through interviews with environmentalists both here and abroad. Moreover, she writes, "The special places that stood out in memory, where people formed a first bond with the natural world, were always part of the regular rhythm of daily life: the garden or nearby lake or forest where people played as children, the summer cabin or grandparents' farm that was visited repeatedly in the course of growing up, favorite hiking trails during the university years. In these places, people became comfortable with being out in the natural world, usually alone or with a small group of family or friends" (19).

There is a place for rage in the defense of nature, for moral indignation, for "speaking truth to power." But what ultimately sustains any effort on earth's behalf is the heart's delight in mystery, in what Barbara Kingsolver calls "[a] willingness to participate in sunlight, and the color red. An agreement to enter into a conspiracy with life, on behalf of both frog and snake, the predator and the prey, in order to come away changed" ("Reprise" 268).

In my memory, a five-year-old child is sitting on the lawn behind her house on the Texas coast. She is bare-footed, and her dog, a black cocker spaniel named Schatzie, is lying beside her. The child is holding a blade of St. Augustine grass, which she tears along the mid-line and then lets fly in the wind. Anchored by the good green earth, immersed in sky, she has no awareness of the world beyond this place. This moment is all she knows. The scene is hardly memorable, in the usual sense of the word, but it is one of my earliest memories of engaging the natural world.

Susan Hanson

Like Barbara Kingsolver, I found my place in the natural order at an early age. Going shirtless whenever I could, and shoeless too, I turned brown in the south Texas sun. I had no woods to roam, and only a neighbor's tree to climb, but I had oyster shell driveways and ditches full of rainwater and beans in a garden that my father helped me plant. Later, I would pick dewberries with my friends, eating half of them on the way home. I lived in no "wilderness." Far from it. But there were creek beds and "unimproved" land, backyard gardens and a sweet-smelling gardenia bush below my bedroom window. These things were enough.

I had no formal "lessons" about the landscape in which I lived, but I had my father's stories—such as the Texas folk wisdom that the call of the yellow-billed cuckoo, or "rain crow," signals an impending storm; and the appearance of the scissor-tailed flycatcher or the leafing out of the honey mesquite means spring has finally come. My father particularly favored mockingbirds, all of whom he addressed as "Oscar," for reasons known only to him. I never thought it odd that he talked to birds, or that he and my mother chose to spend their leisure in the garden. That was simply what one *did,* I concluded; I learned this by osmosis.

We never spoke of *ecology* when I was growing up, and we no doubt broke some cardinal rules—the chief of which was using Malathion and Diazinon to deal with garden pests. It was the sixties, after all. That said, I still grew up with the inexplicable knowledge that I was part of the earth in some tangible, sensual way. Like Barbara Kingsolver, I have my parents primarily to thank for this—not because of what they *consciously* did, but for what they were able to see: "everyday wonders" in an unremarkable land.

Another vignette: I see a young woman dressed in shorts and T-shirt, her two-year-old daughter standing with her in a garden, freshly tilled. The child is looking up expectantly, her tiny hand outstretched for something that the mother wants to give her. It is a seed, most likely squash or bean. The child receives it like communion bread, reflects on it a moment, then carefully buries it in the earth. She is my daughter, a Band-Aid on her knee, and I am the woman, much younger, in my twenties, living out a pattern that I learned decades before. This is the way I pass on what I know, the way I tell her *Be kind to the earth, Let it speak to you, Delight in the life around you.*

These are also words that Barbara Kingsolver's characters—her "children"—have internalized. With the help of their mentors, they have acquired a sense of belonging in the world that brings them confidence and empowers them to lead creative and authentic lives. Overt as she is in developing themes around other issues—social justice, poverty, industrial agriculture—Kingsolver allows character and plot, particularly in *Prodigal Summer,* to quietly make the case that Sobel, Chawla, and others in education and the social sciences have been arguing for years: If we want children to take care of the earth, we must first teach them to love it. And the only way to teach them that love is to take their hand and to wonder with them at the finding of a feather, or a fossil in a rock, or the yellow-green wing of a moth.

Susan Hanson

Together at the Table: *Animal, Vegetable, Miracle* and Thoreau's *Wild Fruits*

Gioia Woods

n her 2007 book *Animal, Vegetable, Miracle: A Year of Food Life,* Barbara Kingsolver asks if "the story of bread, from tilled ground to our table, [is] less relevant to our lives than the history of the thirteen colonies" (9). One hundred and fifty years earlier in his last manuscript, *Wild Fruits,* Henry David Thoreau had also commented on the extra-nutritive value of food: "better for us is the wild cherry than the pineapple . . . not on account of their flavor merely, but the part they play in our education" (5). That Kingsolver should echo Thoreau's belief in the transcendent and educational value of food will come as no surprise to her readers. Thoreau, as Lawrence Buell points out, "stands for nature" in the American environmental imagination. Although Thoreau tends to embody American environmental values, Buell laments that he has not "engendered any canonical progeny, at least within the field of literature" (9). I propose here that the Thoreau of *Wild Fruits,* the later Thoreau who had moved from a lively interest in natural history to a deep, expert familiarity in his local flora and fauna borne of hours of close observation, has indeed left literary progeny. Kingsolver's *Animal, Vegetable, Miracle* is, in many ways, that kin. The pages that follow explore the relationship between the two texts and examine the ways ideological discourses of science, economics, and politics meet to produce a revised aesthetic, an environmental aesthetic. The deep engagement these discourses demand move the reader from passive observer of the beautiful to active constructor of it. But first, what is the common ideological ground, and where are the disparities?

AMERICAN LITERARY CONTEXTS

Values inhere in the arts of a culture. In order to discern a culture's values and attitudes, we should first look to its aesthetic expression. There we will find both a historical repository of values and an active force shaping these values. In American environmental literature we discern, as Buell succinctly writes, "old world desire . . . American cultural nationalism . . . [and] discourse of American exceptionalism" (3–4). These ideological discourses are certainly present in *Wild Fruits,* and two of the three are present in *Animal, Vegetable, Miracle.* The texts share a certain pastoral nostalgia, which in American literature has often stood as an antidote to the ills of urban industrialization: in *Wild Fruits* Thoreau imbues fields with an Arcadian sense of rustic seclusion; Kingsolver valorizes her family's rural experience, from small-town post-office to close-knit neighbors. As for cultural nationalism, Thoreau, in keeping with his time, considers New England the New Eden; Kingsolver practices a twenty-first-century form of romantic nationalism in her quest to illustrate how an exceptional geography can shape a "natural" (locovore) economy. Thoreau's nationalism is closely tied to the rhetoric of American exceptionalism. The nation is distinct because of its rugged, frontier spirit that engenders liberty and egalitarianism and that can be sampled in its wild fruit by those with the appropriate "savage tastes." Thoreau shares the confidence our nation's founders had in the continent's abundant resources; he urges his fellow Americans to deeply appreciate the flavors inherent in those fruits. Kingsolver, on the other hand, while celebrating the *potential* for those distinct American flavors, rejects the geographical link to moral superiority that characterizes exceptionalist ideology. She has made a career of challenging American exceptionalism and continues to do so here. *Animal, Vegetable, Miracle* often reads as a lament for the loss of American potential—the tyranny of consumption has resulted in the loss of local flavors; our wealth has resulted in a loss of health. Perhaps we are exceptional in other areas, she ironically suggests: we do not know where our food comes from, our younger generation has a shorter projected lifespan than their parents, we are engaged in an epic struggle against obesity, and we cannot even speak of an American national cuisine. The wild and savage tastes celebrated by her nineteenth-century forebear are all but lost, hiding in the seeds of an heirloom tomato.

Americanists have written millions of words about how the American frontier became an androcentric trope for pastoral escape or wilderness adventure.[1] Despite his being a long-canonized writer of the American Renaissance, we find a slightly different legacy, neither escape nor adventure, in Thoreau's *Wild Fruits*. Although Thoreau does not engage in what has been termed the gynocentric narrative in response to wilderness—the one that favors gardening and domesticity—he does deeply embed food, the stuff that ultimately sustains culture, with deep and complex meaning.

In the American tradition of environmental literature, the natural world and its edible offerings are often invested with values that exceed their utilitarian capacity. Food not only nourishes the body, it nourishes national identity. From Cabeza de Vaca's 1530s descriptions of food cultures in the American Southwest to Michael Pollen's enormously popular 2006 book *The Omnivore's Dilemma*, the American relationship with food has occupied our national literary imagination. Thoreau himself conflates food culture with national identity: native fruits are far superior to those that are imported; they "fit us to live here" (5). The ideals of freedom from tyranny and independence resonate throughout the work of Thoreau and Kingsolver; choosing local American flavor is often a trope for choosing American values. Thoreau cautions against the belief that "the fruits of New England are mean and insignificant while those of foreign lands are noble and memorable. Our own, whatever they may be, are far more important to us than others can be" (5). Kingsolver, for her part, bemoans the lack of a national cuisine. She points out that "Italians eat Italian food, the Japanese eat Japanese, and so on, honoring the ancient synergies between what their land can give and what their bodies need. Strong food cultures are both aesthetic and functional" (15). Local food culture, in other words, has the potential to develop both national and aesthetic sensibilities.

For each writer, the natural world is the source for all American qualities, not the least of which is social justice; Kingsolver, like Thoreau, has questioned loyalty to a government that supports unjust war. Like Thoreau, Kingsolver calls to our attention the political efficacy of corporate farms filling our table with foreign fruits. Both conduct sustained inquiry into nature's economy, seeking the "true" value of seed and fruit and animal. Thoreau and Kingsolver share certain rhetorical approaches, too: a scriptural prose style, almost jeremiad, exhorting readers to change their attitudes and their lives. Like Thoreau, Kingsolver infuses her nonfiction with an attitude of close, scientific observation. Both Kingsolver and Thoreau demonstrate how ideas can be understood in terms of their practical consequences. Kingsolver's "We went to the farm to live deliberately" echoes the most famous American justification, Thoreau's "I went to the woods because I wished to live deliberately" (Kingsolver 23; Thoreau 343).

DISCOURSE AND BEAUTY

The experience of beauty is that which brings us pleasure, satisfaction, and meaning. The experience of beauty in *Animal, Vegetable, Miracle* and *Wild Fruits* is a deliberate, purposeful activity that requires deep engagement with nature. We cannot be satisfied if we are disinterested viewers; aesthetic appreciation, for Kingsolver and Thoreau, comes when we acknowledge the dirt under our nails and the flavors in our mouths. An environmental aesthetic, in contrast to a classical aesthetic, breaks down the subject-object relationship between "scene" and "viewer." The classical aesthetic proposes a passive viewer; the environmental aesthetic, by contrast, demands the viewer actively engage the natural world. In an article entitled "Contemporary Aesthetics and the Neglect of Natural Beauty," Ronald Hepburn argued that our appreciation of the natural world involves both recognition of its varying character and an acknowledgement of our own multisensory experience of it. Central to the aesthetic appreciation of nature, in this view, is first-hand tactile experience and deep knowledge of nature. The experience of taste and the knowledge of where our food comes from, for Kingsolver and Thoreau, moves us from disinterested viewer to invested participant. There are material and transcendent benefits to be gained from this aesthetic.

In an 1851 journal entry, Thoreau writes of his dedication to becoming a watchman for the divine presence in nature: "We are surrounded by a rich and fertile mystery," he writes, and should "probe it, pry into it, employ ourselves about it" (xii). Kingsolver, too, reaches for a kind of transcendental truth—she wants to respect the "dignity of a spectacular food"; to realign our desires to the virtues of "patience and restraint" (30, 31). Like Thoreau, Kingsolver presents an argument for a massive culture shift; unlike Thoreau, Kingsolver is not searching for the divine in nature. She is searching for "national and biological integrity" through locavore living (17). A local food culture, she explains, "arises out of a place, a soil, a climate, a history, a temperament, a collective sense of belonging" (17).

Environmental aesthetics acknowledges the complexity of the natural world; Thoreau and Kingsolver pay homage to that complexity by constructing their texts as meeting places for the discourses of science, politics, economy, and art. The *scientific* is embodied in the descriptions of how natural systems function, found, for example, in Kingsolver's and Thoreau's observation of botanical history. The *political* emphasizes how power interests serve to value or devalue nature, found, for instance, in Kingsolver's explanation of farmer's marginalization at the hands of government and Thoreau's indictment of urban preference for imported fruits. The *economic* value speaks to the way markets place monetary worth on the natural world, found in Thoreau's lyrical assertion of a fruit's increased value when it has been gathered by the eater, not bought on the market, and in Kingsolver's narrative of her family's choice to "live off the grid." The *artistic* values nature for its beauty and complexity, found in Kingsolver's whimsical analogy of the "vegetannual" and Thoreau's insistence on fruit to "feed the imagination." Each of these discourses—scientific, political, economic, and artistic—meet within these pages. The narrative result is a revision of human values of nature. Ecological criticism, central to my reading of these texts, makes it possible for the critic to examine a text for the way it represents the relationship between humans and nature. As ecocritic Ursula Heise has written, the job of an ecocritic is to analyze texts for evidence of "the value of the natural environment" and its "relation to human needs and goals" (Heise 4).

By examining how diverse discourses meet in the text, the ecocritic can determine how nature is valued and what "use" it has for humans. Natural historians for two millennia have written about the "proper" way to use nature, beginning in the West with Pliny the Elder's multivolume encyclopedia *Naturalis Historia,* circa 77 C.E. The American literary tradition of writing about nature began during the "earliest documented European explorations of North America in the fifteenth century" (Branch xvi). These early observers of the American continent suggested many uses for the natural world, including those encoded long before in Judeo-Christian scriptural traditions. Roderick Nash, in his classic study *Wilderness and the American Mind,* documents the way the natural world was sanctuary, testing ground, a place to exercise freedom, and an antidote from corrupt society. Clearly the legacy of evaluating the natural world and its uses is complex, and made more so by pre–twentieth-century notions of aesthetics. Immanuel Kant argued in *The Critique of Judgment* (1790) that natural beauty is superior to art. Others elaborated on this by downplaying the viewer's background—and even nature's utilitarian purpose—in favor of an aesthetic appreciation of nature based on experiencing nature as if it were art: scenes framed and controlled to produce emotional affect. It is with Henry David Thoreau and other nature writers in the mid-nineteenth century that the aesthetic appreciation of nature moves away from the disinterested viewer to the engaged participator. This tradition, which distinguishes Kingsolver's *Animal, Vegetable, Miracle,* is signaled by a complex meeting of diverse discourses. *Wild Fruits* is no less an example of the ways scientific, economic, and political discourses act to transform what is considered beautiful and valuable than is *Animal, Vegetable, Miracle.*

Animal, Vegetable, Miracle is anchored by a seasonal calendar of planting and harvest and includes recipes for locavores and scientific essays explaining food phenomena. According to *Wild Fruits* editor Bradley Dean, Thoreau referred to his last manuscript as his "Kalendar" after a 1664 text, *Kalendarium Hortense, or Gardner's Almanac,* by John Evelyn (*Wild Fruits* xi). Thoreau's extensive observations of the annual natural phenomena in Concord were to be collected in a single archetypical year. In *Animal, Vegetable, Miracle* and *Wild Fruits,* the authors announce their intentions to make close observation of the natural world. Moreover—and perhaps more significantly for the purpose of my own comparison—each author proceeds to deconstruct the cultural values assigned to fruit and field by calling into question those values that abuse nature's worth and celebrating those values that sustain it. Both texts are concerned with the question of value and thus are engaged with the philosophical quest for the "proper" evaluation of natural resources, especially food. Before fully turning to *Animal, Vegetable, Miracle,* I would like to comment a bit further on *Wild Fruits* by way of developing a Thoreauvian reading of Kingsolver.

THOREAU'S "RICH AND FERTILE MYSTERY"

In the section called "Black Huckleberry," rivaling in development and philosophical insight the more famous "Wild Apples" entry, Thoreau describes the botanical properties, linguistic etymology, natural history, and regional variety of the fruit before explicitly making of the huckleberry a trope that serves as polemic on the experience of freedom. "Liberation and enlargement," Thoreau insists, "such is the fruit which all cultures aim to secure" (57). Spending time picking huckleberries for oneself and one's family would teach more than any book could, allowing for an expansive lesson where one "could not fail to see and hear things worth seeing and hearing" (57). The very demise of American freedom awaits the country once the huckleberry goes to market: "[W]hat becomes of the true value of country life, if you must go to market for it. . . . [W]hat sort of country is that where the huckleberry fields are private property?" (57). What happens, Thoreau explains, is that nature retreats and hides under a veil, the human and the berry become enslaved, our relationship to nature degraded. American authenticity is threatened.

By engaging economic discourse, Thoreau, like Kingsolver, attempts to revise culturally received notions of beauty. He links increased market value, in fact, to decreased beauty: "As long as the berries are free to all comers, they are beautiful," he writes (58). When local fruits are valued only for what they fetch on the market, we "strike only one more blow at a simple and wholesome relationship to nature" (58). Taking the berry to market is a form of domination over nature that ultimately serves to alienate us from it. Theodore Adorno and Max Horkheimer similarly conclude that humans "pay for their increase in power with alienation from that over which they exercise their power" (77). The struggle for power over nature's resource is a key feature of political discourse; for Thoreau, "money comes between a man and his objects" ("Civil Disobedience" 123).

The political was famously personal for Thoreau. In his essay "Civil Disobedience" (1849) he explains that he wishes "to trace the effects of my allegiance" by choosing which taxes to pay and which to boycott (131). He spent a night in jail to publicize his belief that his country "must cease to hold slaves and to make war on Mexico," even if it costs them their identity as a nation (114). One clue can be found in "Civil Disobedience" concerning his insistence that local fruit is a better political choice for Americans than imported fruit. Citizens may say they are opposed to injustice, he explains, but often "postpone the question of freedom to the question of free trade" (115). Choosing local fruit is an exercise of both political and economic freedom—Americans can remove themselves from the market system, which destroys beauty, and become a "majority of one," thus strengthening political power.

In his essay "Wild Apples," the discourses of the political and the economic are most ardently combined. Here Thoreau makes his strongest case for the inherent value of "all natural products," which "cannot be vulgarized, or bought and sold" (74). The doctrine of transcendentalism is operative here, forcing Thoreau to conclude that the very highest value is not material, but spiritual—the struggle for power over nature and the drive to "vulgarize" nature on the market erode the highest ethereal value. Any driver taking the fruit to market "begins to lose his load" as the "evanescent and celestial qualities" are removed from the apples, leaving behind only the "pulp and skin and core" (75). Only an American of a certain character can truly experience the beauty of the wild apple, and that is one who eats the apple out-of-doors, perhaps in the wind; one who has a "savage or wild taste" (87).

Although Thoreau became expert in his observations of natural history during the last decade or so of his life, his prose remained dedicated to the transcendent, mystical value of the natural world. In his introduction to *Wild Fruits*, Bradley Dean suggests that Thoreau would have "encouraged us to read *Wild Fruits* with an appreciation of its many dimensions—its value as natural history and scientific observation and its place as home-grown "American scripture" (xiii). In his journal, Thoreau refers to his growing manuscripts as "my New Testament," wherein parables and morality tales are "to be drawn, not from Egypt or Babylonia, but from New England" (xiii). Thoreau was working on both a metaphorical and literal level: local fruit best nourishes our identity as Americans as does locally grounded sacred writing. It is not my intention to fully analyze the transcendental discourse in *Wild Fruits;* suffice it here to say that the transcendental tradition immeasurably shaped Thoreau as a writer and a thinker. Because transcendentalism shaped Thoreau and he in turn shapes the American environmental imagination, we can read traces of transcendental discourses in Kingsolver. Both texts share what Lawrence Buell terms the "dual-accountability" to both the object-world and the world of imagination.

KINGSOLVER'S FOOD APPRECIATION COURSE

Examples of dual-accountability abound in *Animal, Vegetable, Miracle.* Kingsolver's family's asparagus patch is often recognized by guests as ethereally beautiful. Gardeners are likened to devotees who fast or make pilgrimages to "honor the spirit of what they believe makes our world whole and lovely" (29). In a particularly Thoreau-inspired passage, Kingsolver explains the patience and restraint necessary in establishing a local food culture, how food out of season is "cheapened by our wholesale desires" (31). Establishing a local food culture requires more than a farmer's market, she explains; it is "farmers growing trust" (123). While narrating her foray into making cheese, Kingsolver comments on the extra-edible value of the finished product. The process, she writes, involves "connecting with ... artisans . . . recalling our best memories infused with scents, parental love . . . and the routines of childhood" (123–24). The astute reader will note Kingsolver's denial of food's symbolic value—it is "not symbolic of anything so much as it is the real stuff" (338). Food may not be symbolic—that is, standing in for something else—but the process (Thoreau's "experience") of acquiring food can certainly be a vehicle of transcendence. Elsewhere she describes how her family's heirloom turkeys "are not just large birds but symbols of a precarious hold on vanishing honesty" (335). Kingsolver acknowledges both the objective, material reality of food and points to the imaginative potentiality of it: dual accountability. One textual marker of dual accountability is scientific discourse.

In literature, scientific discourse is signaled within a text by descriptions of how natural systems function. Within these descriptions, the reader can discern the scientific values that inhere in the text. In *Animal, Vegetable, Miracle*, Kingsolver, unlike many environmental writers past and present, does not use scientific discourse to authorize her narrative or to justify her literary project. Instead, the scientific meets other discourses in such a way as to suggest a holistic approach to the problem of sustainability and eating locally. Kingsolver acknowledges the diverse discourses that meet within the pages of her book and even suggests how they should be understood by the reader: "This is not a how-to book aimed at getting you cranking out your own food. . . . think of the agricultural parts of the story as a music appreciation course for food—acquainting yourself with the composers and conductors can improve the quality of your experience" (10). Science as music appreciation, an analogy which suggests that the production of knowledge about that which is beautiful and complex (i.e., the natural world) is tied to the social history of the producers of that beauty. Here Kingsolver rejects classical aesthetics and its theory of disinterestedness, which dissociated the viewer from the object of appreciation and insisted on "framing" the aesthetic object as a conceptual ideal.

By aligning scientific discourse with aesthetic discourse, Kingsolver signals the narrative direction of *Animal, Vegetable, Miracle:* it challenges readers to revise the aesthetics of the picturesque and the sublime and engage in an aesthetics of participation. For the reader less apt to pick up a scientific text, Kingsolver enters scientific discourse through accepted values of the beautiful: a "music appreciation course for food."

The most obvious way the text embeds scientific discourse is within Steven L. Hopp's sidebars, which resemble mini essays. These inserted genres are characteristic of good contemporary science writing: accessible by the general public, made friendly with humorous prose. The sidebars also

point to the multivalent rhetorical purposes of the book—Kingsolver admits
the book may be an argument "for reinstating food-production classes in
school," an antidote to the absence of knowledge of how food grows and
comes to table that "has rendered us a nation of wary label-readers," and
proof "that a family living on or near green land need not depend for its life
on industrial food" (9, 10, 22). As Kingsolver unfolds the story of her family's year of "realigning our lives with the food chain," sidebars by Hopp,
a biologist, are signaled by a strong page break and made distinct by their
typeface. Each sidebar, supported by a resource list in the reference section,
represents not so much a change in narrative tone as a change in generic
register. Instead of being organized by any essential generic characteristics,
or by participating in an established genre, Kingsolver's book is organized
around an ideological notion of genre that allows for it to be flexible and
include a variety of inserted texts—Hopp's sidebars and daughter Camille
Kingsolver's "recipe and reflection" pieces. The central generic characteristic is the *ideology* that seeks to shrink the space between producer and
consumer: the ideology of the locavore. Hopp's sidebars participate in the
formation of this ideology by relying on what readers typically associate
with scientific discourse: he explains, often using numerical data and cause-
and-effect argument, how natural systems function. In "Oily Food," for instance, the book's first sidebar, Hopp illustrates American dependence on
energy. We consume, he writes, "400 gallons of oil a year per citizen"; each
food item in a typical meal travels, on average, 1,500 miles (5). Instead of
creating a doom-and-gloom scenario that overwhelms the would-be environmentalist, Hopp calls upon each reader to imagine his or her own plate.
Changing the source of a typical meal is within the realm of possibility for
most. Hopp relies on the authority of scientific language and the intimation
of positive action—the reader need not be a passive consumer of his or her
next meal, but an active shaper of it. This calls to mind the distinction between passively viewing the beautiful and actively constructing it. As if to
highlight our proper, active role in both the food we eat and the beauty we
create, Hopp calls attention to the reader's role in the functioning of natural
systems. One way he does this is with explicit reference to economic value.
Kingsolver writes, "Steven's sidebars are, in his words, 'fifty-cent buckets of
a dollar's worth of goods," indicating that the reader is getting a good deal
on the bundled information offered there (21).

In "The Global Equation," Hopp compares the worth of farmers in developing countries to the worth of "processors, brokers, shippers, supermar-

kets, and oil companies" who profit from importing foods like bananas" (66). The cost of shipping bananas and potatoes, among other readily available produce, has detrimental affects on developing nations' environment (by burning rain forests) and indigenous populations (by driving farmers into global competition with each other, resulting in a "downward wage spiral") (67).

Economic value is of central concern in *Animal, Vegetable, Miracle*. In "Waiting for Asparagus," Kingsolver recalls her father's search for wild asparagus, "not always the tastiest, but [with] the advantage of being free" (27). More to the point, it is the perceived market value that Kingsolver and her collaborators constantly call into question. While looking at seed catalogs for heirloom vegetables, Kingsolver again asks the reader to challenge given cultural values: "I have seen women looking at jewelry ads with a misty eye and one hand resting on the heart, and I only know what they're feeling because that's how I read the seed catalogs in January" (46). Likewise, in "The Birds and the Bees," Kingsolver waxes poetic about her own turkey hatchlings and the arrival of daughter Lily's twenty-eight mail-order chicks. "It's a good thing," she writes, "that they don't stay this adorable forever" (89). Lily agrees to begin her own "chicken business," factoring in cost of hatchlings and feed as she gathers eggs, arranges them in rainbow-colored collections, and sells them. In narrating Lily's small-time economic venture, Kingsolver reflects on a larger economic venture: the insidious factory farms called concentrated animal feeding operations (CAFOs). By presenting the two economies together, Kingsolver implicitly demands the reader make an evaluative choice. Once again, Hopp's sidebar illuminates the scientific implications involved in choosing between a CAFO chicken and a free-range chicken. Ultimately, the farm is not a picture-like scene to be framed and appreciated by a disinterested viewer. By layering scientific and economic values, Kingsolver urges an environmental aesthetic in which value is ascertained by engagement with nature.

Political discourse makes its appearance throughout *Animal, Vegetable, Miracle* and can hardly be separated from discourses of science and economics. Kingsolver refers to the "war between producer and consumer" that makes certain produce available at market year-round, despite the interests of small farmers, global supply chains, and, of course, the environment itself (28). Year-round availability alters the storied and historical relationship between produce and producer, ultimately stripping produce of its beauty. In "Springing Forward," Kingsolver compares open pollinated

274

heirlooms with genetically modified seeds. The struggle for control over genetically modified seeds and what goes to market is presented, exposé-style, in Hopp's sidebar "The Strange Case of Percy Schmeiser." Some canola plants on Schmeiser's farm contained genes that belonged to the biotech seed producer, Monsanto. The case, highlighting the implications of "letting GM genies out of their bottle," resulted in an ongoing power struggle between Monsanto and like companies and Canadian farmers who grow organic canola (51). Hopp goes on to reveal the efforts of Canadian provinces and U.S. states to block genetically modified products; he documents the way the U.S. federal government has sided with biotech companies and against the consumer. Hopp concludes that in order to amass the political power needed to "keep GM's intellectual paws out of our bodies, and our fields," consumers must "demand full disclosure on what's in our food" (51).

What is in our food, Kingsolver insists throughout, is beauty, if only we remember how to look for it. (I say "remember" purposefully to remind us that nostalgia for the pastoral is a central feature of the Thoreauvian tradition in nature writing.) Hopp's sidebar provides political context to Kingsolver's discussion of genetically modified foods, and in doing so adds depth to the way the beautiful in nature is realized through an environmental aesthetic of appreciation. "Heirloom vegetables are irresistible," she writes, "not just for the poetry in their names but because these titles stand for real stories" (46). Calling to mind a Whitmanesque catalog, Kingsolver takes note of the varieties she considers ordering for her garden: "I swoon over names like Moon and Stars watermelon, Cajun Jewel okra, Gold of Bacau pole bean, Sweet Chocolate pepper, Collective Farm Woman melon, Georgian Crystal garlic, mother-of-thyme" (46). The evocative naming stands in direct contrast to the genetically modified seed that has no history. Every heirloom seed, Kingsolver points out, is collected for a reason: showy color, seasonal production, and of course, flavor. "Heirlooms," Kingsolver explains, "are the tangiest or sweetest tomatoes, the most fragrant melons, the eggplants without a trace of bitterness" (48). By contrast, produce sold in stores are bred because they look alike, are easily packaged, and can be mechanically harvested. Kingsolver traces the "Case of Murdered Flavor" to the upper-class desire for out-of-season produce, "an expensive party trick" that turned national when the combination of fashion, marketing, and the interstate highway got involved (48). Through this example, Kingsolver suggests that political power interests have resulted in the loss of beauty. Like Aldo Leopold's Land Ethic, set forth to help humans maintain the integrity, sta-

Gioia Woods

bility, and beauty of the biotic community, Kingsolver's evaluative revision involves the recognition that humans are *part* of the biotic community, not apart from it. We should eat seasonably, she concludes, like the "earth-enraptured primates we once were" (58).

BEAUTY, AUTHENTICITY, AND THE "GOOD LIFE"

What we learn when we read Kingsolver in the context of Thoreau is that the yearning for a local food culture that celebrates vernacular American flavors has a long tradition in our literature. We also learn that "nation" and "nature" have a long relationship in our literature. We discover Thoreau indeed has a canonical kin. We come to find out that our literature can be a site of encounter among diverse discourses, and that this encounter can work to revise culturally received values. In this case, each writer revisions beauty. Not a static science within a frame, but an active process of engagement, beauty calls out from these texts to be tasted.

This "taste," however, is not just a sensation on a tongue; taste, like beauty, involves a deep engagement with the scientific, economic, and political legacies engendered in that sensation. In short, authenticity refers to the way the conscious self comes to terms with the material world. Authenticity—the result of the self's encounter with nature, the way the self reacts and changes as a result of this encounter—is a central, if not *the* central, area of concern in American nature writing. In this body of literature, authenticity can mask pastoralism, nationalism, and exceptionalism. But for Thoreau and Kingsolver, authenticity is characterized by the predominance of ethical claims for the good life, whether concerning the individual only (Thoreau's preference) or the individual within the group (Kingsolver's preference). Jørgen Habermas refers to these ethical claims, whether "ethical-existential" or "ethical-political" as claims for authenticity. Authenticity claims do not come with an expectation of universal consensus, Habermas explains, but instead focus on the particular values of those whose good is at stake. In *Wild Fruits*, Thoreau argues for an individual ethic characterized by a relationship with nature whose value is not determined by the market, but by the inherent potential for personal growth and education. It is within this argument that Thoreau elevates economic discourse. It is neither the "foreignness or size or nutritive qualities of a fruit that determine its absolute value," nor the possession of them nor the eating of them, but in the charged category Thoreau refers to as the "experience" of them (3–4). Taking the fruit to market always degrades the value of the experience: one "cannot buy that pleasure which it yields to him who truly plucks it" (5). Kingsolver echoes this sentiment as she describes her hopes for the world her children will inherit: "if someday they crave orchards where their kids can climb onto the branches and steal apples, the world will have enough trees with arms to receive them" (271). It is within the embrace of the apple tree, not in the viewing of it, where one finds beauty.

Note

1. Literary critic and historian F. O. Mathiesson is largely credited with creating the "canon" of American literature. His 1941 book, *American Renaissance: Art and Expression in the Age of Emerson and Whitman,* identifies the mid-nineteenth century as a period in which American literature flourished. Mathiesson's work was certainly influenced by the first "Americanist" historian Vernon Lewis Parrington, who wrote *Main Currents in American Thought,* a three-volume history of American letters from colonial times, in 1927. During the mid-twentieth century the American canon began to take shape under the direction of historians and critics like Henry Nash Smith (*Virgin Land: The American West as Symbol and Myth,* 1950) Leo Marx (*The Machine in the Garden: Technology and the Pastoral Ideal in America,* 1967) and later Annette Kolodny (*The Lay of the Land: Metaphor as Experience and History in American Life and Letters,* 1975). These critics worked to identify certain recurring themes in American literature, themes that they claimed illuminated a unique American culture. It is the establishment of this literary canon, which largely argued that American literature was distinct in its symbolization of the American frontier and the natural world, that both Thoreau and Kingsolver work within and perhaps, at times, against.

WORKS CITED

"About Barbara: Bellwether Prize." *Barbara Kingsolver*. Web. 25 July 2006.

Ackerman, Diane. *Deep Play*. New York: Random House, 1999. Print.

Achebe, Chinua. "An Image of Africa: Racism in Conrad's *Heart of Darkness*." *Massachusetts Review* 18.4 (1977): 782–94. Print.

Adorno, Theodor W., and Max Horheimer. "The Logic of Domination." *The Green Studies Reader: From Romanticism to Ecocriticism*. Ed. Laurence Coupe. New York: Routledge Press, 2000. 77–80. Print.

Adorno, Theodor. "Commitment." *Aesthetics and Politics*. London: Verso, 1977. 177–95. Print.

Alcoff, Linda Martín. *Visible Identities: Race, Gender, and the Self*. New York: Oxford Univ. Press, 2006. Print.

Alexie, Sherman. *Indian Killer*. New York: Grand Central Publishing, 1998. Print.

Allen, Chadwick. *Blood Narrative: Indigenous Identity in American Indian and Maori Literary and Activist Texts*. Durham: Duke Univ. Press, 2002. Print.

Allen, Paula Gunn. *Off the Reservation*. Boston: Beacon, 1998. Print.

———. "The Feminine Landscape of Leslie Marmon Silko's *Ceremony*." *Studies in American Indian Literature: Critical Essays and Course Designs*. Ed. Paula Gunn Allen. New York: Modern Language Association of America, 1983. 127–33. Print.

———. *The Sacred Hoop*. Boston: Beacon, 1986. Print.

Alterman, Eric. *What Liberal Media? The Truth about Bias and the News*. New York: Basic Books, 2003. Print.

American Psychiatric Association. *Diagnostic and Statistical Manual of Mental Disorders*. 3rd ed. Washington, DC: APA, 1980. Print.

Amossy, Ruth. "The Cliché in the Reading Process." *SubStance* 2 (1982): 34–45. Print.

Anzaldua, Gloria. *Borderlands/La Frontera: The New Mestiza*. San Francisco: Aunt Lute Books, 1987. Print.

Appelbaum, Paul S., Lisa A. Uyehara, and Mark R. Elin, eds. *Trauma and Memory: Clinical and Legal Controversies*. New York: Oxford Univ. Press, 1997. Print.

Armstrong, Louise. *Rocking the Cradle of Sexual Politics: What Happened When Women Said Incest*. Reading, MA: Addison-Wesley, 1994. Print.

Ashcroft, Bill, Gareth Griffins, and Helen T. Tiffin. *The Empire Writes Back: Theory and Practice in Post-Colonial Literatures*. London: Routledge, 1989. Print.

Baird, Robert. "Going Indian: Discovery, Adoption, and Renaming toward a 'True American' from *Deerslayer* to *Dances with Wolves*." *Dressing in Feathers*. Ed. S. Elizabeth Bird. Boulder: Westview Press, 1996. 195–207. Print.

Bakhtin, Mikhail. *Rabelais and His World.* Trans. Helene Iswolsky. Bloomington: Indiana Univ. Press, 1984. Print.

Bal, Mieke. *Narratology: Introduction to the Theory of Narrative.* Toronto: University of Toronto Press, 1985. Print.

Bangsund, Jenny Christine. "Dwelling among Immortals: Narratives of Disability and Revelation in Twentieth-Century American Fiction." Ph.D. diss., Duquesne Univ., 2007. Print.

Barthes, Roland. *Mythologies.* New York: Hill & Wang, 1972. Print.

"Barbara Kingsolver." *Contemporary Authors Online.* Gale Literary Database. Web. 21 Sept. 2000.

Bauman, Zygmunt. *Mortality, Immortality and Other Life Strategies.* Stanford: Stanford Univ. Press, 1992. Print.

Beattie, L. Elisabeth, ed. "Barbara Kingsolver." *Conversations with Kentucky Writers.* Lexington: Univ. Press of Kentucky, 1996. 149–71. Print.

Benjamin, Walter. "The Task of the Translator." *Illuminations.* New York: Shocken Books, 1969. 69–82. Print.

Bennett, Ronan. *The Catastrophist.* London: Headline Review, 1998. Print.

Benson, Steve, et al. "Aesthetic Tendency and the Politics of Poetry: A Manifesto." *Social Text* 19–20 (Fall 1988): 261–75. Print.

Bent, Geoffrey. "Less Than Divine: Toni Morrison's *Paradise.*" *Southern Review* 35.1 (Winter 1999): 145–49. Print.

Benveniste, Emile. "A Look at the Development of Linguistics." *Problems in General Linguistics.* Trans. Mary Elizabeth Meek. Miami: Univ. of Miami Press, 1971. 17–27. Print.

Berger, James. "Trauma and Literary Theory." *Contemporary Literature* 38 (1997): 569–82. Print.

———. "Trauma without Disability; Disability without Trauma: A Disciplinary Divide." *Journal of Advanced Composition* 24.3 (2004): 563–82. Print.

Berry, Wendell. *Sex, Economy, Freedom & Community.* New York: Pantheon, 1993. Print.

Betterton, Rosemarie. "Promising Monsters: Pregnant Bodies, Artistic Subjectivity, and Maternal Imagination." *Hypatia* 21.1 (2006): 80–100. Print.

Bhabha, Homi. *The Location of Culture.* New York: Routledge, 1994. Print.

Bloom, Sandra L. *Creating Sanctuary: Toward the Evolution of Sane* Societies. New York: Routledge, 1997. Print.

Born, Brad. "Kingsolver's Gospel for Africa: (Western White Female) Heart of Goodness." *Mennonite Life* 56.1 (2001). Web. 12 Nov. 2007.

Brace, Marianne. "To Have and Have Nothing." *Independent [London].* 8 July 2001: 17. Print.

Braidotti, Rosi. "Signs of Wonder and Traces of Doubt: On Teratolog and Embodied Difference." *Between Monsters, Goddesses, and Cyborgs: Feminist Confrontations with Science, Medicine, and Cyberspace.* Ed. Nina Lykke and Rosi Braidotti. London: Zed Books, 1996. Print.

Branch, Michael P., ed. *Reading the Roots: American Nature Writing before Walden*. Athens: Univ. of Georgia Press, 2004. Print.

Brinkmeyer, Robert. *Remapping Southern Literature*. Athens: Univ. of Georgia Press, 2000. Print.

Brown, Laura S. "Not Outside the Range: One Feminist Perspective on Psychic Trauma." Caruth, *Trauma*, 100–112. Print.

Bruchac, Joseph. *Native American Stories*. Golden, CO: Fulcrum, 1991. Print.

Bruner, Jerome. "The Narrative Construction of Reality." *Critical Inquiry* 18 (1991): 1–21.

——. "The 'Remembered' Self." *The Remembering Self: Construction and Accuracy in the Self-Narrative*. Ed. Ulric Neisser and Robyn Fivush. New York: Cambridge Univ. Press, 1994. 41–54. Print.

Buchanan, Linda. "A Study of Maternal Rhetoric: Anne Hutchinson, Monsters, and the Antinomian Controversy." *Rhetoric Review* 25.3 (2006): 239–59. Print.

Buell, Lawrence. *The Environmental Imagination: Thoreau, Nature Writing, and the Formation of American Culture*. Cambridge: Belknap Press of Harvard Univ. Press, 1995. Print.

——. *Writing for an Endangered World: Literature, Culture, and Environment in the U.S. and Beyond*. Cambridge: Belknap, 2001. Print.

Bulbeck, Chilla. *Re-orienting Western Feminisms: Women's Diversity in a Postcolonial World*. Cambridge: Cambridge University Press, 1998. Print.

Butler, Judith. *Gender Trouble: Feminism and the Subversion of Identity*. New York: Routledge, 1990. Print.

——. *Undoing Gender*. New York: Routledge, 2004. Print.

Carson, Rachel. *The Sea Around Us*. New York: Oxford Univ. Press, 2008. Print.

——. *The Sense of Wonder*. New York: HarperCollins, 1998. Print.

——. *Silent Spring*. Boston, Mariner Books, 2002. Print.

Caruth, Cathy, ed. *Trauma: Explorations in Memory*. Baltimore: Johns Hopkins Univ. Press, 1995. Print.

——. *Unclaimed Experience: Trauma, Narrative, and History*. Baltimore: Johns Hopkins Univ. Press, 1996. Print.

Charles, Ron. "Mothers of Nature Howling at the Moon." *Christian Science Monitor* 19 Oct. 2000: 20. Print.

Chawla, Louise. "Life Paths into Effective Environmental Action." *Journal of Environmental Education* 31.1 (1999): 15–26. Print.

Cheng, Anna Anlin. *The Melancholy of Race: Psychoanalysis, Assimilation and Hidden Grief*. Oxford: Oxford Univ. Press, 2001. Print.

Cheyfitz, Erik. *The Poetics of Imperialism: Translation and Colonization from "The Tempest" to "Tarzan."* London: Oxford Univ., 1991. Print.

Chow, Rey. *Ethics after Idealism: Theory-Culture-Ethnicity-Reading*. Bloomington: Indiana Univ. Press, 1998. Print.

Clarke, Deborah. "Domesticating the Car: Women's Road Trips." *Studies in American Fiction* 32.1 (2004): 101–28. Print.

Clifford, James. *Routes: Travel and Translation in the Late Twentieth Century*. Cambridge: Harvard University Press, 1997. Print.

Cockrell, Amanda. "Luna Moth, Coyotes, Sugar Skulls: The Fiction of Barbara Kingsolver." *Hollins Critic* 38.2 (2001): 1–15. Print.

"Colorado River Compact: Triumph of the Hoover Compromise or Environmental Tragedy?" *Curriculum Guides for Education for National History Day Project*. The Herbert Hoover Presidential Library and Museum. Web. 14 August 2009.

Comer, Krista. *Landscapes of the New West: Gender and Geography in Contemporary Women's Writing*. Chapel Hill: Univ. of North Carolina Press, 1999. Print.

———. "Sidestepping Environmental Justice: 'Natural' Landscapes and the Wilderness Plot." *Breaking Boundaries: New Perspectives on Women's Regional Writing*. Ed. Sherrie A. Inness and Diana Royer. Iowa City: Univ. of Iowa Press, 1997. 216–36. Print.

Conrad, Joseph. "Explicitness Is Fatal to Art." *Heart of Darkness. A Norton Critical Edition*. 3rd ed. Ed. Robert Kimbrough. New York: W. W. Norton & Co., 1988. 232–33. Print.

———. *Heart of Darkness and Other Stories*. Ed. Gene Moore. Ware: Wordsworth Editions Limited, 1995. Print.

Coolidge, Calvin. "The Press Under a Free Government." *Calvin Coolidge*. Calvin Coolidge Memorial Foundation. Web. 12 July 2008.

Cranny-Francis, Anne. *Feminist Fiction: Feminist Uses of Generic Fiction*. Cambridge: Polity Press, 1990. Print.

Crenshaw, Kimberlé. "Demarginalizing the Intersection of Race and Sex." *Living with Contradictions*. Ed. Alison M. Jaggar. Boulder: Westview Press, 1994. 39–52. Print.

"Crittenden Compromise of 1860." *Crittenden Compromise of 1860* 1.1 (1997): 1–2. Web. 10 Dec. 2007.

Daugherty, Tracy. "After Murrah: An Essay on Public and Private Pain." *Southwest Review* 83 (1998): 489–511. Print.

"Defining a Literature of Social Change." *The Bellwether Prize for Fiction: In Support of a Literature of Social Change*. Web. 12 Dec. 2007.

de Lauretis, Teresa. *Technologies of Gender: Essays on Theory, Film, and Fiction*. Bloomington: Indiana Univ. Press, 1987. Print.

DeLillo, Don. *Underworld*. New York: Scribner, 1997. Print.

De Man, Paul. "Semiology and Rhetoric." *Allegories of Reading*. New Haven: Yale Univ. Press, 1979. 3–19. Print.

———. "Resistance to Theory." *The Resistance to Theory*. Vol. 33, *Theory and History of Literature*. Minneapolis: University of Minnesota Press, 1990. 1–20. Print.

De Reus, Lee Ann. "Exploring the Matrix of Identity in Barbara Kingsolver's *Animal Dreams*." *Reading the Family Dance: Family Systems Therapy and Literary Study*. Ed. John V. Knapp and Kenneth Womack. Newark: Univ. of Delaware Press, 2003. 93–108. Print.

Deloria, Philip J. *Playing Indian*. New Haven: Yale Univ. Press, 1998. Print.

DeMarr, Mary Jean. *Barbara Kingsolver: A Critical Companion*. Westport, CT: Greenwood, 1999. Print.

———. "Mothers and Children in Barbara Kingsolver's *The Bean Trees.*" *Women in Literature: Reading through the Lens of Gender.* Ed. Jerilyn Fisher, Ellen S. Silber, and David Sadker. Westport, CT: Greenwood, 2003. 26–28. Print.

DeMeester, Karen. "Trauma and Recovery in Virginia Woolf's Mrs. Dalloway." *Modern Fiction Studies* 44 (1998): 649–73. Print.

Demory, Pamela. "Into the Heart of Light: Barbara Kingsolver Rereads *Heart of Darkness.*" *Conradiana: A Journal of Joseph Conrad Studies* 34.3 (2002): 181–93. Print.

Desai, Gaurav, and Supriya Nair, eds. *Postcolonialisms: An Anthology of Cultural Theory and Criticism.* New Brunswick: Rutgers Univ. Press, 2005. Print.

deVries, Marten W. "Trauma in Cultural Perspective." van der Kolk, McFarlane, and Weisaeth, *Traumatic Stress,* 398–413. Print.

De Witte, Ludo. *The Assassination of Lumumba (De Moord op Lumumba).* London: Verso, 1999. Print.

Dirlik, Arif. "The Global in the Local." *Global/Local: Cultural Production and the Transnational Imaginary.* Eds. Rob Wilson and Wimal Dissanayake. Durham: Duke University Press, 1996. 21–45. Print.

Douglas, Mary. *Purity and Danger: An Analysis of the Concepts of Pollution and Taboo.* New York: Routledge, 1966. Print.

Dunaway, David King. "Barbara Kingsolver." *Writing the Southwest.* Albuquerque: Univ. of New Mexico Press, 2003. 93–103. Print.

Epstein, Julia. *Altered Conditions: Disease, Medicine, and Storytelling.* New York: Routledge, 1995. Print.

Epstein, Robin. "Barbara Kingsolver." *Progressive* 60.2 (1996): 33–37. Print.

Erikson, Kai. "Notes on Trauma and Community." Caruth, *Trauma* 183–99. Print.

Evernden, Neil. "Beyond Ecology: Self, Place and the Pathetic Fallacy." *The Ecocriticism Reader: Landmarks in Literary Ecology.* Ed. Cheryll Glotfelty and Harold Fromm. Athens: Univ. of Georgia Press, 1995. 92–104. Print.

Fagan, Kristina. "Adoption as National Fantasy in Barbara Kingsolver's *Pigs in Heaven* and Margaret Laurence's *The Diviners.*" *Imagining Adoption: Essays on Literature and Culture.* Ed. Marianne Novy. Ann Arbor: Univ. of Michigan Press, 2001, 251–66. Print.

Faludi, Susan. *The Terror Dream: Fear and Fantasy in Post-9/11 America.* New York: Metropolitan Books, 2007. Print.

Farn, Regelind. "Colonial and Postcolonial Rewritings of *Heart of Darkness:* A Century of Dialogue with Joseph Conrad." Ph.D. diss., Univ. of Dortmund, 2005. Print.

Felski, Rita. *Literature after Feminism.* Chicago: Univ. of Chicago Press, 2003. Print.

Fiedler, Leslie A. *The Return of the Vanishing American.* New York: Stein and Day, 1971. Print.

Finkel, Mike. "The Ultimate Survivor." *Audubon* 101.3 (1999): 52+. Print.

Foster, John Wilson. "Encountering Traditions." *Nature in Ireland: A Scientific and Cultural History.* Ed. John Wilson Foster. Dublin: Lilliput Press, 1997. 23–70. Print.

Foucault, Michel. *Discipline and Punish: The Birth of the Prison.* New York: Vintage, 1995. Print.

———. *The Birth of the Clinic: An Archaeology of Medical Perception.* New York: Vintage, 1994. Print.

———. *Madness and Civilization: A History of Insanity in an Age of Reason.* New York: Vintage, 1988. Print.

———. *The History of Sexuality: An Introduction.* Vol. 1. New York: Random House, 1978. Print.

———. *Power/Knowledge: Selected Interviews and Other Writings, 1972–1977.* Ed. and trans. Colin Gordon. New York: Pantheon, 1980. Print.

Fox, Stephen D. "Barbara Kingsolver and Keri Hulme: Disability, Family, and Culture." *Critique: Studies in Contemporary Fiction* 45.4 (2004): 405–20. Print.

Fraser, Nancy, and Linda Gordon. "Contract versus Charity: Why Is There No Social Citizenship in the United States?" *The Citizenship Debates: A Reader.* Ed. Gershon Shafir. Minneapolis: Univ. of Minnesota Press, 1998. 113–30. Print.

Freedman, Jill, and Gene Combs. *Narrative Therapy: The Social Construction of Preferred Realities.* New York: Norton, 1996. Print.

Freeman, Mark. *Rewriting the Self: History, Memory, Narrative.* London: Routledge, 1993. Print.

Freud, Sigmund. *Beyond the Pleasure Principle. The Standard Edition of the Complete Psychological Works of Sigmund Freud.* Trans. James Strachey. Vol. 18. London: Hogarth, 1955. 7–64. Print.

Fromm, Harold. "The Hegemonic Form of Othering; or, The Academic's Burden." Gates, *"Race"* 396–99. Print.

Gates, Henry Louis, Jr., ed. *"Race," Writing and Difference.* Chicago: Univ. of Chicago Press, 1985. Print.

George, Rosemary Marangoly. *The Politics of Home: Postcolonial Relocations and Twentieth-Century Fiction.* Berkeley: Univ. of California Press, 1996. Print.

———, ed. "Recycling: Long Routes to and from Domestic Fixes." *Burning Down the House: Recycling Domesticity.* Boulder: Westview Press, 1998. 1–20. Print.

Giles, Jeff. "Getting Back to Nature." *Newsweek* 6 Nov. 2000: 82. Print.

Godfrey, Kathleen. "Barbara Kingsolver's Cherokee Nation: Problems of Representation in *Pigs in Heaven.*" *Western American Literature* 36.3 (2001): 259–77. Print.

Goldberg, Bernard. *100 People Who Are Screwing Up America (and Al Franken Is #37).* New York: HarperCollins, 2005. Print.

Goldblatt, Patricia. "The Implausibility of Marriage." *MultiCultural Review* 10.3 (2001): 42–48. Print.

Goldman, Marlene. "Margaret Atwood's Wilderness Tips: Apocalyptic Cannibal Fiction." *Eating Their Words: Cannibalism and the Boundaries of Identity.* Ed. Kristen Guest. New York: State Univ. of New York Press, 2001. 167–85. Print.

"Grace." *Webster's II New Riverside University Dictionary.* Boston: Houghton Mifflin Co., 1988. Print.

Graulich, Melody. "O Beautiful for Spacious Guys." *The Frontier Experience and the American Dream.* Ed. David Moyer, Mark Busby, and Paul Bryant. College Station: Texas A & M Univ. Press, 1989. 186–201. Print.

Works Cited

Gray, Paul. "On Familiar Ground." *Time* 30 Oct. 2000: 90. Print.

Griffin, Susan. *Woman and Nature: The Roaring Inside Her.* New York: Harper & Row, 1978. Print.

Grosz, Elizabeth. *Space, Time, and Perversion: Essays on the Politics of Bodies.* New York: Routledge, 1995. Print.

Guest, Kristen. "Introduction: Cannibalism and the Boundaries of Identity." *Eating Their Words: Cannibalism and the Boundaries of Identity.* Ed. Kristen Guest. New York: State Univ. of New York Press, 2001. 1–9. Print.

Guth, Hans P. "The Politics of Rhetoric." *College Composition and Communication* 23.1 (Feb. 1972): 30–43. Print.

Haaken, Janice. *Pillar of Salt: Gender, Memory, and the Perils of Looking Back.* New Brunswick, NJ: Rutgers Univ. Press, 1998. Print.

Habermas, Jørgen. *Justification and Application: Remarks on Discourse Ethics.* Trans. C. P. Cronin. Cambridge, MA: MIT Press, 1994. Print.

Hamill, Sam, ed. *Poets against the War.* New York: Nation Books, 2003. Print.

Haraway, Donna. *Simians, Cyborgs, and Women: The Reinvention of Nature.* New York: Routledge, 1991. Print.

Harding, Sandra. *Is Science Multicultural? Postcolonialisms, Feminisms, and Epistemologies.* Bloomington: Indiana University Press, 1998. Print.

Harstock, Nancy. "The Feminist Standpoint: Developing the Ground for a Specifically Feminist Historical Materialism." *The Feminist Standpoint Theory Reader.* Ed. Sandra Harding. New York: Routledge, 2004. 35–53. Print.

Hartley, George. "Textual Politics and the Language Poets." 1989. Web. 17 Nov. 2007.

Hartman, Geoffrey H. "On Traumatic Knowledge and Literary Studies." *New Literary History* 26 (1995): 537–63. Print.

Harvey, David. *Spaces of Hope.* Berkeley: Univ. of California Press, 2000. Print.

Haven, Janet, ed. "The Hoover Dam: Lonely Lands Made Fruitful." *X-Roads Project.* Univ. of Virginia. Web. 21 Dec. 2007.

Heise, Ursula. "Science and Ecocriticism." *American Book Review* 18.5 (1997): 4+. Print.

Hejinian, Lyn. *Writing Is an Aid to Memory.* Los Angeles: Sun & Moon Press, 1996. Print.

Henderson, Margaret. "Subdivisions of Suburbia: The Politics of Place in Melissa Lucashenko's *Steam Pigs* and Amanda Lohrey's *Camille's Bread.*" *Australian Literary Studies* 18.4 (1998): 72–86. Print.

Henke, Suzette A. *Shattered Subjects: Trauma and Testimony in Women's Life-Writing.* New York: St. Martin's, 1998. Print.

Hepburn, R. W. "Contemporary Aesthetics and the Neglect of Natural Beauty." *British Analytical Philosophy.* Ed. B. Williams and A. Montefiore. London: Routledge, 1966. 285–310. Print.

Herman, Judith Lewis. *Trauma and Recovery.* New York: Basic, 1997. Print.

Hill Collins, Patricia. *Black Feminist Thought: Knowledge, Consciousness, and the Politics of Empowerment.* New York: Routledge, 1990. Print.

Himmelwright, Catherine. "Garden of Auto Parts: Kingsolver's Merger of American Western Myth and Native American Myth in *The Bean Trees.*" 27–46.

284

hooks, bell. *Feminism Is for Everybody: Passionate Politics.* Cambridge, MA: South End Press, 2000. Print.

Hunt, Nancy. "Hommes et femmes, sujets du Congo colonial" [Men and women, subjects of the colonial Congo]. *La mémoire du Congo: Le temps colonial.* Tervuren: Musée Royal de l'Afrique Centrale; Gent: Editions Snoeck, 2005. 51–57. Print.

Hurston, Zora Neale. *Dust Tracks on a Road.* New York: Harper Collins, 1991. Print.

Jacobs, Johan. "Translating the 'Heart of Darkness': Cross-Cultural Discourse in the Contemporary Congo Book." *Current Writing: Text and Reception in Southern Africa* 14.2 (2002): 104–17. Print.

Jacobs, Naomi. "Barbara Kingsolver's Anti-Western: 'Unraveling the Myths' in *Animal Dreams.*" *Americana: The Journal of American Popular Culture 1900 to Present* 2.2 (2003). Web. 8 July 2008.

Jakobson, Roman. "Linguistics and Poetics." *Verbal Art, Verbal Sign, Verbal Time.* Ed. Krystyna Pomorska and Stephen Ruby. Minneapolis: University of Minnesota Press, 1985. 62–94. Print.

———. "What Is Poetry?" *Verbal Art, Verbal Sign, Verbal Time.* Ed. Krystyna Pomorska and Stephen Ruby. Minneapolis: University of Minnesota Press, 1985. 368–78. Print.

Johnson, Michael. *New Westers.* Lawrence: University Press of Kansas, 1996. Print.

Jones, Susan. *Conrad and Women.* Oxford: Clarendon Press, 1999. Print.

Jones, Suzanne Whitmore. "The Southern Family Farm as Endangered Species: Possibilities for Survival in Barbara Kingsolver's *Prodigal Summer.*" *Southern Literary Journal* 39.1 (2006): 83–97. Print.

Jussawalla, Feroza. "Reading and Teaching Barbara Kingsolver's *Poisonwood Bible* as Postcolonial." *Revista Alicantina de Estudios Ingleses* 16 (2003): 165–75. Print.

Karbo, Karen. "And Baby Makes Two." Interview with Barbara Kingsolver. *New York Times on the Web.* 27 June 1993. Web. 20 July 2008.

Kentoff, Maureen Meharg. "An Interdimensional Model for Coping with Identity-Based Oppression: Conversations with US Feminist Activists." MA thesis, George Washington Univ., 2007. Print.

Kerr, Sarah. "The Novel as Indictment." *New York Times Magazine* 11 Oct. 1998: 52–55. Web. 13 Apr. 2008.

Kilgour, Maggie. *Communion to Cannibalism: An Anatomy of Metaphors of Incorporation.* Princeton: Princeton Univ. Press, 1990. Print.

King, Nicola. *Memory, Narrative, Identity: Remembering the Self.* Edinburgh: Edinburgh Univ. Press, 2000. Print.

Kingsolver, Barbara. "A Good Farmer." *The Essential Agrarian Reader.* Ed. Norman Wirzba. Lexington: Univ. Press of Kentucky. 11–18. Print.

———. *Animal Dreams.* New York: Harper Collins, 1990. Print.

———. *Another America/Otra America.* Spanish Trans. Rebeca Cartes. New York: Seal Press, 1990. Print.

———. *The Bean Trees.* New York: Harper & Row, 1988. Print.

———. "Careful What You Let in the Door." *High Tide in Tucson* 243–56. Print.

Works Cited

——. "Civil Disobedience at Breakfast." *High Tide in Tucson* 85–98. Print.

——. "Confessions of a Reluctant Rock Goddess." *High Tide in Tucson* 121–34. Print.

——. "Creation Stories." *High Tide in Tucson* 17–22. Print.

——. "Dialogue: Barbara Kingsolver." *Barbara Kingsolver.* HarperCollins. Nov. 2000. Web. 5 July 2008.

——. "FAQ." *Barbara Kingsolver.* Harper Collins. Web. 5 July 2008.

——. "The Forest in the Seeds." *High Tide in Tucson* 236–42. Print.

——. "Foreword." *The Essential Agrarian Reader: The Future of Culture, Community, and the Land.* Ed. Norman Wirzba. Lexington: Univ. Press of Kentucky, 2003. ix–xvii. Print.

——. "God's Wife's Measuring Spoons." *Small Wonder* 246–64. Print.

——. *High Tide in Tucson: Essays from Now or Never.* New York: Harper–Collins, 1995. Print.

——. "High Tide in Tucson." *High Tide in Tucson.* 1–16. Print.

——. *Holding the Line: Women in the Great Arizona Mine Strike of 1983.* Ithaca, NY: ILR Press, 1989. Print.

——. *Homeland and Other Stories.* New York: Harper & Row, 1990. Print.

——. "How Mr. Dewey Decimal Saved My Life." *High Tide in Tucson* 46–53. Print.

——. "In Case You Ever Want to Go Home Again." *High Tide in Tucson* 35–45. Print.

——. "Infernal Paradise." *High Tide in Tucson* 194–206. Print.

——. "Islands on the Moon." *Homeland and Other Stories* 119–47. Print.

——. "Jabberwocky." *High Tide in Tucson* 222–35. Print.

——. "Knowing Our Place." *Small Wonder* 31–40. Print.

——. "Letter to a Daughter at Thirteen." *Small Wonder* 144–59. Print.

——. "Letter to My Mother." *Small Wonder* 160–75. Print.

——. "Life without Go-Go Boots." *High Tide in Tucson* 54–58. Print.

——. "Lily's Chickens." *Small Wonder* 109–30. Print.

——. "Making Peace." *High Tide in Tucson,* 23–34. Print.

——. "Mexican Torture Victims Face Trial." *Militant* 25 July 1980: 5. Print.

——. "The Memory Place." *High Tide in Tucson* 170–80. Print.

——. "The Not-So-Deadly Sin." *High Tide in Tucson.* 257–62. Print.

——. *Pigs in Heaven.* New York: Harper Collins, 1993. Print.

——. *The Poisonwood Bible.* London: Faber and Faber Limited, 1998. Print.

——. *The Poisonwood Bible.* New York: Harper Collins, 1999. Print.

——. *Prodigal Summer.* New York: Harper Collins, 2000. Print.

——. "Postcards from the Imaginary Mom." *High Tide in Tucson* 158–69. Print.

——. "Reprise." *High Tide in Tucson* 263–70. Print.

——. "Saying Grace." *Small Wonder* 22–30. Print.

——. "Semper Fi." *High Tide in Tucson* 66–79. Print.

——. *Small Wonder.* New York: Harper-Collins, 2002. Print.

——. "Small Wonder." *Small Wonder* 1–21. Print.

——. "The Spaces Between." *High Tide in Tucson* 146–57. Print.

——. "Stone Soup." *High Tide in Tucson* 135–45. Print.

———. "Taming the Beast with Two Backs." *Small Wonder.* 222–27. Print.

———. "Tucson Residents Fight Atomic Poisoning." *Militant* 13 July 1979: 3. Print.

Kingsolver, Barbara, and Annie Griffiths Belt. Photographs. *Last Stand: America's Virgin Lands.* New York: Harper Collins, 2002. Print.

Kingsolver, Barbara, with Steven L. Hopp and Camille Kingsolver. *Animal, Vegetable, Miracle: A Year of Food Life.* New York: HarperCollins, 2007. Print.

Koleva, Daniela. "Narrating Nature: Perceptions of the Environment and Attitudes Towards It in Life Stories." *The Roots of Environmental Consciousness: Popular Tradition and Personal Experience.* Ed. Stephen Hussey and Paul Tompson. London: Routledge, 2000. 63–75. Print.

Kolodny, Annette. *The Land before Her.* Chapel Hill: Univ. of North Carolina Press, 1984. Print.

———. *The Lay of the Land: Metaphor as Experience and History in American Life and Letters.* Chapel Hill: Univ. of North Carolina Press, 1975. Print.

Koza, Kimberly A. "The Africa of Two Western Women Writers: Barbara Kingsolver and Margaret Laurence." *Critique* 44.3 (2003): 284–94. Print.

Kunz, Diane. "White Men in Africa: On Barbara Kingsolver's *The Poisonwood Bible.*" *Novel History: Historians and Novelists Confront America's Past (and Each Other).* Ed. Mark C. Carnes. New York: Simon & Schuster, 2001. 285–97. Print.

Kuribayashi, Tomoko, and Julie Tharp. Introduction. *Creating Safe Space: Violence and Women's Writing.* Albany: State Univ. of New York Press, 1998. 1–8. Print.

Kymlicka, Will. "Multicultural Citizenship." *The Citizenship Debates: A Reader.* Ed. Gershon Shafir. Minneapolis: Univ. of Minnesota Press, 1998. 167–88. Print.

LaCapra, Dominick. *Representing the Holocaust: History, Theory, Trauma.* Ithaca: Cornell Univ. Press, 1994. Print.

Laclau, Ernesto, and Chantal Mouffe. *Hegemony and Socialist Strategy: Towards a Radical Democratic Politics.* London: Verso, 1985. Print.

Lai, Larissa. "Foreword." *Other Conundrums: Race, Culture, and Canadian Art.* Ed. Monika Kin Gagnon. Vancouver: Arsenal Pulp Press, 2000. 15–20. Print.

Lear, Linda. *Rachel Carson: Witness for Nature.* New York: Holt, 1997. Print.

Le Guin, Ursula K. "The Fabric of Grace." Rev. of *Animal Dreams,* by Barbara Kingsolver. *Washington Post* 2 Sept. 1990: Book World 1+. Print.

Leeming, David. *Creation Myths.* New York: Oxford Univ. Press, 1994. Print.

Leopold, Aldo. *A Sand County Almanac And Sketches from Here and There.* New York: Oxford Univ. Press, 1949. Print.

Levinas, Emmanuel. "Ethics as First Philosophy." *The Levinas Reader.* Ed. Seán Hand. Oxford: Blackwell, 1989. 75–87. Print.

Lewis, R. W. B. *The American Adam.* Chicago: University of Chicago Press, 1955. Print.

Limón, José E. *American Encounters: Greater Mexico, the United States and the Erotics of Culture.* Boston: Beacon Press, 1998. Print.

Linard, André. "Enfin le bout du tunnel au Congo?" *En Marche* 6 July 2006: 6. Print.

London, Bette. *The Appropriated Voice. Narrative Authority in Conrad, Forster, and Woolf.* Ann Arbor: Univ. of Michigan Press, 1990. Print.

Works Cited

Lopez, Barry. "Children in the Woods." *Being in the World.* Ed. Terrell Dixon and Scott Slovic. New York: Longman, 1992. Print.

——. *Crossing Open Ground.* New York: Vintage, 1988. Print.

Lorde, Audre. "A Burst of Light: Living with Cancer." *A Burst of Light.* Ithaca: Firebrand, 1988. 49–134. Print.

Love, Glen. *Practical Ecocriticism: Literature, Biology and the Environment.* Charlottesville: Univ. of Virginia Press, 2003. Print.

MacEoin, Gary. "Nature Triumphs in Novel Buzzing with Life." *National Catholic Reporter* 9 Nov. 2001: 19. Print.

MacGregor, Sherilyn. *Beyond Mothering Earth: Ecological Citizenship and the Politics of Care.* Vancouver: Univ. of British Columbia Press, 2006. Print.

Madsen, Deborah L. *American Exceptionalism.* Jackson: Univ. Press of Mississippi, 1998. Print.

Manes, Christopher. "Nature and Silence." *The Ecocriticism Reader: Landmarks in Literary Ecology.* Ed. Cheryll Glotfelty and Harold Fromm. Athens: Univ. of Georgia Press, 1995. 15–29. Print.

Marx, Leo. *The Machine in the Garden: Technology and the Pastoral Ideal in America.* London: Oxford Univ. Press, 1967. Print.

Massey, Doreen. *Space, Place, and Gender.* Minneapolis: Univ. of Minnesota Press, 1994. Print.

Massey, Doreen, and Pat Jess, eds. *A Place in the World? Places, Cultures and Globalization.* Oxford: Open University, 1995. Print.

Mathiesson, F. O. *American Renaissance: Art and Expression in the Age of Emerson and Whitman.* New York: Oxford Univ. Press, 1941. Print.

McDowell, Linda. *Gender, Identity and Place: Understanding Feminist Geographies.* Minneapolis: Univ. of Minnesota Press, 1999. Print.

McKee, Patricia. "Geographies of *Paradise.*" *New Centennial Review* 3.1 (2003): 197–223. Print.

McKibben, Bill. *Deep Economy: The Wealth of Communities and the Durable Future.* New York: Henry Holt and Co., 2007. Print.

McWilliams, Carey. *North from Mexico: The Spanish-Speaking People of the United States.* 1948. New ed., updated by Matt S. Meier. New York: Praeger Publishers, 1990. Print.

Mendes, Guy. "'Messing with the Sacred': An Interview with Barbara Kingsolver." *Appalachian Journal* 28.3 (Spring 2001): 304–24. Print.

Michael, Magali Cornier. *New Visions of Community in Contemporary American Fiction: Tan, Kingsolver, Castillo, Morrison.* Iowa City: Univ. of Iowa Press, 2006. Print.

Mies, Maria, and Vandana Shiva. *Ecofeminism.* London: Fernwood Publications (Zed Books), 1993. Print.

Miller, J. Hillis. *Fiction and Repetition: Seven English Novels.* Cambridge: Harvard Univ. Press, 1982. Print.

Morgan, Craig, Craig Morris, and Lance McDaniel. "God, Family and Country." CowboyLyrics.Com. Web. 12 July 2008.

Morris, Robyn. "'What Does It Mean to Be Human?': Racing Monsters, Clones, and Replicants." *Foundation* 91 (2004): 81–96. Print.

Morrison, Toni. "Home." *The House That Race Built*. Ed. Wahneema Lubiano. New York: Pantheon Books, 1997. 3–12. Print.

———. *Playing in the Dark: Whiteness and the Literary Imagination*. Cambridge: Harvard Univ. Press, 1992. Print.

Murphy, Patrick D. "Nature Nurturing Fathers in a World beyond Our Control" *Eco-Man: New Perspectives on Masculinity and Nature*. Ed. Mark Alister. Charlottesville: Univ. Press of Virginia, 2004. 196–210. Print.

Murrey, Loretta Martin. "The Loner and the Matriarchal Community in Barbara Kingsolver's *The Bean Trees* and *Pigs in Heaven*." *Southern Studies: An Interdisciplinary Journal of the South* 5.1–2 (1994): 155–64. Print.

Nabhan, Gary Paul, and Stephen Trimble. *The Geography of Childhood: Why Children Need Wild Places*. Boston: Beacon Press, 1994. Print.

Nash, Roderick. *Wilderness and the American Mind*. 3rd ed. New Haven, CT: Yale University Press, 1982. Print.

Nünning, Ansgar. "Where Historiographic Metafiction and Narratology Meet: Towards an Applied Cultural Narratology." *Style* 38.3 (2004): 352–403. Print.

Ognibene, Elaine R. "The Missionary Position: Barbara Kingsolver's *The Poisonwood Bible*. *College Literature* 30.3 (2003): 19–36. Print.

Owens, Louis. "Apocalypse at the Two-Socks Hop: Dancing with the Vanishing American." *Mixedblood Messages: Literature, Film, Family, Place*. Norman: Univ. of Oklahoma Press, 1998. 113–34. Print.

———. "As If an Indian Were Really an Indian: Native American Voices and Postcolonial Theory." *Native American Representations: First Encounters, Distorted Images, and Literary Appropriations*. Ed. Gretchen M. Bataille. Lincoln: Univ. of Nebraska Press, 2001. 11–25. Print.

Palgi, Phyllis, and Joshua Dorban. "Reflections on the Self of Homo Hippocraticus and the Quest for Symbolic Immortality." *Trauma and Self*. Ed. Charles B. Strozier and Michael Flynn. Lanham, MD: Rowman & Littlefield, 1996. 221–30. Print.

Paredes, Raymund A. "Contemporary Mexican-American Literature, 1960–Present." *A Literary History of the American West*. Ed. Western Literature Association. Fort Worth, TX: Christian University Press, 1987. 1101–18. Print.

Parrington, Vernon Louis. *Main Currents in American Thought: An Interpretation of American Literature from the Beginnings to 1920*. 3 vols. Seattle: University of Washington, 1927–30. Print.

Pence, Amy. "Interview with Barbara Kingsolver." *Poets and Writers Magazine* July–Aug. 1993: 16–21. Print.

Perdue, Theda. *Cherokee Women*. Lincoln: Univ. of Nebraska Press, 1998. Print.

Perry, Donna. "Barbara Kingsolver." *Backtalk: Women Writers Speak Out*. New Brunswick, NJ: Rutgers Univ. Press, 1993. 143–69. Print.

Pierson, Melissa Holbrook. "Losing Home: When Memories No Longer Have a Place to Reside." *Orion Magazine* Sept./Oct. 2007. Web. 8 May 2010..

Pollan, Michael. "The Idea of a Garden." *Second Nature: A Gardener's Education*. New York: Dell, 1991. 209–38. Print.

Pynchon, Thomas. *The Crying of Lot 49*. 1965. Harper: New York, 2006. Print.

Quick, Susan Chamberlain. "Barbara Kingsolver: A Voice of the Southwest—An Annotated Bibliography." *Bulletin of Bibliography* 54.4 (1997): 283–302. Print.

Randall, Margaret. Foreword. *Another America/Otra América*. By Barbara Kingsolver, with Spanish translations by Rebeca Cartes. Seattle: Seal Press, 1992. xi–xiii. Print.

Regier, Ami. "Replacing the Hero with the Reader: Public Story Structure in *The Poisonwood Bible*." *Mennonite Life* 56.1 (2001). Web. 12 Nov. 2007.

Renan, Ernst. "What Is a Nation?" *Becoming National: A Reader*. Eds. Geoff Eley and Ronald Grigor Suny. Oxford: Oxford Univ. Press, 1996. 42–55. Print.

Rich, Adrienne. "Natural Resources." *The Dream of a Common Language: Poems 1974–77*. New York: Norton, 1978. 60–67. Print.

Riva, Silvia. *Nouvelle Histoire de la Littérature du Congo—Kinshasa*. Paris: L'Harmattan, 2006. Print.

Rodriguez, Ralph E. "Men with Guns: The Story John Sayles Can't Tell." *The End of Cinema As We Know It*. Ed. Jon Lewis. New York: New York Univ. Press, 2001. 168–75. Print.

Roses, Lorraine Elena. "Language and Other Barriers." *New York Review of Books* July 1992: 19. Print.

Rubenstein, Roberta. "Homeric Resonances: Longing and Belonging in Barbara Kingsolver's *Animal Dreams*." *Homemaking: Women Writers and the Politics and Poetics of Home*. Ed. Catherine Wiley and Fiona R. Barnes. New York: Garland, 1996. 5–22. Print.

Ryan, Maureen. "Barbara's Kingsolver's Lowfat Fiction." *Journal of American Culture* 18.4 (1995): 77–82. Print.

Ryden, Kent. *Mapping the Invisible Landscape*. Iowa City: Univ. of Iowa Press, 1993. Print.

Rye, Gill. "Registering Trauma: The Body in Childbirth in Contemporary French Women's Writing." *Nottingham French Studies* 45.3 (2006): 92–104. Print.

Saldívar, José David. *Border Matters: Remapping American Cultural Studies*. Berkeley: Univ. of California Press, 1997. Print.

Sanborn, Geoffrey. *The Sign of the Cannibal: Melville and the Making of a Postcolonial Reader*. Durham: Duke Univ. Press, 1998. Print.

Saxton, Martha. *Being Good: Women's Moral Values in Early America*. New York: Hill & Wang, 2003. Print.

Schipper, Minneke. *Conrads Rivier*. Amsterdam/Antwerpen: Uitgeverij Contact, 1994. Print.

Schlissel, Lillian. *Women's Diaries of the Westward Journey*. New York: Schocken Books, 1982. Print.

Schuessler, Jennifer. "Men, Women and Coyotes." *New York Times Book Review* 5 Nov. 2000: 38. Print.

Schwarz, Henry, and Sangeeta Ray, eds. *A Companion to Postcolonial Studies*. Malden: Blackwell Press, 2000. Print.

See, Lisa. "An Interview with Barbara Kingsolver." *Publishers Weekly* 31 Aug. 1990: 46–47. Print.

Works Cited

"Serendipity and the Southwest: A Conversation with Barbara Kingsolver." *Bloomsbury Review* Nov.–Dec. 1990: 3+. Print.

Shafir, Gershon. *The Citizenship Debates: A Reader.* Minneapolis: Univ. of Minnesota Press, 1998. Print.

Sharpe, Jenny. "Postcolonial Studies in the House of US Multiculturalism." *A Companion to Postcolonial Studies.* Ed. Henry Scwarz and Sangeeta Ray. Malden: Blackwell Press, 2000. 112–25. Print.

Shohat, Ella. "The Struggle over Representation: Casting, Coalitions, and the Politics of Identification." *Late Imperial Culture.* Ed. Roman De La Campa, E. Ann Kaplan, and Michael Sprinker. New York: Verso, 1995. 166–78. Print.

Silko, Leslie Marmon. "Books: Notes on Mixtec and Maya Screenfolds, Picture Books of Preconquest Mexico." *Yellow Woman and a Beauty of the Spirit: Essays on Native American Life Today.* Leslie Marmon Silko. New York: Touchstone, 1997. 155–65. Print.

———. *Gardens in the Dunes.* New York: Simon and Schuster, 1999. Print.

Slotkin, Richard. *Gunfighter Nation.* Norman: Univ. of Oklahoma Press, 1992. Print.

———. *Regeneration through Violence.* New York: Harper Collins, 1973. Print.

Smith, Henry Nash. *Virgin Land: The American West as Symbol and Myth.* New York: Vintage Books, 1950. Print.

Smith, Johanna. "'Too Beautiful Altogether': Ideologies of Gender and Empire in *Heart of Darkness.*" *Heart of Darkness.* 2nd ed. Ed. Ross McMurfin. New York: St. Martin's Press, 1996. 169–84. Print.

Smith, Ruth L. "Negotiating Homes: Morality as a Scarce Good." *Cultural Critique* 38 (Winter 1997–98): 177–95. Print.

Snodgrass, Mary Ellen. *Barbara Kingsolver: A Literary Companion.* Jefferson, NC: McFarland and Co., 2004. Print.

Sobel, David. "Beyond Ecophobia." *yes!* magazine (Winter 1999). Web. 30 Oct. 2006.

———. *Childhood and Nature: Design Principles for Educators.* Portland, ME: Stenhouse Publishers, 2008. Print.

Spencer, Nicholas. *After Utopia: The Rise of Critical Space in Twentieth-Century American Fiction.* Lincoln: Univ. of Nebraska Press, 2006. Print.

Spivak, Gayatri. *A Critique of Postcolonial Reason.* Cambridge, MA: Harvard University Press, 1999. Print.

Stegner, Wallace E. *Mormon Country.* 2nd ed. Lincoln: U of Nebraska Press, 2003.

Stevenson, Sheryl. "Trauma and Memory in Kingsolver's *Animal Dreams.*" 87–108.

Stewart, Pamela J., and Andrew Strathern, eds. *Landscape, Memory and History: Anthropological Perspectives.* London: Pluto Press, 2001. Print.

Stout, Janis. *Through the Window, Out the Door.* Tuscaloosa: Univ. Press of Alabama, 1998. Print.

Straus, Nina Pelikan. "The Exclusion of the Intended from Secret Sharing in Conrad's *Heart of Darkness.*" *Joseph Conrad's "Heart of Darkness": A Casebook.* Ed. Gene Moore. Oxford: Oxford Univ. Press, 2004. 197–217. Print.

Sturm, Circe Dawn. *Blood Politics: Race, Culture, and Identity in the Cherokee Nation of Oklahoma.* Berkeley: Univ. of California Press, 2002. Print.

Works Cited

Swartz, Patti Capel. "'Saving Grace': Political and Environmental Issues and the Role of Connections in Barbara Kingsolver's *Animal Dreams.*" *Interdisciplinary Studies in Literature and Environment* 1.1 (1993): 65–79. Print.

Tal, Kali. *Worlds of Hurt: Reading the Literatures of Trauma.* Cambridge: Cambridge Univ. Press, 1996. Print.

The Diane Rhem Show. National Public Radio. WAMU, Washington, DC. 5 Nov. 1998.

"The Hoover Dam: Lonely Lands Made Fruitful." Ed. Janet Haven. *X-Roads Project.* Univ. of Virginia. Web. 21 Dec. 2007.

Thomson, Rosemarie Garland. *Extraordinary Bodies: Figuring Physical Disability in American Culture and Literature.* New York: Columbia Univ. Press, 1997. Print.

Thomas, Rick. "Under Seize: The Indian Child Welfare Act." *Lifting the Veil.* 28 Feb. 2006. Web. 20 July 2008.

Thoreau, Henry David. "Civil Disobedience." *The Portable Thoreau.* Ed. Carl Bode. New York: Penguin Books, 1947. 109–37. Print.

———. *Wild Fruits.* Ed. Bradley P. Dean. New York: W. W. Norton, 2000. Print.

Tompkins, Jane. "'Indians': Textualism, Morality, and the Problem of History." Gates, *"Race"* 59–77. Print.

———. *West of Everything.* Oxford: Oxford Univ. Press, 1992. Print.

Trimble, Stephen. "A Land of One's Own." *The Geography of Childhood.* Ed. Gary Nabhan and Stephen Trimble. Boston: Beacon Press, 1994. 53–75. Print.

Twain, Mark. *Adventures of Huckleberry Finn.* New York: Harper & Row, 1987. Print.

"Update: Barbara Kingsolver." *Barbara Kingsolver.* Harper Collins. Web. 6 Nov. 2000.

Urgo, Joseph R. "The Yoknapatawpha Project: The Map of a Deeper Existence." *Mississippi Quarterly* 57.4 (2004): 639–55. Print.

van der Kolk, Bessel A., Alexander C. McFarlane, and Lars Weisaeth, eds. *Traumatic Stress: The Effects of Overwhelming Experience on Mind, Body, and Society.* New York: Guilford, 1996. Print.

Vizenor, Gerald. *Fugitive Poses: Native American Indian Scenes of Absence and Presence.* Lincoln: Univ. of Nebraska Press, 1998. Print.

Wagner-Martin, Linda. *Barbara Kingsolver.* Great Writers. Philadelphia: Chelsea House, 2004. Print.

Warner, Susan, and Kathryn M. Feltey. "From Victim to Survivor: Recovered Memories and Identity Transformation." Williams and Banyard, *Trauma and Memory,* 161–72. Print.

Welch, Sharon D. *A Feminist Ethic of Risk.* Minneapolis: Fortress, 1990. Print.

Wenz, Peter S. "Leopold's Novel: The Land Ethic in Barbara Kingsolver's *Prodigal Summer.*" *Ethics and the Environment* 8.2 (2003): 106–25. Print.

West, Rinda. *Out of the Shadow: Ecopsychology, Story and Encounters with the Land.* Charlottesville: Univ. of Virginia Press, 2007. Print.

Whisenhunt, Donald W. *President Herbert Hoover.* New York: Nova Science Publishing, Inc., 2006.

Wilde, Oscar. "The Soul of Man Under Socialism." 1891. Molinari Institute. Web. 25 July 2006.

Williams, Linda M., and Victoria L. Banyard, eds. *Trauma and Memory*. Thousand Oaks, CA: Sage, 1999. Print.

Williams, Patricia. *The Alchemy of Race and Rights: Diary of a Law Professor*. Cambridge: Harvard University Press, 1991. Print.

Willis, Meredith Sue. "Barbara Kingsolver, Moving On." *Appalachian Journal: A Regional Studies Review* 22.1 (1994): 79–86. Print.

Wilson, E. O. "The Environmental Ethic." *Listening to the Earth*. Ed. Christopher Hallowell and Walter Levy. New York: Pearson Longman, 2005. 198–207. Print.

Woods, Gioia. "Barbara Kingsolver." *Twentieth-Century American Western Writers: First Series*. Ed. Richard H. Cracroft. *Dictionary of Literary Biography*. Vol. 206. Detroit: Gale Group, 1999. Literature Resource Center. Web. 11 Apr. 2009.

Woolf, Virginia. *Moments of Being: A Collection of Autobiographical Writing*. Ed. Jeanne Schulkind. 2nd ed. New York: Harcourt, 1985. Print.

CONTRIBUTORS

WES BERRY teaches American literature, writing, and environmental humanities at Western Kentucky University, near his native county. He lives on a ridgeline between the Green and Barren Rivers, home to rare mussel species. His unpublished novel, *Boating with the Dead,* was a finalist for the Bellwether Prize for Fiction of Social Change, sponsored by Barbara Kingsolver, in 2008.

ROBIN COHEN is an assistant professor of English at Texas State University–San Marcos, where she teaches courses in Native American and postcolonial literatures. Other teaching and research interests include Katherine Ann Porter, Willa Cather, multicultural American literature, and the literature of the Southwest. She has published and delivered conference papers on Native American literature, particularly the works of Leslie Marmon Silko.

CHRISTINE CUSICK is an assistant professor of English at Seton Hill University. She has published ecocritical studies of contemporary poetry and landscape photography and her own place-based creative nonfiction, which has been recognized as notable by the Best American Essays series. Her edited collection, *Out of the Earth: Ecocritical Readings of Irish Texts,* including her interview with writer and cartographer Tim Robinson, is forthcoming from Cork University Press.

MEAGAN EVANS received an MFA in poetry from Texas State University and is currently completing her Ph.D. in poetry and poetics at the University of Oregon. Her poems have appeared in *Black Warrior Review, Alice Blue Review, DIAGRAM, Iron Horse, W.O.M.B,* and *effing mag.*

SUSAN HANSON is the author of *Icons of Loss and Grace: Moments from the Natural World* and a coeditor of *What Wildness Is This: Women Write about the Southwest.* Her work has appeared in such publications as *Northern Lights, EarthSpirit, ISLE, Southwestern Literature,* and *Texas Parks & Wildlife.* A longtime member of the English faculty at Texas State University, she also worked for nearly twenty years as a journalist and twelve as an Episcopal lay campus chaplain. She and her husband live in San Marcos, Texas, and have a grown daughter.

294

CATHERINE HIMMELWRIGHT teaches at Auburn University. Her critical interests are in twentieth-century American literature as well as southern literature. She has published articles in the *Southern Literary Journal* and *Mississippi Quarterly*.

KRISTIN J. JACOBSON holds a Ph.D. from Pennsylvania State University. In 2005 she joined the faculty at Richard Stockton College of New Jersey, where she teaches courses in American literature, American studies, and women's studies. Incorporating feminist geography and literary analysis, her interdisciplinary book, *Neodomestic American Fiction* (forthcoming from Ohio State University Press), investigates late twentieth-century and early twenty-first-century manifestations of "domestic fiction." She has also published articles in *Genre, Tulsa Studies in Women's Literature,* and *Legacy.*

MAUREEN MEHARG KENTOFF received her master's degree in Women's Studies at George Washington University in Washington, D.C., and is currently pursuing a doctoral degree in English literature. Her pursuit of interdisciplinary scholarship has allowed her to incorporate into her work studies of psychology, philosophy, the humanities, and social activism. Now, with a focus on twentieth- and twenty-first-century American literature, she is exploring themes of identity, agency, and feminism in women's personal narratives. As a burgeoning author and professor, Maureen plans to spend her remaining lives writing, teaching, and promoting anti-oppressionist literature and critical theory.

PRISCILLA LEDER is professor of English at Texas State University–San Marcos, where she has taught for over twenty years. She specializes in nineteenth- and twentieth-century American women writers and has published essays on Kate Chopin, Sarah Orne Jewett, Alice Walker, Fannie Hurst, Julia Peterkin, and Richard Ford. She has taught in Portugal and Belgium on Fulbright lectureships.

HÉLOÏSE MEIRE holds bachelor's and master's degrees in English and German language and literature from the Université Catholique de Louvain in Louvain-la-Neuve, Belgium. As a graduate student, she spent six months as an exchange student at the Flemish University Katholieke Universiteit Leuven and one academic year at Dublin City University. Her master's thesis on *The Poisonwood Bible* and *Heart of Darkness* was nominated for the Belgian Association of Anglicists in Higher Education Award. She is currently studying acting at the Institut des Arts de Diffusion in Louvain-la-Neuve.

JEANNE SOKOLOWSKI is an advanced Ph.D. student at Indiana University, Bloomington, where she is writing her dissertation on how contemporary Asian American and Native American fiction challenges our understanding of the nation. She has also published on citizenship in the work of Mine Okubo and John Okada. A former Fulbright Junior Research grant recipient, Jeanne has lived in Japan, South Korea, and China but now resides in semirural Kentucky.

SHERYL STEVENSON, formerly associate professor of English at the University of Akron, now teaches at the University of Toronto. Much of her published work focuses on modern and contemporary women writers, including Djuna Barnes, Stevie Smith, Muriel Spark, Pat Barker, and Sarah Waters. Marking her interest in disability studies, her 2008 essay "(M)Othering and Autism: Maternal Rhetorics of Self-Revision" was published in the groundbreaking collection *Autism and Representation.*

BREYAN STRICKLER is an assistant professor specializing in American literature at Loras College in Dubuque, Iowa. Her previous articles focus on environmental rhetoric in contemporary American and Australian fiction and on environmental organizations, the rhetoric of social justice, and community-based learning. She is currently working on rhetorical studies of travel literature and science fiction, particularly as they construct intersections between the urban and the natural.

GIOIA WOODS is associate professor of humanities and humanities program coordinator at Northern Arizona University. She is the author of the Western Writers Series monograph *Gary Nabhan,* co-editor of *Western Subjects: Autobiographical Writing in the North American West,* and author of articles on Western literature and culture, ecological criticism, and twentieth-century American literature.

INDEX

activism, 82–84, 219, 232n2
activist, 6, 9–13, 95, 155, 180, 191, 259
adaptation, 14, 54–59, 219, 244
adoption, 7, 11, 145–50, 154, 156n1, 158–72,
 172n3, 183–88, 244
Adorno, Theodor W., 132–43, 269

Bellwether Prize, 19, 84, 194
Benjamin, Walter, 142
Buell, Lawrence, 125, 263–64, 270

child abuse, 19, 32–43, 64, 87, 108, 121, 149,
 183–84
citizenship, 159–60, 165–66, 186, 200, 215,
 230
Comer, Krista, 19–20, 106, 175–77, 182,
 188–93, 198n1
Conrad, Joseph, 71–73, 81–85

DeMarr, Mary Jean, 22n3, 81, 129, 183
Demory, Pamela, 72–73, 81–82, 85n1
determinism, 55, 224–25
DNA, 58, 224, 231

ecology, 5–7, 14, 17–18, 20, 85n5, 215, 261
economics, 22, 205–6, 243, 263, 273
education, 18, 87, 130, 165, 39, 244, 257,
 262–63, 275
Eisenhower, Dwight D., 77, 181, 201
Emerson, Ralph Waldo, 225, 276n1

enfranchisement, 59, 132, 165
Erdrich, Louise, 193, 197
ethnicity, 151, 155, 192–93
Evernden, Neil, 215
exceptionalism, 194, 209, 264, 275,

Fagan, Kristina, 147, 154
Faludi, Susan, 66
Faulkner, William, 197–98
Felski, Rita, 55, 7
feminism, 21, 50, 55, 68, 75, 84
Fiedler, Leslie A., 30, 34, 36
flag, 200, 208–10
folklore, 54, 193
food, 1, 14–16, 37–41, 48, 112–16, 124, 147,
 199–209, 228–30, 232n4, 243–47, 254,
 260, 263–75
forest, 15, 216, 220–222, 239, 259–60, 273
fossil, 202–5, 210, 252, 262
Foucault, Michel, 111, 117
Fox, Stephen D., 18, 76, 109–11
fundamentalist, 77, 204

garden, 16–17, 22, 27–28, 37, 44–45, 203,
 237–47, 260–61, 270, 274
gender, 17–20, 22n3, 52, 59–62, 72–74, 81–
 85, 95, 130, 151–55, 197, 198n4
geography, 22, 176–78, 180, 183, 191–98,
 209, 264
Godfrey, Kathleen, 20, 246, 161, 166, 171,
 175–77, 182
Goldberg, Bernard, 199–210

Goldin, Frances, 7
Griffin, Susan, 110
Grosz, Elizabeth, 50, 55–59, 64, 68nn2–3
Guest, Kristen, 118
Gunn Allen, Paula, 39, 190

Habermas, Jorgen, 275
Haraway, Donna, 535, 60–61
Hartman, Geoffrey, 87
Harvey, David, 179–183, 188–197
Herman, Judith Lewis, 88–91, 96–106, 107nn1–3
Hill Collins, Patricia 55, 61
Hoover dam, 158, 169–70, 173n6
Hurston, Zora Neale, 148
hybridity, 60, 112, 117, 120, 125–26, 147, 152, 180

immigrant, 47, 134, 157
immigration, 19, 64, 186
imperialism, 71–72, 76–77, 81, 84, 132, 157, 169
industrialization, 152, 264

Jacobs, Johan, 18, 80
Jacobs, Naomi, 20, 151, 190–91
Jakobson, Roman, 131–35, 140
Jefferson, Thomas, 199

Kant, Immanuel, 172n4, 267
Kikongo, 13, 78
Kingsolver, Barbara
—essay collections: High Tide in Tucson, 12–14, 21, 47–68, 108n11, 229–31; Small Wonder, 14–15, 66, 199, 206, 229–31
—essays: "Careful What You Let In The Door," 64–65; "Confessions of A Reluctant Rock Goddess," 131; "Creation Stories," 53–54; "The Forest in the Seeds," 67, 214; "Foreward," The Essential Agrarian Reader," 201, 205, 253; God's Wife's Measuring Spoons," 17, 19; "High Tide in Tucson," 52–56, 58–60, 222–25; "How Mr. Dewey Decimal Saved My Life," 3, 63; "In Case You Ever Want to Go Home Again," 3, 7–8, 12, 51, 56; "Infernal Paradise," 54; "Jabberwocky," 19, 64–66; "Knowing Our Place," 180, 213, 227–31; "Letter to a Daughter at Thirteen," 3; "Letter to My Mother," 4; "Life Without Go-Go Boots," 3; "Lily's Chickens," 245–47; "Making Peace," 48; "The Memory Place," 1, 12; "Postcards from the Imaginary Mom," 214; "Reprise," 67, 260; "Saying Grace," 208; "Semper Fi," 60, 225, 236; "Small Wonder," 207–8, 216–21, 251–53, 258; "The Spaces Between," 58, 62–65, 161, 226; "Stone Soup," 12, 57, 107n5, 204; "Taming the Beast with Two Backs," 235
—non-fiction: Animal, Vegetable, Miracle, 15–16, 21–22, 199–202, 206, 210, 230–31, 263–73; Holding the Line, 8–9, 108n8, 108n11, 160, 177; Last Stand: America's Virgin Lands, 15
—novels: Animal Dreams, 9–10, 18–21, 23n4, 87–108, 109–12, 121–26, 147, 150–55, 175–78, 182–192, 198n4, 213; The Bean Trees, 7–8, 10–11, 19–21, 22n3, 23n4, 27–45, 93, 145–49, 153–55, 160–63, 175–88, 195–96, 198n4, 213; Pigs in Heaven, 11–12, 19–21, 23n4, 146–56, 157–72, 176, 184–88, 196, 198n4, 213; The Poisonwood Bible, 13–14, 18–21, 22n3, 71–86, 109–11, 119, 123, 126, 157, 176–82, 195 nn4–5; Prodigal Summer, 14, 18–22, 198n4, 233–49, 251, 254–59, 262
—poetry collection: Another America/Otra America, 10–11, 21, 129–143
—poems: "In Exile," 130; "Justicia," 130; "Possession," 140–41; "Refuge," 136–38,

140; "This House I Cannot Leave,"
138–40; "Waiting for the Invasion," 132;
"Your Mother's Eyes," 141
—short story: "Islands on the Moon," 9
—short story collection: *Homeland and
Other Stories* 8–10
—web site: "Dialogue: Barbara Kingsolver,"
175, 179, 183; "FAQ," 13–14, 233–34
Kolodny, Annette, 27–28, 276n1
Koza, Kimberly, 18, 176–77, 182
Kunz, Diane, 18, 175, 182
Kymlicka, Will, 160

Leopold, Aldo, 15, 233–34
Lessing, Doris, 3, 63
Limón, José E., 185, 198n
locavore, 266, 272
Lopez, Barry, 227–28, 252
Love, Glen, 215, 223
Lumumba, Patrice, 72, 80, 86nn6–7, 178,
181

McDowell, Linda, 180
McKee, Patricia, 194
McKibben, Bill, 210n2, 232n4
Mobutu Sese Seko, 76, 80
Morrison, Toni, 67, 157, 194, 197
Murrey, Loretta Martin 17, 23n4, 171

Nabhan, Gary, 251
nationalism, 208, 264, 274
Native American, 10, 18, 21, 27–45, 58,
145–46, 157–72, 183–84, 187–88, 193,
226
neocolonialism, 75, 157–60, 183
Nunning, Angsar. 70

O'Connor, Flannery, 3, 9
Owens, Louis, 156n1, 158

Paredes, Raymund, 193, 198n1
patriotism, 32, 65, 199–210
pesticide, 218, 225, 233, 258
poetics, 131–33, 143
Pollan, Michael, 22, 237–45
pollution, 16, 20, 94, 201, 220
postcolonialism, 79–80, 126, 157–58, 163,
168, 172n2

racism, 20, 29, 61, 81, 130, 132, 147–48,
157–62
Regier, Ami, 83–74
Rodriguez, Ralph, 187–88
Roses, Lorraine, 130–31
Rubenstein, Roberta, 17, 23n4, 101–3, 183,
190
Ryan, Maureen, 19, 46n6, 106, 152
Ryden, Kent, 226
Rye, Gill, 121, 124

Sanborn, Geoffrey, 163, 172n4
Schlissel. Lillian, 29, 45n1
Schwarz, Henry, 168
Silko, Leslie Marmon, 172n3, 184
Smith, Henry Nash, 34, 276n1
Smith, Johanna, 72, 74–75, 85n4
Sobel, David, 251, 259–60, 262
Spencer, Nicholas, 178–79
stereotype, 21, 135, 147, 150–53, 161, 163–
65, 171, 177, 184, 193
Straus, Nina Pelikan, 72, 74, 77–81
Swartz, Patti Capel, 18, 108n8, 177–78,
210n1

terrorist, 90, 208
Thoreau, Henry David, 15–16, 48–49, 67,
201, 205–6, 214–15, 258, 263–76
Tompkins, Jane, 28–30, 157, 163–64, 183
transcendentalism, 49, 269–70
trauma, 18, 21, 87–107, 109, 117, 120–25

Trimble, Stephen, 251
Tucson, Arizona, 5–7, 11–13, 39, 40, 53, 89, 91–95, 108n11, 141, 162, 176–77, 185, 191, 222

unhome, 137, 139
utopia, 178, 188, 193

Vietnam, 4, 97
Volterra Principle, 237–38

Wagner-Martin, Linda, 4, 79, 236, 22n3
Walden, 16, 48
waste, 16, 119, 126, 201
Wenz, Peter, 233–34
wilderness, 15, 22, 36, 46n3, 49, 75, 169, 179, 190–93, 221, 237–43, 253, 258, 261, 264–65
Willis, Meredith Sue, 17, 188–89, 193, 197
Wilson, E. O., 225–26, 228, 259
woodlands, 15, 253
Woolf, Virginia, 9, 67, 96, 231